THE NATURE OF EVIL

THE NATURE
OF EVIL

DARYL KOEHN

First published in 2005 by
PALGRAVE MACMILLAN™
175 Fifth Avenue, New York, N.Y. 10010 and
Houndmills, Basingstoke, Hampshire, England RG21 6XS
Companies and representatives throughout the world.

PALGRAVE MACMILLAN is the global academic imprint of the Palgrave Macmillan division of St. Martin's Press, LLC and of Palgrave Macmillan Ltd. Macmillan® is a registered trademark in the United States, United Kingdom and other countries. Palgrave is a registered trademark in the European Union and other countries.

ISBN 1–4039–6894–2

Library of Congress Cataloging-in-Publication Data

Koehn, Daryl, 1955–
      The nature of evil / Daryl Koehn.
           p. cm.
      Includes bibliographical references and index.
      ISBN 1–4039–6894–2
        1. Good and evil. I. Title.

BJ1401.K64 2005
170—dc22   2004053468

A catalogue record for this book is available from the British Library.

Design by Newgen Imaging Systems (P) Ltd., Chennai, India.

First edition: March 2005

10 9 8 7 6 5 4 3 2 1

Printed in the United States of America.

For all who have suffered

CONTENTS

Acknowledgments   ix

Introduction   1

1. Evil as Vice   15

2. Evil as Losing the Ability to Act   35

3. Evil as Flight from Narcissistic Boredom   63

4. Evil as Hypocritical Repression   87

5. Evil as Imagined Portent   117

6. Evil as the Loss of Our Humanity   151

7. Evil as Satanizing Self, Others, and God   187

8. Evil as Fanatical Impiety   207

9. Final Thoughts   235

Notes   281

Works Consulted   295

About the Author   301

Index   303

ACKNOWLEDGMENTS

I AM INDEBTED TO THE MANY FRIENDS AND COLLEAGUES WHO HAVE TALKED with me over the years about the nature of evil. The University of St. Thomas provided me with the opportunity to teach a class and to do several talks on the subject. My students pushed me hard; discussions with them generated many insights into the works discussed in this book. My conversations with John Cornell were especially useful in helping me to refine my thinking about this most difficult topic. I would be remiss if I did not acknowledge my large debt to the other scholars who have dared to tackle the intimidating issue of the nature of evil.

I am grateful to Dr. King-tak Ip and the Centre for Applied Ethics at Hong Kong Baptist University for providing me with support that enabled me to finish and refine portions of the book. Julia Traber and Rebecca McCarthy did an excellent job of correcting and proofreading the entire manuscript. Amanda Johnson and Erin Ivy at Palgrave Macmillan and the copy-editing team at Newgen Imaging Systems superbly shepherded the book through production.

INTRODUCTION

Nobody knowingly does evil.

—Plato

CULTURES APPROACH EVIL IN TWO WAYS: THE MORALISTIC WAY AND THE WAY of wisdom. Although the moralistic approach is more common, it does not enable us to understand evil. If we do not grasp evil, we cannot be free of it. Enslaved by our ignorance, we behave in ways that increase our individual and collective suffering. The way of wisdom, by contrast, offers insight into evil and relief from suffering for those who have ears to hear and eyes to see. This book attempts to understand the nature of evil from the perspective of the wisdom tradition.

In order to understand the wisdom tradition perspective and distinguish it from the moralistic approach, we need to work through some examples of suffering. Until that is done, my claims about the superiority of the wisdom tradition's approach will sound overly bold or dogmatic. I, however, want to show my hand a bit in this introduction so that the reader gets some sense of the lay of the land I propose to traverse. I ask the reader's indulgence as I use very broad strokes to distinguish between the moralistic and the wisdom tradition.

VICE VERSUS IGNORANCE OF THE SELF

Moralities equate evil with vice. Vice is the corruption of choice or of the will. Some moralists (e.g., Immanuel Kant) argue that this corruption is identical to a failure to reason consistently and rigorously in a way that is publicly intelligible.[1] This failure gets embodied in acts of violence, malice, or harm. Such acts are evil insofar as they express corrupted practical reason (the will). Other moralists (e.g., Aristotle) locate the corruption in action itself.[2] We act badly because we fail to deliberate. Our ill-considered actions produce bad habits or vices. These vices further compromise our ability to deliberate and thereby cause us great unhappiness.

Both of these moral approaches agree in treating evil as violative vice resulting from the corruption of our will or choice. The wisdom tradition rejects this claim. It does not view violence, malice, or even vice as evil. These are merely symptoms of what the wisdom tradition insists is the true evil—human suffering caused by our lack of self-knowledge. We mistakenly identify the self with something that it is not. The resulting false identity is not stable, and we are left at the mercy of external forces. In an effort to stabilize and maintain our false identity, we adopt a variety of self-defeating, violent, paranoid, masochistic, and sadistic strategies. Our lack of self-knowledge locks us into unsatisfying, quasi-mechanical patterns of behavior.

If we can perceive these mechanical trajectories, we can discover how we have become ensnared in enslaving behaviors. But this "if" is a big one. Moralistically equating evil with vice, we quickly move to praise and blame other people's behavior. We are so busy judging what others have (or have not) done that we do not attend to our behavior. As a result, our reactions and circumstances control us, instead of the reverse. What is more, we often wind up doing—in the name of morality—the very thing for which we condemn others.

The wisdom tradition contends that we spend most of our life asleep, operating on autopilot. We fail to realize that the things that we have taken to be real are merely images or illusions. This does not mean that reality does not exist. Even Buddhist sages who describe the world as an illusion implicitly believe that it is better to see the world as it is than to persist in error. If I did not agree that some ways of thinking and behaving are objectively better than others, I would not have bothered to write this book. Were all lives equally good, there would be no point in trying to improve our understanding of evil. Anyone who writes seriously about good and evil presupposes that some lives are objectively better than others. The difficulty lies in identifying which forms of life are genuinely good.

Voluntary Action versus Unwitting Enslavement

What, then, is a good life? According to the wisdom tradition, a good life need not be saintly. A life is good insofar as human beings find it to be enduringly satisfying or happy. No one needs to advocate that we should pursue happiness. Each of us is doing that already. We desire a good life because desire, by its very nature, aims at satisfaction. We want to be satisfied not just for the next nanosecond but for the foreseeable future. Human desire, by nature, aims at a good or an object capable of permanently satisfying us. From childhood on, we try one thing after another in order to be happy. Although we may mistake what is conducive to the good life, it does not follow that we are not pursuing the good life. At every moment, each of us seeks to realize lasting satisfaction.

Most moralists share the wisdom tradition's view of the good life as an enduringly satisfying existence. Moralists and sages diverge, however, in their understanding of the impediments to living well. If we do not lead a good life, we must, according to moralists, be abusing our free will. We can exercise our will virtuously or viciously. Either way, our willing or choosing is free. Morality equates being human with free agency. As long as we are free, our deeds reflect our freedom and identity. From the moral point of view, every action we perform is thoroughly ours and controllable by us. In other words, our actions are voluntary. Moral systems of praise and blame carefully distinguish voluntary from involuntary actions. They must make this distinction, for praise and blame aim at behavior modification, and we can alter only that behavior that is within our control. Having distinguished voluntary from involuntary actions, moralities label actions that foster community "virtuous." Actions that appear to undermine community are condemned as "vicious" or "criminal." In this manner, morality construes evil as voluntary vice and then assimilates it to crime.

Thinkers whom I would place in the wisdom tradition—Plato, Jesus, Confucius, Buddha, Baruch Spinoza, Johann Wolfgang von Goethe, Dante Alighieri, and Henry James, to name a few—deny that we are born free. Freedom is an achievement, not a birthright. Humanity, too, must be realized; it is not a given. Much of our behavior is not humane precisely because we are not free. Operating with a false sense of self, we enslave ourselves to our passions. When we do harm, we do so unwittingly. It does little good, therefore, to blame us for our crimes. Besides, from the wisdom perspective, we never go unpunished. Our unhappy lives, not civil penalties, are our punishment. Everything is avenged on earth. Mistaking what we want for what we truly need, we suffer terribly. In an effort to distract ourselves from our pain, dread, and emptiness, we lash out at others and excoriate ourselves. On this view, evil is not vice or crime. Evil is frustrated desire stemming from our efforts to preserve a false conception of the self. In an effort to overcome our frustration, we adopt a variety of narcissistic, sadistic, and paranoid strategies. These strategies only intensify our anxiety and rage. Escaping this cycle of dread, anguish, violence, and shame requires that we become wise about who we are. As we come to know ourselves better, our suffering diminishes, and our lives become more rewarding. If we do not become more self-aware, we doom ourselves to behave in unhealthy and sometimes violent ways.

Frustration and pain are real enough, but they stem from illusion. Believing that we already know exactly who we are, we do not investigate the matter any further. We rely on society's opinion-makers to supply us with an identity and to show us the best way to live. Society, though, rarely speaks with one voice. Consequently, we internalize many inconsistent beliefs. Querying his fellow citizens about their most cherished beliefs, Socrates found that they quickly fell into contradiction. Yet, certain of their wisdom, these interlocutors adamantly refused to acknowledge the incoherence of their positions. Little has changed in the intervening two thousand years. Our fear of losing the only identity we have ever known is so great that we prefer to deny the truth and suffer than to forgo our false personas and mistaken positions.

Wisdom tradition thinkers maintain that we see the world through a lens distorted by prejudice and error. Worse still, we do not perceive this distortion, because we have not examined who we are. As a result, our concept of evil is confused. Many think evil is malice or sadism. Some equate evil with harm of any sort. Others restrict evil to hurtful human actions and exclude natural disasters. Instead of sorting through and testing our conflicting notions of evil, we devote ourselves to fighting what we take to be other people's evil. Our moralistic outlook does not value self-examination. Society's system of praise and blame directs our attention outward, encouraging us to emulate, judge, and prosecute other people.

We justify our prosecution of wrongdoers by insisting that these offenders possess the self-knowledge needed to act virtuously and so are accountable for their vicious deeds. Aristotle, for example, explicitly denies that human beings can fail to know who they are: "also [a person] could not be ignorant of the agent; for how could he not know himself?"[3]

I doubt whether matters are as straightforward as Aristotle portrays them to be. If Aristotle's peers could not help but know themselves, why was the injunction "Know Thyself" inscribed on the Greek temple at Delphi? It makes no sense to enjoin people to do what they are already doing. The words at the Delphic shrine reflect the wisdom tradition's key insight, that we do not understand who we truly are. Whether self-knowledge is a given (moralism) or an achievement (wisdom tradition) is very much an open question.

Overcoming Evil: Uncorrupted Choice versus Insight

For moralists, evil is a noun—transgressive vice, crime, or harm stemming from corrupt choice or an impure will. The wisdom tradition conceives of evil more as an adjective—evil is the *frustrated* quality of unsatisfied desire. From the wisdom tradition perspective, to speak of "suffering evil" is redundant. Evil is suffering; it is the pain of frustration caused by our ignorance of what we need to be lastingly satisfied. If evil is suffering, does it follow that we never do evil? We can be said to do evil whenever our futile attempts to maintain our false sense of who we are interfere with our happiness or other people's ability to thrive. The wisdom tradition readily concedes that our ignorance may lead us to affect our fellow human beings in ways that they may deem hurtful. What it does not grant is the moralists' claim that we voluntarily choose to be malicious or to maim others. In our struggle to secure our inherently unstable self-identity, we always pursue that which strikes us as good—that is, as likely to lead to our happiness. After the fact, we may wish we had not behaved in that particular way. But punishment typically accomplishes little. As long as we are ignorant of who we are, we will rely on our habitual strategies for maintaining our sense of self and repressing the dread that threatens to overwhelm us. In order to contain the chaos produced by violence, societies are inevitably driven to identify and isolate aggressive individuals.

Although this societal response is understandable, the wisdom tradition would encourage us to redirect some of the energy we spend punishing wrongdoers toward enabling people to discover their authentic selves. Thinkers in the wisdom tradition invite each of us to unearth the reasons why we so often behave in self-frustrating, pathological ways.

Helping others learn about themselves is itself a tricky proposition. Individuals achieve self-knowledge only by thinking. Becoming thoughtful is akin to waking up. What causes us to wake up? We sleep through thunderstorms, sirens, and alarms. So outside sounds do not wake us up. If we heed the alarm or a spouse's plea to get out of bed, it is only because we are already awakening. Our waking up is the cause of our being awake. There is no additional cause of awakening. Just as we wake up through awakening, so, too, we become thoughtful by thinking. Thinking turns itself on. No one else can force us to think.

I make no claim, therefore, to teach people how to become self-aware or how to liberate themselves from evil. If what I say about the nature of evil appears to you—the reader—to be true, it will be because you have recognized yourself in these pages. It is up to you to examine how far that recognition extends. What I can do is analyze how and why we fall into traps of our own making. Those who see themselves in these portrayals of suffering can try to avoid these pitfalls. If you and I come to appreciate how easy it is to seduce ourselves into behaving self-destructively, we will perhaps be less inclined to satanize others. Checking our rush to judgment is not a bad thing, especially because our propensity to imagine the worst about other people turns out to be among the most seductive and deadly traps.

When we do not think about the dynamics of self-destruction, we condemn ourselves to an unhappy existence. In the subsequent chapters, we meet many such doomed individuals: the talented actor who wants to be recognized for his ability, becomes famous, and unwittingly destroys his talent in the process; the doctor who loses his integrity through his efforts to preserve his social respectability and professionalism; the woman who, in her desperate efforts to save a boy from moral corruption, unknowingly kills this very child; the man who tries to escape his past only to find himself relentlessly pursued by his history; the sanctimonious prosecutor who, in his effort to rid the city of injustice, becomes unjust and impious.

Socrates was right to claim that good and wise poets can write tragedy and comedy equally well. Both modes are dramatic expressions of the same truth: our unexamined lives reveal themselves to be fundamentally incongruous because what we pursue turns out not to be what we want. If circumstances are unfavorable, we die unhappy. If fortune smiles on us, our lives may be longer but not necessarily better. Shakespeare never says that a character lives happily ever after. Every Shakespearean comedy narrowly misses being a tragedy. If circumstances had been just a little different, the play would end with the characters being interred, not getting married. As long as we are not self-aware, we risk profound unhappiness. Whether we are self-aware depends, in turn, on whether we think. The sages in the wisdom tradition consistently deny that they teach anyone anything. By saying many startling things, they try to provoke us into thinking for ourselves. Their claims—"judge not lest ye be judged" (Jesus), or "if heaven is with me, no one can harm" (Confucius), or "all is illusion" (Buddha)—call into question our most deeply held tenets and point to a radically different way of thinking about evil and about human development.

Contrast this approach with that of morality. Morality establishes role models and then dictates that we cultivate a virtuous character through free, voluntary choices, bringing our behavior into compliance with that of these role models and with the rules and mores endorsed by the community. Social theorists and community leaders defend these moral demands on the ground that individual compliance and virtue are necessary for the good of the community. Lovers of wisdom see our life's work in quite different terms. Since evil is not corrupt choice but suffering caused by individual and collective ignorance, we have but one task in life: to gain insight into why we act and react as we do, and into how we fit into the universe. Learning causes our behavior to change spontaneously. As we become more reflective, our old concerns evaporate and past fears dissolve. We do not choose to change. Socrates, Confucius, and Jesus never mention the word "choice." (Translators occasionally introduce the word into Socratic dialogues, Christian Gospels, and Confucian texts, but "choice" does not appear in the original languages of any of these works.) The truth, not willpower or good habits, sets us free. We become free only through an uncoerced moment of insight, the moment at which a glimmer of truth comes to us and we see who we truly are: "Opening one's eyes may take a lifetime. Seeing is done in a flash."[4]

Whereas moralities preach the need to acquire habits of virtue and to avoid rationalizations and excuses, the wisdom tradition, as its name suggests, emphasizes wisdom. Socrates says that virtue is identical to wisdom.[5] Being wise means, in part, acknowledging that we are finite human beings, not gods. We find a similar idea in Chinese wisdom texts. Although these texts distinguish between seekers after enlightenment and demons, the texts explicitly deny that the seekers' character somehow makes them better than the demons. On the contrary, these Chinese works attribute many virtues to the demons. The habits of those who desire enlightenment do not necessarily improve over time. In what respect, then, does the lover of wisdom differ from the demons? Lovers of wisdom try to find their special, but limited, place in the world; they keep themselves open to learning. The demons, by contrast, discover little about the world or themselves because they think they are omnipotent. They attempt to consume or engulf the entire world and view anyone who stands in their way as an enemy.[6] Jesus similarly singles out as evil our propensity to demonize each other.[7] This propensity exists even in those with the best habits and the finest reputations for integrity and honesty. Unless we gain insight into what drives us to portray other people as our enemies, we will remain angry, unhappy, and prone to violence.

True Community

Only at that moment of insight does true community become possible. What counts as true community? When moralists talk about the good of the community, they presuppose that human beings are free. The moral problem then becomes one of figuring out how to devise a political regime that honors human freedom. Democracy generally ends up being deemed the most legitimate and best form of communal regime. Wisdom thinkers consider this approach naïve. They deny that human beings are born free. Most of us are not free most of the time. Since we do not know ourselves, our passions control us. Bound by our illusions, we cannot function as members of a genuine community built around shared work. Lacking self-awareness, we lose focus as we are driven hither and thither by our passions and anxieties. Our unsuccessful attempts to contain our fragmenting selves remove us ever farther from reality. In our ignorant madness, we attempt to transfer our feelings of dread and impotence onto our fellow citizens. By making them feel our pain, we hope to convince ourselves that we remain in total control of our future. What passes for civilized community or democracy is but a thin veneer over our simmering rage at how impotent we feel. This rage is always on the verge of breaking through. Under such conditions, working together is extremely difficult, if not impossible. We cannot realize our shared interests when we do not know where our personal interest truly lies. For Confucius or Socrates, the best community is one that strives to help its members to know themselves and to discover what is in their interest. In the words of Mahatma Gandhi, "In true democracy every man and woman is taught to think for himself or herself."[8]

Examining evil from the perspective of a lover of wisdom means taking a sustained look at a few of the many ways in which human ignorance manifests itself and leads to self-destruction and the loss of true community. It also means considering how communities help or hinder individuals' ability to achieve insight and freedom. I will examine both these aspects in the subsequent chapters. Before outlining how I propose to proceed, I want to mention one topic that I do not discuss. Most authors who discuss evil take one question as central: why does a good God allow evil? I avoid this question for four reasons. First, the question only arises if we put ourselves on par with, or even above, God. This strategy results in the peculiar spectacle wryly described by the philosopher Mary Midgley:

> The inquiry [into why God allows evil] takes the form of a law court, in which Man appearing both as judge and accuser, arraigns God and convicts him of mismanaging his responsibilities. We then get a strange drama, in which two robed and wigged figures apparently sit opposite each other exchanging accusations. . . . If God is not there, the drama cannot arise. If he is there, he is surely something bigger and more mysterious than a corrupt or stupid official.[9]

This "strange drama" is not only comical but also dangerous in many respects. A second reason for avoiding discussions of divine responsibility is that accusing God keeps us from carefully examining our experience of evil and the role we play in causing suffering. We fixate instead on events safely in the past—the Holocaust, the September 11 bombing of the

World Trade Center, the rape of Nanking. Mesmerized by historical terrors, we fail to evaluate our present actions. In singling out spectacular horrors, we do not see that, in W. H. Auden's words, "evil is unspectacular . . . and shares our bed and eats at our table."[10] By focusing on egregious actions, we also overlook the deep connection between what people suffer and what they subsequently do. As a result, violence appears to come out of nowhere. Since the prospect of completely unmotivated actions is itself scary, we are tempted to impute free (i.e., voluntary) malice to evildoers. The question of why God allows dreadful evil to occur prejudices us in favor of a moralistic account of evil built around the notion of free will or intentional choice. I avoid theodicy because it closes down any discussion about the nature of evil.

This last observation brings me to my third reason for setting aside the issue of God's alleged responsibility for evildoing. We cannot possibly think about why a divine being (assuming such a being exists) would permit evil unless we have done some hard thinking about what evil is. This book speaks to the logically prior question: what is the nature or essence of evil? Whether we approach that question from the perspective of morality or of wisdom makes all the difference. The moralist presumes to know what is evil, to judge who is virtuous and who unworthy, and to sanction punishment. Thus, we see the Biblical Job's "friends" explaining that Job's suffering must be a divine punishment for his sins.[11] Since Job feels that he is an innocent victim, the friends' moralistic explanation gives rise to the issue of divine responsibility: why would a loving and just God allow an innocent to suffer? But the lover of wisdom would suggest that the problem has perhaps been wrongly formulated. The divine neither causes us to suffer nor permits other people to inflict suffering upon us. If there is a God, then the individual's place is decreed by God. Nothing anyone or anything else does alters our place in the universe or the satisfaction that goes with realizing who we are. We suffer only to the extent that we are filled with the preoccupations of the illusory self. In that sense, Job is right: he has not transgressed the moral law and merits no punishment. Like the rest of us, he suffers because he lacks self-knowledge. We come to the paradox at the center of every wisdom tradition: we find ourselves only through losing ourselves. The illusory self must die in order for the authentic self to live. We suffer only because we have attached ourselves to a false self. The godhead has nothing to do with this illusion and its attendant suffering. We can detach ourselves at any moment by starting to reflect and to live.

What constitutes truly living is a large topic beyond the scope of this inquiry. If pressed, I would say that wisdom thinkers understand living to mean something like "acting with the consciousness that we are limited beings who can be happy only if we abandon our illusions, including the false belief that we are all-powerful and supremely knowledgeable." As God reminds Job, human beings command neither the heavens nor the earth. Although we may think we have dominion over the animals of the earth, we find ourselves powerless when attacked by a shark or crocodile. An earthquake can destroy one of our big cities in a few seconds. From the wisdom perspective, none of us has a rightful claim against God. A fourth reason for steering clear of this moralistic notion is that it causes us to demonize the divine and rage at the universe's unjust treatment of us. This demonization and rage is itself the primary source of our suffering. That accounts for why Job's suffering stops the moment that the divine grants Job a vision of the whole and his limited place within it. It is also why Job's prosperity after his vision is exactly twice what it was before his sufferings began. The moment his perspective shifts, he regains everything he thought he had lost. The man who suffered was never the real Job, so the real Job never lost anything. From Job's final perspective of "dust and ashes," the losses over which he grieved so mightily are as nothing. In the end, we all die. What makes life worth living is not our illusion of invulnerability or immortality, but our ability to find truth in the life time allotted to us. The problem of human suffering is ours, not God's. I propose, therefore, that we think about our human problem—namely, what, if anything, can we do to minimize the suffering that is evil?

OUTLINE OF THE CHAPTERS

I begin by analyzing Aristotle's discussion of voluntary and involuntary actions. Aristotle treats human beings as initiators of action and equates evil with voluntary vice. His moral system thus serves as a nice foil to the wisdom tradition, which characterizes us as unwitting responders to perceived threats to our self-identity. It is natural to start with Aristotle's account of vice because it has been so influential. Aristotle sets out to aid lawmakers by offering a morality designed to justify the political system of praise and blame, control, and punishment. His distinctions among types of action underpin and guide how modern Western legal systems categorize and react to criminal behavior. Therein lies the danger. Aristotle's moralistic approach underestimates the extent of our ignorance about who we are and fails to appreciate how trapped most of us are in unhealthy dynamics of our making. Assimilating evil to criminal vice makes our actions appear more voluntary than they are and disregards the role that society plays in causing us to behave as we do. It involves us in bad faith as well. For in our heart of hearts, we do not truly believe that every deed originates in free choice. As Kenneth Cauthen points out, when we judge our peers, we talk as if their choices were completely unconditioned. However, when we are accused of wrongdoing, we urge our judges to take into account the different pressures and constraints under which we operated. We "are more likely to magnify freedom when we speak of our enemies."[12]

After examining and rejecting Aristotle's view, I shift gears and explore evil from the perspective of authors whom I locate within the wisdom tradition. Using literature, I examine in detail how our false sense of self dooms us to unhappy lives. Klaus Mann, Patricia Highsmith, Robert Louis Stevenson, and Henry James show how our mistaken self-identity causes us to behave in ways that exacerbate our anxiety and dread. This heightened anxiety makes it still more difficult for us to discover who we truly are and to overcome our dread.

Since narratives or stories unfold over time, they are especially well suited to disclosing how our responses to our suffering often merely compound the problem. Literature has another great advantage. Most philosophical and theological discussions of wickedness label some actions (the Holocaust, the September 11 bombing of the World Trade Center, murder, rape) or people (Adolf Hitler, Osama bin Laden, Timothy McVeigh) as evil. If we do not take care, this approach leads to complacent self-righteousness. We busily detail other people's wrongdoing, never stopping to examine whether we are guilty of similar sins. The best literature lays an ironic trap, catching us in the act of unwittingly doing the very things we condemn as immoral. In the middle chapters, I consider what the existence of these ironic traps teaches us about the nature of evil.

I conclude with an examination of what Dante, Jesus, and Socrates—exemplars of the wisdom tradition—propose as the way to break out of the cycle of alienation, paranoia, narcissistic rage, and violence in which we trap ourselves. If this self-destructive cycle of suffering—not malice or injury per se—constitutes evil, then the most effective way to resist evil is to discover our real or objective self. Dante suggests that we must first experience other people's evil or sin as our own before we can leave our suffering behind. The way to heaven and self-knowledge is through a poetic hell. I say "poetic hell" because our experience of shared sinning is liberating, Dante believes, only when it is simultaneously aesthetic and intellectual. The *Inferno*, Dante's artistic and sensual rendering of his journey through hell, enables us to have this dual experience. For his part, Jesus teaches that, if we want to be free and to enter into new life, we must avoid the deadly dynamics of demonization, see the limits of the law, and stop satanizing our fellow human beings and God. Only then can we experience divine love, transcend our suffering, and achieve a measure of everlasting peace. Socrates would have us stabilize our identity by devoting ourselves to the search for the unchanging, eternal *eidē* or forms. These *eidē*, which are the source of being and truth, enable us to assess objectively the goodness of a proposed course of action. In addition, devoting ourselves to the *eidē* also activates our conscience, understood as the voice of God within us.

All three thinkers argue that our suffering disappears of its own accord as we come to know ourselves better and as we stop converting the world and its inhabitants into obstacles to our happiness. To paraphrase John Knowles's beautiful line: we must stop constructing at infinite cost to ourselves these Maginot Lines against an enemy we think we see across the frontier, an enemy who never attacks that way—if ever he attacks at all; if he is indeed the enemy.[13] If the real enemy is our ignorance of the inner workings of our hearts, we should be seeking to identify our illusions, including our false beliefs about the nature of evil. I now turn to that task.

1

EVIL AS VICE

Each thing is subject to one evil which ruins it; iron to rust,
wool to moth, flocks of sheep to wolves. . . . As then each one of
these things is liable to that which ruins its virtue, let us now
consider what it is which injures the human race, and what it
is which ruins the virtue of a human being.

           —*St. John Crysostom*

THE OLDEST WESTERN RELIGIOUS CONCEPTIONS OF EVIL HAVE LITTLE TO DO
with malice and everything to do with painful frustration. *Kakía*, the New
Testament Greek word for evil, refers to anything that impedes human
thriving—sickness, disease, loss, misfortune.[1] The early Christian writer
Valentinus defined evil as anguish and terror.[2] The ancient Hebrew word
for evil *raʿ* similarly equates evil with identity-threatening anxiety, a
sense of worthlessness, and sadness.[3] Paul Ricoeur has argued that the
early Hebrews thought our primordial experience of evil was one of
dread.[4] These views are consistent with the views of ancient tribal peoples
who identified evil with illness and death, not with malice or trespass.[5]
Sandra Bloom goes so far as to claim that "in every culture evil has been
associated with calamity, misfortune, sorrow, and suffering and, therefore,
with traumatic experience."[6] In all the early views, natural cataclysms or
accidents, as well as human actions, qualify as evil insofar as they cause
human beings to suffer.

The religious concept of evil changed when orthodox Church fathers started to insist that evil was a morally corrupt condition of the heart that causes individuals to trespass against others. This view makes evil intentional and shifts our attention away from suffering toward doing. We should not be surprised, therefore, that many people today do not consider natural disasters or accidents to be evil. If our house floods, we consider the deluge a hassle. When natural catastrophes cause extensive property damage and human suffering, we may characterize the effects as great misfortunes. However, since we do not see any malice in nature, most of us do not deem hurricanes or earthquakes "evil." Nor do we think of accidents as evil. If a workman unintentionally drops a hammer and severely injures us, we may accuse him of negligence. But to call him or his deed "evil" seems perverse, regardless of how much suffering he has caused us. Only nonaccidental, voluntary human actions strike us as evil.

Susan Neiman has argued that Rousseau was the first thinker to identify evil with intentional human action.[7] Writing after the horror of the Lisbon earthquake in 1755, Rousseau rejected the theistic worldview that interpreted cataclysms as divine punishment for human sins. Too many innocents died to make that view plausible. Rousseau believed that human beings might justifiably be punished only for the harm they have caused. Therefore, he drove a wedge between suffering produced by natural events and willful evil. Earthquakes might be bad, but they should not be labeled "evil." That term should be reserved for human injustices.

Neiman contends that Rousseau's Enlightenment view has become the modern perspective:

> On this [modern] view, Lisbon and Auschwitz are two completely different kinds of events. Lisbon denotes the sort of thing insurance companies call natural disasters, to remove them from the sphere of human action. Thus human beings are absolved of responsibility not only for causing or compensating them but even for thinking about them, except in pragmatic and technological terms. Earthquakes and volcanoes, famines and floods inhabit the borders of human meaning. We want to understand just so much about them as might help us gain control. Only traditional—that is, pre-modern—theists will seek in them significance. Auschwitz, by contrast, stands for all this is meant when we use the word evil today; absolute wrongdoing that leaves no room for account or expiation.[8]

So it is that we moderns believe that only primitive people prone to magical thinking would connect a hurricane or earthquake with past human actions, much less view it as a form of divine punishment. Yet, as Neiman notes, our enlightened view leaves us with little to say about suffering in general. The Lisbon earthquake left people howling in despair. Many were so traumatized that they gave up on life. There is something in this pain that calls for a response, yet we dismiss natural, catastrophic suffering as uninteresting and morally irrelevant.

Neiman is right to worry about our fixation on human wrongdoing and our corresponding lack of interest in human suffering. She is mistaken, though, about who set us on this path. Aristotle, not Rousseau, appears to have been the first Western theorist to associate evil with voluntary human action. In the opening chapters of the *Nicomachean Ethics*, Aristotle dismisses the idea that suffering per se can interfere with or diminish our happiness.[9] It is vice, understood as a bad habit and voluntary corruption of choice, that is the true threat and that deserves to be called evil. Although Aristotelian vice produces untoward actions, it need not be intentional. For Aristotle, we become vicious through negligent inattention and laziness. Later, the Church fathers, drawing upon Aristotle's account of vice, construed evil as fully intentional, violative action or sin. In so doing, they removed us even farther from the older idea of evil as pain, suffering, and dread.[10]

This emphasis on action, instead of on anxiety-inducing suffering, is characteristic of the moralistic approach to evil. Aristotle's crystallization of this approach continues to shape our thinking about evil. To comprehend what is at stake in the great divide between the moralistic and wisdom tradition approach to evil, we must understand Aristotle's theory of vice and the many problems with this account.

ARISTOTELIAN VICE

Aristotle says that man is, by nature, a political animal.[11] He means that we can fully realize our human abilities only in communities shaped by a political regime. Like animals, we secure food and shelter by living in social groups. But realizing our highest powers requires living together in a community structured and governed by a regime intent upon enabling its citizens to live in the best possible way.[12] (Even a tyrannical regime, such as that of Saddam Hussein, aims at what it takes to be good for its citizens; however, it may narrowly restrict who qualifies as a "citizen.") This realization of human capabilities, accomplished always within a political community, is goodness, or what Aristotle terms "excellence" or "virtue."

Although regimes differ in what they take to be virtuous, every regime operates with some guiding notion of what is good for human beings. A regime shapes us through its laws and its system of education. Law and education are intrinsically political, and both rely heavily upon praise and blame. That is why Aristotle says that virtue is what we praise and vice is what we blame.[13] If we consistently praise certain sorts of actions and passions, then we must believe, Aristotle argues, that these constitute excellence. We blame those actions and passions that keep us from realizing our distinctively human abilities to discriminate, to form friendships, and to die for a worthy cause. Through praise and blame, the political community attempts to mold all members of the community to act and feel in ways judged to be in the individual and collective interest.

Since there would be no point in praising or blaming actions utterly beyond human control, communities restrict praise and blame to voluntary actions. Aristotle defines voluntary actions as deeds that are within our control and for which we may justifiably be held responsible. As he notes, legislators in all regimes must be concerned with voluntary and involuntary behavior, because they are responsible for drafting enforceable legislation designed to shape the character of the citizenry.[14] The laws they draft become, in turn, the basis for praise and blame and for attributing responsibility and imposing sanctions.

We have plenty of evidence that Aristotle is right about the role of the law in our communities. Hardly a day goes by when our newspapers do not excoriate someone or other as an evildoer and demand that he or she be imprisoned for having chosen to act improperly. In making this demand, we assimilate evil to voluntary vice and vice to crime. It is not obvious, however, that this transitive assimilation is sound. As I noted in the introduction, while moralistic treatments of evil emphasize voluntary wrongdoing, thinkers in the wisdom tradition do not even mention choice or free will. We should consider, therefore, why moralists are so keen on emphasizing the difference between voluntary and involuntary action. Since this distinction lies at the heart of Aristotle's theory of goodness, evil, and responsibility, his analysis can help us to see where and why moral theorists and wisdom thinkers part ways.

Aristotle maintains that only two sorts of actions qualify as genuinely involuntary—actions committed under compulsion and those done out of ignorance.[15] Since we like to be praised but hate being blamed, we are tempted to minimize our blameworthiness by mischaracterizing our voluntary actions as involuntary. To counteract this tendency, Aristotle begins by circumscribing the number of actions that qualify as compelled and excusable. Involuntary actions are ones for which the moving principle is entirely outside of the agent. If a kidnapper grabs a woman and transports her in his car, she involuntarily goes with him. In this case, the moving principle is the kidnapper driving the car. The woman contributes no agency whatsoever to the action. We may pity or pardon her plight, but we should not accuse her of evildoing or viciousness. She does not deserve to be blamed.

Let us suppose, though, that this same woman is sailing her boat with some friends when a storm comes up. As the boat starts to take on water, she jettisons some goods. Is she "forced" to do so, or is her jettisoning a voluntary act, subject to praise or blame? Aristotle's answer is that her act is not compelled and, therefore, qualifies as voluntary.[16] Although the woman has not caused the storm to appear on the horizon, she does contribute her agency to the action of throwing goods overboard. It is within her power to act well or badly as she goes about responding to the storm threat. Many factors should be considered: when the goods should be jettisoned, which ones should go, and so on. If she deliberates well, considering all of these relevant issues, she merits our praise. If she panics, throwing more goods overboard than necessary, or if she opts to dispose of a friend instead of a keg of beer, she becomes blameworthy in our eyes.

Aristotle concedes that, in the abstract, her action might be judged involuntary.[17] After all, no one of sound mind goes out on a sailing party with a view to discarding the very things—food, drink—that make for a good party. However, our actions never occur in the abstract. We act in specific, concrete circumstances. Doing the right thing or acting virtuously means making the correct determination with respect to a host of particular factors—who must act, what they must do, when and how they should act, with what instruments the deed should be attempted, and so on. If teachers and parents have raised us well, and if we exert ourselves to be as thoughtful as possible about our choices, we can act virtuously in the concrete. Despite the fact that discarding goods is not an act that we would perform, other things being equal, we do contribute agency to the act—by deliberating or by failing to rouse ourselves to deliberate. Whenever an action can be determined by deliberation, the action is voluntary. Only actions resulting from a moving principle that is entirely outside of the agent should be called involuntary.

Even when we act under duress or pain of death, our deeds may be voluntary. Sometimes we do something we would prefer not to do because we fear some greater evil or because we have a noble goal in mind. To take Aristotle's example: assume that a dictator kidnaps our parents or children. He demands that we do something base in return for his not murdering them. Under these conditions, we may be sorely tempted to act ignobly. Still, our response to the threat is not compelled. It is up to us to determine which goals are worthy of what type and degree of sacrifice. As Aristotle puts it, we praise those who endure great pains for noble objects but blame those who endure needless suffering or who act basely for venal gains.[18]

Evaluating the situation will reveal that we have options. Perhaps we can trick the dictator or counter with a threat of our own. Our options may be limited, but that does not make our action involuntary. On the contrary, the difficulty of choosing means we must use all of our faculties and have our wits about us if we are to act well. The fact that there are such difficulties, Aristotle thinks, accounts for why we praise those people who rise to the occasion and blame those who do not. In some cases, the cost of doing the right thing may be so enormous that the pressure threatens to overstrain our nature. Aristotle concedes that, if no one could withstand such pressure (e.g., extreme torture), our response may merit pity or pardon, not blame. Yet here again he hesitates: "some acts, perhaps, we cannot be forced to do, but ought rather to face death after the most fearful sufferings."[19] He is cautious because he believes that we are all prone to excuse away our base actions, claiming that we were forced to do an awful thing or arguing that anyone in our position would have behaved ignobly.

Aristotle thinks that we will never live a good life unless we are willing, at some point, to take a stand and show our true character. Even in the face of death, we must claim for ourselves the right to shape our lives in a maximally satisfying way. After all, each of us dies at some point. Biological persistence cannot be the goal of our existence. Persistence is possible without the use of human intelligence of imagination. (Think of people in comas.) Our faculties exist to be used, and so living well must involve developing and exercising our ability to discriminate among ways of life. It is no accident that Aristotle lists courage as the first virtue or excellence. There are two kinds of courage: genuine courage and political courage.[20] The genuinely courageous person discriminates among goals, choosing to fight only for those that are most worthy of defense. The politically courageous fight for their country, right or wrong. Although political courage is less good than genuine, unqualified courage, it nonetheless merits praise. Those men and women who take a stand, knowing the potential cost to them and their families, are on the road to virtue. They grasp that there is more to life than doing whatever it takes to stay alive. In acting on this intuition, they show that they are capable of rousing themselves to excel. That is why sworn enemies respect each other's courage. We hear an echo of Aristotle in Samuel Johnson's claim: "Courage is a quality so necessary for maintaining virtue, that it is always respected, even when it is associated with vice."[21]

Those who lack the virtue of courage slink away from the life-threatening danger or, equally blameworthily, throw themselves recklessly into battle, regardless of the danger to themselves or to their comrades. Either way, these individuals forfeit a little of their humanity because they fail to judge well. Faculties that we fail to use atrophy. Over time we habit-uate ourselves to not deliberating and judging. We make ourselves into reactors who unthinkingly and almost mechanically respond to situations. Evil or vice might be defined as a failure to deliberate that leads to the destruction of our humanity. Humanity and the faculty of deliberation are, Aristotle contends, ultimately one and the same. Vice is the voluntary destruction of the moving principle, which Aristotle calls "deliberative desire."[22] Man is this "moving principle."[23]

If vice destroys the person who originates action, does it follow that vicious behavior is involuntary and that the wicked are not responsible for their actions? Is there a person left to be held accountable after vice has taken its toll? Each of us creates our habits through actions that admit of deliberation. We also develop habits through our inaction, our failure to attempt to deliberate as best we can. Permitting our faculties to atrophy through negligent laziness, we eventually become incapable of behaving in any way different from our habitual modes of reacting. Vice is uncon-scious of itself.[24] But it does not follow, according to Aristotle, that society should let us off the moral hook. What does follow is that the community should collectively set the bar for involuntary actions quite high, restricting what legitimately counts as a compelled, pardonable act. Consequently, Aristotle defines the compulsory quite narrowly: "the compulsory, then, seems to be that whose moving principle is outside, the person compelled contributing nothing."[25] By raising the bar, the political community acts to curb our cowardly tendency to excuse away our ignoble behavior. By collectively holding our moral feet to the fire in this fashion, we create an incentive for all of us to think hard before initiating an action. Our reflection will open up new possibilities for action and suggest ways to avoid baseness. To refuse to rally our wits is, in Aristotle's view, to begin the slide toward self-deception and to destroy our ability to discriminate and judge well.

Aristotle argues for a similarly high bar with respect to actions involving ignorance. Whether such actions are involuntary depends crucially upon the type of ignorance behind the act. Actions done in ignorance differ greatly from those done by reason of unavoidable ignorance.[26] Those who attack others in a fit of rage or who drink themselves silly often claim that they did not realize what they were doing. Although it may well be true that they acted in ignorance, their lack of knowledge does not excuse their action. According to Aristotle, their attempt to avoid blame is itself a hallmark of evil or vicious passivity. Such people do not understand that there is a fundamental difference between self-caused and unavoidable ignorance. Given that human beings are limited creatures, it is not possible for us to have full and complete knowledge of the circumstances in which we act. Some ignorance is inescapable. This unavoidable ignorance is excusable; self-caused ignorance is not. Those who make themselves drunk or indulge their anger cause themselves to be oblivious to circumstances. No one forces drunkards to drink too much. No one coerces the enraged to become angry. The drunkard and the angry individual uncritically accept some course of action as good. They fail to deliberate because they have rendered themselves unable to do so. They initiated the attitudes and actions causing the impairment of their critical faculties. Aristotle maintains that they alone are to blame for the harm they have inflicted upon themselves and perhaps on others as well.[27]

It might be objected that the drunkard or angry person is ignorant of the right way to behave and does not know what is in his or her true interest. That objection does not mitigate the person's responsibility but merely redescribes his or her plight: "Now every wicked man is ignorant of what he ought to do and what he ought to abstain from, and it is by reason of error of this kind that men become unjust and in general bad."[28] In Aristotle's view, which underpins most Western legal systems, wickedness or evil is our self-caused, voluntary lack of clarity as to what we must do if we are to lead humanly satisfying lives. Our habitual indiscriminate indulgence of our appetites and passions prevents us from thinking clearly. In our confusion, we act stupidly, risking our lives and endangering our friends, colleagues, and fellow citizens. Having freely and irretrievably compromised our ability to reason well about the best way to act, we threaten the communal welfare and so deserve to be described as evil and punished for our wickedness.

Why do we fail to deliberate? Aristotle answers: we have not exerted ourselves to the fullest. Becoming good at choosing, like becoming a fine musician or top athlete, is difficult. It requires effort and attention. Practice alone does not make us perfect. The great coach Vince Lombardi spoke as a true Aristotelian when he maintained, "only perfect practice makes perfect."[29] If we fail to use our muscles in the correct way, they eventually become unusable. By taking the lazy way out and pursuing whatever strikes us as pleasurable, we destroy our faculty of judgment. In the Aristotelian language of St. John Crysostom, the failure to judge is the specific vice or evil that corrupts judgment and destroys the human being. As our ability to judge disappears, we become progressively less able to draw crucial distinctions of the sort Aristotle has made. To make matters worse, instead of blaming ourselves when we act badly and taking measures to overcome our voluntary ignorance of the right way to act, we say, "the devil made me do it" or "my mother (father, wife, husband, or whoever) has driven me to drink."

When we do something that garners praise, we are quite happy to accept that our deeds are entirely voluntary and worthy of accolades. This asymmetry in our attitudes toward our responsibility can be corrected, Aristotle believes, only if we are quite clear about which actions are in our control and which are not. Actions done in ignorance of the right principle (i.e., actions initiated without deliberation) are voluntary. Actions stemming from our ignorance of some particular circumstance or detail (e.g., of what we are doing, of whom we are affecting, of which instrument we are using, of which end or goal we are pursuing, or of our manner) may be involuntary. If a man unwittingly uses a defective foil that breaks during a fencing match and kills his opponent, he has not voluntarily killed his opponent. If he has properly inspected and stored his equipment, both he and his dead opponent are victims of unforeseeable, unfortunate circumstances. To take another case: if a woman gives her child what she believes is healing serum to counteract the effect of a snakebite to the child's leg, but it turns out that her child is allergic to this serum and falls ill, the woman did not voluntarily sicken her child. In the first case, the man is ignorant of the particular instrument (he thinks the foil is safely intact when, in fact, the weapon is dangerously defective); in the second case, the woman is ignorant of her goal (she thinks she is saving her child, but she is impairing the child's health).

Although we might quarrel with some of the details of this Aristotelian account, his basic thesis is clear enough: ignorance resulting from laziness or laxity is blameworthy because it is evil or vicious. Only involuntary ignorance, which occurs because human beings cannot foresee every contingency, is pardonable or pitiable. To say that our ignorance is involuntary does not mean that it is painless. The woman who accidentally kills her child may grieve for years over her loss; the fencer who unknowingly impales his opponent may be overwhelmed by a sense of shame and feelings of remorse. Insofar as suffering prevents us from feeling that our life is an excellent one, we might be said, in a loose sense, to have experienced evil. Aristotle concedes, for example, that it is a blow to a person's happiness when a good friend dies or suffers many reversals.[30] But these sufferings, Aristotle argues, pale in comparison with the permanent unhappiness we bring upon ourselves if we become criminally wicked, vicious, evil. Suffering passes; wickedness is permanent. In addition, suffering can lead to understanding. The grieving mother may become more humane, coming to a fuller appreciation of human vulnerability and of the losses others have suffered. In the process of making amends to the family of his dead opponent, the fencer may develop a lasting friendship with them. The possibility that accidental suffering might work to refine our judgment and to enrich our lives explains why an Aristotelian moralist will consider neither the action nor the person of the mother or fencer to be evil.

By contrast, when we voluntarily do something that warrants blame, we reap only a bitter reward. We lose our humanity and become like automatons. We go through life thoughtlessly reacting to stimuli and pursuing temptations that are often in conflict with each and that become less pleasurable over time. To sort out these conflicts and to fathom why the pleasures are diminishing requires that we use the critical faculty of judgment or discernment. However, our vice has destroyed precisely this faculty, which Aristotle calls the first principle of human action.[31] As our frustrations mount, we try a variety of things to escape our unhappiness. Everything we try compounds our problems. We enter a hell of our own making, a hell that is doubly tormenting because we cannot see where we are, whence we have come, or whither we are going. The vicious literally have no prospects. Vice destroys the person in a way that causing or undergoing involuntary suffering does not. That is why Aristotle takes evil to be a matter of vice.

Dangers of Equating Evil with Vice

Aristotle's moralistic account of evil has two strengths. First, the account offers an explanation of why political regimes so roundly condemn evil. Every community is held together by its culture. For the moralist, culture is a set of inherited habits and norms designed to maximize human satisfaction. These habits reflect our accumulated wisdom regarding the behaviors that are conducive to happiness and those that are not. Since no culture can anticipate every contingency, every political morality is inevitably partial. This inadequacy does not mean that the morality is utterly arbitrary or that we could do without it. The moralist will insist that the happiness of each of us depends in a thousand ways upon the larger culture in which we live. Aristotle's account seeks to disclose the profound intuitions about evil underlying our system of praise and blame and the laws that both reflect and sustain that system of behavior modification. By becoming clearer about these intuitions, we can make better distinctions and write improved laws, thereby enriching our lives and those of our children.

Moralists, like Aristotle, argue that evil is not blameworthy only because culture condemns it. Every society resorts to praise and blame in order to prevent human beings from destroying their faculties of judgment and acting in ways that undermine individual and collective happiness. In punishing the vicious, the community simply does that which we have asked it to do. The moralist's assimilation of evil to vice and vice to crime aims at revealing and reinforcing the role that culture plays in enabling us to lead satisfying lives. We need to examine how the wisdom tradition deals with the need for laws and this crucial role of culture.

The second strength of Aristotle's moralistic account is its refusal to equate all evil with conscious wrongdoing. We tend to think of evil as active—as an act intended to harm another. Although Aristotle does not rule out malice, his focus is on the evil of neglect, indifference, and laziness.[32] Evil is primarily our failure to exert ourselves to attend critically to what we are doing. This laxity causes our powers of choice and deliberation to atrophy. Evil is less something we consciously choose and more the destruction of choice itself. Hence, we find Aristotle making the startling claim that the vicious person does not, in the strict sense, choose. For choice is deliberate or reasoned desire and vice destroys reason (what Aristotle calls the "principle" or "source").[33] Evil is the void in the agent where the potential for choice was present until the agent freely destroyed that power by acting without proper deliberation. That is why people who are bestial or brutish—people who are diseased or who have acted badly from birth—are, in Aristotle's view, less evil than the vicious.[34] Since such people never had the potential for choice, they cannot be said to have corrupted it and so are not truly wicked.

From Aristotle's perspective, virtue alone is active and dynamic. Virtuous action is the result of an attentive struggle for balance and for the right kind and measure of control. To be courageous, we must steer clear of both cowardice and overconfident foolhardiness. Living a human life means considering the different forms of error and taking care to avoid them. Unlike virtue, vice is unconscious of itself.[35] It is inattention, a letting go of life. Once this letting go occurs, life is irretrievable. As Aristotle puts it, it was once open to the self-indulgent man not to be such, but this is no longer so.[36] He would say the same of confirmed gluttons, spendthrifts, and sadists.

I argue in subsequent chapters that we are quite capable of acting violently and sadistically with the best of intentions. Therefore, Aristotle's linking of evil with the destruction of our critical faculty, instead of with malicious intent, is a step in the right direction. In other respects, though, his treatment of evil as criminal vice and his focus on individual actions and agency are seriously misleading. There are five major problems with this approach.

First, it overlooks the way in which the social system of praise and blame itself operates as a force diminishing our humanity. As I noted above, communal norms comprise, at best, a partial morality. Every system contains inconsistencies and favors some personas or roles at the expense of others. Behavior stigmatized as deviant may not be as bad as a given society would have its members believe. The individual human being is always more than a particular persona or role. To say that someone is individual means that he or she is unique. By definition, the individual acts in ways that do not conform to majority expectations. Behavior that is perceived as strange easily gets demonized as unhealthy, dangerous, or not fully human. If we take Aristotle's route and identify evil with vice, we will not see, much less properly analyze, the mechanics of demonization. We will judge as vicious that which is merely unfamiliar.

Individuals may outwardly conform to communal norms, while inwardly they seethe. The anger we feel for having been forced to conform can fuel a social dynamic of envy and resentment. As Nietzsche famously observed, "Chastity is a virtue in some, but in many it is almost a vice. To be sure, they abstain, but the bitch 'sensuality' glances enviously out of everything they do."[37] Reflecting on the individual's response to overly rigid social demands, Honoré de Balzac concluded that society had a built-in safety release valve: "when law becomes despotic, morals are relaxed, and vice versa." Whether society has such a homeostatic mechanism is an open question. Still, at a minimum, we can agree with Nietzsche and Balzac that the practices of praise and blame are not neutral. In the words of Garrath Williams, "Judgments of desert are also actions."[38] Praising and blaming should not be treated as if they were activities beyond reproach. I will examine the mechanics and consequences of the political system of praise and blame more closely in later chapters.

Second, this approach locates vice/evil primarily within the agent. The moralist contends that each of us is born with a set of distinctively human capacities. Through effort and care, we develop these capacities and bring them to fruition. Or we destroy them through carelessness. This view treats a human being as the primary origin, moving principle, or cause. Although praise and blame can influence our attitudes and behavior, these practices, in Aristotle's view, do not cause us to act in any particular way. On the contrary, the community's attempt to modify the behavior of its members assumes that each individual freely initiates his or her actions. That is why we praise and blame only voluntary actions and pity or pardon the involuntary ones. In this fashion, moralists place responsibility for vicious or virtuous actions squarely on the person who initiates (or fails to initiate) the action in question.

Since no society could exist for long if it could not hold its members accountable for breaches of its laws and mores, it is perhaps inevitable that communities attribute agency to citizens and punish those who appear to deviate from their laws and mores. The problem with this practice is that it makes it difficult to understand phenomena such as mass hysteria and witch-hunts. In these cases, evil is larger than any single individual. It is as if evil moves through the entire community, leading people to think and do things that they normally would not. The spasm seizes us and then passes. To understand these phenomena, we need an account of evil that does not make such a firm distinction between the righteous person and the deviant sinner.

Aristotle's account is flawed in a third way. Like other moralists, he assumes that we can disinterestedly survey evil and remain above the fray. Christopher Kutz puts it well: "Much philosophical writing about moral responsibility takes a juridical perspective, from which the disinterested writer metes out the appropriate deserts to the offending agent." Kutz contends "[t]his tendency wholly fails to capture the way in which agents and respondents are mutually engaged in moral, social, and legal relationships."[39] It overlooks how readily we get drawn into evil at the very moment we presume to blame the wickedness of other people. In the parable of the wheat and the tares, Jesus warns against assuming that it is so easy to distinguish the good from the evil. Tares are weeds that look remarkably similar to wheat. They grow among the wheat and the roots of both become intertwined.[40] In removing the tares, we risk tearing up the wheat as well. Henry David Thoreau worried a good deal about the close relationship between virtue and vice: "We are double-edged blades, and every time we whet our virtue the return stroke straps our vice. Where is the skillful swordsman who can give clean wounds, and not rip up his work with the other edge?"[41] In the less metaphorical language of Oliver Goldsmith: "There are some faults so nearly allied to excellence that we can scarce weed out the vice without eradicating the virtue."[42]

The drive toward excellence easily becomes self-righteous zeal. Vice frequently masquerades as virtue. Our prejudices and biases incline us to see wickedness where there is none. Moralists generally ignore these problems. The consequences of this oversight can be seen if we return to Aristotle for a moment and closely attend to his discussion of ignorance. When we have injured someone because our knowledge of the circumstances is partial, Aristotle contends that we should not be blamed as long as we show remorse.[43] If we accidentally kill someone and are not in the least bit sorry, our action, in Aristotle's view, begins to resemble an absolutely wrong, unforgivable, vicious act. Although we did not intend the death, our indifference to the pain and suffering we have caused reveals us to be uncaring and lax, the kind of person who could have voluntarily caused the death. Only if we are genuinely sorry can we escape blame. That is why our legal judges take into account a convicted party's contrition (or lack thereof) when determining the punishment. But here a difficulty arises. If vice can assume "some mark of virtue in his outward parts," how are we to know when an individual is truly remorseful?[44] Some individuals are more expressive of their emotions than others. Cultural differences compound the problem. Some cultures stress self-control and the desirability of not showing what one is feeling. Are we such excellent judges of cross-cultural character that we can, without any qualms, impose harsh sentences on those we judge to be cold, unfeeling, vicious, and evil?

We should remember as well that moralities evolve. As Amitai Etzioni argues, we cannot equate goodness with whatever a particular community happens to endorse.[45] It has not been that long since supposedly decent Americans turned a blind eye to the lynching of blacks; some private clubs in America still discriminate against women, Catholics, and Jews. Positive change comes about as individuals challenge the theories of human nature used to justify such acts, and as they disobey discriminatory laws they deem unjust. In these cases of civil disobedience, individuals do not exhibit remorse because they do not feel that they have acted badly. If we assimilate evil to criminal vice, then we will view this absence of contrition as confirmation that the individual is thoroughly corrupt. Yet, in this instance, the lack of remorse might serve as a sign of the person's essential soundness.

When we assume the role of superior spectators casting our supposedly impartial eye on the virtues and vices of others, we make ourselves into enforcers of communal mores. Forgetting that every political system is fraught with contradiction, we cling to the mores that serve as the source of our authority and power. Backed by the authority of the law, we become smug in our self-righteousness. Certain in our rectitude, we proclaim, along with Aristotle, that the wicked should be punished and shunned.[46] This stance risks locking us into a rigid antagonism toward our fellow citizens. We refuse to acknowledge our sins because doing so would require that we ask for others' mercy. Having loudly proclaimed that voluntary wickedness must never be forgiven, we are afraid to own up to our shortcomings. Instead, we become even more dogmatic and harsh in a frantic effort to prove our sanctity.

Socrates had a good eye for perceiving the fissures and inconsistencies in politically sanctioned moral systems. He routinely caught the self-righteous in contradictions. The Athenians retaliated by murdering him. Jesus, who reserved his most scathing comments for hypocrites, suffered a similar fate. Yet moralists have strikingly little to say about hypocrisy, the expression of evil most discussed by thinkers in the wisdom tradition. The moralists who rail against vice typically (and unwittingly) overlook hypocrisy because they do not perceive how profoundly incoherent many inherited social beliefs are. Consequently, they fail to grasp how common it is for us to say one thing and then to do another. It falls to ironic thinkers such as Jesus, Nietzsche, Spinoza, and Socrates to lay bare our hypocrisy.

Their radical suggestions for exposing, and coping with, hypocrisy ("when someone strikes you, turn the other cheek" (Jesus); "it is far better to suffer injustice than to do it" (Socrates)) undermine many of the cherished beliefs drummed into us by authority figures (e.g., "stand up and fight for your rights"; "prosecute all offenders"). Instead of rethinking our entrenched beliefs, we resist any suggestion that appears to threaten our socially reinforced self-image. We will murder before we will relinquish our habitual and "virtuous" self.

Hannah Arendt is onto us when she writes: "What makes it so plausible to assume that hypocrisy is the vice of vices is that integrity can . . . exist under the cover of all other vices except this one. . . . Only the hypocrite is really rotten to the core."[47] Integrity and Aristotelian vice can indeed coexist. Aristotle concedes as much when he argues that each person has a single characteristic weakness that he or she should try to overcome. You may be prone to overindulging in food, and I may be too fearful. So you have more of the virtue of courage, and I possess more temperance. However, both of us start out as fundamentally sound. By conforming to communal norms, deliberating well, and being appropriately remorseful, each of us can build on the integrity we already possess to overcome our propensity toward vice. Or so moralism would have us believe.

Against this optimistic moralistic view, I would oppose the wisdom perspective's insistence that evil is a beast forever crouching at our door. We are in eternal danger because we are anxious hypocrites who hide our deep-seated insecurity from ourselves. Arendt is quite correct to call attention to our hypocrisy. She is wrong to name it the "vice of vices." That description reduces hypocrisy to a form of deviancy. Hypocrisy is not a vice. It is our way of life insofar as we refuse to admit that we are limited beings who lack a complete, consistent understanding of ourselves or of the world. Unless we comprehend and admit the extent of our hypocrisy, we will live in dread of exposure. In the chapters that follow, we will see how this dread leads to cruelty and violence, sometimes on a large scale. Unlike vice, hypocritical evil has a systemic dimension. The fear and rage that gripped the Athenians and drove them to murder Socrates was larger than a single man or woman. Locating evil in the failure of individuals to deliberate well prevents us from seeing these larger dynamics and from doing something about them.

A case drawn from the annals of slavery illustrates the problem. Slave traders usually separated family members and transported people from different tribes so that they could not communicate with each other and mutiny. Occasionally, though, large numbers of people from a single tribe were brought over on the same ship. In one such case, the abducted Africans reached an understanding that they would not allow themselves to be enslaved. When the boat came to shore, they disembarked and then turned *en masse*, walked out into the sea, and drowned themselves. One cannot help but be moved by their courageous resolution. Aristotle would say that their action merits our praise: they knew they were moving principles and chose to preserve their dignity by dying. Yet there is more to be said about this case. It could be argued that any system that forces people to choose between dying and living enslaved is cruel and unjust. The key issue is not whether the trapped men and women acted voluntarily and merit our praise—the more important questions take us into the realm of communal hypocrisy: why did the system of slavery develop? And why did supposedly good Christian men and women allow it to exist for so long?

Blame typically operates with a "retrospective focus" and hones in on the "attributes of the culprit rather than the situation" he or she faced.[48] The whole question of responsibility becomes more complicated when we look at the larger setting in which individuals find themselves acting. If we are honest, we will admit that some individuals seem better positioned than others to be Aristotelian initiators or "moving principles." One Victorian woman insisted "virtue and vice suppose the freedom to choose . . . but what can be the morals of a woman who is not even in possession of herself, who has nothing of her own, and who has all her life been trained to extricate herself from the arbitrary by ruse, from constraint by using her charms? . . . As long as she is subject to man's yoke or to prejudice, as long as she receives no professional education, as long as she is deprived of her civil rights, there can be no moral law for her!"[49] Moralism stresses the free will of individuals: the criminal could have acted other than he or she did. Yet moral philosophers are remarkably silent when it comes to specifying what these other, supposedly viable options were.

Kenneth Cauthen's point about our asymmetrical judgment (quoted in the introduction) is relevant here. When assessing other people's behavior and imposing punishment, we always emphasize their unfettered choice or will. Yet, when it comes time to account for our actions, we cite the many situational factors constraining us. Moralists attribute this asymmetry to special pleading and chalk up our protests as another blameworthy offense. The wisdom tradition provides another explanation—namely, that we are not born free but must become free by reflecting on our experience, identifying impediments to our ability to act, determining which barriers we (individually and collectively) can overcome, and then taking such steps as we can to remove these obstacles. Moralism forecloses this reflection by defining human beings and choice/will as free. The wisdom tradition cannot guarantee reflection but it at least encourages it by interpreting freedom as an achievement, not as a given. In the following chapters, I argue that we unconsciously lock ourselves into individual and collective patterns of behavior with a perverse, controlling logic all their own. The majority of us spend most of our lives being reactors, not agents. We can become free only if we are able to see these controlling logics, yet we get little help from morality. Morality has little to say about the dynamics of dread, rage, narcissism, demonization, and hypocrisy. We should think twice, therefore, before endorsing the moralistic perspective.

Fourth, the moral justification for praise and blame is not completely consistent. Recall that praise and blame are intended to modify the individual's free behavior. Yet, if through action we acquire habits and become irretrievably vicious ("it was once open to the drunkard to be sober, but it is no longer"; "he has made himself into the sort of being who easily becomes enraged"), then it hardly makes sense to blame us for our behavior. The vicious cannot help themselves once vice has destroyed the moving principle—the human being. Or so Aristotle would have us believe. Yet this claim smacks of hubris. Sometimes alcoholics do reform themselves. I do not presume to attempt here a definitive answer on how such reform is possible. However, I would say that such counterexamples suggest that the moralistic account of human development is deeply flawed. Indeed, the practices of praise and blame make the most sense if we grant that even vicious characters are capable of reforming themselves. But, to the extent that moralists insist that our voluntarily acquired character becomes our fate, they cannot countenance this possibility.

The final difficulty with reducing evil to vice is that the reduction tempts us to think of evil as deviance. Society condemns as vicious acts those behaviors that do not conform to its idea of what makes for a healthy human being. Both moralists and wisdom thinkers agree that some behaviors leave us frustrated and unhappy and should be avoided. For my part, I do not dismiss political sanctions as entirely arbitrary. In some cases, they can perhaps help foster wisdom, a possibility I explore in the final chapter. What concerns me here is our moral blind spot. Having conflated evil with deviant vice, we refuse to entertain other accounts of why people become violent or behave sadistically. Violence may erupt when the community frustrates common, natural, and healthy impulses. Or people may lash out if they feel that their identity is being threatened. Divorcing evil from natural impulses and commonplace fears makes evil seem utterly foreign, a kind of demonic invasion. Once we delve more deeply into the connections among violence, frustration, paranoia, and mistaken identity, evil looks a lot less alien.

While the French proverb "Tout comprendre, c'est tout pardonner" ("To understand all is to forgive all") may overstate the case, we should, at least, strive to comprehend why behaviors occur. Unless we attain a measure of clarity on this score, we cannot hope to respond appropriately to acts that we deem evil. Our responses are more helpful the less we are spooked by evil and the clearer we are about our possible complicity in the actions and suffering we are wont to condemn. Even if our complicity is not great, we have a responsibility as members of the community to address the situation created by those whom we accuse and blame. We cannot act to prevent or curtail such actions in the future if we do not try to understand why the offender acted as he or she did. Moreover, our compassion grows as we see that we, too, are capable of violence and cruelty. Acknowledging this fact is part of what it means to be a responsible citizen. Hypocrites who will not admit their own propensity to violence are often the most dangerous of human beings. In the words of Richard Steele, "No vice or wickedness, which people fall into from indulgence to desires which are natural to all, ought to place them below the compassion of the virtuous part of the world; which indeed often makes me a little apt to suspect the sincerity of their virtue, who are too warmly provoked at other people's personal sins."[50] In our outrage, we may sink lower than those we condemn: "One is absolutely sickened, not by the crimes that the wicked have committed, but by the punishments that the good have inflicted; and a community is infinitely more brutalized by the habitual employment of punishment than it is by the occasional occurrence of crime."[51]

For all these reasons, we need a richer picture of evil. To begin painting that picture, I turn to a literary portrayal of evil—Klaus Mann's *Mephisto*. Although Mann, like Aristotle, associates evil with passivity and cowardice, he does not conflate evil with social deviance or blameworthy crime. Quite the reverse. Mann shows how we can lose the ability to act by means of a thoroughly moral impulse—the desire to avoid shame and to be respected and praised by society.

2

EVIL AS LOSING THE ABILITY TO ACT

All men's failings I forgive in actors; No actor's failings will I forgive in men.

—*Johann Wolfgang von Goethe*

WE TEND TO THINK OF EVIL AS SOMETHING DRAMATIC AND GLAMOROUS, a view reinforced by popular culture. Films and magazines portray evil as the rare work of genius. The French philosopher Simone Weil attacked this view, arguing that, whereas "fictional evil is varied and intriguing, attractive, profound and full of charm," real evil is stupid and insipid.[1] Weil is not entirely correct in her assessment. As we will see, evil assumes a variety of forms and hides itself from itself. In this respect, evil deserves to be called cunning, not dismissed as stupid. Weil, however, is also partly right. The shrewdly articulate film villain Hannibal Lector titillates more than the obviously sick Charles Manson. The clever criminal captures our imagination and seduces us into believing that evil involves complex, malicious motives. Therein lies the problem, for evildoers are more ignorant than malicious. They are trapped in unsatisfying, neurotic modes of behavior. Since they do not know who they are, they cannot escape their self-inflicted suffering. They behave almost mechanically, not creatively. In that respect, both real and fictional evil is, to use Weil's adjective, insipid.

In this chapter and in chapter 3, I want to challenge popular culture's view of evil as sinister brilliance and Aristotle's notion that evil is identical to vice. Analyzing the behavior of two characters who take themselves to be geniuses, I make the case that evil is better understood as self-inflicted suffering born of ignorance rather than as intentional malice. As I noted in the introduction, the wisdom tradition has long equated evil with suffering. Although the novelist Klaus Mann does not explicitly place himself in this tradition, he does so implicitly with his novel *Mephisto*. Mann's protagonist Hendrik Höfgen, whom Mann modeled on his brother-in-law Gustav Gründgens, suffers and commits evil, yet his motives are neither complex nor especially deviant. His evil lies in his impulse to avoid at all cost personal shame and the pain of embarrassment. Aristotle describes our desire to be respected by other people and to avoid shame as the condition of all virtue and human goodness.[2] That is why Aristotle considers shame a quasi-virtue.[3] Mann rejects this view of shame. He shows how our supposedly moral desire to escape social embarrassment functions as the source of evil. *Mephisto* explores the evil that unfolds when our desire to be esteemed is so great that that we will do almost anything to have our worth affirmed by others.

The novel portrays the ambitious actor Hendrik Höfgen's rise to power as the Nazis gain ascendancy. These parallel paths turn out to have much in common. With few exceptions, all the characters in the book are actors who have made their self-respect contingent upon the approval and admiration of other people. Like Aristotelian vice, this practice destroys our humanity, but the cause of the destruction is different. We are doomed by our need to feel loved, not by corrupt choice or laxity. This desire for societal approval of our talents converts us into hypocrites racked by anxiety and dread, and it costs us our ability to act.

THE AMBIGUOUS QUEST FOR RESPECT

Human rights activists proclaim that people are owed respect. Many philosophers contend that only actions showing respect for others qualify as morally good actions. Yet respect is a fundamentally ambiguous notion. For rights theorists and activists, respect means honoring the innate dignity of every human being. However, we more commonly equate respect with the act of honoring the excellence or power of someone or something. Those who have lived through a hurricane respect the force of nature's winds; we respect those who show great courage or who succeed by overcoming huge obstacles. This common usage is closest to the Latin root of "respect," which means to "to look at (*spectare*) again (*re-*)." To be respected means to command a second look, to make people sit up and take notice.

Some moralists acknowledge, but then dismiss, this second usage as quaint and irrelevant to moral discourse. Yet every morality that bases itself upon shame implicitly connects our worth to the way in which we *appear* to another. As Leon Kass has argued, we experience shame only when we feel that we have fallen short in the *eyes* of our fellow human beings.[4] We fear that our peers will sever relations with us and that we will never merit a second look from them. Our colloquial usage does have moral import. And there's the rub. In equating respect with the second look, we bind ourselves to the public. Our deeds, gestures, and speech are all calculated to catch the public eye. The more respected we are, the more likely we are to lack any internal compass by which to guide our actions because we have given control of our lives over to the many. From childhood on, we are conditioned to believe that without this audience we are nothing. We thereby acquire a taste for the drug of approval, appreciation, and adoration.

The protagonists in *Mephisto* are obsessed with the impression they are making on each other. The novel opens with a grand spectacle. The Nazi air force general is throwing a lavish party in the Opera House. All the elite, including many members of the nobility, are present. The guests are busy admiring others while congratulating themselves on their stunning appearance. The room sparkles as the light flashes off the many medals of the men. The women are dazzling in their lamé gowns and expensive, glittering jewelry. Throughout the novel, Mann takes care to describe the eyes of the characters. The iridescence of Höfgen's gray-green eyes "made one think of precious but cursed stones or of the greedy eyes of some evil and menacing fish." Lotte, the second-rate provincial actress who has become the general's wife, has "large, round, protruding cow-like eyes . . . of a moist, shining blue." When the minister of propaganda arrives at the party, the crowd feels as if an "evil, solitary and cruel god had clambered down among the everyday bustle of pleasure-seeking, cowardly, pitiful mortals." His eyes bear "a malicious, abstracted smile as they [flit] over the group of millionaires, ambassadors, regimental commanders and film stars." Höfgen's rival, the poet and Privy Councilor Caesar von Muck, has steel-blue eyes "whose piercing and fiery purity had been commented on admiringly in many articles."[5] The angry, mocking playwright Marder has a restless piercing gaze that turns cold and lustful as he gazes at the actress Nicoletta. With her gleaming "cat's eyes," she is the perfect match for him.[6] The eyes of these glitterati shine. Or I should say: they turn into hard surfaces, endlessly reflecting the light of the eyes of other people who are equally brittle and lacking in depth. Only the dark blue, almost black eyes of Barbara, Höfgen's thoughtful wife, are different. Her deep eyes take in the world around her as she gravely searches to understand what she is seeing.[7]

If these guests, who are clawing their way up the social ladder and who are reveling in the admiration of the crowd, are all actors on the public stage, so, too, are we. We appear before our fellow citizens, and they presume to judge our worth. Even our secret deeds have a way of emerging from the darkness into the daylight of public scrutiny. Although we sometimes wish we could avoid such scrutiny, we feel a surge of pride if we are lucky enough to be invited to join the elite and powerful people who exist to see and be seen. Mann slyly asks us to become part of the select, chosen crowd watching in fascination as Höfgen, Lotte, the air force general, and the minister of propaganda meet:

> Here they stood, offered to the burning curiosity of selected members of their public: four powers of this land, four wielders of force, four actors. Here were the publicity manager, the specialist in death sentences and bomber flights, the sentimental wife and pale-faced intriguer. The chosen public watched as the fat leader slapped the theater director hard on the shoulder and asked, laughing, "How's it going, Mephisto?"[8]

At this very moment—when the eyes of the crowd and of the reader are focused upon four actors who feel themselves roundly admired—Mann introduces another paradox of respect: the more self-respect we derive from the many, the less lasting is our dignity. Our dignity becomes a quite fragile thing, because some of us are judged to possess a more striking appearance than others. Even the compelling Hendrik slips a notch or two in our estimation when we realize how relative our aesthetic judgments are:

> Aesthetically, Höfgen showed to great advantage. Next to the far too well fleshed couple he looked slim, and in contrast to the deformed

propaganda dwarf he appeared tall and comely. His face, too, however pale and gaunt it might appear, contrasted agreeably with the three faces about him. With the sensitive temples and strong outline of the chin, his features seemed to be those of a man who had lived and suffered. The face of his fleshy protector, on the other hand, was a bloated mask, that of the actress a mindless larva, and that of the propagandist a grotesque caricature.[9]

To look good relative to a larva and a dwarf is not a grand achievement. Hendrik himself is aware that he may not appear so imposing in the presence of more acute and penetrating individuals. By the end of the novel, he fears and flees the dark gaze of his estranged wife Barbara and of anyone else who may call him to task for his past betrayals. He returns home to nestle in the bosom of his mother, the one person in whose eyes he can do no wrong. Yet this vapid woman can give him no lasting comfort. Hendrik may appear to be the shining boy wonder to his mother and to the adoring audience of Nazi supporters. Still, somewhere in the crowd are the dark and searching eyes of those who have not sold their souls in order to be respected. The moment this gaze alights upon an actor, his or her dignity evaporates.

Genuine dignity depends upon an inward turn. We must measure ourselves relative to some nonhuman, nonarbitrary standard. Only after we pass muster are we entitled to claim dignity as our right. I take up the question of what this nonhuman standard is in chapter 8. At this point, I wish to note this paradox: human dignity depends upon that which is nonhuman. Human societies with their carefully constructed moralities, laws, and role models have trouble acknowledging this fact.

RESPECT, MASOCHISTIC ANXIETY, AND THE OBSESSION WITH PURITY

We do not have to embrace vice in order to lose our dignity or our ability to act. The actor Hendrik Höfgen never intends to commit dastardly deeds. Therefore, if we reduce evil to vice, Hendrik's behavior will not strike us as all that egregious. Although he does betray a man whom he considers his friend, he is but a bit player in the entire Nazi drama. Even his vices seem rather minor in the grand scheme of things. He is prone to massive temper tantrums and fits. Like many of us, he eats too much and is overweight. We might judge him to be, at worst, intemperate. Yet, Mann goes further, portraying Hendrik as Mephisto, a demonic hypocrite. In what sense can a man or woman be demonic? How does one become a devilish character? The answers lie in the process by which we prostitute our talents of real value "for the sake of some tawdry fame."[10]

When we court the approval of the many, we create a self-respect that is inherently unstable and that brings into play an array of other impulses that ultimately destroy our ability to act justly, compassionately, and lovingly. This process of self-obliteration goes beyond mere badness or criminal violation of the law. Mann thinks it deserves to be called "evil" because it strikes at our core, eviscerating our humanity. He who cannot be a Mensch ceases to be a man. Our cunning remains intact as we become corrupt, but our honesty and compassion disappear. All that remains is a feverish desire to gain whatever will make us happy. We become little devils in the sense that we will do anything to or for others in a vain effort to convince ourselves that we are honorable human beings.

We take the first step on this slippery slope toward losing our soul when we bind ourselves to the crowd. When we do not care why we are being admired, then the quantity, not the quality, of the respect we garner becomes our main concern. Being adored by many appears better than being honorable in our own eyes. Höfgen, Lotte, the general, and the propaganda minister require the admiration of a crowd because they can see themselves only in the reflective glint of surrounding eyes. They have no objective standard against which they can assess their worth. Like so many of us, they crave their fifteen minutes' worth of fame. After we get this fame, we continue to feel dissatisfied and anxious, sensing that the edifice of self we have built on the shifting sands of public esteem will come crashing down at any moment. Although we may shine in one setting, we are likely to appear to disadvantage in another. To make matters worse, the setting keeps shifting. We actors cannot control the stage on which we appear. So, as we bask in the glow of public regard, we simultaneously suspect that we are worthless.

To allay this anxiety, we devise ways to acknowledge, while simultaneously denying, our predicament. As Höfgen's career begins to take off, he starts to visit Princess Tenab, an African tap dancer who supplements her income through prostitution. Hendrik pays Tenab to abuse him and to compel him to dance until he is exhausted. When Hendrik begins to tire and his feet turn leaden, she whips him with his riding crop, shouting, "What have you got in your bones? You want to be a man, you want to be an actor and have people pay money to watch you? You wretched little lump!"[11] By submitting to another's insults, we can confess, "Yes, I am worthless," without having to address our addiction to other people's approval, which is the real source of our anxiety. We remain actors in search of an audience.

The proof that nothing about our existence has changed is that we never permit this staged abasement to get out of hand. Although we grovel, we still believe that we are superior and are in charge of our destiny. To admit to ourselves that we truly are despicable would force the issue of what it truly means to merit respect. Hence, our duplicitous strategy: we say we are utterly unworthy while we carefully manage just how worthless we are. Hendrik immediately puts a stop to Tenab's tormenting when she tries to lash his face. Since we need our face to impress and to command the admiration of the crowd, we must not lose face. Hendrik knows that to "arrive in the theater in the evening with a blood-red strip from his forehead to his chin would be going too far—that much was clear."[12]

In addition to managing the level of abuse, we take care to select the type of tormentor our ruse requires. Hendrik is drawn to Princess Tenab not because of her title (although that is agreeable because it indirectly confers status on him) but on account of her "ferociously darting eyes."[13] Having abdicated our throne of judgment, we require a prying and preying eye to ferret out and to affirm what we already suspect—that our self-respect is not worth much. Our need for a tormentor shows the problem with equating evil with sadism. In Hendrik, we have a case where our failure to judge ourselves relative to the true standard of dignity—a failure or omission that might be termed "negative evil" as opposed to "positive or intentional evil"—is not sadistic but masochistic. Our need to be abused functions as a perverse form of self-affirmation. We feel ourselves to be a "lump" or worm, and so get others to confirm that we are such.

This insight points to a second paradox: the public must not learn of our masochistic need for its approval. Hendrik dimly perceives that he would not appear to advantage if the many were ever to see him in his "childish and ridiculous getup consisting of black sneakers, short white socks . . . [and] shorts of shiny black satin such as little boys wear at gym class."[14] Our weakness must be simultaneously public and private. We require an audience (e.g., a Tenab) to confirm our suspicions about ourselves. But we must control who sees and affirms our weakness. Without such control, we are in danger of losing the respect that comes from public approval. Yet the effort required to keep our weakness in the shadows debilitates us further. We live in terror of having our abjectness exposed by our tormentors, our Tenabs. The princess has only to threaten to show up at the theater for Hendrik to be thrown into a panic.

Let us take stock of what we have discovered thus far. Our failure to develop our ability to judge what is truly worthy of esteem makes us dependent upon the praise and blame of other people. We think we have worth if and only if others esteem us. This belief inevitably makes us anxious because the public is fickle and so our worth is beyond our control. In an effort to allay anxiety and to shore up our image of ourselves, we devise masochistic strategies that paradoxically exacerbate, instead of alleviate, our anxiety. Evil could be defined as our unconscious development and execution of strategies to preserve our self-esteem. Mann's account challenges Aristotle's concept of evil. Although devilish evil is, like Aristotelian vice, a failure to develop our ability to judge well, Mann thinks evil manifests itself with desperate cunning. *Pace* Aristotle, the social system of praise and blame does not assure our accountability because we masochistically use this very system to avoid the moment of final reckoning.

I fear I will be misunderstood. I am not saying that the desire to possess self-esteem is evil. We naturally cling to the self-esteem that makes our life worth living. Without it, we feel alienated from the universe and start to think life is pointless. The struggle to maintain our self-esteem is not, in and of itself, evil. What is problematic is the unconscious and self-defeating quality of our efforts. Our desperate efforts to gain some measure of self-respect become ever more manic. We come to crave an ecstasy that will free us (however temporarily) from our deadening anxiety. Our abusers must be able to transport us out of ourselves. It does us no good to have our worthlessness affirmed by one who is as worthless as we are. His or her judgment would not be trustworthy. We need the liberating gaze of one who is completely other than we are. Consequently,

Hendrik worships Tenab's black otherness, which gives her the

> awesome mask of a strange god, a god enthroned in a secret place in
> the deepest jungle and crying out for human sacrifice. A human body
> is brought to her and blood poured over her feet; through distended
> nostrils she breathes in the sweet stench. . . . Around her the slaves
> dance in ecstasy: they swing their arms and legs, leap in the air, sway
> and stagger. Their roar becomes a long moan of joy, and the moan-
> ing becomes a subdued panting, and they sink to the ground before
> the feet of the black god they love and worship with all their hearts,
> as men can only worship the one to whom they have sacrificed that
> which is beyond price—blood.[15]

To escape the shackles of the many and to feel free, we must be
liberated from the gaze of our peers. Unable to conceive of any basis for
self-worth apart from external approval, we abase ourselves before
a "strange god" with an "awesome mask" totally lacking in human
features—the ultimate other. This strange god we worship demands blood
sacrifice. The human must give way before absolute, divine otherness.
What is human in us must die in order for the actor in us to feel alive.
Who provides the sacrificial blood? In one sense, every party within our
sphere is a potential victim of our anxiety. We will sacrifice our friends,
lovers, and family members in order to escape the anxiety that haunts our
every move. In another sense, the sacrificial blood drains from our own
veins. Höfgen becomes progressively more pale as he binds himself ever
more tightly to senior Nazi officials. Like the minister of propaganda,
Lotte, or the general, Höfgen will assume any role if doing so delights the
crowd.[16] Developing his talent would require submitting to the demands
of his craft and of the characters he is attempting to enact. Refusing to
delve deeply into any role, Höfgen settles for an increase in pay and a
good night at the house. Early in the story he "throws off" the role of
Hamlet after only a few hours of practice. He gets away with this sloppy
performance because the crowd and critics love him.

When we make our self-respect contingent upon the approval of
others, we slip into pure subjectivity and lose any discipline or art. Like
Hendrik, we cease to be able to act in the strict sense of the term. To give
a realistic portrayal of a stage character, an actor must understand

the thinking and the circumstances of his or her fellow human beings and the causes of their behavior. Acting that is disciplined and genuine can make us more compassionate by showing us our limitations and by disclosing how we unconsciously self-destruct. Disciplined acting is not limited to professional actors. Every time we thoughtfully enter into another person's plight with a view to better understanding him or her, we become an actor of sorts. Through this critically imaginative act, we discover points of commonality and develop sympathy with those around us. We discern analogies between our life and the existence of others. Good acting creates community. Catering to the whims of the public destroys it, for pandering does not promote understanding. It confirms members of the audience in their delusions, including their belief in their virtue and their right to a clear conscience. In this theater of the false, the Nazi air force general's wife can assume the role of Lessing's Minna von Barnhelm, declaiming "the lines of a Jewish playwright who [she and her husband] would have harassed and hounded if he had been their contemporary."[17]

In binding ourselves over to the many, we also lose the ability to love other people who, like us, are doing their best to become content. Hendrik can love no one. He can only worship and fear the strange god who appears to give him life. Princess Tenab is nothing but his "black Venus."[18] She has no independent being, no status as an individual with her own character, likes, dislikes, and aspirations. Our Tenabs are simply the other (usually of the gender we are not and thus more other). They merely serve a psychological function in our personal drama as we send them "hurrying hither and thither in the service of [our] suffering and desire."[19] Adoration and blood sacrifice are possible, but not true love.

Acting justly becomes impossible as well. Justice demands that we render to individuals what is their due. Determining what is due to another person entails having some sense of who the other person is. If our world is not peopled but only occupied by symbols, we cannot discern what justice requires of us. At no point does Hendrik wonder about the justice of joining the Nazi regime or abandoning his wife Barbara. He goes through life reacting to inner compulsions, which enslave him because he does not understand them. Since the Nazi regime consists of and is supported by people like Hendrik, the community as a whole is equally enslaved and unconsciously marches toward its doom. The Germans party in rooms filled with artificial fragrance, ignoring the "stale, sweet stench of blood, which permeated the entire country" and behaving as though "never would this radiance fall from [them]; never would the tortured by avenged; never would darkness reach out to engulf [them]."[20]

Historically, evil has been identified with impurity or defilement.[21] Mann clarifies why evil takes the form of an obsession with purity. Like the Nazis, who extol the virtue of racial purity and idolize the Aryan type, Hendrik cannot tolerate any imperfection in his dominatrix-lover. Hendrik confides to Tenab that he loves her because she is so pure. Our god can serve to allay our anxiety over our self-worth only if its divinity is in no way divided or compromised. If the divine were flawed in any way— if it were the same as we are—then it would cease to be worthy of our worship and blood sacrifice, and could not function to shore up our self-esteem. That is why Höfgen cannot see that Princess Tenab is not a Venus but instead a deeply unhappy, scheming woman with a drinking problem.

Our desire to be publicly respectable removes us from the real world of living human beings. Evil de-centers us. When we live for others, we never develop an internal compass for directing our lives. Nor do we acquire the discipline to develop our human power to act within a community of actors. Refinement of our powers and craft occurs only when we are sufficiently in touch with reality to perceive the objective possibilities and limitations of action and actors. When we live in a fantasy world, we renounce creative growth and development. By the end of the story, Höfgen can excel in only one role—Mephistopheles, the anti-life spirit of destruction and denial. This part he can play to perfection because no craft or discipline is required. He performs no role because he has become Mephisto.

Our Good and Bad Angels

Insofar as doing evil is identical with unwittingly destroying our power to act and our humanity, evil is a failure to develop. In that sense, evil is negative. As the philosopher Mary Midgley notes, we have some positive capacities (e.g., the ability to be generous and compassionate). The failure to bring these capabilities to fruition is sufficiently bad. As Midgley puts it, we do not need to posit special or extra capacities for meanness, cowardice, or injustice in order to understand evil.[22]

Midgley's observation is correct as far as it goes. But what moralists like Aristotle and Midgley do not see is that our failure to thrive occurs because we try to secure happiness by devising paradoxical and self-thwarting strategies for success, strategies which have a relentless logic all their own. Having based our self-esteem on public approval, we begin to live in a fantasy world. Removed from reality, we cannot form an appropriate and objective assessment of our worth and so swing between poles of self-aggrandizement and self-loathing. Adored by the many, we begin to imagine we are gods. However, the objective world breaks through in a variety of ways, reminding us that we are mere humans. Feeling that we have no value, we aggressively assert our "worm nature" by creating and then worshipping a strange god who confirms that we are dirt. The catch is that we cannot accept this assessment and go on living. As our unease escalates, we shift tactics. We start to look for a new god, one who will unconditionally affirm our worth and thereby save us from ourselves.

Shortly after Hendrik meets Barbara, the daughter of a well-respected, learned university professor, he proposes marriage to her. If Tenab is his bad angel, she will be his "good angel" and rescue him from his fate:

> Hendrik sank to his knees and burst into tears. "I need you," he sobbed, his head in her lap. "Without you I shall go completely to pieces. There is so much that's bad in me. Alone I can't muster the force to get the better of it. But you will make what is best in me strong."[23]

Barbara, like Princess Tenab, is merely another symbolic star in the firmament of the actor's dream world. Hendrik knows little about her and does not bother to investigate any further. When they are together, he prattles on about his professional woes, his lonely childhood, and his ideals. Barbara exists for Hendrik only to the extent that he believes she can assist him in some way.

We do not ask that our good angel save us by forcing us to confront our illusions. The good angel is to confirm us in our belief that we are good or even great. So we place conditions on how we are to be liberated from our hell: our good angel must bring out the best in us. This requirement enables us to carry on without making any real change in our lives. If we fail, it must be the fault of our good angel—our savior did not work hard enough to nurture our native goodness. Given that we have not altered our outlook in any fundamental way, it should come as no surprise that our good angel is the exact correlate of our bad angel. In seeking out

Barbara, Hendrik repeats the old unsatisfying pattern. He will be worthy of respect only if a special divinity bestows her seal of approval upon him. To save Hendrik from himself, the new lover Barbara must be every bit as divine and pure as Hendrik's black Venus, the bad angel Tenab. If Barbara were in any way unworthy, she would not be able to save Hendrik from his corrupt ways. She would be as degraded as he feels himself to be and, therefore, could not function as the other on whose alterity he relies to save him from his unworthy self.

Such logic, though, is fatally flawed. Our good angel inevitably disappoints us. Whomever we cast in that role will, at some point, deviate from our idealized vision of what a savior should be. The truth is that no one else can save us from ourselves. Only we can reflect upon and reform our ways. The approval of our good angel does not free us from our dependence on our bad angel. On the one hand, since our bad angel makes our worthlessness real to us, we need to remain involved with our dark god in order to feel shame. For, if we feel no shame, from what is our good angel saving us? On the other hand, in order for our good angel to save us, we must stop all intercourse with our bad angel. Meeting and marrying Barbara does not resolve Hendrik's predicament but only deepens his crisis:

> The thought of his meeting with Princess Tenab the following morning filled Hendrik with anxiety. He must ask his dance mistress not to visit him any more—his new deep feeling for Barbara demanded that. But it already hurt him to think of no longer seeing [the princess].[24]

Yet the actor never gives up Princess Tenab with her green leather boots and red whip. Barbara eventually sees that Hendrik will never change. The two separate. By the end of the novel, Hendrik has married the untalented but ambitious actress Nicoletta, whom he outfits with red boots and a green whip.

As long as we look to others to affirm our worth, we are caught in an anxiety trap. Neither our good, nor our dark, angel has the power to redeem us. Undaunted, we try for a composite or compromise angel. Since we need both our good and bad angels, we attempt to overcome the opposition between the two by melding them into one. Our good angel must not be too independent. The best savior is a failed actor who, like us, has spent his or her life catering to the tastes and whims of other people. The awful actress Nicoletta, Hendrik's second wife and newest "good" angel, is a clone of the "bad" angel Tenab. Only the colors of the boots and whip have changed.

Demonic Arithmetic

Hendrik is not unique in his plight. Many of us marry, divorce, and then remarry a second spouse with an uncanny resemblance to the first. This pattern persists for as long as we continue look to other people to save us from ourselves. Throughout our quest, we remain the same tormented beings we have always been. When this strategy to secure self-esteem fails, we become ever more desperate. Since the world keeps threatening to break through the illusions we have fostered, we evolve a supplemental strategy to help us suppress our doubts about our self-worth. We create a simulacrum of a morality, a way to acknowledge our defects without ever having to admit the full extent of our abasement.

Hendrik is able to rationalize all of his actions by telling himself that although some of his acts may have been questionable, he has done enough good deeds to build up credits on his moral balance sheet and to cancel any of his debits. Although Hendrik mocks the Nazis and, in the presence of his good-angel wife Barbara, swears undying enmity to the regime, he readily reconciles himself to the Nazis when the air force general offers him patronage and the directorship of the State Theater.[25] Feeling the contradiction, he avoids coming into contact with Barbara (how could he endure her penetrating stare?) and tells himself that he will use his success to accomplish good things. He assures himself that he is not a collaborator; the Nazi patronage fell into his lap. Unlike his idealistic friends, he is a pragmatist who realizes that he can get things done only if he works within the system. He feels that it has required admirable self-discipline on his part to "bring himself to the point of howling with the wolves." After all, by toadying to Nazi officials, he is able to persuade the Nazis to free his old communist friend Otto Ulrichs. After he gets Otto a job at the State Theater, Hendrik proudly tells himself, "I rescued a man. . . . That is a good deed" and records a credit on his moral balance sheet.[26]

Our calculations, though, are never honest. We ensure that our credits will outweigh any debits by minimizing our many betrayals. While

Hendrik is assiduously cultivating senior Nazi officials, many of his friends are arrested by these same Nazis. Hendrik does nothing, telling himself that only "when he himself was finally rescued (that is, safe by virtue of his dramatic successes) could he perhaps be useful to the others." This mantra is "the formula with which he warded off any thought of the sufferers."[27] Now we can see why evil is sometimes thought of as a pact with the devil. A pact always involves a perceived trade-off. We give up something of value in order to get something we believe to be of greater value. Whenever we start to imagine that our deeds will produce a net moral gain, we have entered the world of the pact. In this world, nothing is absolutely forbidden to us. Every act, in principle, can be redeemed by an offsetting or compensating deed.[28] Yes, indulging our desires comes at a high price, but we do not focus on that cost. Like Faust, who sells his soul to the devil Mephistopheles, we choose to remain conveniently vague about the "costs" we are incurring. This failure to examine what we are doing is precisely what makes the pact seem attractive. Our inattention allows us to relegate the dangers of our position to the shadows or periphery of our consciousness and to proceed to reap the supposed benefits.

In treating every act as a matter of trade-offs, we subtly change the nature of our behavior. From childhood on, we sometimes act badly. By "act badly," I mean that we behave in ways that cause us shame. But our bad acts do not mean that we are thoroughly corrupt. As long as we retain some vestige of humanity—as long as we feel that there will be a final reckoning using objective ethical standards—we are not corrupt. We continue to feel shame because some part of us understands that we can thrive only if we conform ourselves to the objective requirements that the universe imposes upon us. But once we, like Hendrik and Faust, embrace a calculus of trade-offs and deny the existence of such objective requirements, we cease to be capable of real shame. It then becomes impossible for us to alter our behavior because we never admit that we have been behaving inappropriately.

At this point, our thoughtlessness and carelessness become a matter of system or policy. Using our moral arithmetic of trade-offs, we can rationalize anything we do. In refusing to acknowledge the existence of an objective order in which we must operate in order to thrive, we unwittingly divorce our deeds from the end or good that we are trying to realize. Consequently, whatever we do to make ourselves happy leaves us dissatisfied.

Actions, in the strictest sense of the word, cease to exist. Everything we do is a pointless gesture. Having done nothing to save his friend Otto Ulrichs, Hendrik arranges for an anonymous gift to be sent to Otto's mother. The gift accomplishes and means nothing. But Hendrik counts the gesture as a credit to cancel any debit he might have created when he failed his longtime loyal friend.

Having denied the existence of an objective, constraining order, we try to salvage happiness by creating a world in which our acts are redeemable at a price that we get to set. At that moment, the Faustian bargain is struck. We do not have to worry about losing our life in the future; we have already relinquished it. We reduce our life to a series of futile trade-offs. That is why, in many versions of the Mephisto tale, the devil's document is not only signed with our precious blood but also written in it. Dead to love and compassion and unable to change, we become devilish. I do not mean that we become cruel or that we rejoice in causing harm. I mean rather that we forfeit the last vestige of our humanity—our sense that we have failed ourselves.

In this context, the devil is our dark side, that part of us that misleads, obfuscates, and provides us with the rationalizations we find ourselves needing in our masochistic quest to be unconditionally admired and respected by other people. Although we sign the pact with our blood, the devil provides no signature. Since the devil and we are one at this point, our agreement suffices to bind the devil as well. Having relinquished our humanity and dignity, we are content to live a life of lies, denial, and rationalization. We cease to struggle against our feelings of unworthiness and become reconciled to them. Self-pity takes the place of shame. Folk wisdom depicts the devil as a liar and a supreme hypocrite: the devil is both the "Evil One" and "Good Fellow." Having made a pact with the devil, our anxiety causes us to share in this satanic duplicity. Deep down we know that any respect we garner from those who are stupid, base, or fearful is not worth much. Even Hendrik, a man obsessed with fame, understands that the German press lavishly praises the horrific acting of Lotte Lindenthal for only one reason: she is the wife of the German air force general, and the critics are afraid to tell the truth. Nevertheless, he bases his self-worth upon the press's assessment of him. Dimly discerning his dilemma, Höfgen whines, "One asks more from life than just to be a well-paid entertainer who becomes completely absorbed in a profession one claims to despise in one's heart of hearts."[29] Yet, those of us who have no source of self-respect apart from other people's regard must find some way of living as actors while assuring ourselves that we are superior to mere crowd pleasers. Soon we are in hot pursuit of a strategy that permits us to be hypocrites while denying that we are such. We soon find ourselves desperate for a devilish strategy that will enable us to be both a "Good Fellow" and the "Evil One."

Our strategy can take a variety of forms. Often we employ several forms at the same time. Employing a sham moral calculus of the sort described above is one such strategy. Compartmentalizing our life into different personae is another. We may take pains to be perceived as good parents while doing whatever it takes to advance our careers. We may develop a caring front to hide the seamier side of our existence. Or we may create an alternative professional personality to deflect attention from our shameful behavior. Hendrik represents himself as a Communist who is devoted to the revolution. From early on in his career, Hendrik assures his left-wing friends that he will support the Revolutionary Theater and stage productions on its behalf. While assiduously catering to Nazi tastes, Hendrik clings to his revolutionary faith, "this rare mark of validity that so favourably distinguished him from the general run of Berlin actors." His demonic moral calculus again comes to his aid. He explains that he cannot mount revolutionary productions until both he and his acting ensemble are successful. So the "Revolutionary Theater . . . was advanced as the pretext for staging box-office successes," and Höfgen's "revolutionary tactics amounted to daily thinking up new reasons why a start could not be made on rehearsals for the Revolutionary Theater."[30]

Insofar as other people are equally party to our pact with the devil, hypocrisy is a collective matter. The hypocrisy of the actor Höfgen mirrors that which pervades the entire Nazi regime. Hitler orchestrates the murder of millions, while priding himself on a love of life so great that he cannot bear to eat meat. Although members of the Nazi Senate of Culture profess to be refined, they panic when someone suggests reading a chapter from a book. They opt instead to imitate the baying of hounds and the clucking of hens.[31] The air force general (modeled on Hermann Göring) executes thousands, all the while representing himself as a great man of culture with a profound understanding of humanity. The general is smitten by Höfgen's portrayal of Mephistopheles because it enables the general to deny his responsibility for murdering and torturing his fellow citizens. According to the general, a little bit of Mephisto lives in each of us.[32] We are all a bit guilty. And when all are guilty, no one is.

If each of us has a Mephistophelean side, we should worry about that possibility, not use it to justify our corrupt dealings with others and ourselves. A little bit of Mephisto has a way of becoming the whole of our existence. Like the general, we fall in love with the idea that we are entitled to be—nay, we must be—merciless if we are to preserve our honor and self-respect. Soon we are we assuring ourselves that our inner Mephisto provides the cunning and strength needed to succeed in life. The idea that we are all Mephistophelean also permits us to excuse our faults. Although the air force general murders men and women who defile racial purity by marrying Jews or consorting with blacks and gypsies, he perceives no great problem when he learns of Höfgen's liaison with Princess Tenab. After all, he explains to Hendrik, no one is a pure angel.[33] In other words, Höfgen is devilish at the periphery but sound at the core. Such a claim pleases and soothes Hendrik because the actor is quite familiar with this type of reasoning. Here we have another instance of the hypocritical calculus we employ to repress, rather than deal with, our feelings of unworthiness and shame.

THE SENTIMENTALITY AND ROMANTICISM OF EVIL

Hypocrisy comfortably exists alongside sentimentality and romanticism in the corrupt, masochistic individual. The romantic in us believes in self-expression and the spontaneous overflowing of powerful feeling. For the romantic, goodness is a natural trait, not an achievement. The naturally good individual should be allowed to operate without restraint. The romantic soul rebels against the strictures of reason, science, and tradition. If an actor like Höfgen can inspire great feeling in others using little or no craft, so much the better.

Having embraced a sham moral calculus and rationalized our hypocrisy, we feel no shame when it comes to manipulating and pleasing the audience. Signing a pact with the devil is identical to becoming addicted to the enthusiastic adoration of the crowd. The validation provided by the many makes it easier for us to indulge our whims without feeling any regret. We can assure ourselves that we are promoting human advancement when we encourage our fellow human beings to give themselves over to their surging, romantic feelings. Hitler (who was a cabaret actor in his youth) sees in Hendrik a fellow traveler and immediately pronounces the ambitious actor an asset to the regime. As Mann's Hitler tells Hendrik, "the interests of our Nordic culture require the positive commitment of an energetic, racially self-assertive and target-oriented individual."[34] The romantic masochist is "energetic." Having assented to the lie within our soul, we lose our place in the objective world. We have nothing to fall back upon except our subjective will and feelings. So we indulge any and all sentiments to the full.

Since the romantic's ability to feel strong emotions provides welcome reassurance that he is still alive, Hendrik is not in the least troubled by the wild mood swings he exhibits over the course of a single hour. His young associate Miklas, an early supporter of the Nazis, is similarly emotional. The youth rages at the injustices he feels he has experienced at the hands of the bourgeoisie. When the Nazis do not give him the recognition he believes he deserves, Miklas does not stop to consider whether his faith was misplaced. Instead, he turns his wrath upon the Nazis. As always, the logic of purity is at work as we indulge our sentiments. Any deed can be excused as long as the romantic is "good at heart." Although the air force general daily torments his wife Lotte Lindenthal when he is not busy murdering Jews, tears well up in her eyes as she explains that, at the core, he is a good man who nightly stands in homage before the portrait of his dead first wife.

When desire is entirely subjective—when we are motivated only by a desire to please other people and are unconstrained by tradition, public checks and balances, and, most importantly, a love of wisdom and objective truth—our passions control us. The reigning emotions in this novel are pity, self-pity, and rage. Höfgen and the other Nazis pity the less successful and strong. Their pity stems from a sense of their own superiority and strength. Although the Nazis in the novel continually blather about the need for self-discipline, they are, ironically, at the utter mercy of their sentiments. They rage at the world in a futile attempt to change it through self-assertion. Or they indulge in self-pity, complaining that the world has misunderstood them and that they deserve to be better treated because they are basically good people. In both cases, they blame their lack of success on a hostile and unfair world.

This romanticism is akin to magical thinking. Magical thinking tries to influence or control human and natural events by accessing some external force existing beyond the ordinary human sphere. We have already seen how Höfgen prostrates himself before Princess Tenab, his awesome and strange god. He uses her "as a wicked inanimate force to refresh and renew his energies."[35] When he dances, he does so for this god. He enters a strange ecstatic, Bacchic state.[36] As we give ourselves over completely to our feelings, we come to feel that we have entered another world, transcending ordinary human existence. In the ordinary world, we are subject to objective physical and logical constraints. By becoming a slave to the divinity we create, we, like Höfgen, seek to slip these bonds of earthly existence.

Our idol is always formed in our image. Tenab, Hendrik's "black Venus," exhibits only those traits with which Hendrik's psyche endows her. Hendrik, however, does not understand that he is worshipping his projection of himself. His religion is but another attempt to control the world through willful self-assertion. Hendrik's father-in-law Bruckner (based on Thomas Mann) describes Hendrik as an undistinguished man who, when the floodlights are on him, becomes a "colorful, magical figure."[37] The description aptly characterizes all of us who are in league with the devil. Romantic and sentimental, we prostitute our talent, abandoning ourselves to our passions and dancing before our idol god as we seek to compel the audience to adore us.

THE COMICAL NARCISSISM OF EVIL

Narcissism, the obsession with one's self-image, is usually thought of as a vice or as one evil among many. This conception of narcissism may be incorrect. Evil, understood as a descent into romantic, masochistic subjectivity, is intrinsically narcissistic. This narcissism embodies two paradoxes. First, the more we become obsessed with our self-image, the less we have a centered self. Having denied the existence of an objective good, we have no order to which to appeal in order to ground the self. We live derivatively through the approval and respect of other people. Like Narcissus, who was entranced by his reflection staring back at him, we feel alive only when the glittering, reflective eyes of another are upon us.

Second, although we make our self-worth entirely contingent upon the approval of members of the community, we fail to grasp that our admirers are people in their own right. Implicitly believing that the world and our success in it are entirely of our making, everything exists for us only in relation to our desires and feelings. Our world consists of nothing but things to be used and gods to be worshipped. When the Nazi leaders make threatening noises about Hendrik's past involvement with the communists, Hendrik sets out to seduce Lotte Lindenthal. He sees the actress not as a person but as a fortress he must successfully storm if he is to have a dazzling career. "Lotte Lindenthal must be made to love him." No matter "how full-bosomed and cow-eyed she might be, no matter how provincial and homespun she might look, with her double chin and her blond permanent wave, for him she was as desirable as a goddess."[38]

At the same time as we worship a strange god of our own making, we demand that everyone else idolize us. Hendrik marries Barbara because he believes that she can save him from his wicked angel Tenab and because her family's aristocratic connections can assist him in his career.[39] Although he is impotent with his wife Barbara, he tells himself that this failure is of no concern. After all, he brings to the marriage "the excitement of his presence, the intoxication of his closeness."[40] When Barbara refuses to share with him the letters her friends write to her, Hendrik is enraged that his wife dares to have a life of her own. Since he believes the whole world revolves around him, he is certain that she and her friends poke fun at him in their correspondence.[41] Sensing her disapproval of him, he sets out to win her over. She, too, must be made to love him. He "cannot stand to have someone around him who does not admire and believe in him."[42]

Our desire to be worshipped far exceeds our value. The relation between the two is incongruous, and the incongruous is comical. Early in his career Hendrik had lived with a landlady who, he imagines, views him with derision. After creating a big splash in the theater, Höfgen makes a point of returning to Hamburg to visit Frau Monkeberg. She, too, must see him in his glory. He is enraged to learn that his landlady has died. Her death is not a natural event but a calculated insult to his respect: "That was just like her: rather than face a meeting that would have been painful she had taken refuge in flight."[43] The real Frau Monkeberg would not have found such a meeting uncomfortable. However, the romantic within spins whatever fantasy accords with our sentiments. Hendrik's self-pity inclines him to envisage the landlady embracing death instead of having to admit his glory. Still, the disappointment rankles. Here is another person close to Hendrik who has refused to admire him. The old anxiety rears its ugly head. Perhaps his success is not worth all that much if the better people like Barbara and Frau Monkeberg, the "gentry without money but with a noble past," stubbornly remain outside the reach of his charm.[44] Only when he can "step out into a bright spotlight and shine . . . [does] a sense of security return to him."[45]

The False Sense of Shame

As I noted at the beginning of this chapter, moralists take a person's sense of shame as evidence that the agent is capable of developing into a better individual. Mann takes us deeper into the concept of shame. Whether shame is ennobling depends on what the basis of shame is. At different points in his career, Hendrik feels what he takes to be shame. Unable to consummate his marriage to Barbara, he leans on her bed and confides one of his frightful little memories. As a child, he had been a choirboy. The boys' choir was to sing at a wedding.

> It was a great occasion and we were all pretty excited. But I was pos-
> sessed by the devil: I wanted to turn the thing into a great personal
> success. So when our choir began its pious hymn, I had such an
> enormously high opinion of my voice that I really thought it would
> make a charming effect if my shrill tones echoed in the church vaults.
> There I was, swollen with pride, letting out a piercing yell. The
> music teacher who was conducting gave me a look that was more
> sickened than punishing and said, "Shut up, you!" Do you under-
> stand Barbara . . . how appalling that was? I who took myself to be a
> caroling archangel. . . .[46]

Notice that Hendrik does not feel disgraced for having spoiled the wedding by trying to steal the show. He feels mortified only because he did not succeed in making the occasion a personal triumph. Having made our self-worth contingent upon others' approval, we experience no dishonor for having failed to act in accordance with our humanity. True shame arises when we do not act as a human being should act. We experi-ence other-directed shame when we fail to command a second look. Other-directed or false shame is intensely romantic, narcissistic, and masochistic.

False shame does not sensitize us to the feelings of those around us. Nor does it lead us to wonder whether our aspirations, intentions, or self-image are flawed. Instead, it reinforces our desire to impress and our tendency toward irritable self-pity. When Barbara indicates that she is not troubled by any such childhood memories, Höfgen whirls on her, incensed that she does not share his sense of failure. Only he must descend into the hell of shame. Rage combined with self-pity—the typical response of magical narcissists when their worldview is questioned—coexists comfortably with false shame. If Barbara does not share Hendrik's past, all the more reason for him to feel bad—he must have failed where others have succeeded!—and to wallow in self-pity.

Our Final Act: A Nonperformance

Where do our self-pitying rage, false shame, and double-dealing lead us? Deeper into dissatisfaction and to the ultimate betrayal—the repudiation of our talent and the collapse of our world. Mann's *Mephisto* ends where it must—with a final pathetic performance by the actor Hendrik, a performance that is a nonperformance by one who has forfeited his art and become a mere shell of a man.

Hendrik's longtime friend Otto is arrested for his work in the resistance. Hendrik makes a half-hearted attempt to intervene with the general to save Otto but curtails his efforts when the general warns him not to meddle with events that do not concern him. Always sensitive to attitudes and events that might threaten his career, Hendrik ceases trying to help Otto while assuring himself that he will assist his friend at some future time:

> Hendrik realized that he would be in danger of losing the favor of the godhead if he tried to help his old friend any further at that moment. I shall let a few days go by, he thought. Then, if I find the fat man in a better temper, I shall cautiously try to go back to the subject. In one way or another, I shall succeed in getting Otto out of the Columbiahaus jail or the concentration camp. But that shall have to be the end of it. . . . His senseless rashness, his childish notion of heroism, are going to get me into appalling trouble.[47]

Although he inwardly vows to rescue his friend Otto, Hendrik washes his hands of the entire matter. He cannot be expected to help at the cost of his safety. Hendrik does nothing for his friend, completely forgetting about Otto for two days. After several days have passed, he calls Lotte Lindenthal. She tells him that he need not worry about Otto. Otto is dead. In typical Höfgen fashion, Hendrik sends an untraceable donation to Otto's mother to pay for a gravestone. Having sent the donation, he is relieved because "on the page in his heart where he listed 'insurance' there was once again a credit balance."[48] As we have seen, the gesture is meaningless; it cannot redeem the betrayal of a close friend. But, in the demonic person's world, everything is a matter of willpower. If Hendrik desires a credit on his ethical balance sheet, the requisite sum magically appears.

At the same time that Hendrik is betraying his friend, he is renouncing his lifelong vocation. Selected to play Hamlet, Hendrik finds himself unable to realize the character. When he was younger, he had tossed off the role. Now, as an experienced but thoroughly corrupt actor, he finds that the Danish prince keeps eluding him. This failure shatters him. Hendrik has always justified his collaboration with the Nazis by arguing that talented and true actors must work within the political system to keep great art alive. Shakespeare's plays qualify as great art. Therefore, if Hendrik cannot successfully portray Hamlet, his elaborate calculus of rationalization and double-dealing will crumble. Hendrik pleads with an imaginary Hamlet:

> I've got to play you. If I fail at playing you, I'll have failed at everything. You're my ordeal by fire; I've got to pass. My whole life, all the sins I've committed, my great betrayal, all my shame can only be vindicated by my art. But I'm an artist only if I can play Hamlet.[49]

Whine though he will, Hendrik cannot interpret Hamlet's role successfully because he has not cultivated any artistic discipline and does not appreciate human character and motivation. He has spent his entire life manipulating other people. They have existed only as pawns in his game to become a successful actor. Lacking any sense of their objective features and traits and largely unreflective about his motives, he possesses no imaginative resources on which to draw in order to come up with a plausible, compelling, and coherent interpretation of Hamlet.

Still, Hendrik feels tormented because he has one remaining scruple. Despite his addiction to the admiration of the crowd, Hendrik knows good acting differs from bad. He must insist on this difference, because he has rationalized his collaboration by telling himself that he is raising the standard of theater in Germany. A mediocre performance of Hamlet will damn him. His sense that he must do a great Hamlet paralyzes him. Hendrik finds he can play Hamlet only by letting go of this one remaining objective standard. He imputes energy, virility, and assertiveness to Hamlet, portraying the Prince of Denmark as a "slightly neurotic Prussian lieutenant."[50] Throughout his life, he has been prone to fits, which he now incorporates into his professional persona. At one moment, his Hamlet stands rigidly; a moment later he faints to the ground in a hysterical fit. Although Hendrik's interpretation completely ignores Hamlet's indecisiveness (which has some affinities with Hendrik's paralysis), the crowd loves this Nazified Hamlet. German colleagues and journalists extol Hendrik's rendition. They argue that Shakespeare's Hamlet is poor in deed and rich in thought, and, as such, "Hamlet is a danger for the German people."[51] Hendrik is to be praised for turning *Hamlet* into the "exemplary German drama" by creating a character who willfully overcomes his brooding isolation and springs into action. Given that the Germans were engaged in murdering millions, one would not have thought that they needed to worry about being "poor in deed." However, such ironies are lost on the Nazis and on Hendrik because their magical thinking lets them perceive only what it suits them to see.

The drama of *Mephisto* draws to its inevitable close. Drama, the representation of human action, must end when we have destroyed our ability to act as a human being. Human action is possible only in a world of constraints and limitations. Once we let go of our scruples, we enter a world of magical thinking or madness from which there is no return. In the end, the only role at which Hendrik can excel is Mephisto. As Hendrik's Jewish colleague Dora Martin observes, Hendrik makes a fine Mephisto because both are utterly devoid of scruples. Hendrik does not have to play at being Mephisto. This role requires no talent. He only has to be himself to succeed in the mad milieu of Nazi Germany.

By now it should be clear that not all evil is sadistic or dramatic. Some forms of evil may be, in a profound sense, antidramatic. When we start to live for the respect of other people, we betray ourselves. The warning uttered by Hamlet's ghost should serve as a caution to us all: true nobility and a career are sometimes incompatible. We find ourselves forced to commit to a life with dignity or to an anxiety-ridden existence. The two lives are objectively different and irreconcilable. Evil consists not so much in choosing the wrong path but in refusing to acknowledge the difference between a dignified, peaceful life and one filled with dread. To muddle along by rationalizing our vapid gestures and masochistically worshipping false gods is to be in league with our inner devil or spirit of destruction.

Even as the Berlin public and press rave about Hendrik's novel interpretation of the character of Hamlet, his old doubts about his worth return. Not even the prospect of being whipped by his new wife Nicoletta can restore his self-confidence. Princess Tenab calmed his anxiety by feeding the energy he poured into his acting career. However, he has destroyed his talent. Since he has just let Otto die, Hendrik cannot fall back on the old, comfortable lie that he is a major player in the German resistance. These betrayals of his friend and of his talent are two sides of the same coin—the repudiation of his humanity. Hendrik settles for the illusion of nobility. Real nobility would require that he do what is genuinely honorable. He would have to seek an objective measure of worth and renounce his desire to impress an unruly mob consisting of the very people he claims to disdain. Trapped by his false sense of self-worth, he cannot bring himself to make this renunciation.

Hendrik's confidence is further shaken by the sudden appearance of one of Otto's colleagues in the Resistance. The colleague warns Höfgen that the Resistance has a long memory and will not forget that Höfgen, the man who paraded his Communist credentials and railed against the Nazis, later joined forces with the foe. Hendrik's ancient fear that the situation will change and that he will no longer be the darling of the regime comes back to haunt him. Suddenly his life does not seem to have much value.

When our world collapses, we turn to those who have loved us in the past. Who loves us most unconditionally? Our mothers. Sobbing, Hendrik collapses into his mother's lap. This fit of pique and self-pity is his final nonperformance. It was his mother who urged him to become an actor and believed in him throughout his career. Our mothers are the perfect audience. They sympathize with us and do not press too hard to learn where our truth ends and our falsity begins. Like Hendrik, we can confide our great betrayals to our mothers without worrying whether our remorse is genuine. In their welcoming arms, we try to return to childhood and to shed our unhappy selves.

If we are honest with ourselves, we understand only too well Hendrik's lapse into self-pity and his cry, "What do men want from me? Why do they pursue me? Why are they so hard? All I am is a perfectly ordinary actor—"[52] When our lives are in shambles, we deny our past. Hendrik would have everyone believe that he is, and always has been, a perfectly ordinary actor. Forget the Hendrik with the exotic stage name who raged each time a critic mistakenly used the common and vulgar "Henrik." Forget the actor who became a major political player, pandering to the tastes of Nazis in his role as director of the State Theater. Forget the actor who had his lover Princess Tenab imprisoned in order to scare her out of the country. In his mother's arms, he is once again the simple son "Heinz," the good-hearted choirboy who deserves our pity, not our scorn.

Tempting though it is to return to childhood, we cannot live in the all-forgiving embrace of our mothers. Having destroyed our ability to act, we seek to revoke our identity and to avoid our destiny. But we cannot avoid unwittingly speaking and enacting the truth. Hendrik's final, melodramatic collapse into his mother's arms is, ironically, the one true performance of his career. He is more right than he knows: he never was a great actor. His falseness is his truth.

This final scene derives its truth from Klaus Mann's art, not Hendrik's. Mann is the true artist because he understands that the evil we live cannot be magically exorcised. The hypocrisy, narcissism, sentimentality, romanticism, and subjectivism of evil are real. Every attempt we make to deny that we have fallen on evil days only confirms that we are in league with our inner devil. The self-justifying lines that Goethe gives to Mephisto are truer and more damning than we like to admit: "What you may call the realm of sin, / And nothing there but evil see, / Is where I live and have to be."[53]

Mann begins his portrayal of evil by quoting Goethe's maxim: "All men's failings I forgive in actors; no actor's failings will I forgive in men."[54] What is the unforgivable failing of an actor? We fail as actors when we do not realize our talent through discipline, generous appreciation of humanity, and steadfast devotion to the truth. In basing our self-esteem on the admiration and approval of the many and devoting our energy to preserving our reputation, we turn our back on wisdom and, consequently, lose our gravitas, our humanity, and our ability to act. Having denied the objective existence of the world, we drift like insubstantial shades over the face of the earth.

While we may tell ourselves that we are in control of the trade-offs we make, we cannot sell our souls and still come out ahead. As Thoreau shrewdly observes, "Nature hates calculators." In the long run, we inevitably find "the cost of a thing is the amount of . . . life which is required to be exchanged for it."[55] Our Puritan forefathers knew a thing or two when they imagined the devil as a "savings' box, with the till-hole between his teeth," a figure who appears "all the time [to be] going through some process of mental arithmetic; doing sums with dollars and cents: his very mouth, wrinkled and drawn up at the corners, look[ing] like a purse."[56] In this era in which everything has a price, we reckon all costs except the one that matters most: the loss of our ability to act. Like the shades we will soon meet in Dante's *Inferno*, we become frozen in our self-pity and unhappy destiny. Then, like Mephisto, we are forever where we have to be.

3

EVIL AS FLIGHT FROM NARCISSISTIC BOREDOM

Life is first boredom, then fear.
—*Phillip Larkin*

WHEN WE FIRST MEET TOM RIPLEY, THE FAVORITE PROTAGONIST OF NOVELIST Patricia Highsmith, we do not suspect that he is a serial killer in the making. Granted, he is involved in a bit of mail fraud. However, he never cashes any of the checks he receives. He appears personable and friendly enough. When Herbert Greenleaf asks Tom to go to Italy and to persuade his son Dickie to return home, Tom readily agrees, telling himself that he can do the senior Greenleaf a good turn. He appears to want little from life but the chance to see Europe and to acquire some culture.

By the time Highsmith's novel *The Talented Mr. Ripley* ends, Tom has bludgeoned Dickie to death, sunk the body in the ocean, and assumed Dickie's identity for a period of several weeks. Forced to reappear as Tom, he tells the Italian police and Dickie's friend Marge that Dickie has decided to withdraw from his friends and to concentrate on painting. When Dickie's old friend Freddie Miles begins to suspect that Tom has lied about Dickie's whereabouts, Tom murders Freddie. When Marge discovers that Tom possesses Dickie's rings, Tom coolly contemplates beating her to death with the wooden heel of a shoe. He eventually convinces the Greenleafs that their son has committed suicide. By forging Dickie's will, he inherits Dickie's substantial estate and sets off for a vacation in Greece.[1]

Although some American and European academics argue that evil is a social construct, Highsmith is not in this camp.[2] All her novels involve an encounter with real, amoral evil; Highsmith rejects the "liberal humanist faith" that a rising standard of living or the embracing of democratic institutions will rid the world of this personal, psychological, and political evil.[3] Her concept of evil, however, does not fit the moralist's model. Tom Ripley's evil is not intentional. A close examination of the Highsmith's tale shows that Tom's plotting (if that is the word) occurs pre-rationally. Nor would it be correct to view his evil as a matter of the untoward deed. Tom Ripley is not evil because he murders. He murders because he is in thrall to evil.

So how are we to understand this evil, if not in moral terms? The wisdom tradition's approach is helpful. As I noted in the introduction, this tradition focuses on suffering and its causes. It understands evil as the pain and frustration we unwittingly inflict upon ourselves as we adopt ever more perverse strategies to escape our unhappy selves. Like Hendrik, Tom aspires to be a famous actor. Like Hendrik, Tom increasingly compromises his ability to act. But Highsmith's tale brings to the foreground the deep connection between evil and our quest for a stable identity and lasting satisfaction. Although we may be inclined to deny any kinship with the masochistic Hendrik, distancing ourselves from the bored Tom Ripley is not so easy. Tom is more violent than Hendrik, but, in his ennui and lethargy, he also more obviously resembles us. Who among us has not felt at some time or another dissatisfied with life for reasons we cannot state? Tom's anxiety is ours and so, by implication, is his violence. Instead of dismissing Tom as sociopathic, we should pay attention to how our vague dissatisfaction can cause us to self-destruct and to harm others in the process. We ignore Highsmith's tale at our peril.

ALIENATED BOREDOM

Tom Ripley is dissatisfied with the world and with himself. He has held a series of jobs, working in a warehouse, on a banana boat, and for the Internal Revenue Service. In his view, none of these jobs is commensurate with his talents. He put up with them because he needs the cash, but he is "bored, God-damned bloody bored, bored."[4] When the story opens, his boredom has escalated to the point where he abhors going to dinner parties hosted by people with whom he does not want to dine in the first place. The evenings seem to go on forever, and he worries that his life will be a series of monotonous jobs and encounters.[5] When Mr. Greenleaf approaches Tom about talking to Dickie, Tom initially finds this conversation, like all his interactions with his associates, uninteresting and repellent.[6]

When we suffer from ennui, we think the world owes it to us to be intriguing and engaging. Tom expects the handsome and urbane Dickie to be scintillatingly clever. When Dickie fails to entertain Tom, Tom grouses, "Christ, Dickie had been a bore that day!"[7] We know what Tom is feeling. One employee survey after another has shown that people hate their jobs and wish for greater stimulation in their lives. Yet stimulation from external sources cannot rid us of our boredom. It only reinforces the passivity at the root of our ennui. We need to become thinkers, identifying the objective constraints governing our efforts to become happy. Instead, we behave like children. We have some need or desire, so the universe must fulfill it! We do not consider the possibility that the universe does not exist in order to cater to our every whim. Our failure to think means we have no sense of ourselves as beings who are a part of a larger whole with its own logic and necessity. We become narcissists who reduce the universe to the size of our infantile self.

In the process, we undermine the objective self. By objective self, I mean the self that derives a lasting satisfaction from comprehending its place in the larger whole. In the absence of such an understanding, unlimited ambition fills the void. Although Tom finds other people uninteresting, he is certain that he is extraordinarily talented and fascinating. Once we turn ourselves into the world, we see ourselves as equal to any challenge. We cannot abide the thought that other people may find us dull or lacking in ability. If their perception were correct, it would call into question our self-conception and leave us completely at a loss. For what in the world could be more interesting than our world-self?

Highsmith's genius lies in her perception that the line between deviant serial killers and normal decent folk is a fine one. Dickie Greenleaf resembles his friend Tom Ripley in many ways. He has rebelled against his father by refusing to work in the family shipyard. Although he has a flair for drawing and designing boats, Dickie prefers to dabble at landscape painting. Living off checks from his father, he drifts through the day, swimming, sunning, and priding himself on his mediocre Italian and poorly executed paintings. Dickie's discipline is not much better than Tom's, and he shares Tom's inflated sense of his abilities.

The boredom of the two men is not a character flaw. We have elevated our boredom into a quasi-virtue. As one French journalist writes, "There are moments when, faced with our lack of success, I wonder whether we are failures, proud but impotent. One thing reassures me as to our value: the boredom that afflicts us. It is the hallmark of quality in modern men."[8] In other words, our boredom proves our superiority! Yet we feel deeply dissatisfied and barely alive. We try to overcome the deadness within by garnering attention. Reality TV shows proliferate as ever more of us come to believe that we deserve recognition. Being on TV or in the newspaper confirms, in turn, that we are the talented people we take ourselves to be. Once we conflate the self with the world, naked ambition and a craving for celebrity start to preempt real achievement.

Many of us are frozen in adolescence, that stage in which it appears that everyone else is watching what we do. As the modern joke goes, "You know you are mature when you realize that other people are too self-preoccupied to pay any attention to you." Our feeble attempt at humor merely confirms the extent of our boredom and alienation from our selves. It never occurs to us that true maturity means discovering an intrinsically satisfying way to exist. If we do not make this discovery, we become increasingly restless. Frustrated by the world's indifference toward us, we revenge ourselves upon the world.[9]

As *The Talented Mr. Ripley* opens, we learn that Tom has been frightening taxpayers into making unnecessary remittances to the mythical IRS clerk George McAlpin, one of Tom's many personae. The first time through the book, the reader finds his tactics puzzling. Tom does not appear to care whether he makes any money from the scam. Why, then, is he running the risk of being imprisoned for mail fraud? When we reread the opening in the light of Tom's subsequent murders, his little "game" is more intelligible and more chilling. At one level, the postal scam serves to alleviate boredom. Tom has no qualms, because his actions are merely "good clean sport. He wasn't stealing money from anybody."[10] At another level though, Tom is deadly earnest about this game. Since his targets have all written their checks to the IRS instead of to George McAlpin, Tom has not been able to cash the checks. Nevertheless, he keeps them as evidence that he is smarter than these poor dupes and so merits the fame that eludes him. He needs this proof to sustain his self-image and will do anything to obtain it. That is why he cannot give up his game playing. In *Ripley's Game*, the sequel to *The Talented Mr. Ripley*, Tom takes revenge on a sick man who has insulted him by starting a rumor that the man is about to die from leukemia.[11]

Tom's behavior is tactical insofar as it has a purpose: it functions to distract him from his boredom and to support his image of himself as a talented individual who merits the world's accolades. These tactics are not conscious, as is evinced by Tom's inability to admit his scam to himself or his peers. He has constructed his personality around one sustaining belief: he is a talented brilliant artist. Such a man would never condescend to small-time thievery. The fraud must be termed merely "sport" in order for Tom's personality to remain intact.

Each of us has a self-inflicted blind spot, and we all use tactics of one sort or another to shore up our identity. Our behavior is far from random. It has a logic and so could be described as purposive. But our activity is not purposeful or consciously intentional. Aristotle would say that Tom, like Hendrik, fails to deliberate well. What Aristotle does not apprehend is the cause of the failure. Both men are caught up in trajectories that unfold with a logic they neither understand nor control. We cannot escape these purposive trajectories through an act of willpower or exertion. Any action we might take would follow this same trajectory. Escaping requires that we become aware of this logic and come to know ourselves. This awareness and self-knowledge develop together. Instead of blaming people for their actions, we should be trying to comprehend the logic of alienation. By delving deeper into the way in which Tom tries to escape his boredom, we may be able to identify some of our blind spots and to avoid Tom's fate.

The Obsessive Desire for Money

For many people, wealth appears to be the ticket to Paradise. Tom downplays his tax fraud by insisting that he is not a thief, yet he is obsessed with money. When Mr. Greenleaf asks him to retrieve Dickie from Europe, Tom suddenly recalls that Dickie is a tall blond fellow with lots of money. Later Tom tries to involve Dickie in a smuggling operation that will net each man over three hundred dollars. Murdering Dickie appears to be an attractive course because Tom can "set up an apartment in Rome or Paris, receive Dickie's check every month and forge Dickie's signature on it."[12]

Like Tom, we delude ourselves into believing that money will enable us to become the fascinating people we take ourselves to be. Individuals with money are typically admired, so money becomes a source of self-esteem for us. The greater our alienation, the more we desire material wealth. The desire for money and the need to be admired by others are inseparable. While he is figuring out how to use Mr. Greenleaf to get a free trip to Europe, Tom is assuring himself that he will acquit himself well with Dickie and "Mr. Greenleaf would know that he had, and would respect him for it."[13] Tom cannot help but get emotionally involved in his quest to retrieve Dickie. To fail would mean that he is not as talented as he takes himself to be. The only way to escape his boring life is "to make Dickie like him. That he wanted more than anything else in the world."[14]

We think that having money will make us more likeable. Being likeable, in turn, will bring us still more money, status, and self-esteem. The problem is that acquiring money does not make us happy or provide us with a stable identity. Even after Tom has stolen Dickie's money and identity, Tom continues to worry about how others view him. He makes a point of getting invited into the chic houses of wealthy French associates. Since the French are especially reticent, these invitations are proof that the new Tom—Dickie Greenleaf—must be likeable.[15] Why, then, does the new Tom hate these parties as much as the old Tom did?

We would not be bored if we were able to engage the world in an objective way. I consider what this engagement looks like in the closing chapters. Now I want to emphasize the need for an objective approach. When we seek to appreciate the nature of things and allow the world to disclose to us who we are, we are taken out of ourselves into the world. We allow genius to find us instead of seeking to transform ourselves into geniuses or celebrities. As we comprehend the essential nature of things, we stop worrying about how we are viewed by our fellow human beings. Our life becomes intrinsically satisfying. If, however, we fail to engage with life in this objective way, we are thrown back entirely onto ourselves.

Like Hendrik, Tom discovers that the isolated self, disengaged from reality, has no way to measure its worth. This atomistic self is a disordered succession of passing emotions and fears. Detached from the world, it feels uncentered, adrift, and unreal. Our obsessive quest for wealth is an attempt to acquire an identity, to make a name for ourselves, and to live an ordered existence. As Tom puts it, it takes possessions to give "a man self-respect. . . . Possessions reminded [Tom] that he existed, and made him enjoy his existence."[16]

When Tom finds he must rid himself of Dickie a second time, relinquish the Greenleaf persona, and return to being Tom Ripley, he starts to cry:

> He hated becoming Thomas Ripley again, hated being nobody, hated putting on his old set of habits again, and feeling that people looked down on him and were bored with him unless he put on an act for them like a clown, feeling incompetent and incapable of doing anything with himself. . . . He hated going back to himself as he would have hated putting on a shabby suit of clothes, a grease-spotted, unpressed suit of clothes that had not been very good even when it was new . . . As he packed he began to reckon up defiantly the things of Dickie's that he could still keep because they had no initials, or because no one would remember that they were Dickie's and not his own.[17]

As this quotation shows, conceiving of narcissists as people in love with themselves is a mistake. Narcissists despise their bored and boring selves. They will do anything to escape their sense that they are doomed to be unhappy. Tom wants nothing more than to leave his ordinary existence behind and to become Dickie, a man whose wealth permits him to lead what Tom romantically perceives to be a cosmopolitan and exotic existence.

We should not be surprised that Tom steals Dickie's two signet rings after killing his friend. Tom stares at the rings of just about every man he meets. Signet rings have long been a symbol of identity, power, and status, all of which Tom has lusted after his entire life. Tom wastes no time in appropriating Dickie's status-bestowing possessions and selling Dickie's house and boat to garner the money needed to make others take note of his good taste:

> [I]t had been impossible to make a beginning at acquiring anything of his own on forty dollars a week. It would have taken him the best years of his life, even if he had economized stringently, to buy the things he wanted. Dickie's money had given him only an added momentum on the road he had been traveling. The money gave him the leisure to see Greece, to collect Etruscan pottery if he wanted to (he had recently seen an interesting book on that subject by an American living in Rome), to join art societies if he cared to and to donate to their work.[18]

Narcissists, who have mistaken the self for the world, believe that becoming wealthy will cause everyone to esteem and like them. This esteem is, after all, their natural due. They believe that they alone deserve to be valued and esteemed. When Tom observes Mr. Greenleaf's affection for Dickie's friend Marge, he becomes extremely jealous.[19] Believing that we are much superior to everyone else, we begrudge others any love or attention that they receive.

Let me recapitulate the dynamics of narcissism. Disengaged from the world, we become bored. Our strategies for eliminating boredom fail. We are left feeling dead. However, we still believe that we are infinitely talented, superior to everyone else, and therefore worthy of adulation. We are alienated from others, yet desperate for the public adulation that confirms we are still alive. Since we believe that we deserve this adulation more than our less talented peers, our appetite for other people's approval is insatiable. The respect of others becomes our drug, our high of self-respect. Like a drug addict, we are always thinking about our next fix. Since at any moment we may feel our esteem threatened, we need a reserve or stash of external esteem. Dependent on others to give us self-worth, we monitor and measure the exact amounts of affection our peers are receiving. If those around us appear to be receiving as much (or more) respect than we are, then we conclude that we are no one special. We convert esteem into a scarce good and resent it when anyone else receives affection that should, in our minds, be coming to us.

The narcissistic self is endlessly inventive. When no outsider is available to supply us with the admiration we crave, we elevate ourselves by deprecating others. Like heroin users who must content themselves with methadone, we settle for a fake or synthetic form of respect. We amuse and reassure ourselves by analyzing the stupidity of our peers and associates. Here, then, is another one of the many paradoxes connected with evil: although we depend upon others to supply us with a desirable self-image, we come to despise those who fulfill this need. Bob, the only one of Tom's acquaintances who offers him a place to stay in New York, is, according to Tom, nothing but a "crummy bum."[20] When Bob and his associates come to Tom's cabin to see him off, Tom feels that these "second-rate people" have contaminated his cabin.[21] The men and women whom Tom defrauds are "idiots."[22] When Mrs. Greenleaf shows him pictures of Dickie as a child, Tom (who lost his mother when he was quite young) immediately demotes the beloved Dickie: "Tom could not help feeling that Richard was not very intelligent, or else he loved to be photographed and thought he looked best with his mouth spread from ear to ear, which was not very intelligent of him, either."[23] Dickie's friend Marge speaks "abominably" and is so stupid that she is, in Tom's view, easy to manipulate.[24] The reporters who cover the story of Dickie's disappearance are mere "dopes . . . who haven't got any clues at all about anything."[25] The American detective whom Mr. Greenleaf hires to track down Dickie strikes Tom as "moderately bright, but only moderately."[26] In Tom's judgment, the Italian inspector who investigates the disappearance of Dickie is not "particularly bright."[27] The harder the police press him to account for his past whereabouts, the more Tom views them with contempt. Tom needs them to be stupid in order for him to feel confident. Consequently, the police go from being "not bright" to full-fledged "idiots" within the space of a few pages.

By degrading our fellow human beings, we hope to make ourselves more lovable. Our reasoning is convoluted. We convince ourselves that the very people whom we despise should love us more. Since we are smarter or lovelier than they are, we are more deserving of people's esteem and affection. The more affection we merit, the greater our stature (in our own eyes) becomes. Our self-elevation makes us appear even more worthy of everyone's esteem, including the respect of people whom we feel entitled to victimize because they are not worthy to live. This self-validating circle is completely subjective and leaves us immune to criticism. Anyone who dares to criticize us gets dismissed as ignorant and unworthy of consideration.

The Irritated and Melodramatic Self

The example of Tom Ripley shows that evil is not one character trait among many. Evil is the frustration and suffering we experience because we have unwittingly embraced a delusional and paradoxical way of being in the world. This way of being permeates all our traits, perceptions, and actions. It would perhaps be more accurate to refer to this purely subjective, narcissistic existence as a way of not being. What passes for the self is little more than a succession of fears, rages, bewilderments, ecstatic highs, and self-pitying lows. To quote Gertrude Stein: "There is no there there."[28] Evil is the self's destruction of the self.

Doing evil is not separable from suffering evil. Doing evil means adopting different interrelated strategies (e.g., assuming another's identity, stealing other people's wealth) in a vain attempt to escape a deadening sense of alienation and boredom. Each of these strategies can be traced back to our painful alienation. Our practice of treating people with contempt is the flip side of our desperate quest to find external sources to validate our worth and importance. Our hubristic belief in our many wonderful talents is the converse of our deep-seated fear that we might be judged as boring as those whom we despise. These strategies and beliefs become habitual. It should not surprise us that so-called narcissistic personality disorder has proven resistant to therapy. If Highsmith's understanding of evil is correct, narcissism bred of boredom is not a feature of the personality. Narcissism is the personality, where a personality is understood as an individual's habitual way of acting and reacting. (Even to speak of the mere "individual" in this case is misleading because this term suggests a contained, ordered self. At the mercy of passion, the narcissist is little more than an identifiable set of habits or, as we like to say, a "complex.") Curing a person of narcissism would entail destroying the only personality the individual has ever known and thrusting him or her into a world that has no objective existence for this individual. Alienated narcissists will dismiss their therapists as stupid or untrustworthy before they will dismantle their personalities.

Alienated subjectivity, like the false shame explored in chapter 2, expresses itself mechanically. Every expression of evil appears to possess its own internal, inflexible logic. The logic is rigid because it always involves rationalization. Rationalization occurs when we operate entirely subjectively, steadfastly avoiding any encounter with our true self. Instead of asking ourselves why our behavior is leaving us unhappy, we blame the world for giving us a raw deal and continually lapse into self-pity. When the Greenleafs send Tom a fruit basket as a send-off gift, Tom cannot appreciate the gesture. Bemoaning his inability to afford such an item, he breaks down and starts to sob.[29] Orphaned at a young age, Tom is raised by his Aunt Dottie. Instead of being grateful for this maiden aunt's assistance, Tom rails at her for failing to provide him with more. Although she continues to send checks to her fully grown nephew, Tom complains that this money is an insult "considering what Aunt Dottie might have sent him."[30] Instead of acknowledging and valuing Mr. Greenleaf's willingness to send him to Europe, Tom feels mortally wounded when the Greenleafs decide that Dickie will not return from Europe to take over the family business. When Herbert Greenleaf writes to thank Tom for his efforts, Tom resents this "final blow. . . . Mr. Greenleaf had simply cut him off. He had failed."[31]

Since the world continues to go its own way, refusing to conform to our whims and delusions, our subjective personality proves quite fragile. Early on we find that we, like Tom Ripley, must tell ourselves lies or stories in order to preserve our sense of self. The world, though, is a far richer place than our habitual rationalizations and deceptions. That is why genuine reason leaves behind habitual modes of imagining and perceiving. In Hannah Arendt's striking phrase, genuine reason "thinks without banisters."[32] Cunning, by contrast, needs a stable of well-worn tricks and strategies to sustain it. Compared with genuine reason, cunning always appears mechanical.

Mechanical actions, by definition, are insensitive to other people's needs, desires, and interests. Other people are relevant only insofar as they impede or facilitate the forward motion of the narcissist. Like Tom, we become perennially irritated at a world that does not conform to our expectations and demands. Given this undercurrent of irritation, our happiness and depression readily convert into rage at the "injustices" we are forced to suffer. Feeling irritated and alienated, we experience no shame when we treat other people badly. We see them only as hindrances or helpmates, never as full-bodied people with feelings to be understood and appreciated. However, it would be a mistake to think that narcissistic individuals are completely lacking in empathy. Tom Ripley is adept at intuiting what others are thinking and at manipulating them by telling them what they already believe or want to hear. If empathy consists of being able to see the world from another's perspective, the Tom Ripleys of this world are empathetic in the extreme. What alienated selves lack is the ability to feel any concern for what happens to other people except insofar as these happenings further or impede their narcissistic plans.

At no point does Tom consider how much Dickie's disappearance has confused, hurt, and disappointed Dickie's parents or Dickie's friend Marge. As long as Tom sees Marge as a potential competitor for Dickie's affection, Tom hates Marge for interfering with the bond he imagines exists between the two men.[33] After Tom has murdered Dickie, Tom finds Marge getting on his nerves as she speculates about the absent Dickie's latest movements: "Marge was optimistic, he could see that. Even now she had that energetic buoyancy that made Tom think of the typical Girl Scout . . . She irritated him intensely suddenly."[34] A few days later, after Marge has come round to thinking that Dickie has committed suicide, Tom suddenly starts viewing her as an ally. She becomes "good old Marge." Tom feels "almost affectionate towards her. . . . Marge was an asset rather than a liability."[35] Note that his irritation remains. Alienated individuals feel "almost" affectionate toward others, but never truly so. Determined to escape our boredom, we relentlessly pursue what we take to be in our interest. The moment someone proves resistant to our manipulation, he or she becomes hateful to us. The aphorism— "Withhold admiration from a narcissist and be disliked. Give it and be treated with indifference"—succinctly expresses the alienated individual's relationships with other people.[36]

Tom's willingness to use other people is reminiscent of Hendrik's strategies for garnering respect. Both men crave respect, but Tom's career more clearly exhibits the incipiently violent nature of the narcissist. Tom feels that he—not those whom he manipulates, defrauds, or murders—is the victim. We see how close rage is to the surface in Tom's aggrieved reaction to the police request that he stick around for further interrogation. How dare the police question him and force him to revise his plans! He must move all his suitcases, those for Dickie Greenleaf and those for Tom Ripley, to a new hotel: "He had packed them for such a different purpose. And now this!"[37] Tom wants to go to Greece posing as Dickie but soon finds he must abandon this plan because of police pressure. He laments:

> But would it happen that he couldn't see Greece as Dickie Greenleaf?
> Would one thing after another come up to thwart him—murder,

suspicion, people? He hadn't wanted to murder, it had been a necessity. The idea of going to Greece, trudging over the Acropolis as Tom Ripley, American tourist, held no charm for him at all. He would as soon not go. Tears came in his eyes as he stared up at the campanile of the cathedral, and then he turned away and began to walk down a new street.[38]

Our self-pity, coupled with our rage, produces a melodramatic outlook. We inevitably overestimate the significance of events when we evaluate them with reference only to ourselves. Things strike us as terribly important that do not matter one whit to those around us. Lacking any objective measure for ascertaining significance, we unconsciously imbue events with our emotions. How threatening an event is depends on how blue we happen to be feeling on a given day. Tom is convinced that he had the worst of all possible childhoods. When Dickie asks him if he is going home for the holidays, Tom immediately reads malice into this query. Dickie should have known that poor Tom has no home.

Our reactions tend toward the maudlin. Mr. Greenleaf's letter thanking Tom for his assistance strikes Tom as the "final" blow.[39] When Tom relinquishes Dickie's identity, he feels "identifying himself as Thomas Phelps Ripley was going to be one of the saddest things he had ever done in his life."[40] After the private detective asks to meet with Tom, Tom looks out the window at his Rome apartment house: it "was like a last glimpse . . . the view across the canal to where his house stood . . . he might never see it again."[41] Extreme lows quickly turn into manic highs. Our mood swings wildly when we do not engage with the world, because the self is not grounded in the larger reality. As long as Tom can bask in the affection of Dickie, he is happy. The moment he begins to suspect that Dickie's friend Marge does not like him, he becomes restless and discontent. The most innocuous comment pushes him over the edge into rage.

The Connection between Boredom
and Violence

Our alienated boredom leaves us in dread. Unable to pinpoint the source of our unhappiness, we begin to feel that our future has been irremediably compromised. Although we tell ourselves that money and status will make us happy, we simultaneously suspect that we will never thrive. To become lastingly happy, we must ask ourselves some hard questions: Who are we? How is our self-conception impeding our development? Why are we subject to such severe mood swings? In short, we must use our reason in a rigorous and probing way to discover how exactly we fit into the world. Until we do so, we will continue to feel trapped. It is no wonder that Ripley's favorite bar is the Green Cage.[42]

Instead of reflecting on our plight, we act impulsively and childishly. Deeply fearful, we grasp at any straw of salvation. We would be happier if we were more disciplined. But discipline, like lasting satisfaction, presupposes an objective outlook. In the strict sense, discipline is a union between mind and object that occurs when the mind is able to discern the nature of an object or the inner laws governing the object being perceived or investigated.[43] The disciplined violinist learns and comes to respect what the instrument's objective capabilities are. The disciplined actor submits to the requirements of the plot, language, and role. The object controls and regulates the thinking and emotions of the actor. Objects have no controlling power for those who believe they are innately talented beyond measure. Although Tom claims to want to be an actor, he refuses to work at his craft. He gets angry when he is rejected for several roles and settles for mimicking other people at parties.[44]

Bereft of discipline, we expect instantaneous results and gratification and so doom ourselves to frustration. Tom does not last long in any job. Again, the world is to blame: "He had a talent for mathematics. Why in hell didn't they pay him for it, somewhere?"[45] Although Tom is vague about who the "they" are, he is certain that he deserves better treatment than he has received to date. As our alienation increases, we feel progressively less shame about using any means to get what we deserve. After Tom is fired from a job, he steals a loaf of bread and devours it, "feeling that the world owed a loaf of bread to him, and more."[46]

Unable to discern the role our illusions have played in our failures, we imagine that some malign force necessitates our action. This belief serves to distance us from our wrongdoing. Others may try to hold us accountable, but such people are little more than troublesome gnats. Superior people like us can easily swat them. Moreover, since we believe the world has forced us to eliminate people who stand in our way, we are buoyed by our innocence:

> The [police detective] was waiting for [Tom] to contribute something more. Tom felt quite comfortable now. It was going just as he had hoped in his more optimistic moments: the police held nothing against him at all, and they suspected him of nothing. Tom felt suddenly innocent and strong, as free of guilt as his old suitcase from which he had carefully scrubbed the [telltale] sticker.[47]

We do not do evil because we are violent. We are violent because we are enslaved to a false self-image that causes us pain. Our frustration, coupled with our lack of shame, grandiose self-perception, and mechanical approach to life, makes it easy for us to perform violent acts. This toxic combination results in another paradox: at the same time that we are assuring ourselves that we are smart enough to avoid being caught and prosecuted for our crimes, we are busily convincing ourselves that we have done absolutely nothing wrong. Whenever the truth threatens to break through—that we have committed a crime—we immediately move to cancel or subvert that bothersome truth.

Sometimes, though, truth does break through. When it does, we panic. We are so accustomed to living a lie that we do not know how to dwell in truth. After Tom confides his humble origins to the Greenleafs, he is suddenly afraid. He has come dangerously close to confessing that he is not the extraordinary talented man he must believe himself to be. The alienated narcissist fears speaking the truth more than telling lies:

> That had been the only time tonight when he had felt uncomfortable, unreal, the way he might have felt if he had been lying, yet it had been practically the only thing he had said that *was* true: My parents died when I was very small. I was raised by my aunt in Boston. Mr. Greenleaf came into the room. His figure seemed to pulsate and grow larger and larger. Tom blinked his eyes, feeling a sudden terror of him, an impulse to attack him before he was attacked.[48]

Violence is our way of evacuating our dread onto others. We do not freely choose to act violently if by "freely choose" we mean "originate spontaneously." Our violence is more akin to an instinctive self-defense, a programmed response. We may be mistaken about who the self is, but if our illusory self is the only one we know, our response is predictable, not spontaneous or unconstrained. Admitting failure is not an option for the narcissist. When Tom begins to suspect that Dickie is not going to be his bosom buddy and that the two are not going to live together forever on Dickie's money, he quickly moves to murder Dickie and—this is key— to assume Dickie's identity:

> A crazy emotion of hate, of affection, of impatience and frustration was welling in [Tom], hampering his breathing. He wanted to kill Dickie. It was not the first time had thought of it. Before, once or twice or three times, it had been an impulse caused by anger or disappointment, an impulse that vanished immediately and left him with a feeling of shame. Now he thought about it for an entire minute, two minutes, because he was leaving Dickie anyway, and what was there to be ashamed of any more? He had failed with Dickie, in every way. He hated Dickie, because, however he looked at what had happened, his failing had not been his own fault, not due to anything he had done, but due to Dickie's inhuman stubbornness. And his blatant rudeness! . . . If he killed him on this trip, Tom thought, he could simply say that some accident had happened. He could—He had just thought of something brilliant: he could become Dickie Greenleaf himself.[49]

Note how Tom minimizes the violence he contemplates. He contends that he is not doing anything wrong because he is the victim, not Dickie. Tom need not feel any shame for his shortcomings, because Dickie is responsible for Tom's failure to realize his full potential. Besides, Dickie, with his "inhuman" stubbornness, barely qualifies as a person. Therefore, if Tom kills him, his act will not count as murder. And, in any case, Tom will not be responsible for anything he himself has done because he will be the charming and wealthy Dickie Greenleaf. Indeed, there will not have been any murder. Since Tom will have become Dickie, Dickie will still be very much alive!

At one level, Tom's assumption of Dickie's identity ratifies the similarity between the two men. In their boredom, they are virtually indistinguishable from each other or, it must be said, from most of us. As I noted earlier, Highsmith's probing of Tom's psyche functions as an exposé of the modern condition of alienation. At a deeper level, however, Tom's transformation into Dickie is meant to disclose the mechanics of alienation. When we feel alienated from ourselves, we implicitly divide our lives in two. There exists, on the one hand, the supposedly real and fascinatingly talented self (Dickie Greenleaf) and, on the other, the fake nobody (Tom Ripley) from whom we desperately wish to escape. Having a double nature not only enables us to preserve our fragile subjective self, but also provides us with plausible deniability in case we are driven to violence—we can alienate our violence, imputing it to our unreal self.

Tom repeatedly assumes the identity of other men as his career unfolds. He delights in fooling others. His victims' gullibility reinforces his sense of superiority. But something more is at stake. Tom murders a stranger when the man sees through Tom's impersonation and threatens to turn him in to the authorities. The one failure we cannot tolerate is a lapse or breakdown in our self-disguise. If we cannot successfully shift identities, then we might be exposed. Although being seen as an incompetent fraud would be humiliating, losing our ability to escape into a delusion of self-grandeur would be far worse. If we have spent our entire life avoiding the truth about ourselves, our existence becomes meaningless the moment we must admit to being a nobody.

Our existential duplicity results in moral doublespeak. We deny that moral standards apply to us, life's victims. We may not even see ourselves as agents. Tom consistently considers himself a spectator, a distanced viewer who is watching a play unfold around him. At the same time, we are excessively moralistic when it comes to other people's behavior and are perfectly willing to apply moral standards to friends and associates. Strange as it seems, Tom, who has murdered four people, indignantly turns down a request to carry out a contract hit on the grounds that he has a reputation to protect.[50]

The language of morality appeals to the narcissist within us because it enables us to assert our superiority. We are driven to use the language to garner praise and to criticize other people. Yet we have a terrible fear of being blamed. So we apply moral language selectively, avoiding any mention of our failures while congratulating ourselves on our virtue. We inventively impute small virtues to ourselves in order to minimize our larger faults. Like Hendrik, Tom employs a moral calculus in which he gets to determine the worth of his acts. Tom will kill Dickie in order to get his friend's estate, but he refuses to stoop to putting the touch on

Mr. Greenleaf: "At least, he thought proudly, he hadn't tried to wheedle any more money out of Mr. Greenleaf, and he might have. . . . Anybody else would have, Tom thought, anybody, but he hadn't, and that counted for something."[51] Instead of wheedling the money, Tom steals it by manufacturing a forged version of Dickie's will.

At other times, we create a fantasy version of ourselves, a scrupulously proper self. Forging yet another persona becomes easy when we are fundamentally divided. Since virtue is praiseworthy, what could be a better way of alleviating dread than to imagine ourselves as paragons of virtue? Tom convinces himself that he will be a better son to the Greenleafs than the one he has just murdered: Tom "would have made up for all Dickie's negligence and unconcern for his parents in the past."[52] The Greenleafs would not see matters in this light, but Tom is so self-congratulatory that he is beyond the reach of irony. Having murdered Dickie's friend Freddy Miles, Tom sails for Greece, the home of the great Greek warriors. Alone at the prow of the ship, he imagines himself to be a hero:

> A defiant courage rose in him. What if the radioman were receiving at this very minute a message to arrest Tom Ripley? He would stand up just as bravely as he was standing now. Or he might hurl himself over the ship's gunwale—which for him would be supreme act of courage as well as escape.[53]

Given that Tom is terrified of water, this scenario hardly qualifies as a plan of action. The fantasy serves instead to reinforce Tom's sense that he is an especially noble creature, a superior being who is entitled to use the language of morality to assess other people's behavior. In Tom's eyes, the authorities' pursuit of him is unjust. He is a heroic savior, not a man who has committed two murders and coolly contemplated a third. On the trip to Greece, Tom imagines himself jumping into the water and rescuing a passenger who has fallen overboard. He might even rescue the entire ship by "fighting through the waters of a ruptured bulkhead to close the breach with his own body."[54]

This fantasy is especially revealing of the way in which we hide from ourselves the truth about ourselves. Instead of owning up to what we have done (Dickie's body is under water, not Tom's), we rewrite the past, making ourselves into active victims (Tom substitutes his body for Dickie's). We first convert ourselves from agents into victims who, as such, have contributed nothing to past events. Victims, though, are uninteresting and boring. If we are to escape our boredom, we must perform glorious deeds. Therefore, we quickly reconfigure our identity. Gone is the passive suffering victim. In his or her place is the heroic individual who willingly and consciously becomes a victim for a virtuous cause and who deserves public adoration.

ALIENATION, RISK-TAKING, AND PARANOIA

Alienated, we trace a trajectory from boredom through contempt, irritation, rage, fantasy, and violence only to wind up where we began: we are, in the words of the modern poet John Berryman, "heavy bored."[55] None of our attempts to hide this truth from ourselves can succeed. Our hypocritical strategies ignore the root problem—our subjectivity, lack of discipline, and failure to use our reason to discover the basis for an objective self. This failure drives us to up the ante in order to make ourselves feel more vital and alive. Desperate to thrive, we become addicted to risk-taking and to the thrill of escaping detection. Casinos and gambling boats provide us with an illusion of contentment. Folk wisdom gets it right when it paints the devil, the West's most popular symbol for evil incarnate, as an enthusiastic and inveterate gambler.[56]

The stakes are higher than mere money. Tom does not risk currency; he stakes his freedom on his belief that he is a great actor. Priding himself on having fooled the Italian police into thinking he had nothing to do with Dickie Greenleaf's disappearance, Tom suddenly conceives the notion of forging Dickie's will. A forgery is tricky. Tom must reproduce Dickie's signature and convince the Greenleafs that he and Dickie were sufficiently friendly for Dickie to designate Tom as heir to Dickie's estate. If Tom benefits from Dickie's death, then the police may again become interested in him. Far from dissuading Tom, this heightened risk draws him like a moth to the flame. The murder did not provide him with the satisfaction for which he had hoped. A more daring course is required if he is to secure his happiness.

As I noted previously, the alienated self is little more than a series of passing emotions, reactions, and events. Lacking any objective standard by which to evaluate and order their identity, bored individuals experience the world as one big casino. They embrace chance. No place excites Tom like the Côte d'Azur, the gambling Mecca of the world.[57] Needing the "fix" provided by our risk-taking, we are willing to do anything to remain at the poker table of life. Stealing, lying, and murder become just so many chips in our game. We do not intend these actions. We can truthfully say, along with Tom Ripley, that we do not *want* to be murderers or liars.[58] Like him, we may be able to repress what we have done—for a while. Our past, though, is never far behind. Ripley's story opens with him believing that the police are after him, and it ends the same way. As he disembarks in Crete and sees four policemen on the shore, he tensely wonders: "Was he going to see policemen waiting for him on every pier that he ever approached? In Alexandria? Istanbul? Bombay?"[59]

As we have seen, the alienated self veers toward the melodramatic. Imagining ourselves to be innocent victims who have in no way contributed to our suffering, we feel at the mercy of the world. We continually fear that the worst will befall us. This sense that some unspecified disaster awaits us around the corner makes us paranoid. "Paranoia" means "that which is beyond (*para-*) the grasp of our intuitive understanding (*nous*)." In our alienation, we cannot specify what form the disaster we fear will assume. Like Tom, we want to believe that we are the best and smartest people in the world. Our narcissism does not permit us to entertain consciously the possibility that we might be exposed as frauds or criminals by someone whom we deem to be our inferior. We push such thoughts to the periphery of our consciousness, saying that there is no point in thinking about that. The "that," however, will not leave us alone. Immediately after telling himself that there is "no use spoiling his trip worrying about imaginary policemen," Tom starts to fret.[60] He reassures himself that, even if there were policemen on the pier, it would not necessarily mean trouble. Yet, precisely because we are driven to protect our fragile identity at any cost, we are not free to ignore the threats the world poses for our persona. We are always of two minds when it comes to our future security. This duality means that the source of our fear is always beyond what we are able to face. Consequently, our fear haunts us.

The Locus of Evil

I have intentionally used the pronoun "we" throughout this chapter to remind us of our kinship with Tom Ripley. I am not suggesting that each of us is a serial killer. Hannah Arendt is right: when everyone is guilty of a particular crime, then no one is. Primo Levi, who writes so eloquently about his experience at Auschwitz, warns against any cheap suggestion that we are all murderers:

> I do not know, and it does not much interest me to know, whether in my depths there lurks a murderer, but I do know that I was a guiltless victim and I was not a murderer. I know that the murderers existed, not only in Germany, and still exist, retired or on active duty, and that to confuse them with their victims is a moral disease or an aesthetic affectation or a sinister sign of complicity; above all, it is a precious service rendered (intentionally or not) to the negators of truth.[61]

I grant that we must not lose sight of differences in behavior. Primo Levi did not murder his fellow Jews anymore than you or I killed Dickie Greenleaf. Tom Ripley has bludgeoned Dickie, and the police are, from a moral point of view (see chapter 1), right to pursue him. I wonder, though, whether matters are quite as clear-cut as Levi would have us believe. If murder sometimes is, as I have been arguing, an attempt to escape a state of alienated boredom, locating evil exclusively, or even primarily, in the criminal deed is misleading. To the extent that evil is the human experience of a dread-inducing and frustrating boredom, each of us has at some point lived evil.

Morality requires that we distinguish between murderers and their victims. By punishing those who break the law, we hope to contain the violence simmering below the surface of civilization. Convicting and imprisoning murderers and child molesters may prevent them from acting out their frustration. However, if we are honest, we will admit that criminals also are victims. In making this claim, I am not restating the well-known fact that abusers frequently turn out to have been abused as children. I mean instead that we, like Tom Ripley, victimize ourselves because we misconceive who we are. This point is not, as Levi implies, an "aesthetic affectation" that sinisterly conflates the victim and the victimizer. The realization that we victimize ourselves is a genuine insight into the nature of evil, which literature is able to convey masterfully for two reasons.

First, any literary plot with a beginning, middle, and end has an internal driving necessity. Since self-inflicted suffering traces a mechanical trajectory, plays and novels are perfect vehicles for exhibiting the operation of evil. Second, because novels rely upon a narrator, they draw the reader into the perspective of the one who is telling the tale. We become interested in that perspective and, for the duration of our engagement, that perspective becomes ours. The novel *The Talented Mr. Ripley* succeeds only to the extent that we at least partially identify with the young Ripley who, as the novel opens, feels he is being pursued. As readers, we want to be taken out of ourselves for the time it takes us to read and appreciate Tom's tale. In this respect, the reader is akin to Tom. We, too, want to leave our life and become someone else.

Highsmith brilliantly forces the question: why do we moderns love our novels so? Why do we want to become the murderer Ripley, if just for a few hours? We enter the alternative world of fiction because we are every bit as bored as Tom. While we may not be murderers, we are sufficiently alienated to empathize with Tom's anxiety and his desire to be respected and loved by his peers. This desire for respect is normal. No one goes through adolescence without experiencing the desperate craving to be liked and popular. Tom's preoccupation with how other people see him does not strike us initially as either alien or abnormal. We slip easily into Tom's world and come to share what Wendy Lesser perceptively describes as Ripley's "free-floating anxiety."[62] The anxiety floats because the alienated self has no center. It drifts not just from Tom the sophisticated and consummate actor to Tom the pathetic orphan to Tom's alter ego Dickie Greenleaf. This evil floats to us, novel-loving readers, as well.

Those of us who want to know why Tom assumes Dickie's identity soon cease to be curious about whether Ripley is going to get away with the murder. The interest of the novel lies in Ripley's futile efforts to escape himself. His growing paranoia is his punishment. Whether he happens to get caught is beside the point. Lacking an objective self, Tom will continue to adopt others people's identities and attack anyone who comes close to unmasking him. We do not have to read all six of Highsmith's Ripley novels to reach this conclusion.

If we are struggling to understand who we truly are, then Ripley's career loses its fascination for us. However, if we are not doing this soul work, the boundary between Ripley and us remains permeable. His anxiety will infect us, and we will attempt to lose ourselves in this character, compulsively reading one novel after the next. Novels, though, will never provide us with the closure we seek. Highsmith's artistic rendering of the serial killer Ripley asks: who are we? If we do not address this challenge, we will be swept out into sea of anxiety, caught in a riptide of serial reading.

4

EVIL AS HYPOCRITICAL REPRESSION

Unable to create a meaningful life for itself, the personality takes its own revenge: from the lower depths comes a regressive form of spontaneity: raw animality forms a counterpoise to the meaningless stimuli and the vicarious life to which the ordinary man is conditioned.

—*Lewis Mumford*

EVERYONE HAS HEARD OF *THE STRANGE TALE OF DR. JEKYLL AND MR. HYDE* by Robert Louis Stevenson.[1] The story is usually thought to be a creepy science fiction account of a terrifying creature run amok or a psychological drama depicting the monster lurking in the heart of every man and woman. The reality is both more complicated and more terrifying. The tale depicts the consequences of our collective refusal to encounter ourselves. Like Klaus Mann and Patricia Highsmith, Stevenson thinks that masochistic and sadistic acts are symptomatic of a deeper evil—our profound ignorance of who we are. Science fiction monsters are rare; deluded, self-evading people are common. We are more like Dr. Jekyll and Mr. Hyde than we suspect.

Mann and Highsmith focus on the role individuals play in their self-delusion. Stevenson builds upon and extends such insights by exposing the way in which societal hypocrisy prevents us from becoming self-aware. From childhood on, society teaches us to repress certain feelings and notions. As a consequence, each of us has a dark side, a part of ourselves that we have not expressed and so do not know. The feelings and images we have suppressed do not disappear. Vaguely aware that we are not living fully, we become filled with dread and melancholic. Every pop psychologist knows this much. What Stevenson understands is that anxiety is not just the individual's problem. The social collective contributes to our melancholia by demanding that we conform to certain personas. Then, when we rebel against these strictures, our oppressors vicariously live through the outbreak of our animal spirits. Morality settles for blaming deviance; Stevenson shows how morality is the hypocritical engine behind the deviance.

Most people know only the movie or folk version of Stevenson's tale. As a result, they do not realize that the story is as much about other people's reactions to Hyde as about the dual nature of Dr. Jekyll. Therefore, before I consider how society's moral hypocrisy contributes to Dr. Jekyll's personality split, I want to summarize the tale's plot.

A BRIEF PLOT SUMMARY

Dr. Jekyll, a well-respected physician and scientist, finds himself increasingly dissatisfied with existence. From youth, Jekyll has practiced a strict regimen of self-denial. His "morbid sense of shame" does not permit him to indulge the high spirits of his youth or to do anything that might be construed as the least bit undignified or unrespectable.[2] Jekyll begins to fantasize about how wonderful it would be if he could separate his "good" part from his lower, undignified, and "evil" portion. After years of reflection and experimentation, Jekyll discovers that the natural body is merely an "aura and effulgence" of the powers of the human spirit.[3] He compounds a drug that shakes the prison door of his personality. In Jekyll's own words, this drug is "neither diabolical [n]or divine."[4] The drug merely overcomes Jekyll's inhibitions and allows for the expression of "a second form and countenance."[5] According to Jekyll, this alternative form bears the stamp of the "lower elements" of the soul. The discovery enthralls the doctor, and soon he is regularly assuming the form of Edward Hyde, his alter ego, in order to indulge his hitherto suppressed fantasies. As Hyde, he takes a separate set of rooms in Soho where he lives out his second existence, returning to Jekyll's home and laboratory when he feels the need to take the drug and to revert to his professional self.

One evening on his way back to Jekyll's house, Hyde collides with a young girl. A Mr. Enfield witnesses his actions. Horrified by what he has seen, Enfield intervenes and forces Hyde to provide recompense to the girl's family. Enfield subsequently tells this story to his friend and older cousin Gabriel John Utterson. Utterson, a lawyer, recognizes that the house to which Hyde was returning that night belongs to his old school-boy friend Dr. Jekyll. Utterson's interest is piqued because he knows that Jekyll's will contains a peculiar clause: in the event Jekyll should disappear for more than three months, a Mr. Hyde is to inherit Jekyll's entire estate. What, Utterson wonders, could possibly be the relationship between the upstanding Dr. Jekyll and this horror-inspiring lowlife Hyde?

The mystery deepens as Utterson investigates. Utterson tracks down Hyde. Even when seen at a distance, Hyde fills Utterson with disquietude. Although he confronts Hyde, Utterson cannot allay his misgivings about the man. When he subsequently asks Jekyll about Hyde, Jekyll is evasive and will only say that he takes a strong and special interest in the young Hyde. When Hyde is later seen murdering a prominent acquaintance of Utterson's, the lawyer becomes still more alarmed. Jekyll appears withdrawn and to be covering for Hyde, a confirmed murderer.

For a few months, Hyde disappears. Jekyll returns to his normal, gregarious self. Utterson's concerns subside until Jekyll abruptly retreats into seclusion and refuses to see his old friend. Unbeknownst to Utterson, Jekyll has vowed never again to adopt the form of the monstrous Hyde. However, to his horror, Jekyll finds that he has begun spontaneously and unwillingly to assume the form of the felon Hyde. The doctor, therefore, can no longer appear in public. What is worse, the drug appears to be losing its effectiveness. Jekyll finds it increasingly difficult to effect the transition back from Hyde. Whenever he sleeps, relaxes, indulges in fanciful thoughts, or recollects some bodily pleasure, Jekyll slips into the form of Hyde. Confined to his laboratory, Jekyll–Hyde frantically tries to compound an effective version of the drug.

Jekyll's servants begin to suspect foul play. For over a week, they do not see nor hear any sign of their master Jekyll. At one point, Jekyll's manservant Poole glimpses a terrible looking, doubled-over creature dart into the doctor's cabinet or consultation room. Neither the voice nor the pacing footfalls of the man locked in the cabinet belong to the master the servants have respected and obeyed for many years. Frightened, Poole summons Utterson. The two break down the door to the doctor's inner chamber. Inside they find the still-twitching corpse of the man they know as Hyde and a packet of letters addressed to Utterson. The first letter from Dr. Lanyon, a lifelong friend of Jekyll's, relates how Lanyon came to witness the despised and hunted Hyde transform himself into Dr. Jekyll. A second letter—"Dr. Jekyll's Confession"—describes how and why Jekyll came to metamorphose into Hyde.

Up until this point, the reader, like Utterson, Enfield, and Jekyll's servants, does not realize that the two men Hyde and Jekyll are one. Jekyll's confession reveals all. Or at least it appears to do so.

HATED SELF

If these bare bones of the story were the entirety of this strange tale, we might be inclined to concur with Dr. Jekyll's moralistic view that evil is identical with sadistic cruelty and that Hyde, therefore, is "purely evil." The story would be a Victorian morality tale, warning us not to delight in cruel or self-indulgent deeds lest we unwittingly develop a habit of performing vicious deeds. The story would echo Aristotle's moral teaching: repeated acts confirm us in our wrongdoing, destroy our power of choice, and make us irredeemably evil, a lesson that Jekyll, to his horror, learns too late.

The tale has often been read in this comforting way. By identifying evil with vicious habits of the individual, we can locate evil in a single individual and tell ourselves that we—thank God—are not like that loathsome soul Jekyll–Hyde. However, matters are not so tidily and reassuringly simple. While evil does manifest itself over the course of this tale, it cannot be located in and confined to either Dr. Jekyll or his alter ego, Edward Hyde. The belief that we can readily identify objective evil and assign it to a single soul turns out to be one of the ruses of an evil that hides itself.

We should not forget that we see Hyde exclusively through the eyes of other people. Our informants are, for the most part, men. Stevenson's tale teems with older professional men: Dr. Jekyll, Jekyll's friends Dr. Lanyon and the lawyer Utterson, Mr. Enfield, and Hyde. The plot features only a few women—Hyde's Soho housekeeper, a cook, and a hysterical housemaid who work for Jekyll, the young girl on whom Hyde is seen to trod, and a woman servant who sees Hyde murder Danvers Carew. These women have no names and are relegated to the shadows. Any connection the characters have with women is suppressed, and this suppression is, we will see, part of the problem.

The tale has a second key dimension. Although many who encounter Hyde are horrified by him, none can give an objective description of the man. Enfield explains: Hyde is "an extraordinary looking man . . . yet I really can name nothing out of the way . . . I can make no hand of it; I can't describe him. And it's not want of memory; for I declare I can see him this moment."[6] The most Enfield can say is that Hyde "gives a strong feeling of deformity."[7] The lawyer Utterson sees "a pale and dwarfish" Hyde with a displeasing smile, who speaks in a whispering and broken voice.[8] Like Enfield, Utterson experiences "an impression of deformity without any nameable malformation."[9] Utterson is overwhelmed by a "hitherto unknown disgust, loathing and fear."[10] He quickly decides that Hyde must be concealing something:

> There must be something else . . . There is something more, if I could find a name for it. God bless me, the man seems hardly human! Something troglodytic, shall we say? . . . [O]r is it the mere radiance of a foul soul that thus transpires through, and transfigures, its clay continent? The last, I think: for O my poor old Harry Jekyll, if ever I read Satan's signature upon a face, it is on that of your new friend.[11]

Jekyll's schoolboy chum Lanyon is struck by Hyde's "ludicrous accoutrement."[12] Instead of seeing a tormented, poorly dressed man, Lanyon perceives "something abnormal and misbegotten in the very essence of the creature . . . something seizing, surprising and revolting."[13] Like Utterson, Lanyon is seized by an urge, a "disgustful curiosity"[14] to get to the bottom of Hyde and to know his "origin, his life, his fortune and status in the world."[15] Jekyll himself perceptively observes, "when I wore the semblance of Edward Hyde, none would come near me at first without a visible misgiving of the flesh."[16]

Those who have met Hyde cannot agree on what he looks like, and no photograph of Hyde exists. Hyde cannot be known objectively. We know him only subjectively, because Hyde represents the hidden aspect of our personality that we have come to fear or loathe. Each of us has a vision of who we are and would like to be, a vision shaped by outside forces. However, the self is always more than this socially promoted ideal. The self has an inner drive and a felt need to realize its unique talents. Under pressure from society and family, we deny and hide those of our traits and talents that do not accord with our envisioned ideal self. But these things do not disappear; they just retreat into the shadows and become our "Hyde."

Dr. Jekyll is psychologically astute. Unlike the other characters in this tale, he acknowledges that he is a composite being. He knows and admits he has been leading a double life since childhood:

> I was born in the year 18— to a large fortune, endowed besides with excellent parts, inclined by nature to industry, fond of the respect of the wise and good among my fellow-men, and thus, as might have been supposed, with every guarantee of an honorable and distinguished future. And indeed, the worst of my faults was a certain impatient gaiety of disposition, such as has made the happiness of many, but such as I found it hard to reconcile with my imperious desire to carry my head high, and wear a more than commonly grave countenance before the public. Hence it came about that I concealed my pleasures; and that when I reached years of reflection, and began to look round me and take stock of my progress and position in the world, I stood already committed to a profound duplicity of life. Many a man would have even blazoned such irregularities as I was guilty of; but from the high views that I had set before me, I regarded and hid them with an almost morbid sense of shame. It was thus rather the exacting nature of my aspirations than any particular degradation in my faults, that made me what I was and, with even a deeper trench than in the majority of men, severed in me those provinces of good and ill which divide and compound man's dual nature. In this case, I was driven to reflect deeply and inveterately on the hard law of life, which lies at the root of religion and is one of the most plentiful springs of distress. Though so profound a double-dealer, I was in no sense a hypocrite, both sides of me were in dead earnest; I was no more my self when I laid aside restraint and plunged in shame, than when I labored, in the eye of day, at the furtherance of knowledge or the relief of sorrow and suffering. And it chanced that the direction of my scientific studies, which led wholly towards the mystic and the transcendental, reacted and shed a strong light on this consciousness of the perennial war among my members. With every day and from both sides of my intelligence, the moral and the

intellectual, I thus drew steadily nearer to that truth, by whose partial discovery I have been doomed to such a dreadful shipwreck: that man is not truly one, but truly two. I say two, because the state of my own knowledge does not pass beyond that point. Others will follow, others will outstrip me on the same lines; and I hazard the guess that man will be ultimately known for a mere polity of multifarious, incongruous and independent denizens. I for my part, from the nature of my life, advanced infallibly in one direction and in one direction only. It was on the moral side, and in my own person, that I learned to recognize the thorough and primitive duality of man; I saw that, of the two natures that contended in the field of my consciousness, even if I could rightly be said to be either, it was only because I was radically both; and from an early date, even before the course of my scientific discoveries had begun to suggest the most naked possibility of such a miracle, I had learned to dwell with pleasure, as a beloved daydream, on the thought of the separation of these elements. If each, I told myself, could but be housed in separate identities, life would be relieved of all that was unbearable; the unjust might go his way delivered from the aspirations and remorse of his more upright twin; and the just could walk steadfastly and securely on his upward path, doing the good things in which he found his pleasure, and no longer exposed to disgrace and penitence by the hands of this extraneous evil. It was the curse of mankind that these incongruous faggots were thus bound together—that in the agonized womb of consciousness, these polar twins should be continuously struggling.[17]

Hyde is more than the expression of all that Jekyll finds shameful. Hyde represents the universal or archetypal shadow self whom we disown and hide. Given that each of us finds different traits shameful, we cannot specify the features of the universal shadow. Perhaps the most we can say is that the shadow tends to be the same sex as the person feeling shame because the hidden traits could, in theory, be integrated into that individual's public self. Since the main characters in this tale are male, the shadow Hyde is also masculine.

Why do we hate some dimensions of our self? Is our hidden self—our Hyde—evil? From childhood on, we construct idealized selves. Our parents promote specific ideals and virtues, reinforcing some of our attitudes and behaviors with praise, while blaming actions they judge less desirable.

Teachers and religious figures provide guidance and enforce strictures. How we appear to ourselves is thus a function of how we appear to others. Those traits or behaviors others deem reprehensible seem shameful to us. If we are attracted to these behaviors, we are driven to dissemble in order to avoid blame and punishment. Since the feeling of embarrassment is not pleasant, we begin to lie to ourselves about what we think is good and worth experiencing.

Hyde is the half of our personality that is supported neither by society nor by our conscious, controlling self. Our Hyde can strike us as repellent, because some repressed, shameful behaviors are objectively unjust and, therefore, should be discouraged. Impulses to murder, rape, or steal should not be indulged because such acts undermine the community and interfere with the individual's development. The thief comes to think of the world as his or her property instead of as a dwelling place to be shared with other people. The world, though, is not our property or private playground. Believing it to be so inevitably causes problems for the thief. A similar point applies to violent individuals. We fear such people and will not tell them the unpleasant truths they need to hear. Unaware of facts, the violent move through life as if they are dreaming and become enraged when reality fails to conform to their illusions. As we saw in the earlier chapters, such rage slides toward paranoia, leaving the person unhappy and frustrated.

I have no problem, therefore, with children being taught to curtail some desires. Not everything, though, that a particular society finds shameful is, in fact, so. We miss the power of Stevenson's tale if we think of Hyde as our unacknowledged, vicious impulses. Midgley makes this mistake when she equates Hyde with Jekyll's corrupt desire to become dissipated.[18] Jekyll describes the impulses he has been driven to repress in more neutral terms. In his view, the adolescent Jekyll's "irregularities" are initially little more than the expression of "a certain impatient gaiety of disposition" that does not comport well with the common Victorian image of a sober and grave doctor.[19] For years Jekyll tries to deny this frivolous, light-hearted side of himself. When he finally gives expression to this lively spirit—to his shadow, Hyde, who acts and feels "like a schoolboy at liberty"—Jekyll feels more alive, satisfied, and at peace with himself.[20]

Although Jekyll's confessional letter describes Hyde as "pure evil," this judgment is unwarranted. Just as Jekyll is not purely virtuous—he is extremely proud and quite willing to lie to his friends—so, too, Hyde is not completely vicious. Hyde is part and parcel of the doctor, a man who heals and tries to relieve suffering and who is more self-aware than many of his peers. Before encountering Enfield, Hyde has moved freely about London for nine years, enjoying his pleasures. He attracts no particular notice because he does nothing out of the ordinary. Our hidden side is not intrinsically evil. Our second half has talents or abilities that need to be encouraged if we are to be whole or well-integrated individuals. When we acknowledge our hidden talents, we feel more alive because we are strengthening a hitherto unexercised part of our being. This expression and exercise of previously repressed traits is a civilizing force as well. Civilization advances when individuals discern new modes of communication or hit upon undiscovered ways to perform tasks. These ideas begin in our fancy or imagination. The imagination makes present what is absent and gives rise to inventions. Civilization progresses and our tastes mature when we draw on the resources and energy of our imaginative and suppressed selves.

Although the other characters are wont to describe Hyde as an "apelike" savage or animal, we should be leery of taking these descriptions at face value. When Utterson and the police inspector Newcomen enter Hyde's lodgings in Soho after Hyde has murdered Sir Danvers Carew, they are surprised to find rooms "furnished with luxury and good taste."[21] The lodgings are every bit as civilized and refined as Utterson's or Jekyll's. The apartment boasts exquisite napery, beautiful carpets, and a closet full of wine. Utterson infers that the fine picture on the wall must be a gift from Jekyll because Utterson sees Hyde as a bestial being. Yet, in a letter to a critic who found Hyde's taste too sophisticated, Stevenson comes to Hyde's defense. Stevenson writes, "I rather meant that Hyde had bought [the painting] himself; and Utterson's hypothesis of the gift [is] an error."[22] When Utterson and the butler Poole later break into the consulting room where Hyde has been dwelling for days, they find an ordered, refined space. An easy chair is pulled up to the fire. The kettle is boiling, and a tea set is next to the chair. Papers are neatly arranged on the business table. The room is "the most commonplace that night in London."[23] The servant Poole and Utterson, not Hyde, are the ones who create chaos as they barge into the doctor's office. Jekyll's friend Lanyon unwittingly speaks the truth when Hyde appears before him. Barely able to contain his horror of Hyde, Lanyon writes of the "odd, subjective disturbance" he feels in the presence of the man. In each of these cases, Hyde reflects the prejudices and fears of those who encounter him.

Viewed objectively, Jekyll's Hyde differs little from the rest of us. He is no less a cultured gentleman than the professionals—Utterson, Enfield, Lanyon—who view him with horror and contempt. Our unacknowledged impulses, if recognized, can be integrated as part of our personality and can serve to develop and refine us. Evil lies not in our repressed impulses but in our failure to acknowledge and to integrate select hidden talents and abilities. As Mary Midgley succinctly puts it, "The acknowledged shadow may be terrible enough. But it is the unacknowledged one which is the real killer."[24] I stress again that I am not maintaining that every impulse should be indulged. A talent for pickpocketing or for psychologically manipulating other people is best left undeveloped. But if we are selectively to develop our talents, we must acknowledge those features of our self that we have suppressed or ignored. Until we turn our attention to our dark side, we will not be able to know, much less discriminate among, these abilities.

Still, a mystery remains. Jekyll does acknowledge his personal Hyde. For a period, both Jekyll and Hyde thrive, but Jekyll–Hyde dies a broken and unhappy man. What forces interfere with or prevent successful integration? Are such forces "evil"?

Indiscriminate Indulgence and Repression Strengthen the Shadow

We catch our first glimpse of Hyde through the eyes of Mr. Enfield. One night around three a.m., Mr. Enfield sees "a little man who was stumping along eastward at a good walk."[25] This man collides at the corner with a girl of around eight or ten years old who has been sent to fetch a doctor. The collision at the corner is natural enough: the two didn't see each other. What Enfield finds horrifying is the man's reaction: "the man trampled calmly over the child's body and left her screaming on the ground."[26] Enfield explains that, while the story sounds, "nothing to hear . . . it was hellish to see. It wasn't like a man: it was like some damned juggernaut."[27] Immediately a crowd gathers, including the young girl's family. The apothecary, whom the girl had summoned, arrives on the scene.

The crowd quickly determines that the accident has left the girl more frightened than hurt. What, then, is so repulsive and terrifying about Hyde? Although Hyde may have been callous, he did not attack this child. Hyde collided with, and stepped on, the child. Perhaps Hyde's singleness of purpose is what frightens us. Stevenson repeatedly compares the small or "dwarfish" Hyde to an impish child or a schoolboy.[28] Hyde represents the undeveloped, childish part of us, the part with high animal spirits. When Hyde treads on the child, he reproduces what has been done to him by his "father" Jekyll. Jekyll has spent years mortifying those desires that society deems inappropriate. Denied its pleasures, our inner child never matures and fails to channel its high spirits and cravings into more sophisticated and refined pleasures. When the schoolboy Hyde is finally given some scope, he shows himself to have fine artistic tastes. However, the decades of repressions have taken their toll. Like a tyrannical spoiled child, Hyde has become intent on one thing: getting what he wants. Jekyll does nothing to educate his childish, desiring self. Instead, he gives Hyde completely free rein.

If we take no responsibility for our undeveloped talents and abilities, that part of our self goes untutored. Although our Hyde is not evil, our irresponsible indulgence of previously repressed desires or impulses may qualify as such. Evil resides less in the mischief (often unintended) caused by our overly indulged appetites and more in our careless refusal to educate our desires and to use our reason to explore which talents are worthy of being realized. Under pressure from the collective, we treat those desires that do not accord with our social persona as wicked and as completely alien to us. Although Hyde and Jekyll are one man, Jekyll starts to dissociate himself completely from the persecuted Hyde and to drive his desires ever deeper into the shadows. Uninstructed and unexamined, these alienated desires wreak havoc.

Repression, as well as overindulgence, strengthens our hidden side. As the example of Jekyll shows, our ignored desires do not go away. They persist and typically clamor ever more loudly for satisfaction the longer we refuse to admit their existence. As we age, we become more cunning and learn new ways to rationalize our behavior. Since the shadow is part of us, our newly acquired psychic resources are at the disposal of the shadow, as well of the rational, conscious self. Our hidden self uses these resources in order to get its way. As Jekyll puts it, he has been committed to duplicity from his earliest years, and his Hyde has learned all these tricks.

Let us summarize what we have learned. Evil is not a matter of having or acting upon twisted or sadistic desires. Since overindulgence of our appetites interferes with our ability to refine our desires, we find it tempting to define evil as habitual immoderation. But such a definition, Stevenson suggests, obscures as much as it clarifies. Treating evil as a vice implies that evil is always a matter of action. Evil can be a matter of inaction. Repressing and refusing to act on desire, especially the desire to develop our talents and to realize who we are, deforms our appetites.

Equating vice with evil is problematic for a second reason. Defining evil as practical vice focuses our attention exclusively on the individual who originates the deeds we find shameful. Stevenson's account of evil is subtler. Psychic repression is a collective, as well as individual, evil. The more others react to Hyde with hatred and cruelty, the stronger and more sadistic Hyde becomes. Enfield confesses that he "had taken a loathing to [Hyde] at first sight."[29] Enfield is predisposed to hate Hyde even before he meets the man. Walking alone down the deserted London streets, Enfield so spooks himself that he longs for the sight of a policeman. He sees bogey-men lurking everywhere. When Hyde suddenly appears out of the dark, Enfield finds it all too easy to imagine Hyde to be a satanic fiend. Having demonized Hyde, Enfield has no difficulty assaulting the smallish man.

The reaction of the apothecary, whom the young girl had been sent to summon, is equally noteworthy. This man who is "about as emotional as a bagpipe" cannot look at Hyde without turning "sick and white with the desire" to kill him.[30] The apothecary did not see Hyde collide with the child, yet he conceives a murderous hatred of this young man. Hyde has done nothing to that child that is any worse than what these two men have done to their inner child. Like Dr. Jekyll, the stern, unemotional apothe-cary has spent his life denying that he has any feelings or an imagination. For his part, Enfield, a single man about town, passes his evenings at "some place at the end of the world."[31] While the dry apothecary errs on the side of repression, Enfield appears to have gone too far in the direc-tion of overindulgence. Stevenson hints that Enfield's pleasures might not withstand close scrutiny. Perhaps that is why Enfield consistently travels under the cover of darkness.

The two men's murderous rage is an overblown reaction born of bad faith. Hyde's appearance and action remind them of the supposedly sinful desires they have secreted deep within their psyches. Instead of excavating and selectively educating these desires, the two men take their fiendish steps to punish Hyde and to make it difficult for him ever to show his face again:

> [K]illing being out of the question, we did the next best. We told the man we could and would make such a scandal out of this, as should make his name stink from one end of London to the other. If he had any friends or any credit, we undertook that he should lose them. And all the time, as we were pitching it in red hot, we were keeping the women off him as best we could, for they were as wild as harpies. I never saw . . . such hateful faces.[32]

Note how quickly the crowd turns into a mob ready to lynch this man who has stepped on a child. The crowd's concern for the child is hysterical. Like the rage of Enfield and the doctor, the crowd's hysteria stems from bad faith. The child's family ordered their small daughter to travel unprotected through the streets of London at three a.m. to fetch a doctor. Later, the girl's father and other family members rush to the scene of the collision. Why did not one or more of these able-bodied adults go out into the night to summon the doctor? Their callous indifference, not Hyde's accidental collision with the child, has put the girl at risk. Instead of owning up to this neglect, the parents and other adult members of the crowd project their sense of shame onto Hyde and convert him into a child-molesting monster. The girl's family cares no more for this girl than Jekyll has cared for his inner child Hyde. Yet, at some level, the parents understand that this child is an integral part of themselves. When the girl appears to be threatened, their self-interest kicks in and prompts the adults to rush to the aid of the child they have ignored in the past.

Although the apothecary, Enfield, and the girl's father refrain from murder, they have no compunction about taking the law into their hands. Instead of getting the police, the three form a scheme to blackmail Hyde. They impute a noble motive to themselves: they are taking money from Hyde to help the girl. The girl is not hurt, but the father sees a chance to make a sizable sum of 100 pounds, a small fortune by today's standards. Enfield and the doctor embrace the illicit scheme because it provides them with a surreptitious way to drive Hyde underground. If they were to kill him, their deed would come to light. No member of the mob, though, will object to a spot of blackmail. The men's victimizing of the childlike Hyde will stay hidden.

I have dwelt on Stevenson's opening description because most readers and critics skip over the mob scene and treat the tale as a crudely schematic story of good men and women (Jekyll, Lanyon, Utterson, Enfield) versus wickedness incarnate (Hyde). To proceed in that manner is to participate unwittingly in the collective repression of our hidden selves. Stevenson would deny us that pleasure. As long as Hyde is the shadow side of Jekyll alone, Hyde remains relatively innocuous. Stevenson begins his tale at the point at which Hyde becomes far more dangerous—the point at which Hyde starts to function as our collective projection of the hated part of our selves, a part that we have so repressed, denied, and starved that it appears deformed to us. Hyde is propelled by the energy and hatred of the collective. Evil is inside Jekyll insofar as the doctor suffers dreadfully because he has failed to do the necessary psychic work to integrate his Hyde. However, this internal evil is inextricably entwined with an external evil—our collective practice of deforming ourselves through repression or overindulgence of those parts of our selves that do not readily conform to the ideal personas favored by our society.

We are all composite Jekylls, a point beautifully and subtly illustrated by the way in which Stevenson first introduces us to Hyde. Remember that we first learn of Hyde through the strange tale Enfield relates to his friend Utterson. Utterson subsequently takes over the role of narrator as he becomes obsessed with uncovering Hyde's identity and destroying him. Utterson and Enfield go walking together every Sunday. The youthful Enfield is a "well-known man about town" who disports himself into the wee hours of the night.[33] Gabriel Utterson, by contrast, is a stern lawyer possessing "a rugged countenance, that was never lighted by a smile."[34] He is "cold . . . lean, long, dusty, dreamy and yet somehow lovable."[35] Only when he permits himself to drink wine does "something eminently human" gleam in his eye.[36] He prides himself on his "approved tolerance for others" and his inclination "to help rather than to reprove."[37] As a result, Utterson finds it his "fortune to be the last reputable acquaintance and the last good influence in the lives of down-going men."[38] What can Enfield and Utterson possibly have in common?

The relationship between the two men exactly parallels that between Dr. Jekyll and Mr. Hyde. Enfield embodies "low" society. He is young, rakish, and high-spirited. Like Hyde, he moves under the cover of darkness. Enfield appears to qualify as one of the youthful souls on the skids whom

Utterson loves to help. Like Dr. Jekyll, Utterson is a reserved, upper-class professional. He greatly values his reputation and has always kept a strict check on his impulses. He "mortifies" his taste for good wine, forcing himself to imbibe the less palatable gin. He rations his pleasures, while continually wondering, "almost with envy,"[39] at the high pressure of animal spirits in the young men whom he counsels. Just as Dr. Jekyll is drawn by his gaiety of disposition to experience "irregular" pleasures, so the gaiety and *joie de vivre* of young men beckon Utterson.[40]

Although outsiders watching the two men cannot figure out the nature of their relationship, Utterson and his cousin Enfield have always "put the greatest store by these excursions, counted them the chief jewel of each week, and not only set aside occasions of pleasure, but even resisted the calls of business, that they might enjoy them uninterrupted."[41] The two are kinsmen in the deepest possible sense. They represent the two sides of the human personality: Utterson is the controlling persona, Enfield the repressed appetite that insists on taking its pleasures. Taken singly, neither is well integrated. Only when Utterson sets aside his professional duties and Enfield resists indulging his pleasures do they come together to form something like a whole human being.

This twosome can never be truly healthy. Each of us must come to know, honor, and unite the different parts of our selves. Our failure to do this psychic work harms not only us but also other people. We use friends and family members to avoid the psychic labor of uniting reason with appetite. Enfield and Utterson live vicariously through each other, and the result is every bit as troubling as Dr. Jekyll's effort to indulge all of his appetites through the person of Hyde. By making a public appearance every Sunday with the morally upstanding Utterson, Enfield hopes to establish his bona fides. Utterson functions as Enfield's vicar. As Samuel Butler reminds us, the word "vicar" drives from "vicarious":

> The clergyman is expected to be a kind of human Sunday. Things must not be done in him, which are venial in the week-day classes. He is paid for this business of leading a stricter life than other people. It is his raison d'etre. If his parishioners feel that he does this, they approve of him, for they look upon him as their own contribution towards what they deem a holy life. This is why the clergyman is so often called a vicar—he being the person whose vicarious goodness is to stand for that of those entrusted to his charge.[42]

For his part, Utterson enjoys Enfield's risqué tales of his night ventures. Enfield operates as Utterson's hidden self, engaging in the lawless and immoderate behavior that Utterson finds attractive but never permits himself. Utterson is quite taken with Enfield's gossipy story about the man who collides with the child. He presses his kinsman for the name of the man who stepped on the child. Although the check Hyde gives to his blackmailers is drawn on Dr. Jekyll's account, Enfield somehow has managed to learn Hyde's name and tells it to Utterson. Enfield has probably secured the name with a view to blackmailing Hyde at some future date. Enfield also has made special note of Jekyll's name and the address on the check. Later we learn that Enfield has been looking into the circumstances of Dr. Jekyll's life, probably with a view to extorting money from Jekyll.[43] None of these facts interests the rational lawyer in the least. Utterson overlooks the suspect motives of his licentious kinsman because Enfield is a self-confessed blackmailer. The lawyer is concerned only with hearing some juicy stories and protecting the good name of his friend Dr. Jekyll and, by implication, his own reputation. Enfield is free to victimize as many people as he wishes as long as this behavior does not threaten Utterson's professional persona.

The blindness of Utterson, the very man on whom we readers rely to utter the truth about Jekyll and Hyde, reveals an unpleasant truth. At the moment we become certain that another person is evil incarnate, we often unwittingly become complicitous in evil (understood as the failure to integrate our Hyde into our lives). When we set out to prove how dastardly someone else is, we stop attending to the whole of reality and to our biases and presuppositions. We begin to live in a world reflecting our fears and suspicions, and we overlook problematic facts staring us in the face.

Since Utterson has been inside Dr. Jekyll's house many times, he knows from the beginning of Enfield's tale that the door through which Hyde entered opens into a secret courtyard behind Jekyll's residence. Utterson conceals what he knows and manipulates Enfield into providing more information: is Enfield certain that Hyde used a key to enter? Hyde's free access into Jekyll's house worries the lawyer, for why would his upstanding boyhood friend Jekyll have dealings with a lowlife like Hyde? He starts to act like his namesake, the avenging angel Gabriel. Utterson jumps to the conclusion that Hyde is a blackmailer and determines that he must act to save his noble friend and alter ego Jekyll. Observe Utterson's projection: Utterson's shadow, Enfield, is a blackmailer, and Utterson now converts Hyde into one. In his eagerness to hunt down and punish Hyde, Utterson, the sworn upholder of the law, turns a blind eye to the blackmailing by his kinsman Enfield. He continues to count Enfield as an imprudent, but basically sound, friend at the same time as he turns Hyde, a man whom he has never met, into a satanic enemy.

The Strange Tale of Dr. Jekyll and Mr. Hyde is indeed peculiar. It appears that the upright actions of Utterson, like those of the enraged Enfield, the apothecary, and the father, are prompted by motives of which he is entirely unaware. Yet, if these other characters also have their hidden side, why have generations of readers focused only on Jekyll's supposedly vicious alter ego? Has our fear of Hyde made us as uncomprehending and as complicitous in evil as Jekyll's fellow citizens?

The Socially Hated Self Becomes Hateful

Desire drives our development by urging us to explore the world and to try out new ways of being and of feeling. We cannot develop unless we heed the prompting of desire. Our reason can help us evaluate the wisdom of pursuing what desire represents as good. By persuading us of the undesirability of some habits, reason enables us to rid ourselves of them. However, because our understanding is always partial, reason can take us only so far. Sometimes we must act on a hunch, on our sense that there exists some part of us that needs to be given a chance to see the light of day. Reason must not merely persuade and deny. It must also know its limits. If reason does not acknowledge the right of the transcending self to realize itself, we find ourselves stunted, a sick child like Hyde.

If we, like Dr. Jekyll, insist on conforming to society's ideals, then our hated self soon becomes hateful. As our shadow discovers the hypocrisy permeating society, inwardly we begin to seethe. Craving expression, our hidden self is always looking for ways to justify its claim to be honored and gratified. This sensitivity on the part of our Hyde makes us acutely aware of other people's tendency to violate social norms, and then to deny ever having strayed from the straight and narrow path. The pressure within us builds as our individually repressed appetites see through our collective hypocrisy and demand that they, too, have their day in the sun.

We try to lock the ideal and suppressed sides of our personality into separate compartments (the upright Jekyll versus the monstrous Hyde) so that the left hand will not know, and cannot be responsible for, what the right hand is doing. By creating this false separation, we hope to function as two selves as distinct as Utterson and Enfield or Jekyll and Hyde. As each of us adopts this strategy, individual hypocrisy gets multiplied a million times over. Individual hypocrisy becomes collective hypocrisy. From our pulpits we rail against sin. We promulgate laws and preach professionalism. And then we violate all these standards and rules. When our hidden selves discern the hypocrisy of our peers and clamor to be expressed, they find that the collective denies them a hearing. The hated self then becomes hateful and starts to despise the social order that appears to be the cause of its unhappiness. So we should not be surprised that Jekyll–Hyde's second offense is an attack on the social order.

One year after colliding with the young girl, Dr. Jekyll again transforms himself into Mr. Hyde. This time "the devil came out roaring."[44] Hyde bludgeons an old man to death. In his final confession, Jekyll describes how the murder came about. Two months earlier, the doctor had bidden "a resolute farewell to the liberty, the comparative youth, the light step, leaping impulses and secret pleasures" of Hyde.[45] Assuring himself that he prefers the ideal self or persona of "the elderly and discontented doctor," Jekyll–Hyde chooses a life of rigid severity. In return, he is rewarded by the esteem of his illustrious peers (i.e., Utterson and Dr. Lanyon) and by the approval of his conscience.[46] However, this persona of the socially esteemed professional necessarily fails to satisfy him because the self is always more than a persona. The more the upstanding (yet composite) Jekyll succumbs to society's vision of who he is, the more Hyde appeals to him. Unable to resist this appeal, he reverts to Hyde.

When, late one night, an old man approaches Hyde and greets him graciously, Hyde snaps and assaults the gentleman. His victim turns out to be the illustrious Sir Danvers Carew, a Member of Parliament. London society is horrified by this crime of singular ferocity. Virtuous folk revel in their goodness and are shocked that anyone would dare to attack one of their own. But is Carew so virtuous? We might wonder why this fellow, like Mr. Enfield, is wandering around London in the middle of the night with a purse full of money and a gold watch but no identification.[47] Was he approaching young men under the cover of night in order to ask directions to the postbox? Or was he, like Dr. Jekyll/Hyde, in pursuit of pleasures the community has deemed illicit? Danvers turns out to be a client of the lawyer Utterson. Was he one of those "down-going" men in whose legal problems Utterson specializes?

"Good society" romanticizes those whom it claims for its own. Just as Enfield witnesses Hyde's collision with the child, so a woman sees this murder. A maidservant, alone in her master's house, sits at her bedroom window. Midnight is approaching. The moon is full, and she falls into a dreamy musing. While feeling utterly at peace with the world, she becomes aware of "an aged and beautiful gentleman with white hair."[48] She sees, but pays scant attention to, the "very small gentleman" who is approaching from the opposite direction.[49] The two men meet. The elderly man bows and, with pretty manners, accosts the other man. The maid dreamily watches the scene, enjoying the way the moonlight shines on the face of the elderly man, revealing "an innocent and old-world kindness of disposition, yet with something high, too, as of a well-founded self-content."[50] With a start, she realizes that the smallish person is Mr. Hyde, a man who had once visited her master and whom she immediately disliked. The maid overhears nothing of what the older gentleman says, but she sees Hyde listen impatiently and then erupt in "a great flame of anger."[51] Hyde raises his heavy cane and repeatedly strikes the old man, causing him to fall to earth. Then, "with ape-like fury," he stomps on the victim and strikes him repeatedly.[52] Upon hearing the kindly old man's bones break, the maid faints dead away.

Although the maid perceives a kindly, refined father figure, this figure is every bit as much her projection as the purely evil Hyde is a creation of Utterson, Enfield, Lanyon, and Jekyll. Danvers may be an MP, but that does not make him a saint. Like Dr. Jekyll, Danvers basks in society's approval and uses this commendation to feather his nest. Both men hide behind their civility, using their reputation for goodness and lawfulness as protection while they pursue pleasures condemned by polite society. This hypocrisy incenses Hyde and provokes the attack.

Hyde bludgeons Danvers with a cane given to Jekyll by Utterson. The use of the cane is symbolically appropriate in two ways. Utterson, the sworn upholder of the law who prides himself on punctiliously observing legal niceties, has been happily ignoring the law to protect his old friend Jekyll. For Utterson, the law is little more than an instrument or weapon he uses whenever it suits him to do so. Moreover, the law plays a role in Carew's murder. The community legislates which pleasures are to be deemed illicit and foists different socially correct personae on us. By demanding that we deny a part of ourselves, the law engenders rebellion in us, which society then decries and uses to justify further repression. Every action has an opposite but unequal reaction. Society's repression produces a self-magnifying hatred. Is it so surprising that Stevenson found "civilized places" were bad for his health?

The social demand that we lop off and hide a part of ourselves should shock us as much as Carew's murder. But it does not. The murder is visible; the repression, by definition, hides itself. All of society is abuzz about this crime committed against a man of such high position. Yet none of us discerns, much less opposes, the brutal demands we daily enforce on each other. These legal, repressive demands are perhaps the truer evil. Laws cause us to suffer, yet they are supported by the consent of millions and taken for granted. Like Carew, we complacently uphold the very system that brutalizes us from childhood on. This tension eventually erupts. Although Jekyll has idolized his father for years, at the end of the story he slashes his father's portrait, expressing his rage at the man who would not recognize the Hyde in his son Jekyll.

After falling victim to impulses we have helped to create, we deny that these impulses are thoroughly human. We demonize them, describing them as satanic or bestial. Mr. Hyde, whose human hide we all share, is repeatedly described as an animal.[53] At least the "evil" Hyde owns up to his pleasures and deeds. Most of us are like the "civilized" Utterson, who wallows vicariously. The lawyer, who denies himself wine and who enjoys the theater yet has not gone to a play for twenty years, is only too happy to listen to his cousin Enfield dish the dirt about other people he knows. Utterson's desires to sin are not under control; the quest for satisfaction has been driven underground. Like Hyde, he enters his soul through the cellar door. His human side emerges only when he is drunk.[54] As the story progresses, Utterson increasingly comes to resemble Jekyll and Hyde. He gnaws on his fingers like Jekyll and whispers like Hyde. We can discern a kind of ironic justice in the frisson of fear, the terror of the law, felt by Utterson as he works with the police inspector to track down Hyde.[55]

THE PERSECUTED SHADOW BECOMES
IMPOSSIBLE TO INTEGRATE

The dynamic of repression is as follows: we individually and collectively abhor some desires; this repression deforms our desire; then, because we think that our suppressed desires are repulsive, we feel justified in repressing our impulses without bothering to try to understand them. The more we repress a part of our hidden self, the more hateful and twisted it becomes. When we eventually explode in anger at the hypocrisy we see everywhere, we feel frightened and still more justified in savagely suppressing our Hyde. So the cycle repeats itself, and our anger intensifies.

At this juncture, we may resolve to become "good." As the psychologist John Sanford notes, making such a resolution brings us to a dangerous point:

> To deny the life of the shadow entirely . . . is to run the risk of having our life energies dry up. There are times when we must allow some of the unlived life within us to live if we are to get new energies for living . . . [I]f we strive to be only good and perfect, we become hateful, for too much of the vital energy within us is being denied. For this reason, there are few people more dangerous in life than those who set out to be good. It can even be said that whenever we try to exceed our capacity for natural goodness we bring about evil, not more good, because our unnatural stance generates an accumulation of darkness in the unconscious.[56]

The resolution to be good is a declaration of war on our selves, a war that renders the self unintegrable. The war takes two forms. Shunning our hidden self entirely, we become over-identified with a particular figure, type, or role. Horrified at Hyde's murder of Carew, Jekyll commits himself to a life of virtue:

> The veil of self-indulgence was rent from head to foot, I saw my life as a whole: I followed it up from the days of childhood, when I had walked with my father's hand, and through the self-denying toils of my professional life, to arrive again and again, with the same sense of unreality, at the damned horrors of the evening.[57]

One cannot help but be struck by how much Jekyll idolizes the father figure and all that is manly. Jekyll sees himself as Hyde's father and fantasizes about the good old days when he walked hand in hand with his father.[58]

None of the men in this strange tale is married. Utterson, Jekyll, and Lanyon are obsessed with maintaining a professional façade and obtaining the approval of their male peers.

Jekyll's "self-denying toil" entails, ruthlessly repressing any impulse that is warm, caring, or archetypically feminine.[59] After murdering Carew, Hyde is accosted by a woman who emerges from the London night and offers him a box of matches.[60] Unable to bear the presence of any woman, Hyde strikes her in the face, and she flees into the darkness. Once we commit our selves to conforming to an ideal persona, enlightenment becomes impossible. We need to learn from our Hyde, from the otherness that emerges from the darkness. In denying that we have undeveloped dimensions to our personality and identifying only with our public "good" self, we make it impossible to learn from or to integrate these dimensions.

The war on the shadow assumes a second form. Unhappy, we actively disown our hidden self. After the murder of Carew, Jekyll refuses to admit that Hyde continues to be a part of him. He refers to Hyde only in the third person, distancing himself from any guilt he might feel for what Hyde has done.[61] This disowning of Hyde is the culmination of our failure to integrate ourselves. Jekyll initially takes the drug to escape his hateful life and the guilt he feels for having illicit desires. With each dose, he injures himself further. The action of the drug parallels a wounding. When first compounded, the impure solution blazes red, then bubbles purple and finally, like bruised flesh, subsides into a sickly green. By seeking to escape from our life instead of trying to understand why we are so unhappy, we mortally harm ourselves. In our weakened state, we are still less able to integrate our Hyde in a thoughtful and responsible fashion. Like Jekyll, we say, "I need feel no guilt for the acts of my other self because that self is not me." Guilt, though, can be a sign of health. When we feel guilty about an act or feeling, our guilt prompts us to acknowledge and consider our emotions or behavior. Guilt can point us in the direction of wholeness.

However, as we saw in chapter 2, feeling guilty or ashamed is not an unqualifiedly good thing. A sense of guilt is helpful only if other people support our efforts at integration. Guilt quickly turns morbid if our friends, family members, or colleagues refuse to acknowledge their hidden selves. In that case, these deniers project their fears onto us, try to live through us, and then demand that we bear their burden of guilt. When those around us persecute their hidden selves and shift the guilt, we can be so overwhelmed that we find it impossible to integrate ourselves. Hyde is our collective shadow and creation, and, if we are not careful, we all become part of the war on Hyde and the dynamic that fosters hate and rage.

Hyde does not begin life as a monster. He becomes monstrous as the do-gooders begin to hound him. They have taken it upon themselves to rid the world of that which they deem evil. We have seen how Enfield joins with members of a mob to blackmail Hyde. Enfield's insistence that Hyde is satanic prompts Utterson to unmask this fiend whom the lawyer imagines to be threatening Dr. Jekyll. Although Utterson portrays himself as a tolerant soul who lets each man "go to the devil in his own way,"[62] he becomes obsessed with Hyde:

> Mr. Utterson began to haunt the door [through which Hyde entered]. In the morning before office hours; at noon when business was plenty . . . at night under the face of the fogged city moon . . . the lawyer was to be found on his chosen post. "If he be Mr. Hyde," he had thought, "I shall be Mr. Seek."[63]

Jekyll begs Utterson to leave Hyde alone, but Utterson will not let the question of Hyde's identity drop. He persists in characterizing Hyde as a blackmailer, telling himself that, yes, Jekyll "was wild when he was young; a long while ago to be sure, but in the law of God, there is no statute of limitations. Ay, it must be that; the ghost of some old sin, the cancer of some concealed disgrace."[64] Like Enfield, Utterson embarks on a course of blackmail, reasoning that this "Mister Hyde, if he were studied . . . must have secrets of his own; black secrets by the look of him; secrets compared to which poor Jekyll's worst would be like sunshine."[65] If Hyde is a juggernaut, it is because Utterson has resolved to put his "shoulder to the wheel" and to gain control over the disgust-inspiring Hyde.[66]

Endeavoring to be free of our shadow, we inadvertently enslave ourselves to it. Hyde represents our imagination or fancy. Our imagination often yields unexpected insights, proffering images that allow us to synthesize previously unconnected thoughts and feelings. This synthesis is not something that we can force or control. Insight happens spontaneously. From the outset, Jekyll is frustrated by the drug's unpredictability. Sometimes he can wake the fanciful Hyde; other times Hyde will not appear. But at least Jekyll is attuned to his fanciful side. The doctor sees beauty where others perceive only deformity, and he initially welcomes the appearance of Hyde. By acknowledging our fancy, we create an opportunity to learn more about ourselves. Conversely, if we suppress our imagination, we soon become dominated by our fantasies.

Utterson is a case in point. He views himself as utterly pragmatic. Anything "fanciful" is to be shunned as "immodest." Yet the lawyer is completely oblivious because he is ruled by imagined fears and presentiments. He is so plagued by his suspicions about Hyde that he suffers waking nightmares:

> [The question of Hyde's identity] had touched him on the intellectual side alone; but now his imagination also was engaged or rather enslaved; and as he lay and tossed in the gross darkness of the night . . . Mr. Enfield's tale went by before his mind in a scroll of lighted pictures. He would be aware of the great field of lamps of a nocturnal city; then of the figure of a man walking swiftly; then of a child running from the doctor's; and then these met, and that human Juggernaut trod the child down and passed on regardless of her screams. Or else he would see a room in a rich house, where his friend lay asleep, dreaming and smiling at his dreams; and then the door of that room would be opened, the curtains of the bed plucked apart, the sleeper recalled, and lo! there would stand by his side a figure to whom power was given, and even at that dead hour, he must rise and do its bidding.[67]

In Utterson's dream, it appears to be his sleeping friend Jekyll who must rise and do the faceless phantasm's bidding. In reality, the staid and moderate lawyer Utterson is the one seized by a "singularly strong, almost . . . inordinate curiosity" to find and see the face of Hyde.[68] The lawyer hates the terms of Jekyll's bequest to Hyde (Hyde gets all of Jekyll's worldly goods if Jekyll disappears for more than three months). Utterson chafes at his ignorance of Hyde. This ignorance swells his indignation and gives his fancy a nasty turn. He unconsciously clothes Hyde with "detestable attributes; and out of the shifting, insubstantial mists that had so long baffled [Utterson's] eye, there leaped up the sudden, definite presentment of a fiend."[69] This fear and loathing of Hyde, coupled with our Uttersonian desire to make the mystery of Hyde "roll away," imbues the shadow juggernaut with fiendish energy.[70]

This hatred of the fanciful leaves both Jekyll and Hyde utterly isolated. With no one supporting his efforts at self-integration, Jekyll slips into self-hatred and despair. Having declared war on Hyde, we leave ourselves with no way out of our unhappiness. To be satisfied, we need to address our inchoate longings. Like Jekyll, we need to give them form by embodying them in our life. If we refuse to admit that these longings even exist, they lurk in the recesses of our soul. Left alone, these desires grow because they are unchecked by reason and common sense. As we have seen, we come to fear and hate the hidden self still more. If society reinforces this fear and impedes our efforts to integrate our shadow traits, we soon lose any interest in doing so.

Our repressed longings are not intrinsically evil. Each person has hidden talents and proclivities. We experience evil—we become desperate in our frustration—as we war against the hidden self. Then we slip into self-loathing, wounded by ourselves and by the larger society. At that point, integration becomes almost impossible. Our failure to incorporate our Hyde becomes an established fact. We no longer experience guilt and we lose touch with who we are and with what we are doing. In our intense suffering and ignorance of the cause of our pain, we may resort to violence in a futile effort to rid ourselves of this pain and dread.

The Unintegrable Self

The Strange Tale of Dr. Jekyll and Mr. Hyde ends at this point of no return with the story coming full circle. While on one of their Sunday walks, Utterson and Enfield return to the back door, the neglected side, of Jekyll's house.[71] Here is the door through which Enfield, many months earlier, saw Hyde enter to retrieve the check to pay his blackmailers. On this day, the two men find Jekyll staring down at them, sadly brooding behind the bars covering the windows of his office. While they watch, Jekyll has one of the spontaneous seizures that transform him into Hyde. Yet Utterson and Enfield, both of whom have accosted Hyde in person, fail to recognize Hyde behind the façade of Jekyll's residence. Why are they unable to identify the monstrous Hyde? Why do they perceive only a dejected and broken man? The reason is telling. They have so demonized Hyde that they cannot imagine that Hyde is a part of their respected friend Jekyll. They cannot even entertain this possibility because the two of them—Utterson representing repressive duty, Enfield embodying untutored desire—remain separate and dissociated. Since they do not know what integration would look like, they cannot perceive disintegration.

Nor can the melancholy Jekyll confide his secret to these men. They would not understand his plight. Even if he wanted to describe his condition, the despairing Jekyll might not be able to do so. As the persecuted Hyde becomes more spiteful and violent, Jekyll feels increasingly estranged from this part of himself. In his final confession, Jekyll acknowledges that he at first believed Hyde was a beautiful part of himself. After his first success at self-transformation, Jekyll reports that he felt "younger, lighter, happier in body."[72] Looking at himself in the mirror, Jekyll feels "a leap of welcome" and proudly proclaims, "this, too, was myself."[73] After the murder, the doctor cannot bring himself to refer to Hyde in the first person. Hyde becomes, in Jekyll's eyes, someone who is in no way part of him.

The tale closes with Utterson enlisting Jekyll's servant Poole to help him break into Jekyll's study. There they find a dead Hyde and a packet containing Jekyll's final will and a confession. The confession describes Jekyll's experiments and reveals the secret of the tale: Jekyll and Hyde are the same man. When the story first appeared, readers were astounded by this revelation. Since the secret is so well known today, we do not feel the shock and outrage that those first readers experienced. But we would do well not to be too complacent. The ending is a series of traps within traps. The traps exist and work to the extent that we, like Jekyll and Stevenson's peers, try to distance ourselves from our Hyde. While we modern-day readers appear to avoid the obvious trap of thinking that Hyde and Jekyll are two different people, we stumble into more subtle snares because we are parties to the same collective and individual repression that destroys Jekyll and Hyde.

Like earlier readers, we accept Jekyll's confessional assessment that Hyde is utterly morally corrupt. We do not stop to ponder who wrote this confession. Utterson tells us that the document is written in Jekyll's hand, but this observation is not decisive. In the past, Hyde has forged Jekyll's handwriting and signature on checks.[74] Hyde has no difficulty adopting Jekyll's style. When Hyde taunts the good doctor Lanyon and challenges the doctor to watch what happens when Hyde drinks the drug he has compounded, Hyde's jeremiad is distinctly Jekyllian in tone. Jekyll prides himself on his psychological acuity, but Hyde is equally astute. When Jekyll awakens in his home to the strange sensation that he is in his Soho flat, he begins to analyze his sensations. He is some minutes into his reverie before he realizes that Hyde, not Jekyll, is lolling in the doctor's bed.[75] Mr. Hyde, not Dr. Jekyll, has been performing the psychological analysis!

Hyde may even be recording his psychological observations. After murdering Carew, Hyde rushes to his Soho apartment in order to burn papers. Why would Jekyll be keeping his notes in Hyde's *pied à terre*? Doing so would only increase the risk of exposure, a risk Jekyll is at pains to minimize. Given that Hyde has furnished his Soho apartment with taste, we might hypothesize that Hyde is quite literate as well. We are pushed to think along these lines if we are to make sense of the tale. Understanding why Jekyll wishes to live as Hyde is easy. The staid doctor enjoys acting as Hyde, reveling in Hyde's sensual adventures. But what prompts Hyde to voluntarily take the drug to revert to Jekyll? Jekyll's confession attributes the reversion to Hyde's animal fear of the scaffold. In the early days, though, Hyde had nothing to fear from remaining in the person of Hyde. Hyde's desire and willingness to resume life as Jekyll is incomprehensible unless we posit a deep and abiding affinity and kinship between the two men.

Although the signs of this affinity are everywhere in the text, we cannot see them unless we are willing to admit that we, too, have a hidden side that is valuable and worth exploring and expressing. Determined to demonize Hyde, we overlook the Hyde that is right under our nose. Certain of Hyde's complete otherness, we do not countenance the possibility that Jekyll's story is a composite work—that Hyde is helping to write it and that it truly is the strange tale of Dr. Jekyll *and* Mr. Hyde. Writing an autobiography is an imaginative act well suited to fancy, the very faculty Hyde has in abundance. Hyde and Jekyll have always shared memories; the author of the confession tells us so. He speaks truly, for Jekyll is aware that Hyde has collided with the child, murdered Carew, and struck a woman selling matches. The moment we grant the possibility of joint authorship, several inconsistent details fall into place.

The putative author Jekyll confides that he is writing the confession under the influence of the few remaining dosages of the drug. A week earlier he had discovered that he was running out of the salts needed to compound the drug. In a panic, he writes notes sending Poole scurrying all over town to obtain more of the necessary salts. None of the replacement salts works. Poole corroborates this part of the confession but adds an interesting twist. Poole summons Utterson because he suspects foul play. He insists that, for the past week, there has been no sign of his master. The voice Poole hears sounds like a crying woman and the pacing footfalls in the doctor's room are not those of his master Jekyll. Poole comes across a man rummaging around in the doctor's laboratory but this doubled-over creature is not Jekyll. If Poole's testimony is to be trusted, only one person is present in the doctor's cabinet during the last week of the period when the confession is being written—Hyde.[76]

The confession corroborates Poole's account and this inference. The author tells us that by early January of the final year of Jekyll–Hyde's life, the drug had already lost much of its potency. Whenever Jekyll falls asleep or daydreams, he awakens as Hyde. No drug is necessary to become the more imaginative Hyde; however, double dosages are required to restore the persona of Jekyll. Or so the writer of the confession tells us. In truth, we do not know whether, in the final days, Hyde ever succeeds in reverting to Jekyll. If the author were able to slip back into Jekyll's person, why would he take the risk of leaving the room as Hyde and being spotted by the servant Poole? It makes more sense to suppose that Hyde is present much of the time at the end and is authoring, or at least coauthoring, parts of the confession.

Hyde must be present insofar as a hidden or suppressed self is, by definition, still part of the self. Our Hyde joins in all of our activities, whether or not we know it. Therefore, to accept the confession as Jekyll's alone is to fall into a second trap. We stumble into a third trap when we take everything that is said in the confession at face value. If, however, we resist the temptation to demonize Hyde and read the ending in a more accepting spirit, we uncover evidence of a Hyde very different from the one described in parts of the confession. The writer maligns Hyde, claiming that Hyde will destroy anything Jekyll writes. The writer also maintains that Hyde lives in fear that Jekyll will kill himself, thereby putting an end to Hyde as well. Events show the first claim to be false. When Utterson and Poole break into the study, they find Jekyll's revised will. The supposedly selfish Hyde does not destroy Jekyll's will, even though the revised will makes Utterson, not Hyde, the beneficiary of Jekyll's estate. This will is in the doctor's study in more or less plain view from the early part of January through the end of March; Hyde does not touch it.

The second claim is more intriguing: why doesn't the doctor kill himself once he has determined that he can never return to his professional life and is doomed to live as Hyde? By committing suicide, Jekyll could die in the person of the doctor and take his secret to the grave. The answer, again, is hidden in plain sight. Hyde, the hidden self, feels that he should be recognized. Hyde participates in the drafting of the confession, thereby giving himself substance and making it clear that he is an integral, and initially beloved, part of the good doctor. The vital, animal spirit Hyde keeps the writer alive until the confession is complete. The confession also indirectly bestows upon Hyde a measure of dignity for those who know where to look. Recall that Jekyll portrays Hyde as a lower life form who lacks the courage to kill himself. Yet when Utterson and Poole break into the study, whose body do they find? They discover the corpse of Hyde, the man who, according to Jekyll, was utterly lacking in human courage. To the very end, Jekyll underestimates Hyde's humanity. We do so as well insofar as we read Jekyll's confession as though Hyde were not present during its composition.

And thus we are ensnared by a fourth trap. The written confession comes into Utterson's hands. Utterson has no incentive to make the tale public. The opposite appears true, given that the lawyer has been determined from the beginning to preserve the good name of his upstanding friend Jekyll. How, then, does the tale become public and fall into our hands? Stevenson appears to be suggesting that we are deceived in our implicit belief that we can permanently sever our public persona Jekyll from our hidden self Hyde. This complete dissociation of the two is what springs the other three traps. The reality is that our Hyde will not stay hidden. Our suppressed traits, talents, and abilities always come to the fore one way or the other. The only question is whether we will welcome our hidden self or meet it with scorn and hatred. Whether integration occurs depends crucially upon our response.

Our response depends upon our individual understanding and the structure of the society in which we live. I discuss the ways in which art, law, and education help or impede individual integration in the last three chapters. Before doing that, however, I want to examine the part played by our collective imagination in the delusional dynamics leading to the destruction of the self. Although we like to treat Hyde as a moral monster, he is our creature through and through. Hyde functions as our collective shadow, and our collective imagining of the hidden self energizes this shadow and affects how it gets expressed. If so, we ought to examine more carefully our complicity in the delusional dynamics that lead to madness and so often, to mayhem and murder.

5

EVIL AS IMAGINED PORTENT

Less delicately terrible, perhaps, than the vagaries of departed spirits, but to the full extent as interesting . . . are the number-less possible forms of human malignity.

—*Henry James*

THE PREVIOUS THREE CHAPTERS EXAMINE HOW WE BECOME MORE DANGEROUS as we struggle to preserve an intrinsically unstable or false sense of ourselves. We may, like Hendrik Höfgen, be driven by the morally sanctioned desire to be respected. In other cases, our struggle, like Tom Ripley's, may be fueled by an overwhelming wish to escape our boring lives. These desires are two sides of the same coin. Unhappy with who we are, we strive to acquire a more engaging, respectable identity. Our quest requires other people's help. Their interest and approval confirm that we finally have become whom we hope to be. Both Mann and Highsmith understand that the self is never satisfied by this quest because the self is not a persona or role. Stevenson develops this point further by disclosing the way in which society pressures us to identify with a respectable role but then proceeds to live vicariously through our immorality when we rebel against societal pressure. This social hypocrisy increases the likelihood that the self will fragment and descend into madness. In all these cases, the protagonists use imagination to anticipate threats, suggest possibilities, and rationalize their attempts to preserve their fragile personas. As their efforts unfold, imaginative cunning supplants reason. In this chapter, I explore what happens when the human imagination is allowed to operate unchecked.

No writer has more thoroughly explored the power of our imagination than Henry James. His tale *The Turn of the Screw* ranks as one of the most horrifying stories in the English language. Little happens in the story, yet the account is infused with ominous portent. The young governess who narrates the story perceives this portentousness. Her belief in a mystery to be solved drives the plot. We are only too happy to assist her in her fight to identify and eliminate a dreadful evil. Writing about public reaction to this tale, James insisted that his values were "blanks." It is we who fill in these blanks, happily using our imagination to do so. To use James's metaphor: our imagination enjoys "scoring one entirely off its own bat." This tale, with its "tone of suspected and felt trouble, of an inordinate and incalculable sort," is perfectly suited to engage the imagination.[1] What could better stimulate our efforts to solve a mystery than a mystery that has no bottom—that is "incalculable"? Our imagination responds to the teasing challenge and begins to take on a life of its own. The seed of evil lies in this autonomy of the imagination.

The Setting

We can best see the problems with the imagination if we reproduce the governess's encounters with evil. A brief overview of the storyline will help us get our bearings.

An inexperienced young governess travels to the isolated country estate of Bly to look after two orphaned children, ten-year-old Miles and his younger sister Flora. The children's uncle, known only as the "Master," engages the governess as a replacement for a predecessor who has died while in service. The Master has sent some of his servants to staff Bly while he remains in London to care of some unspecified business. The housekeeper, Mrs. Grose, has been looking after Flora and also Miles whenever he is on holiday from school. The children need a proper governess, so the young woman is hired with the curious and mysterious stipulation that she must never communicate with or trouble the absent Master. This unusual condition becomes relevant when, a few days after her arrival, the governess receives an official letter from the school. The letter states that Miles cannot return to school. Just as the uncle gives no reason for his condition, so the letter is silent on why the school has rejected Miles.

The reader and the governess alike wonder why this beautiful child has been sent down. The governess soon suspects that Miles is not as innocent as he appears. As if this development were not sufficiently worrisome, the governess encounters a male intruder at Bly. After consulting with Mrs. Grose, who had appeared "inordinately glad" to have the governess for company, the governess establishes that the horrifying intruder is none other than the Master's dead valet Peter Quint. Shortly after encountering Quint, the governess sees a woman in black. Again, with the help of Mrs. Grose, the governess identifies this vile creature. This horror is Miss Jessel, her dead predecessor. The governess comes to believe that the morally corrupt Quint and Miss Jessel have returned from the dead to get hold of the children. It falls to the governess to save them.[2]

In the preface to this tale, James writes that he strove to create a "pair of abnormal agents" who would cause "the situation to reek with the air of Evil."[3] He succeeds magnificently. James's contemporaries damned him for offering such a scandalously "monstrous" and "indecent" tale.[4] Damning James is easy. It is much harder to ascertain exactly where the evil in this tale lies. Are the twin apparitions of Quint and Jessel evil? The two children? Or are the governess and Mrs. Grose, or the governess and the reader the "pair of abnormal agents"? Is there some particular trait or behavior that makes a person evil? If there are "numberless possible forms of human malignancy," as James maintains, is evil beyond our grasp? Answering these questions requires that we examine how the imagined air of this tale comes to reek with evil.

The "Evil" Apparitions

The First Sighting: Evil as an Unfathomed, Violative Threat to Our Identity

The governess settles in with the two children and quickly establishes a routine. Although she claims to enjoy the long days in the presence of the children, she especially cherishes that time of the day—her hour—after the children have gone to bed. Then she can stroll around the lands surrounding the house, enjoying her reveries. It is on one such stroll that the governess first encounters the male figure:

> It was plump . . . in the middle of my very hour: the children were tucked away and I had come out for a stroll. One of the thoughts that . . . used to be with me in these wanderings was that it would be as charming as a charming story suddenly to meet some one. Some one would appear there at the turn of the path and would stand before me and smile and approve [of the job I was doing]. . . . That was exactly present to me—by which I mean the face was—when . . . at the end of a long June day, I stopped short on emerging from one of the plantations and coming into view of the house. What arrested me on the spot—and with a shock much greater than any vision had allowed for—was the sense that my imagination had, in a flash, turned real. He did stand there!—but high up, beyond the lawn and at the very top of the tower to which, on that first morning, little Flora had conducted me. The tower was one of a pair . . . I admired them, had fancies about them . . . yet it was not at such an elevation that the figure I had so often invoked seemed most in place.[5]

The apparition troubles her because it is out of place. The governess had fantasized about meeting a man outside; this figure is inside the house. She had envisioned encountering the man as a peer, as a fellow human being out for a stroll. But this man towers above her.

The vision is doubly spooky because the governess suddenly realizes that the man meeting her eyes is not the figure she had initially supposed:

> An unknown man in a lonely place is a permitted object of fear to a young woman privately bred; and the figure that faced me was—a few more seconds assured me—as little any one else I knew as it was the image that had been in my mind. . . . The place, moreover, in the strangest way in the world, had on the instant and by the very fact of its appearance become a solitude. . . . It was as if, while I took in what I did take in, all the rest of the scene had been stricken with death.

Like the governess, we feel troubled by the man's strangeness. We are concerned for her. The youngest child of a parson, she has previously lived only at home. This post is her first. Twenty years old, she has seen little of the world. The mystery of the man's identity makes her more vulnerable. Who is he and what does he want? His mysterious presence heightens our sense that she is utterly alone in the world. He is staring directly at her; no protective master is just around the turn.

Without making a conscious decision, we cast our lot with the governess. Our imagination and protective feelings are engaged. We must be with her because she is telling us the story. If something happens to her, we will not have our tale. And we want it. The figure's unknown quality intensifies our sense of danger not only because it is potentially threatening to the governess but also because it is so interesting to us. The man on the tower positively invites us to join the governess in speculating about his identity. Yet, try as she will, the governess cannot place the man on the tower. Her inability to place the man increases our imaginative stake and our terror in two ways.

If the governess cannot figure out who the man is, the figure ceases to be simply an unknown presence at Bly. He turns into an *intruder* and a *violator* who has compromised the safety of the children by entering the house unbidden by the governess. Regardless of who he is, his presence is felt to be violative because his intentions are unclear. The figure stares at the governess in a bold and fixed manner. He may have designs upon her, yet he is ominously silent. This silence or reserve threatens the governess's sense of identity. The governess bridles "a little with the sense of how [her] office seemed to require that there should be no such ignorance and no such person."[6] As governess, she is the protector of the children. If a man, unbeknownst to her, has ventured into the house, she must not be doing her job. She is not the governess that she takes herself to be. Having assumed her cause as our own, we feel that she must uncover who he is.

As readers, we begin to search for clues that the governess may have missed. Indeed, the more sophisticated and smarter we think we are, the harder we work to discover clues that this naïve young woman may have missed. Our imagination is fully engaged, busily making present what is absent and filling in the blanks. Since the initial details are so sparse, our imagination must work overtime to figure out the man on the tower. The more possibilities we imagine, the less innocent the figure appears. The figure becomes still harder to place and thus more sinister.

That something or someone is out of place does not make it evil. If we misplace an object, the object does not thereby become evil. Something or someone appears to be evil when it is out of place in a particular sort of way. We feel that we are in the presence of evil when something engages us but then appears to resist our efforts to specify who or what it is. The object's interesting elusiveness—its refusal to conform to our expectation that it disclose itself—causes us to feel that the object has, in some vague way, violated us. All at once our identity appears less secure, and we experience the uncontained anxiety and dread that haunt Hendrik and Tom. Evil is a felt transgression or violation of our identity whose exact consequences or import we cannot specify. James hints that evil is a perceived transgression akin to the breaching of a taboo. Although taboos state what we must not do, they do not tell us what will happen if we disobey the prohibition. The consequences of performing the transgressive, proscribed action are left to our imagination.

It is our imagination that gives evil its portentous quality, a quality about which morality has nothing to say. Social moralities always state the consequences, the punishment that will ensue if we behave in criminally vicious ways. This moral explicitness is the antithesis of portentousness. Wisdom accounts or portrayals, which link evil to our desperate attempts to secure our identity against any imaginable threat, have more to say about the shadowy realm of spooky figures and unsettled feelings. James understands that the portentousness of the evil object is directly proportional to the demands we place upon it. When we base our identity on our office, we are tempted to demand total knowledge. How can we possibly do our job if we are kept in the dark? The governess insists that, even if the man's presence has an innocent explanation, she should have been informed of his identity. It is she, and she alone, who has the authority to determine to whom and on what terms the children are exposed. Unless her authority is recognized, the governess cannot know where she stands or what the future holds for her. She then becomes the one who is out of place. For who is she, if not the "governess"? And, if she does not know who she is, how can she claim to know anything of the world? Everything becomes obscure the moment the unknown figure appears on the tower. In this sense, evil might be said to cast a shadow over the entire world.

The more we seek to control the situation completely, the more paranoid we become. Soon, whatever is out of place and unfathomed turns sinister. Staring at the man intently, the governess realizes that he exhibits "a touch of . . . strange freedom . . . in the sign of familiarity of his wearing no hat."[7] This small, innocent detail becomes a piece of a paranoid puzzle. A real gentleman would never appear in public without wearing a hat! The figure's disregard for this taboo must mean that he recognizes no limits. The figure appears infinitely transgressive, the epitome of evil.

His hard stare reinforces our sense that he is deeply sinister. It is the mark of good manners and breeding to know when to avert our eyes. Individuals who stare too long thereby signal that they do not recognize the need for, or desirability of, social taboos. They have, as we say, "the evil eye" because they are willing to gaze upon anything or anyone, even when doing so is strictly forbidden. In this case, the figure does little but stare and that is enough to make it horrifying:

> He was in one of the angles. . . . So I saw him as I see the letters I form on this page; then, exactly, after a minute, as if to add to the spectacle, he slowly changed his place—passed, looking at me hard all the while, to the opposite corner of the platform. Yes, it was intense to me that during this transit he never took his eyes from me, and I can see at this moment the way his hand, as he went, moved from one of the crenellations to the next. He stopped at the other corner, but less long, and even as he turned away still markedly fixed me. He turned away; that was all I knew.[8]

When the figure finally does move, his manner heightens our foreboding. The man changes place slowly. We imagine that he feels the governess poses no threat to him and is therefore content to take his transgressive time. The man's hand traces every crenellation, a motion that, in the governess's words, "adds to the spectacle" by calling our attention to the insouciance of his movement. The contemptuous sensuousness and invasiveness of the movement compound our horror. No nook or cranny can shield us from this man with the evil eye. Everything about this figure now disturbs us: his moving presence is as portentously transgressive as his silence and lack of a hat.

After seeing the man on the tower and discreetly investigating the matter, the governess ascertains that she has not been the victim of a game or the brunt of some servant's joke. So

> there was but one sane inference: some one had taken a liberty rather monstrous. . . . We had been, collectively, subject to an

intrusion . . . some unscrupulous traveler . . . had made his way unobserved, enjoyed the prospect from the best point of view and then stolen out as he came. If he had given . . . such a bold hard stare, that was but part of his indiscretion. The good thing . . . was that we should surely see no more of him.[9]

Whether this inference is sane, and whether it is the only one to draw, are questions that we should ask ourselves. However, once we have begun to suspect an enemy is in our midst, it is easy to succumb to fearful imaginings. We do not bother to investigate the intentions of our supposed enemies, nor do we realistically assess the nature and extent of the danger they pose. Instead, we imagine the worst without being aware that our imagination is operating in hyperdrive.

The Second Sighting: Evil as Violative Certainty

A few days later, the governess prepares to take the children on a walk. Remembering that she has left behind her gloves, she returns to the dining room to recover them. In the dim gray light of the afternoon, she discovers a man at the window.

> The person looking straight in was the person who had already appeared to me. He appeared thus again with I won't say greater distinctness, for that was impossible, but with a nearness that represented a forward stride in our intercourse and made me, as I met him, catch my breath and turn cold. He was the same—he was the same, and seen, this time, as he had been seen before, from the waist up, the window . . . not going down to the terrace on which he stood. His face was close to the glass, yet the effect of this better view was, strangely, just to show how intense the former had been. He remained but a few seconds—long enough to convince me he also saw and recognized; but it was as if I had been looking at him for years and had known him always. Something, however, happened this time that had not happened before; his stare into my face, through the glass and across the room, was as deep and hard as then, but it quitted me for a moment during which I could still watch it, see it fix successively several other things. On the spot there came to me the added shock of a certitude that it was not for me he had come.[10]

This vision is indeed shocking, disturbing, and profoundly disorienting. As before, the figure's deep and hard gaze violates the home and the governess. But now the governess feels that she has always known this figure. She knows evil every bit as well as it knows her.

Evil is peculiarly well adapted to be perceived by us. As the governess observes, the horrifying figure of evil is simultaneously strange and utterly familiar. It is strange insofar as it is transgressively out of place; it refuses to be confined by our conventions and mores. Yet, while the figure is alien in this respect, it is not supernatural or superhuman. Neither the reader nor the governess is the least bit surprised to find evil in a human form. I would suggest that portentous evil is an imagined human transgression against humanity. The possibility of suffering such a transgression or, we should note, of performing one has been with us our entire lives. In that sense, we, along with the governess, have always known the figure of evil.

Although evil as such never alters its essential character, our relationship with evil changes and develops. The first time the governess encounters the figure, it is outside the house; this time it comes closer, with a nearness that, the governess tells us, represents an advance in the "intercourse" between her and the evil violator. If evil itself is unalterable in character, it follows that the two parties can draw closer only if the governess herself has become more evil or sinisterly transgressive. Since the story is being told from the governess's perspective, we quite naturally tend to see things from her point of view. It is she who frames each of our encounters with evil. But let us try to change our point of view and look back in at the governess through the window of the text. When we shift our perspective, we discover that the governess stares back at the figure every bit as hard as he stares at her. She never takes her eyes off him, even after he looks away to other objects in the room. If his stare is transgressive, hers is equally so.

If we, as readers, can maintain a dual awareness—sharing the governess's perspective while avoiding identifying too much with her anxiety—we can learn a much about the nature of transgressive evil from this second sighting. The apparition "fixes" the governess and whatever it glances upon, and she "fixes" it right back. This activity of fixing suggests a fury or tenacity of purpose. James suggests that it is this fury, not the content, of the purpose, that is most worrisome. Whenever our purpose is so focused that it eliminates all ambiguity, uncertainty, or doubt, we are in the presence of transgressive evil. The relationship between us, the perceivers of evil, and that which we deem evil is reciprocal. No sooner does the evil eye fix upon objects in the room than the governess becomes fixated. She is absolutely certain that she is in the presence of an evil out to get hold of the children.

She never specifies, and we never learn, what exactly is meant by the phrase "getting hold" of the children. Nevertheless, the mutual intensity of the stare suffices to produce in the governess a flash of "knowledge" and to start "a sudden vibration of duty and courage" within her breast.[11] She rushes out to confront the figure. When she cannot find him, it is "confusedly present" to her that she should place herself exactly where the man had been standing:

> I placed my face to the pane and looked, as he had looked, into the room. As if, at this moment, to show me exactly what his range had been, Mrs. Grose, as I had done for himself just before, came in from the hall. With this I had the full image of a repetition of what had already occurred. She saw me as I had seen my own visitant; she pulled up short as I had done; I gave her something of the shock that I had received.[12]

The governess has assumed the place of the evil figure. What is more, she produces in others the same horror she felt when she encountered the evil figure. She asks Mrs. Grose if she had looked very queer through the window. To which Mrs. Grose replies, "Dreadful!" The governess, though, is not in the least apologetic. When we think we have taken a just stand against evil, we readily imagine ourselves to be heroes. We like this heroic feeling so much that we are only too happy to have others confirm our interpretation of events.

The governess is no exception. The second sighting and her heroic response make her still more certain that her interpretation of the figure's sinister intentions is correct. Others must affirm what she reads into her encounters with the evil enemy, and she is willing to use her status and power to obtain their endorsement of her vision. Although the governess is aware that Mrs. Grose has no desire to be frightened further, she forces the housekeeper to listen to her story about the man on the tower and at the window. Mrs. Grose "knew too well her place not to be ready to share with me any marked inconvenience. Oh it was quite settled that she must share."[13]

In our zeal to confront evil, we seek to enlist others in our moral quest. Our certainty that we have met the enemy not only justifies (in our eyes) the war on evil; it also leads to pressuring our allies to join in the war. We will not tolerate any doubt, for that would render us less certain. Our identity and persona require that we be in control and in the right. We do not hesitate to coerce others into going along with us. Having put the housekeeper in her place, the governess describes the figure, adding "stroke to stroke." As critics have noted, the governess's rendering of the figure is curious. She begins by avowing that the man is "like nobody." Only after she senses that this vague, but portentous, claim has stirred some recognition in Mrs. Grose does she fill in the frame, revealing features she neglected to mention in her prior descriptions of the man:

> He has red hair, very red, close-curling, and a pale face, long in shape, with straight good features and little rather queer whiskers that are as red as his hair. His eyebrows are somehow darker; they look particularly arched and as if they might move a good deal. His eyes are sharp, strange—awfully, but I only know clearly that they're rather small and very fixed. His mouth's wide, and his lips are thin, and except for his little whiskers he's quite clean-shaven. He gives me a sort of sense of looking like an actor. . . . He's tall, active, erect . . . but never—no, never!—a gentleman. . . .[14]

The governess's description reiterates the transgressive quality of evil apparent at the first sighting. This time, though, she speaks with greater authority, confidence, and, it must be said, fury. Her hatless man at the window is *never* a gentleman.

Our certainty that someone else is evil itself becomes violative. Ceasing to see objectively, we discern only that which we wish, or need, to perceive. Having figured out that the man is a demonic "horror," her description of the figure alters accordingly. The governess's detailed description evokes the folk stereotype of the devil or Satan. The figure at the window is a man with red hair and whiskers who haunts houses, especially at dusk.[15] This invocation of the archetypical devil is not done consciously. We turn to both archetypes and stereotypes when we are not thinking. Since these types are, by definition, widely accepted, our appeal to them enables us to give expression to our subjective feelings and to fill in the frame in a way that resonates with other people and brings them over to our side.

This approval of our allies gives us greater scope for action, making us more dangerous. When we begin to see the world only as we would like it to be, we start to lose our sanity and treat innocent parties violently. It is no accident that this advance in intercourse between evil and the governess is accompanied by a chilling development: the figure has come not for the governess but for the little children.

The Third Sighting: Evil as Self-Righteous Certainty

With some prompting from the governess, Mrs. Grose identifies the figure painted by the governess as the Master's former valet Peter Quint, a man feared by the housekeeper because he "was so clever—he was so deep."[16] This description profoundly affects the governess, who admits, "I took this in more than I probably showed."[17] But another shock awaits her and us. If Quint was terrifying when he was at Bly, his appearance to the governess makes him twice as horrible. For Peter Quint is dead!

Our anxiety gets ratcheted a notch higher as we join the governess in imagining that this figure, who was "too free" with the children when he was alive, has come to consort with them again.[18] This possibility engenders another disturbing line of thought. Given that the children spent so much time with Quint when he was alive, is it not mystifying, or even downright sinister, that they have never referred to the valet in the governess's presence? Why this strange silence on the part of Miles and Flora? Like the governess, we feel we must be on our guard not to miss a single clue. We share her concern and applaud her courage when she renews her vow to protect the children:

> It was an immense help to me—I confess I rather applaud myself as I look back!—that I saw my response so strongly and so simply. I was there to protect and defend the little creatures in the world the most bereaved and most lovable, the appeal of whose helplessness had suddenly become only too explicit, a deep constant ache of one's own engaged affection. We were cut off, really, together; we were united in our danger. They had nothing but me, and I—well, I had *them*. . . . This chance presented itself to me in an image richly material. I was a screen—I was to stand before them. The more I saw the less they would. I began to watch them in a stifled suspense,

a disguised tension, that might well, had it continued too long, have turned to something like madness. What saved me, as I now see it, was that it turned to another matter altogether. It didn't last as suspense—it was superseded by horrible proofs. Proofs, I say, yes— from the moment I really took hold.[19]

The proofs are not long in coming. Having fixed upon what her response will be in the event that she again sees the figure, the young woman immediately has another encounter with an apparition. This time, Flora and she have gone out for a walk. The governess is silently watching from a bench overlooking the pond, which Flora is pretending is the Sea of Azof. As she watches, the governess begins to take in "with certitude and yet without direct vision the presence, a good way off, of a third person."[20] The governess perceives "no ambiguity in anything." She knows what she will see when she looks up from her stitching. She goes through the motions of reminding herself that it would be perfectly natural for a man—"a messenger, a postman, or a tradesman's boy, from the village"—to be in the neighborhood. These ruminations have no effect upon either her "practical certitude" or "the character and attitude of [the] visitor" because "nothing was more natural than that these things should be the other things they absolutely were not."[21]

Certain that we know how to recognize and defeat evil, we soon see it everywhere. Like the governess, we will have our "proofs." We need such evidence in order to prove to ourselves and to others that we are not crazy. Like the governess, we anticipate the presence of evil, and it obligingly appears before our very eyes. Or does it? What does the governess see when she finally looks up? In one sense, she sees nothing. She narrates what leads up to the moment of the encounter, but does not directly relate the encounter itself. As in the case of the earlier encounters, her world goes silent when she senses the presence of evil. At this moment, the governess judges that Flora is no longer engaged in spontaneous play. After watching Flora intently screw one piece of wood into a small hole in another, the governess finally lifts her head to meet the intruder's gaze. We learn nothing more about this scene until the governess returns to Bly and throws herself into the welcoming arms of the motherly but gullible Mrs. Grose. Then we hear what the young woman has worked up for the housekeeper. The governess has seen not a man but a woman, "a figure of quite as unmistakable horror and evil: a woman in black, pale and dreadful—with such an air also, and such a face!—on the other side of the lake. I was there with the child—quiet for an hour; and in the midst of it she came."[22]

We learn as much about evil from what the governess does not say as from what she chooses to relate. Despite the fact that she was certain she would see a man, she is not especially troubled when events prove her wrong. She neither acknowledges nor accounts for her mistake. Instead, she remains unassailably certain that she seen the face of evil. If we come to believe that some party is infinitely hostile toward us, no evidence can prove us wrong. We become unshakeable because we are not testing evidence against hypotheses to arrive at our "proofs." We begin and end in certainty. Our "proofs" are a reflection of our state of mind and of the strategies we employ to assure our allies and ourselves that we are not mad. The moment we become passionately and absolutely convinced that we are not and cannot be mad, our subjectivity truly takes hold. Our feelings as to what must be true lead us, in the governess's phrase, to "read into" events whatever signs and clues we need to justify these feelings. Perceived portents substitute for and function as our evidence. With respect to her second encounter with the male figure, the governess tells us that the figure "was there or was not there: not there if I didn't see [it]."[23] This third sighting of an apparition adds another twist: the figure must be present if the governess sees it because she certainly is not deluded.

Perhaps we most grossly violate our fellow human beings—perhaps we are most in the grip of delusion—when we behave as if they have no independent existence apart from ourselves. If so, the governess might be said to do evil when she unwittingly substitutes subjective for objective thinking, and then resolutely denies having made the substitution. Her transgressive reasoning acquires the manic intensity she imputes to the evil figures who have come to take hold of the children. Therefore, it is perfectly fitting that this third sighting takes the form of a woman who resembles the governess in every particular. Both women are young; both are described as pale and dreadful. The apparition stares fixedly at the child Flora just as the governess had done prior to lifting her eyes to face the horror. In the process of perceiving, naming, and battling transgressive evil, the governess has become the enemy without knowing it.

Having already "thought it all out," the governess seeks to persuade Mrs. Grose that the woman at the pond was the dead Miss Jessel, the previous governess. She insists as well that Miles and Flora "know" that Quint and Jessel are haunting their every move. When the housekeeper repeatedly expresses some skepticism about the figure being Miss Jessel and Flora's consciousness of Miss Jessel's presence, the governess triumphantly produces her proof for both claims. Miss Jessel "gave me never a glance. She only fixed the child . . . with a determination—indescribable . . . to get hold of her."[24] The governess concedes that Flora never looked at this woman in black, but the child's apparent nonresponsiveness is, the governess insists, additional proof of the evil figure's power to corrupt children. Flora the governess maintains, was dissembling when she turned her back on the figure of Miss Jessel and pretended not to see it.

As evil takes hold of us, anything can be made to serve as a proof of what we subjectively imagine. The negative (Flora did not look at the figure) supports the positive (Flora was fully aware of the dead Miss Jessel). No objection that anyone might raise can survive the twists and turns of our imaginative cunning. We contort reality to conform to whatever we imagine to be true. Whatever does not support our view, we conveniently overlook. Or we overstate the case. Although the governess has never seen Miles with Miss Jessel, she claims that both children are in cahoots with the dead governess. As subjectivity substitutes for objectivity, our world becomes silent, unable to speak to us. We join the governess in a fugue state in which the only voice we heed is the internal one urging us to do—what? That remains to be seen.

The Fourth Sighting: Evil as Living, Detestable Human Presence

Are there any limits to the portentous evil we are capable of imagining? Not if we give free rein to our imagination. After identifying the female figure as Miss Jessel, the governess and housekeeper share their salacious speculations about the predecessor's tenure at, and departure from, Bly. Mrs. Grose explains, "Of her real reason for leaving? Oh yes-as to that. She couldn't have stayed. Fancy it here—for a governess! And afterwards I imagined—and I still imagine. And what I imagine is dreadful." To which the governess replies, "Not so dreadful as what *I* do, I replied; on which I must have shown her—as I was indeed but too conscious—a front of miserable defeat . . . at the renewed touch of her kindness my power to resist broke down."[25]

To resist what? Not the figures of evil. As we will see, the governess feels herself quite up to that task. What she cannot resist is giving in to her suspicions. She needs only the suggestion from Mrs. Grose that Quint took liberties with everyone, including the children, to infer that Flora and Miles have been despoiled (in some unspecified way) by these evil servants. Although Miles has done nothing more sinister than stay at home to read a book, the governess concludes that Miles wishes to commune uninterruptedly with the horrific Quint while his sister plays at the pond in the presence of Miss Jessel.

Portentous, imagined evil has no locus. It can be everywhere at the same time. As we imagine the worst, evil becomes, in James's precise phrase, "inordinate and incalculable."[26] Confronted with a powerful, limitless evil, we slide into melancholia and despair. Although the governess is supposed to be instructing the children, she spends most of her day obsessing about how to deal with the corrupted children and the omni-present evil figures. The children do their best to distract her, dreaming up clever charades in a frantic attempt to cheer her and to distract her from this obsession. But the suspicious think no gesture is innocent. Miles is so adept at reading the governess that we join her in wondering, on the one hand, how one so young can be so precocious and, on the other hand, what Miles could possibly have done to get himself sent down from school. We unconsciously draw the "logical" conclusion: the problem with the boy must be moral instead of intellectual. Without making any explicit decision to side with the governess, we start to conjecture as to the source and nature of this moral turpitude and wonder whether our young, inexperienced heroine will be able to save the children from the two sinister figures.

Her employer has forbidden her to consult with him, and she does not trust the corrupted Miles to give her a straight answer as to why he is not permitted to return to school. Unable to see her way to a solution, the governess drifts from day to day. Lessons of a sort continue, with her suffering from intermittent outbreaks of vulgarity, madness, or both. We get hints of these outbreaks, although she glosses over them, and the reader does not notice them until he or she begins to doubt the governess's reliability:

> Sometimes perhaps indeed (when I dropped into coarseness) I came across traces of little understandings between them by which one of them should keep me occupied while the other slipped away. There is a naïf side, I suppose, in all diplomacy; but if my pupils practiced upon me it was surely with the minimum of grossness. It was all in the other quarter that, after a lull, the grossness broke out.[27]

If the children are practicing "diplomacy" and devising ways to escape from her, it is not, I suspect, because they are communing with demons but because they have begun to fear her. However, having cast herself as the protector of the children, the governess cannot admit that she, like all of us, has a dark side. It is time for the "real" enemy to put in an appearance again. Quint obligingly does so. This time, though, the evil is, if possible, even more palpable.

Feeling that something is astir inside the house, the governess gets up to investigate. She congratulates herself on her courage and deliberation, leaves the library and her Gothic novel behind, and goes to investigate. Her candle suddenly goes out.

> Without it, the next instant I knew that there was a figure on the stair. . . . I required no lapse of seconds to stiffen myself for a third encounter with Quint. The apparition had reached the landing halfway up and was therefore on the spot nearest the window, where, at sight of me, it stopped short and fixed me exactly as it had fixed me from the tower and from the garden. He knew me as well as I knew him; and so, in the cold faint twilight, with a glimmer in the high glass and another on the polish of the oak stair below, we faced each other with our common intensity. He was absolutely, on this occasion, a living detestable dangerous presence. But that was not the wonder of wonders; I reserve this distinction for quite another circumstance: the circumstance that dread had unmistakably quitted me and that there was nothing in me unable to meet and measure him. . . . I had no terror. And he knew I hadn't . . . I felt in a fierce rigor of confidence, that if I stood my ground for a minute I should cease . . . to have him to reckon with; and during the minute, accordingly, the thing was as human and hideous as a real interview: hideous

just because it *was* human, as human as to have met alone . . . in a sleeping house, some enemy. . . . It was the dead silence of our long gaze at such close quarters that gave the whole horror . . . its only note of the unnatural . . . The moment was so prolonged that it would have taken but little more to make me doubt if even *I* were in life. I can't express what followed it save by saying that the silence itself—which was indeed in a manner an attestation of my strength— became the element into which I saw the figure disappear; in which I definitely saw it turn . . . and pass . . . straight down the staircase and into the darkness. . . .[28]

Our certainty that evil is omnipresent makes us more suggestible. A stimulation from one quarter that sets our imagination afire easily starts a blaze in another quarter, especially since speculative despair makes us paranoid. The governess reads her Gothic romance and then knows that she will find an evil figure in the house if she leaves her room to investigate. In a parallel manner, we readers devour this creepy little Jamesian romance and, at each turn, are ready to believe anything the governess tells us about her experience of evil. When we reach this point of heightened sensitivity, evil has drawn near indeed. In the symbolic terms of this tale, the horror has moved inside our house. No longer is there a great distance or pane of glass between the governess, us, and the figure of evil. The imagined enemy dwells within.

To think that we know the face of evil is equivalent to asserting mastery over it. We wrongly believe that if we can know evil fully and name it with certainty, we can gain ascendancy. Recall that the evil figure first appears above, and then on a level with, the governess. Having identified the male figure as Quint, the governess towers above him during their third encounter. It appears she finally has realized her fantasy of being the mistress of the house, the fancy she had been entertaining when she first encountered the sinister figure on the tower. But her position is tenuous. The rigidly erect Quint threatens her authority, seeking to mount the stairs to where the children sleep. It is up to the governess to stand between evil and her charges. She must conquer her fear to match her enemy. If she fails to stiffen her resolve and to protect the children, she loses her identity and her position as governess. Her parents are experiencing some unspecified difficulty, so she cannot return there. Everything depends upon her knowing evil and being able to "take its measure."

I stress again that the evil we envision and seek to defeat is not super-natural. It is horrifying because is so distinctly human. Anything that is utterly alien to human life would appear strange, not terrifying. To expe-rience horror, we must be able to compare and assimilate the encountered thing (the man on the tower) to other parts of ordinary, natural, day-to-day human existence (the master's valet Quint). That is why evil has the feel of the familiarly human. We inevitably share a "common intensity" with the human image we fashion as we figure out who or what is evil. The greater our commitment to our view, the more intensely we experience evil. The intensity, in turn, dissipates our dread and any doubts we might have had about our perceptions and conclusions. We stop dreading and worrying about the future because we think we know its shape. We lose ourselves in our representation of the present evil. Like the governess on the stairs, we enter into a fugue state, staring at our Quints for an eternity. This fugue state persists because we have nothing left to discover in the figure of evil. Our Quints have nothing to do and nowhere to go unless we give them something to do. We stare at them, and they stare back until they evaporate into the silence we create the moment we become sure we can master evil.

This silence is deadly, so much so that we may begin to wonder whether we are alive. Real life is filled with surprises. It forces us to reeval-uate our claims and beliefs. When we become self-proclaimed masters of the universe, we murder not sleep but life itself. We transfer our life energy to our visions of evil. Our imagined evils become "living detestable dangerous" presences. The more alive they are, the more dead we feel. The governess feels "up" and "high" as long as everything in the world of Bly appears interesting and favorable to her; however, she repeatedly "falls" into depression as she comes to suspect that evil lurks everywhere and that she will never be mistress of the house. As the real world loses its ability to engage and enchant, the governess retreats into the world of books and her charming imagination.

The Fifth Sighting: Evil as Mad Courage

After Quint departs into silence, the governess leaves the steps and returns to the room she shares with Flora. Flora has left her bed and is at the window, intently looking out at something. Upon being questioned, Flora denies that she has seen anything. Since the governess perceives evil as omnipresent, she instantly and absolutely believes the child is lying. Flora's obvious willingness to lie, in turn, intensifies the governess's suspicions. She stays up late, prowling about the house in search of the indwelling evil and soon finds it.

Her fifth sighting takes the form of the dead governess:

> I just missed on the staircase . . . a different adventure. Looking down from the top I once recognized the presence of a woman seated on one of the lower steps with her back presented to me, her body half-bowed and her head, in an attitude of woe, in her hands. I had been there but an instant, however, when she vanished without look-ing round at me. I knew, for all that, exactly what dreadful face she had to show; and I wondered whether, if instead of being above I had been below, I should have had the same nerve for going up that I had lately shown Quint.[29]

This sighting discloses the ambiguity of the heroic virtue we display when confronted with that which we deem evil. We pride ourselves on, and praise others for, exhibitions of courage. But does our courage in the face of evil enable us to triumph over it? Or is the source of our courage our belief that we have mastered evil? The governess's courage belongs to the second class. Only insofar as she is the master—only insofar as she is "above" evil—is she able to look evil in the face. Otherwise she lacks the courage to go "up" and confront her Quint. However, the governess has got the matter backward. As long as we think we are on top of evil, we can never see its face. In our certainty, we supply the face of evil without knowing or admitting that we are doing so. The governess knows "exactly what dreadful face" Miss Jessel has to show without even looking at the figure.

Believing that we have courageously mastered evil is a form of madness. Madness is movement along a path in which we encounter only ourselves without knowing that we are doing so. The governess does know the dreadful face this apparition would present. The face is, ironi-cally, her own. Mrs. Grose comments on how "dreadful" the governess looks with her face pressed up to the pane. When the governess describes the "awful eyes" of the dead woman, Mrs. Grose stares at her eyes as if these living eyes "might really have resembled" those of the dead woman.[30] The governess hits upon the truth without realizing it: "I was conscious as I spoke that I looked prodigious things . . . for I got the slow reflection of them in my companion's face."[31] Later, while walking with Miles, the governess seems "to see in the beautiful face with which he watched me how ugly and queer I looked."[32]

Are we mad, then, each time we encounter an evil figure? If evil is our misbegotten attempt to secure happiness for a self we have misconceived, we cannot encounter evil. For evil is not some positive or independent malicious force. Imagining evil as a bogeyman out to get our children or us is a delusion of frustrated desire. The violence and pain engendered by this frustration are real enough, but they, too, stem from our frustrated attempts to preserve a false sense of the self. In later chapters, I examine whether we are responsible for our delusions. What I wish to stress here is that, although evil is not an independent external force, we might describe it as semi-autonomous. We did not individually or collectively invent the delusional dynamic we have been tracing. The trajectory of the unchecked human imagination ensnares us in the most cunning of traps—a trap that we unthinkingly devise and then spring.

James's art discloses the spring mechanism of our imagination at the same time as it draws us ever deeper into the governess's delusional world. James thereby points to one possible way to avoid the trap. If we can remain skeptical of our judgments and resist the heroic temptation to save the world from those whom we deem evil, we can retain our sanity. We always empower the demons we fight. By staying calm and scrupulously skeptical, we cease to provide evil with its energy. However, no guarantees of safety exist. We should remain skeptical about even our sanity. If we become absolutely certain that we are not deranged and set out to prove that we are sane, we may inadvertently join the governess on her descent into madness.

The Sixth Sighting: Evil as Manipulative Control of Vulnerable People

As our certainty that we have fully grasped and understood evil becomes habitual, we no longer need to experience evil directly in order to perceive it everywhere. Quint makes his fourth appearance in an indirect fashion. Awakened from a light slumber, the governess again witnesses Flora staring out into the night:

> That she now saw . . . was proved to me by the fact that she was
> disturbed neither by my re-illumination (of the candle) nor by the
> haste I made to get into slippers . . . She was face to face with the
> apparition we had met at the lake, and could now communicate with
> it as she had not then been able to do. . . . There were empty rooms
> enough at Bly, and it was only a question of choosing the right one.
> The right one suddenly presented itself to me as the lower one . . .
> in the solid corner of the house . . . of . . . the old tower. . . . I uncov-
> ered the glass without a sound. . . . The moon made the night extra-
> ordinarily penetrable and showed me on the lawn a person,
> diminished by distance, who stood there motionless and as if fasci-
> nated, looking up to where I had appeared—looking . . . not so much
> straight at me as at something that was apparently above me. There
> was clearly another person above me—there was a person on the
> tower; but the presence on the lawn was not in the last what I had
> conceived and had confidently hurried to meet. The presence on the
> lawn—I felt sick as I made it out—was poor little Miles himself.[33]

According to the governess, Quint appears to Miles as she watches the boy
from the bedroom up in the tower. The boy himself never admits to
communing with Quint. For all we know, Miles could be looking up at the
governess. He later intimates as much, hinting that he and Flora have
staged the entire performance for the governess's benefit.[34] If so, it is
entirely natural that he should look up to check whether she is watching.
The governess fills in the blank—she supplies Quint—because she has
convinced herself that the children are having intercourse with the dead
servants whenever she is not there to protect them. Now that she is aware
of the children's practice, she ought to be able to catch them in the act.
Surprise, surprise—here she does exactly that.

What is her evidence that Quint is present to the boy? Her "proof"
consists of nothing but her claim "there was clearly another person above
me." Our certainty that evil is present functions as the proof that it is so.
We are the masters of meaning and need look no further for evidence.
The governess climbs the tower, ascending to the place of mastery where
Quint once stood, looking down on her with his violative and transgressive stare. It is she who looks down with a stare able to penetrate the night.

What does this reversal of roles tell us about the nature of evil? And what does it signify that the child Miles occupies the place where both the governess and we expect to find pure evil? At some point in our war on evil, we unwittingly mutate from savior into fiend. The transformation occurs subtly and seamlessly. We rationalize every surprise that "evil" throws our way as we strive to make evil conform to our suppositions about it. Vowing to permit nothing to divert us from our mission to defeat evil, we become a righteous juggernaut, willing to destroy in order to save. Just when we are most certain that nothing can defeat us, the delusional dynamic succeeds at diverting us through inverting our role: we put the very people we claim to be protecting at grave risk.

This inverted dynamic is most evident with respect to children. Children are highly susceptible to being harmed. They are physically smaller and so are easily hurt when an adult gets hold of them. They lack experience of the world and, consequently, have difficulty interpreting the motives and behaviors of those around them. I do not want to overstate the case. Children are amazingly sensitive and resilient beings. Miles and Flora know the governess is disturbed long before anyone else in the house draws that conclusion. Nevertheless, they are vulnerable because they lack authority. If they were to complain about their caretaker, they would probably find themselves at the mercy of an extremely angry adult. Miles and Flora may have staged their nighttime antics in order to get other adults in the house to see just how strange their governess is. Or, as Miles later tells the governess, he may have acted "badly" in order to force her to send him back to school. Once free from her control, he would be in a better position to get the school authorities to inform the absent uncle about the governess's strange behavior. In any case, if the children were driven to such tricks, it only shows how few resources they have to combat the power of adults. Our unchecked imagination can cunningly justify just about any practice. When we permit our imagination to run wild, children become, in James's words, "as exposed as we can humanly conceive children to be."[35]

Although every human being is susceptible to suffering, children are most at risk. The more fixated the governess becomes, the more her fury shifts from the evil Quint and Miss Jessel toward Miles and, to a lesser extent, his sister Flora. The governess will have her victory over evil at all costs. Having victory means controlling children. If we cannot govern children, who are the easiest creatures for us to control and manipulate, we are not the masters we think we are. If our charges dare to resist our authority, their naughtiness "proves" that they need us to save them lest they become yet more evil. At every turn, we have our children in our clutches.

The Seventh Sighting: Evil as Denial

Matters come to a head when Mrs. Grose pressures the governess to ask the uncle to take the children away to a safe place, and when Miles demands to be allowed to return to school. When the governess refuses to give a straight answer to Miles, he threatens to get his uncle to come down to Bly to resolve the issue. Unnerved by Miles's "unnatural" and "sudden revelation of a consciousness and a plan," the governess considers abandoning her duty and fleeing her post.[36] In despair, she collapses onto the bottom stair. She rests there until she recalls with a sudden fright that she is sitting exactly where she had seen Miss Jessel,

> the most horrible of women. At this I was able to straighten myself . . . and made, in my turmoil, for the schoolroom. . . . Seated at my own table in the clear noonday light I saw a person whom, without my previous experience, I should have taken . . . for some housemaid . . . who, availing herself of . . . the schoolroom table and my pens . . . had applied herself to the considerable effort of a letter to her sweetheart. . . . [A]t the moment I took this in I had already become aware that, in spite of my entrance, her attitude strangely persisted. Then it was—with the very act of announcing itself—that her identity flared in a change of posture. She rose, not as if she had heard me, but with an indescribable grand melancholy of indifference and detachment, and . . . stood there as my vile predecessor. . . . [E]ven as I fixed and, for memory, secured it, the awful image passed away. Dark as midnight in her black dress, her haggard beauty and her unutterable woe, she had looked at me long enough to appear to say that her right to sit at my table was as good as mine to sit at hers. While these instants lasted . . . I had the extraordinary chill of a feeling that it was I who was the intruder. . . . I heard myself break into a sound that . . . rang through the long passage and the empty house . . . but I . . . recovered myself and cleared the air. There was nothing in the room the next minute but the sunshine and the sense that I must stay.[37]

We have seen how those of us who declare war on evil come to resemble the very enemy we have vowed to destroy. The governess, who has committed herself to winning the war on evil, now sits exactly where the loathsome Miss Jessel once rested so dejectedly. Such reversals suggest that we cannot eliminate evil from this world. The more we imagine that other people are involved in wrongdoing, the more we risk substituting our fancies for helpful, practical responses. Instead of asking Miles why the school said he could not return, the governess entertains all sorts of possibilities. She starts to second-guess her responses and those of the people around her. Meanwhile nothing gets done about Miles's absence from school. The longer she puts off dealing with the problem, the more difficult it becomes to address it and the more depressed she becomes. Our unconstrained speculations about a pending crisis tend to provoke one.

When we do finally respond, our reactions are more extreme than they would have been if we had curtailed our imaginings. All we know for certain about Miss Jessel is that she left Bly to return home. Yet both the reader and the governess get so caught up in mystification and in the dread of what might happen to the children that the figure in the schoolroom appears as the "most horrible of all women." Our imagination takes the governess and us ever deeper into dark depths of worry and concern. It is no wonder that the seated governess is bowed with the weight of all the woe of the world. Since every attempt to master the imagined crisis provokes another one, our horror inevitably escalates. Our propensity to fear the worst leads to overreactions and tragedy.

We have difficulty accepting the possibility that we may be complicitous in the evil we envision. Having entered into a war on evil, we cast ourselves in the role of savior. Neither the world nor we admit of any ambiguity. If we are not entirely good, then we must be wretchedly vile. Either we are high, or we are low. Like the governess, we are repelled by the thought that we might be akin to the enemy. And so we respond to any flicker of doubt by reasserting our authority and girding ourselves to again enter the fray. This response to ambiguity does not solve the problem of how best to resist evil. We reassert our mastery only to have it challenged again. As soon as we imagine we have plumbed the depths of evil, it reappears in a different form. Having banished the thought that she resembles her most vile predecessor, the governess enters the schoolroom and finds a woman at her desk. How can there be an inferior woman—a mere housemaid—at her desk? This inferior is struggling to do exactly what the governess is being pressured to do—to write a letter to "her sweetheart," the uncle with whom the governess has fallen in love. Indeed, it is the prospect of having to write this letter that causes the governess feel so low and inferior. To write is to admit her inability to deal with the crisis at hand and to disappoint the Master.

The governess is not alone in resisting a drop in status. When we declare war on evil and make ourselves into saviors, we implicitly conceive of ourselves as masters. We are the high ones, the ones chosen to do God's work. How can we relinquish this status without simultaneously forfeiting our identity? None of us wishes to be a nobody. That is why we readers so readily ally ourselves with the young governess in her battle with demons. Yet, because every attempt by us to solve one imagined crisis provokes another one, we remain plagued by the suspicion that we are not the mistresses of our houses, much less of the entire world. Although the governess stands at the door, the lowly housemaid-intruder at the desk will not relinquish the governess's place.

Doubting the righteousness of our cause only prompts us to dedicate ourselves more fully. We vow to "stay the course." Denial becomes a matter of policy for us, rendering us less able to discern alternatives and to explore options. The governess can identify only three possibilities: she must flee, write to the absent Master and lose her post, or stay to fight evil. Other options exist. For example, she could write to her employer and see what happens. That alternative, though, would require that she admit the existence of uncertainty and learn to live with it. That is one thing we masters of the universe cannot do. Instead, we vainly attempt to salvage our position by bringing on yet another proof.

The Eighth Sighting: Evil as the Creation of Enemies

The more anxious we feel, the more obsessed we become with protecting our children. When the governess, who has been listening to Miles play piano, realizes that Flora has gone out without taking her hat (an ominous transgression!), she sounds the alarm.[38] She insists to Mrs. Grose that Miles is in the schoolroom with Quint, while Flora has gone out to meet Miss Jessel. The governess goes out in search of Flora, dragging Mrs. Grose in her wake. The governess leads the way to where she first saw Miss Jessel, promising Mrs. Grose that the housekeeper, too, "beyond a doubt . . . shall see."[39] After they find Flora, the governess confronts the child, demanding to know where Miss Jessel is. Almost immediately

> the whole thing was upon us. . . . [T]he quick smitten glare with which the child's face now received [the name of Miss Jessel] . . . likened my breach of the silence to the smash of a pane of glass. It added to the interposing cry, as if to stay the blow, that Mrs. Grose at the same instant uttered over my violence—the shriek of a creature scared, or rather wounded, which, in turn, within a few seconds, was completed by a gasp of my own. I seized my colleague's arm. "She's there, she's there!" Miss Jessel stood before us on the opposite bank exactly as she had stood the other time, and I remember, strangely, as the first feeling now produced in me, my thrill of joy at having brought on a proof. She was there, so I was justified; she was there, so I was neither cruel nor mad. She was there for poor scared Mrs. Grose, but she was there most for Flora. . . . She rose erect on the spot my friend and I had lately quitted, and there wasn't in all the long reach of her desire an inch of her evil that fell short.[40]

Flora is not impressed and does not even "feign to glance in the direction of the prodigy" the governess has announced. Instead, Flora turns and looks at the governess with "an expression of hard still gravity, an expression absolutely new and unprecedented and that appeared to read and accuse and judge me—this was the stroke that somehow converted the little girl herself into a figure portentous" and "vulgarly pert."[41] When Mrs. Grose sees nothing, the governess feels her "situation crumble." Her position deteriorates further when Flora pleads to be taken away from the governess. At that point, another amazing transformation occurs: Flora's "incomparable childish beauty had suddenly failed, had quite vanished . . . she was literally, she was hideously hard; she had turned common and almost ugly."[42]

Having committed ourselves to a campaign against evil, we require that others see the world exactly as we do. They are either for us or against us. What happens when our fellow human beings resist our vision or express some doubt? We cannot tolerate this resistance. Since people have different experiences and perceptions, some divergence in points of view is inevitable. But, in our role as saviors, we cannot endure any opposition that might introduce an element of doubt into our mission. We most especially cannot abide resistance from those whom we are supposedly protecting. We must deny the relevance of their objections because, if they do not want our help, then we, like the governess, feel our position crumble horribly.

Desperate, we set about marginalizing those who resist our assistance. Like the "vulgarly pert" Flora, these ingrates are surely in league with evil forces. The devil is putting words into their mouths. Our opponents start to take on the quality that, for James, most characterizes evil— portentousness. The innocent Floras of this world turn into something hard, vulgar, and infinitely sinister. Former allies take on dark depths as we guess and second-guess their every move and generate a variety of reasons for explaining why they have gone over to the other side.

The Ninth Sighting: Evil as the Attempt to Master Ambiguity

The governess has her remedy for exorcising the demon who has possessed Miles. She will give Miles "a little more time . . . to bring it out."[43] Feeling that she has, at last, "mastered it, [seen] it all," the governess confides her plan to the housekeeper. She must get Miles to admit his crime: "I'll get it out of him. He'll meet me. He'll confess. If he confesses he's saved. And if he's saved—." Mrs. Grose completes the chain of reasoning for the governess, chiming in "Then *you* are?"[44] In our war on evil, we are the victors (i.e., good people) or the losers (i.e., evil demons). No middle ground exists. We require enemies in order to be victors. The governess needs Miles as much as, or even more than, the boy needs her. Committed to converting others to her point of view, the governess no longer registers the boy's desires. Any desires Miles might have must be corrupt, given that he has been cavorting with Quint.

Someone may protest: "People can object to our unwelcome efforts on their behalf. Such objections will deter us." I am skeptical. Identified with our cause and our image of ourselves as saviors, we cannot hear these protests for what they are. Nothing anyone can say will divert us from our mission. We endlessly parse the nuance and tone of what others say as we desperately try to take the measure of evil and shore up our position.

Sometimes people, sensing the danger they are in, seek to appease us by telling us what we want to hear. The newspapers regularly report cases of alleged child abuse in which judges throw out the testimony given by children. Grilled for hours by parents, police, and social workers probing for evidence of abuse, the children eventually offer up "evidence" that they have been molested. Critics often object that the children have been coached. But that objection misrepresents the deeper issue. The question we should be asking is whether the children have been so frightened by the intensity of their saviors that they seek some respite by trying to guess what their inquisitors wish to hear them say. The children who, like Flora, "decline to be puzzled" by our questions may escape our inquisition.[45] Those who, like Miles, seek to figure out what we want to hear enter unknowingly into our game of mystification and thereby place themselves at far greater risk.

Miles is afraid of the governess.[46] When others fear us, we ought to stop and wonder: have we become akin to the very evil we seek to defeat? Instead, our messianic streak leads us to interpret our wards' fear as proof that our efforts at salvation are on the right track. Does not their fear prove that they are capable of shame and feel some guilt? Their fear of us becomes another "splendid portent" that our victory is near.[47] We must make others afraid for their own good. As these "sinners" become more afraid of us, they speak less. Things are left unsaid. Yet, for the heroic savior, no silence is innocent. Everything is evidence or proof of something. Like the governess and Miles, we and our sinners circle "about with terrors and scruples, fighters not daring to close."[48] Each round is another turning of the screw in our torturous war on evil.

Where and how does our evil war on evil end? James's tale ends ambiguously. Pleading a prior engagement, Miles seeks to escape the governess and her interrogation. She stays him by asking that he tell her just one small thing, "a mere fraction of whole."[49] The governess had learned from Mrs. Grose that someone had removed the letter she had written to the Master in London. The governess wants to know: did Miles take the letter she had written? The moment she asks this question, the male apparition is on the scene:

> I sprang straight up . . . getting hold of [Miles]. . . . The appearance was full upon us. . . . Peter Quint had come into view like a sentinel

before a prison. The next thing I saw was that, from outside, he had reached the window, and then I knew that, close to the glass and glaring in through it, he offered once more to the room his white face of damnation. . . . It came to me in the very horror of the immediate presence . . . to keep the boy himself unaware. . . . It was like fighting with a demon for a human soul, and I saw how the human soul—held out, in the tremor of my hands, at arms' length—had a perfect dew of sweat on a lovely childish forehead. The face that was close to mine was as white as the face against the glass, and out of it presently came a sound . . . "Yes, I took it."

Quint (whose name in Latin means "five") has appeared to the governess five times—on the tower, at the window, on the staircase, on the tower, and now again at the window. Victory cannot be had. If we do not relinquish our quest to master ambiguity, if we do not give up our belief that we possess the screw or key to portentous mysteries, we find that we must exert still more pressure to achieve our goal. One suspicion leads ineluctably to another. Although we, like the governess, exultingly predict that we will "surely get *all*,"[50] this all is never forthcoming. The governess cannot rest easy with Miles's confession that, yes, he did take the letter. She sternly asks whether he stole things at school. When he denies being a thief, she presses to know why he was kicked out of school. When he admits to having said things, she demands that he reveal what he said and to whom. Her figurative pressing becomes a literal one as she holds him ever closer to her to shield him from either seeing or being seen by Quint.

Others are indeed damned—when we insist on regarding them as evil! Consider the plight of Miles. If he admits to having stolen the letter, he confirms the governess's suspicion that he is a thief. If he is that evil, then he is capable of worse. He must confess all before she will give him his freedom. If he denies having taken it, he must still be in the grips of an evil, demonic spirit. She cannot let him go lest he be lost forever to her ministering spirit. Like Quint, she is the guard or screw, the sentinel at the prison door. Sinners have difficulty escaping their saviors, while the saviors can never secure the total victory they crave.

I argued in chapter 1 that evil is not the same as viciousness. Moralities locate vice in the individual. Delusional and semi-autonomous evil, by contrast, acts through us "as a perfectly transparent and non-resistant medium and then passes through" to others.[51] Evil is impersonal in a way that vice never is. It is a mistake therefore, to equate evil with a particular person. As chapter 3 shows, evil can float from person to person. We are readily drawn into imagining the worst and into victimizing those we claim to love. I do not mean to suggest, though, that we are completely innocent victimizers. The delusional dynamic often works in the service of our desires and fantasies. The governess wants to be mistress of Bly, and the apparitions provide her with the opportunity to be such. As readers, we wish to escape our boring lives and to be titillated by a tale of incalculable evil. In some cases, evil's victims are not totally innocent either. When they start trying to figure out the victimizer, they enter into the game of mystification. Their participation is unwitting, but so, I would argue, is that of the victimizers. The governess, a perfectly "charming" and "agreeable woman" who would have been "worthy of any [position],"[52] does not choose to encounter Quint or Miss Jessel. The figures simply appear.

How, then, can we escape this "darker obscure," this "confounding and bottomless" hell of speculation, interpretation, and second-guessing?[53] At the moment the governess exults in her final victory, she suffers a doubt. Miles's confession does not amount to much, and "within a minute there had come to me out of my very pity the appalling alarm of his being perhaps innocent . . . for if he were innocent what then on earth was I?"[54] Paralyzed by doubt, she releases Miles for a moment. However, when Miles tries to leave the room, she again pounces. She feels "all the return of . . . battle" as the "white face of damnation" reappears at the window. Seizing Miles, she screams, "No more, no more, no more!" Intuiting that the governess sees someone, Miles feverishly glances around the room. Seeing nothing himself, he tries to guess what she perceives. He hazards the name of "Miss Jessel," only to be told "It's not Miss Jessel! But it's at the window—straight before us. It's there—the coward horror." Miles takes another guess: "It's he?"[55]

Then we have the final exchange between the governess and her ward: "I was so determined to have all my proof that I flashed into ice to challenge him. 'Whom do you mean by "he"?'" Barely able to breathe in the governess's rigid clasp, Miles gasps, "Peter Quint—you devil! . . . Where?" At last the governess gets the words she has longed to have the child utter. Or does she? Miles's response is ambiguous. Is the child completely innocent, or is he—as the governess believes—duplicitous to the end? Has she saved him, or does she lose him to the devilish Quint? Has Miles at last owned up to seeing Quint, or is he accusing the governess, who has him in her tight hold, of being the devil?

Critics have debated these issues for over one hundred years, and the arguments show no sign of abating. The debate only increases the mystery, inviting further speculation and interpretation. That is the point: the ambiguity we confront when interpreting events, character, speech, actions, motives, and intentions is limitless. I do not mean that all interpretations are equally good or that we cannot progress in our understanding of the matters we investigate. I am suggesting that imagining we can eliminate ambiguity and uncertainty is another of evil's many guises. In life, as in this tale, the Master is resolutely absent. We have no one to whom we can appeal to explain every action and to tell us how to respond. We are thrown back on ourselves. It becomes our responsibility to know ourselves, to scrutinize our ways of interrogating the world, and to assess the wisdom of our interpretations.

We might define evil as the human attempt to control or govern every event. Evil is not a feature or trait of things, but our misbegotten attempt to do what cannot be done. Refusing to admit that some events happen randomly while others may be imponderable, we devote ourselves to figuring out what is occurring and why. Insofar as we rely upon our imagination to get to the bottom of things, we are left feeling frustrated. For one possibility gives birth to a hundred more. Although critics have dismissed the governess as a sexual hysteric, and although it is true that the governess is smitten with the absent Master, she is, I think, better understood as an interpretive hysteric. Although it is convenient and comforting for us to believe that she is mad whereas we are entirely rational, the truth is more complicated. Anyone who takes pleasure in fiction exhibits some measure of the governess's "cultivated credulity." Without it, we could not enjoy losing ourselves in the story. If we experience even a moment of what James refers to as "sacred terror" while reading this tale, it is because we are thoroughly implicated in the governess's imaginings. Like her, we read our preoccupations, interests, and concerns, sexual or otherwise, into the events. The better we are as readers, the more hypotheses we entertain and the more deeply we are drawn into the governess's convoluted and deadly mystification. She deserves to be called a "sophisticated interpreter." And who among us has not aspired to that label?

Like Mann and Highsmith, James locates evil in our attempts to contain and dominate our dread. But he increases the stakes. Understanding evil ceases to be a spectator sport. Evil starts to operate through us when we set ourselves the task of figuring it out and resisting it. I am not, of course, arguing that we should stop reading fiction or interpreting the world around us. I *am* saying that we will be less likely to suffer or do harm if we explore the nature of evil instead of accusing particular individuals of wickedness. James's response to his critics is pertinent here. When a reader complained that James had a dirty mind and took imaginative license with the children in this tale, James retorted that he claimed only one "license"—the right of disavowal: "There is not only from beginning to end of the matter not an inch of expatiation, but my values are positively all blanks save so far as an excited horror, a promoted pity, a created expertness. . . ."[56] The evil figures of Quint and Miss Jessel are vivacious without doing a single thing. Our moral values do everything for them. That is the most spine-tingling fact of all.

6

EVIL AS THE LOSS OF OUR HUMANITY

From love issues the human being. Everything in him which falls out of the range of love's radiance falls into inhumanity, bestiality.

—*St. Augustine*

WHEN WE EXAMINE INSTANCES OF EVIL IN OPERATION, WE DISCOVER THAT evil arises from our attachment to a false and inherently unstable identity. Anxious and insecure, we become narcissistic and paranoid. We may become violent or aggressive as well, but aggression per se is not evil. The root of the problem, the core evil, is the suffering stemming from mistaken identity. Our error takes a variety of forms. We may equate the self with a role. Dr. Jekyll overidentifies with his professional persona, the governess with her sense of herself as a savior. Or we may liken ourselves to gods as Tom Ripley does. Either way, the result is the same: our inadequate and inaccurate self-understanding engenders dread and drives us to attempt to transfer our pain and anxiety onto others.

Like other thinkers in the wisdom tradition, Dante, the great Italian poet of the fourteenth century, equates evil with self-inflicted suffering or injury. The *Divine Comedy*, Dante's three-part poem, recounts his mid-life crisis, his journey through the circles of hell (the *Inferno*) and purgatory (*Purgatorio*), and his eventual salvation as he ascends through the levels of heaven (*Paradiso*). In hell, Dante encounters the shades.[1] The shades are sinners who have rendered themselves less than fully human. In some cases, those whom Dante meets still roam the surface of the earth. Although the residents of Dante's hell may not be "dead" in the biological sense of the term, they are psychologically dead, having made themselves immune to love and joy. Again, this suffering takes the form of a false identity. We see how the sinners in hell have lost their humanity and have become nothing but their sins. Dante and his guide Virgil see and speak with sinners who have trapped themselves in obsessive or neurotic modes of behavior. In this respect, Dante's shades resemble James's governess, Dr. Jekyll, and the other tormented characters considered in the previous chapters. I have included Dante in this book not because of his focus on obsession but because of the insight he provides into the degrees of evil. Although some moralists have tried to create scales of evil, they have based their scales on the number of people hurt or the extent of the pain inflicted on others.[2] Dante's scale, by contrast, considers the extent of self-imposed suffering and the relations among the forms of self-maiming or sinning. His hell has many distinct levels. Every sinner gets cast into a particular region associated with a specific type of sin. As we venture ever deeper into hell, we find that the injustice the sinners do to themselves becomes greater and their sinning more damning.

This journey raises many questions: Why is sinning irredeemable? How does it differ from vicious, yet correctable, behavior? Are the degrees of evil or sinning related to each other in some intelligible way? The best way to address these questions is to proceed through the circles of Dante's hell, examining the nature of evil as manifested in each level. The journey makes more sense if we begin with a sketch or road map of the structure of hell. This brief overview gets fleshed out and documented as we work our way through the infernal regions.

HELLISH HIERARCHY

Dante's hell has three regions, corresponding to three types of sins: sins of incontinence, malice, and bestiality. Although Dante takes this trifold distinction from Aristotle's discussion of vice, he assigns each of these terms a technical meaning quite distinct from Aristotle's usage. Recall from chapter 1 that Aristotle conceives of vice as the destruction of our faculty of choice. For Aristotle, the vicious are permanently wicked or evil. Dante, however, does not believe that vice is permanent. On the contrary, he conceives of vice as an unhealthy, habitual attitude that can be altered because the vicious agent's appetite and reason have not been perverted or corrupted. The vicious go wrong with respect to the object of desire. Those of us with vices remain capable of self-discipline because we have not reduced ourselves to our suffering. Salvation is possible if we reorient ourselves toward goods of the spirit. By learning in purgatory to alter the object of our desire, we can become free of the vice. To take an example from Dante's *Purgatorio*: the angry must learn to direct their anger at the right objects, not to eliminate it completely. Unlike sinful lust, anger is not always bad. Dante thinks we are right to be angry at injustice. By disciplining ourselves not to flare up so easily, we become able to channel our anger appropriately. Sin, though, is another matter. Sin is the enactment of perverse appetites and, in some cases, of twisted reason. Behaving perversely, the sinner enters the realm of illusion. Changing the object of desire is not an option because sin severs desire from real objects. As a result, we sinners lose our freedom and ability to act. Locked into fruitless pursuits and enslaved by our passions, we suffer terribly as we endlessly repeat our error. Our torment is our sin, and our sin is our punishment. The sinner becomes indistinguishable from the sin. That is why the gate to Dante's hell proclaims "Abandon hope all ye who enter here."[3]

Dante's three regions of hell correspond to three types of sins, not vices. Every sin severely injures or deforms our human essence. Those in the upper region of hell have committed sins of incontinence. These sins injure us by placing us at the mercy of our passions. The incontinent have become addicted to the sensation of being moved by emotion. However, to be lastingly happy, we must be guided by reason, not by our passions. Although thinking alone will not save us—for reasons I discuss at the end of this chapter—we must think in order to lead satisfied lives. We will be content if and only if we can find our place in a universe ordered and unified by divine love. Reasoning is necessary to bring our lives into accordance with the harmonious order of the universe. In giving ourselves over to passions, we place ourselves in thrall to the imagination. The objects of sinful desire are projected images produced by emotion, not reality. By pursuing these images, we become deluded and incapable of experiencing divine love.

Those in the lower regions of hell are guilty of the sins of malice. These sins also injure us. However, unlike sins of incontinence, malice harms other people at the same time as it maims the agent. All the sins of malice are species of injustice. For Dante, malice does not mean a self-conscious, active intent to harm another. Sinners in this lower region are every bit as driven by illusion as those in the upper level of hell. Their behavior, like that of James's governess or Tom Ripley, possesses an internal logic and so can be said to be purposive. But their sinning is not self-consciously purposeful. Dante's sinners, like Mann's Hendrik Höfgen, have lost the ability to intend or to act. They move in an almost mechanical fashion.

In what sense, then, are these sins malicious? Dante characterizes them as malicious for two reasons. First, sins of malice result not from passion but from a kind of cunning or plotting. The passionately incontinent fail to use their reason and so pursue objects with no objective reality; the malicious enlist reason in the service of the illusion, thereby distorting intellect as they follow their corrupt appetites. Since reason is a distinctly human faculty, our debasing of our reason constitutes a far greater blow to our humanity than does a passionate sin of incontinence. Second, since these sins not only deform the self but also make it difficult for human beings to live together, they are exceptionally evil (*mal*).[4] In his book *Convivio*, Dante equates the proper use of reason with justice, the most desirable of virtues:

> To the extent that its goodness is more proper [to us], something is that much more beloved, whence it comes that while every virtue is desirable in men, that one is most loved in him which is most human, and that virtue is justice, which is solely of the rational or, really, intellectual part.[5]

Conversely, unjust behavior that destroys our intellect is inhumane in the extreme and, therefore, deserves to be described as malicious.

Dante reserves the deepest region of hell for those who have committed sins of bestiality. As the name suggests, these people have utterly destroyed their humanity through their sin. We become bestial when our behavior is no longer rooted in any way in what is natural and objective, and when we are so completely in the grip of illusion that we deserve to be called "mad." At this point, we are incapable of giving or receiving human affection. Since loving a fellow human being is our way of participating in divine love, bestial sins are worse than a falling away from God.

They constitute a renunciation of God and love. Cold hatred consumes those betrayers of friends, country, and God who reside in the innermost, icy circles of hell.

The essence of Dantean evil is reflected in the geography of hell. Like James and Highsmith, Dante sees evil as a descent into torment and a progressive loss of human freedom. Evil so understood differs markedly from Aristotelian vice. All Aristotelian vices are equally evil insofar as vice is a habit that destroys a person's ability to choose.[6] Aristotle does order the moral virtues, categorizing them according to the extent to which they can be inculcated through habit. Courage is the most habitual, while justice requires the ability to make fine distinctions and so requires a honed intellect. Aristotle does not, however, rank vices from better to worse. Dante, by contrast, thinks sins must be ranked, because some behaviors are more deluded than others. To understand a sin entails locating it in relation to other sins or delusions. That, in turn, requires perceiving and understanding how, in what sense, and to what degree the sin injures our personal and collective humanity. The geography of Dante's hell reflects this gradation of evil in different ways. Each successive circle of hell "girdles a smaller space and greater pain, /Which spurs more lamentation."[7] The tighter the circle, the more suffering or evil we experience. The geography also hints at ordered connections among sins. Many of the circles are linked by bridges, which suggests that one form of sin leads to another. Unlike Aristotle, Dante does not believe that we can become happy by deliberating and choosing well. Rather, in order to avoid a slippery slope of suffering, we must perceive and understand the hierarchy of infernal sin.

Aristotle and Dante differ in another crucial way. Aristotle emphasizes the character we create through our actions. For Aristotle, character refers to our habitual way of acting. By deliberating, we foster good habits. These habits, in turn, enable us to choose well in the future. Bad or vicious habits stem from laziness and prevent us from exerting ourselves in appropriate ways. The ethical challenge, from Aristotle's perspective, is to exert ourselves appropriately before our laziness becomes so habitual that we become incapable of altering our character. Dante, though, does not mention habits in the *Inferno*. He takes up habits in the *Purgatario*. As Cogan has shown, the geography of the *Inferno* centers on the individual or singular sin, which does not depend on habit. Dante's hierarchy of evil is thoroughly Christian in that he thinks we can commit a mortal sin with a single act, if the act involves giving ourselves over to passion or calculated rage. Cogan observes that "even the worst of human sins, Judas' betrayal of Jesus, can [in Dante's view] only be understood as a singular action, not as the result of a depraved habit or habits."[8]

This concept of sin leads Dante to emphasize more than Aristotle the role that reason plays in our happiness. According to Aristotle, we begin to acquire virtue by imitating the good behavior of others. True, to become genuinely virtuous we need to realize our powers of deliberation so that our actions and virtues will be most fully ours. Imitation alone will never make us fully just or courageous. But imitation of the virtuous will put us on the right road. In Dante's ethical world, imitation is worthless. Each sin can be traced back to a particular deformation of appetite. As long as our appetite is disordered, so is our behavior. Insight, not habit, sets us on the path to happiness. Ordering the appetite becomes possible only when we have grasped what is deadly about sins such as gluttony or betrayal. Lacking an adequate apprehension of the nature of each sin, what we are gripped by illusion and pursue what we should not. How exactly we achieve an adequate apprehension remains to be seen. But one thing is clear: insofar as the hierarchy of sins is rational in its structure, reason pays a crucial role in avoiding evil. So does the journey. Only after we have traversed the whole geography of hell can we discern the hierarchy of sin.

There exists a third key difference between Aristotle and Dante. Aristotle makes us responsible for our character. We are happy or unhappy according to whether we choose well or fail to choose. Although Dante stresses the need for reason, he links our escape from evil to the help of guides. The *Divine Comedy* opens with Dante lost and in despair. He tries to leave the valley of despair through his initiative but finds his ascent blocked by beasts. Dante makes progress only after his beloved Beatrice, who is now in heaven, sends the poet Virgil to help him.[9] Beatrice's help, in turn, is motivated by her experience of God's love. We escape evil, Dante suggests, through the love of God working through other people, not through our efforts alone. Therefore, we will need to consider how divine love enables us to overcome the suffering that is sin.

The Upper Region of Hell: Sins of Concupiscence

Lust: Evil as Loving an Image

The first circle of hell proper contains the lustful. Dantean lust is a driving passion. Cleopatra, Dido, Helen, Achilles, Paris, and Tristan—all are swept round and round by a "storm of warring winds." These lovers' passion is a hurricane of hell in "perpetual motion." They know no rest or respite from anguish because they are entirely at the mercy of their desire, "their reason mastered by desire, suborned."[10] Dante tries to summon one pair of lovers to come and speak with him. He does not understand that the couple cannot decide to come to him. Since these lovers can initiate nothing, they are not in control of their desires. Virgil explains that Dante must wait until the wind causes them to "drift closer—then entreat them hither./ In the name of love that leads them: they will respond." As the "merciless weather" batters the pair of lovers toward him, Dante summons them with a "loving call."[11] Then, compelled by their desire to relive their story, they come to Dante.

How has the reason of this lustful pair come to be suborned? Dante learns that the two are his contemporaries Francesca and Paolo, a couple famous for their adulterous liaison. Francesca, while married to Gianciotto Malatesta of Rimini, became involved with his brother Paolo. Gianciotto murdered the two of them when he discovered them in bed together. Francesca rationalizes their liaison, arguing "love which absolves/ None who are loved from loving, made my heart burn/ With joy so strong that as you see it cleaves/ Still to him, here." Entranced by her tale, Dante presses for greater detail: "tell me, in the hours/ Of sweetest sighing, how and in what shape/ Or manner did Love first show you those desires/ So hemmed by doubt?" Francesca responds to Dante's "great craving" by confessing:

> One day, for pleasure,/ We read of Lancelot, by love constrained:/ Alone, suspecting nothing, at our leisure./ Sometimes at what we read our glances joined,/ Looking from the book each to the other's eyes,/ And then the color in our faces drained./ But one particular moment alone it was/ Defeated us: *the longed-for smile*, it said,/ *Was kissed by that most noble lover*: at this,/ This one, who now will never leave my side/ Kissed my mouth, trembling. A Galeotto, that book!/ And so was he who wrote it; that day we read/ No further."[12]

Francesca and Paolo do not love each other because they bring out the best in each other or because they are able to teach one another how to live well. The two fall into each other's arms because their love, like that of Lancelot and Guinevere, is forbidden. Even before they kiss, they are caught by lust. Francesca admits that they set about reading the Arthurian romance for the pure pleasure and thrill of doing something they should not. Titillated by the tale, they turn toward each other. In their state of mind, anyone would suffice as a sexual partner. Paolo has no objective existence for the lustful Francesca, so he appropriately remains silent and unnamed throughout Dante's exchange with Francesca. The two are in love with the idea of being in love. Each desires an image of a lover, the lover as portrayed in Arthurian romance. They have been seduced by the book.

Reason plays no role here in directing the passion. The lustful do not stop to evaluate their romanticized view of love. When we are lustful, we indulge our desire. Like Francesco and Paolo, we go with the flow of our passion, enjoying the sense of being transported. As a result, our distinctively human faculty of reason goes unused and undeveloped. We reduce ourselves to mere bodies. Francesca reports, "love" seized Paolo "for my fair body."[13] Her sentence is ambiguous: either her fair body seized Paolo, or Paolo was seized by love for her body. Either way, lust impedes the development of our humanity.

Our submission to the pulse of passion means that we never experience the liberation of true love, the joyful and fulfilling sense that we are drawing ever closer to being the persons we are. Later in his journey, Dante encounters Beatrice, the woman he fell in love with years ago. Having come down from heaven to purgatory to guide him along his journey, she berates him for failing in his love for her. Like Francesca and Paolo, Dante had long held a romantic view of the beloved. Before the *Divine Comedy*, Dante wrote books extolling passion. His romanticism prevented him from comprehending what his love for Beatrice had been trying to tell him. Francesca rightly perceives Dante's craving to speak with her: he is completely mesmerized by the lovers' tale of forbidden desire. Only as Dante writes and creates this new story of himself—a view of love from the perspective of one who, through the love of God, has escaped from the hell of the passions—can he liberate himself from his tendency to indulge his fancy. At this point in his journey, he requires assistance to escape this vortex of lust. He is aided by Virgil, who well understands the dangers of the passions. Dante is so overwhelmed by his heartfelt compassion for Francesca's plight (which is, at this juncture of his journey, identical to his personal romantic torment) that he swoons. He becomes like a dead body, entirely at the mercy of external forces. Virgil must carry him away from Francesca, Paolo, and all the rest of those who are in the grip of romanticized lust.

Gluttony: Evil as the Perversion of Natural Desire

Upon awakening, Dante finds himself in a quagmire of mud and endless rain. Hail and tainted rain mix with snow and descend upon the gluttonous "emptinesses" who reside in this shadowy realm.[14] The triple-throated monster Cerberus, who barks like a dog, uses his talons to shred the gluttons, who desperately turn this way and that in a vain attempt to avoid him. In order to speak with these poor souls, Virgil must silence this repellent canine. He does so by picking up huge clods of earth and throwing these down Cerberus's voracious gullets.[15]

The sin of gluttony brings into stark relief the difference between Dante's notion of sinful evil and Aristotelian vice. The Aristotelian glutton is one who habitually eats unhealthily, either consuming too much or eating the wrong mix of meats, breads, and vegetables. If we want to avoid the vice of intemperance, we must force ourselves not to eat vast amounts of chocolate cake and potato chips. By compelling ourselves to adhere to what our body and society tell us is a healthy diet, we can choose to become what Aristotle terms "continent."[16] Continence approximates virtue, resembling it in external appearance. Although the continent still have cravings for unhealthy food, they have overcome these longings sufficiently to be able to do the right thing, eating as they should. Through self-discipline, what starts out as continence converts to the virtue of genuine temperance. As we acquire the settled virtue of temperance, we lose the desire to eat what we should not and contentedly eat as we should, free from any bothersome cravings.

For Dante, the sin of gluttony does not involve eating the wrong quality or quantity of food. His focus is not on the object of desire but on the quality of the appetite. We become sinfully gluttonous when we pervert the natural desire for food and cease to be conscious of what we are eating. Not thinking about what human beings need for satisfaction, we sever the natural connection between food and nutrition. No longer are we eating to satisfy our hunger. Instead, we consume in a fruitless effort to fill the vast psychic emptiness that can be filled only when we find our place in the universe. Our consumption becomes limitless.

The ethical problem is not that the gluttons in hell fail to bring their behavior into line with the norms of healthy eating. The problem is instead that they, like the lustful, do not see things in terms of the structure of the universe. We become gluttonous when we do not perceive how the object we desire either sustains or destroys our humanity. In a proper and harmonious state of affairs, our appetites are regulated by the divine order of the universe. In this harmonious state, we desire only what we truly need to fully realize our humanity; the object we pursue perfectly suits our ordered appetite. Desire becomes sinful when we fail to understand our appetite as part of this larger whole. Instead of using our reason to find our place in the universe, we wind up trying to become the universe. In our gluttony, we neither perceive nor think about the particular features of different things. We become consumers gorging ourselves on undifferentiated stuff. Like the dog Cerberus, we seek (albeit unconsciously) to wolf down the world itself.

Living in a world of undistinguished matter, the glutton is in danger of losing his or her human form. It takes a while before Dante realizes that he and Virgil are treading on the gluttons. The gluttons are the mud in which they lie. The gluttons' life-world is one big morass, obliterating the distinction between what is them and what is not them. Only after one sinner hauls himself out of the mud and states his name does Dante know him as one who was once a man. I say "once a man" because Ciacco is in danger of ceasing to be such. His name "Ciacco," "pig" in Italian, says it all. When our reason is not directed toward discovering the structure of the universe, we turn into pigs, consuming whatever is before us. Ciacco is so mired in endless consumption that he can barely emerge from the ooze, prompting Dante to empathize with his "heavy misery."[17]

Since the desire to consume, and thereby become, the world is more perverse and deluded than simple lust, the gluttons are more deformed and suffer more than Francesca and Paolo. Although the lustful mistake an image of a person for the beloved, they are engaged with another person. As Dante learns from Beatrice, we are drawn toward what is lastingly good through our love for our fellow human beings. Having sex with a fellow human being is an attempt to achieve that harmony and unity with the universe; in that respect, intercourse is an entirely natural and necessary dimension of our existence. Lust is a sin not because sex is unnatural, but because the lustful mistake an image produced by desire (a body) for the true object of love (satisfying goodness and oneness with the universe). Eating, like sexual union, is both natural and necessary. Affection and food are what the ancients described as "goods in them-selves." Goods in themselves derive their value because they are necessary to human life. If anything qualifies as good (as an appropriate object of desire), food and sex do. As long as we eat to provide nutrients for our bodies so that our soul may live, we commit no sin and in no way injure ourselves. But, when we gluttonously use food as a substitute for the experience of satisfying love, we pervert this natural human desire for nutrition. Food ceases to be a source of nutrition. Anything that can be consumed becomes food for us. Just as the lustful lover embraces an image of a person, so the glutton consumes a simulacrum of food. Since formless matter (the mud into which the gluttons are sinking) is further removed from satisfying food than the image of a person is from a real person, lust retains more of the form of the correct object than gluttony. Trying to join with the universe is closer to love than trying to consume the universe. Lust, therefore, perverts or frustrates desire to a lesser degree than gluttony does, and so is less injurious.

To put the point in Dante's poetic terms: the lustful Francesca and Paolo are human beings desperately searching for human love. They retain some sense that they need love in order to be fulfilled as human beings. The gluttonous Ciacco does not understand that he needs the love of God and of his fellow human beings, who are children of the universal God. He tries to find happiness in material stuff, which cannot reciprocate love. Ciacco thereby condemns himself to wallow with other pigs in a mud that is slowly swallowing them.

Having recognized Ciacco as a fellow Florentine, Dante wants to know which political party—Guelph or Ghibelline—will triumph. He grills Ciacco about the fate of several politicians whom Dante character-izes as men of good reason who always acted with the best of intentions.[18] Dante reveals himself to be a glutton for information and greedily gobbles up whatever tidbits Ciacco throws his way. Yet political victories have little to do with personal salvation. What does it matter who is winning office and who losing if we fail to do the soul work needed to realize our individual humanity? The fact that every one of Dante's admirable politicians is in hell only serves to show that Dante the journeyer does not yet grasp what good reason truly is. He mistakes political speculation for salvific understanding. Small wonder that Virgil admonishes Dante to "go back to your science."[19] Only if we are guided by reason in the service of objective necessity can we discern the meaning and significance of human behavior and events, and avoid becoming gluttons for earthly detritus that will never satisfy us.

Hoarding and Spending Wantonly: Evil as Wanting to Want

Hoarders and spendthrifts occupy the next circle of hell. These sinners are like

> waves of Charybdis, each crashing apart /Against the one it rushes to meet, here gather/People who hurry forward till they must meet and dance their round . . . Each pushes a weight against his chest, and howls/At his opponent each time that they clash:/"Why do you squander?" and "why do you hoard?" Each wheels/To roll his weight back round again: they rush/Toward the circle's opposite point, collide/Painfully once more, and curse each other afresh.[20]

Dante treats the hoarders and spendthrifts as interchangeable because they represent two sides of the same coin. Both have divorced their desire from natural needs, such as the need for love or food. They spend their whole lives thinking about money—how to get it or how to spend it. They do not want the money for anything in particular. Getting and spending are ways of exercising their desire and feeling alive. They want in order to want more. Given that the precise object of desire is irrelevant, reason plays no role in determining their behavior. The object desired functions merely as a weight or ballast to set these sinners in motion, driving them forward until they collide and then return, only to rush toward each other again.

This circle of sinners seamlessly segues into the next: the realm of the sullen and the wrathful. These two types of sinners dwell in a marsh of purple-black water. Overcome with anger, the wrathful spend their lives throwing themselves at their equally enraged compatriots. Meanwhile, the grim and sullen, immersed under water, cause the surface to bubble with their sighs and moans about their dismal condition. The wrathful and sullen rightly occupy the same region as the hoarders and spendthrifts. The dynamics of appetite are the same in both cases:

> [A]s the collisions between hoarders and spendthrifts embody fruitless energy directed at the material world, a fruitless, stagnant energy characterizes what might be thought of as the emotional stinginess of the sullen and the emotional wastefulness of the wrathful.[21]

Although the wrathful and sullen may injure other people, any such injury is incidental to their desire:

> Though the wrathful commit injury, it is not the end . . . of their action. . . . The end is anger in itself, as if it were actually pleasant. Anger is not naturally a pleasant emotion . . . it is revenge that is pleasant to a person angry in a natural way. But the wrathful find anger pleasant in itself. Anger is properly a response to a perceived prior injury. The wrathful apparently can be angry almost spontaneously.[22]

Since the wrathful enjoy becoming angry, they will use any object as a pretext for doing so. The sullen similarly find that any object will suffice to trigger their brooding.

Once the specific character of the object of desire ceases to matter, anything can become an object of desire. Hoarders and spendthrifts make money their object. Money, however, has no value apart from its relationship to particular desirable objects. Therefore, the sin in this case consists of treating what is not a good in itself (money) as if it were such. Only someone who is profoundly alienated from the order of the universe would pursue money for its own sake. The wrathful and sullen reside even deeper in hell because they go a step further. Their desire has no material object whatsoever. They convert desire itself (or, more precisely, the driving energy of desire) into the object of desire. The wrathful delight in venting the rage arising from their frustration; the sullen take a perverse pleasure in not expressing their dissatisfaction and in not enjoying life.

Either way, these sinners divorce themselves from the true satisfaction that comes only from pursuing objects capable of satiating desire.

Lessons about Evil from the Upper Circles of Hell

Before continuing with Dante to the lowest regions of hell, let us pause and consider what we have learned about evil from the sinners in the upper levels. All these sinners have injured themselves in the past and continue to do so. Evil consists of obsessive, self-inflicted suffering. Whenever we allow ourselves to be controlled by our passions and imagination, we doom ourselves to unhappiness. In order to ascertain which objects are most worthy of pursuit, we must use our reason. Yet, when we are in the grip of a great passion, we are, by definition, not thinking. The sinners in the upper region of hell can barely speak, much less advance, or follow, an argument. The hoarders and spendthrifts spend their time leveling accusations against each other. The sullen "gargle from the craw, unable to speak whole words."[23] The wrathful cannot speak at all.

The objects these sinners pursue are better understood as imaginative projects, things possessing no objective features. What is desired merely reflects the perverse quality of the sinners' desire. Francesca's Paolo is silent because he has no independent existence: he is her projection of what a romantic lover should be. The spendthrifts and hoarders clutch and push heavy weights in front of them as they rush to collide with each other. These weights are oppressively heavy because these sinners' desire to get and spend crushes every other desire or potential. Sin or projective desire is especially destructive of our ability to love. The Francescas and Ciaccos of this world do not perceive other people as fellow participants in a universe ordered and held together by divine love. Consumed by passion, they experience others as obstacles to their happiness. They blame peers and family members for their self-caused suffering, and this transferred hostility prevents them from loving.

Some readers of the *Inferno* have observed that the punishment of the sinners fits their sins. But this formulation does not get Dante's insight quite right. *We speak more accurately if we say that our lives are our rewards or punishments.* Remember that some sinners whom Dante encounters in hell are still moving about Florence. Because their sin removes them from reality and love and causes them suffering, they are dead to life. God does not inflict punishment upon the sinner. As we unfold our lives, we reap what we sow. In that respect, the punishments depicted in hell are entirely just: insofar as the life we live is our punishment or reward, we are rendered exactly what is our due. In reenacting the same sin, we perfect the sin with every repetition, making the torment ever more a part of our lives. Since our obsessive sinning is endless, the punishment we live is eternally and perfectly just.[24]

Dante's portrayal of sin is consistent with the other manifestations of evil we have considered. In all the cases we have examined, evil has turned out to be self-inflicted suffering. In sinning, we unwittingly trap ourselves in unhappy lives from which we cannot escape. We become obsessive, not because we are malicious but because we mistake our projections for real objects. When we do not know what it means to be a human being, what we pursue as good turns out not to be lastingly satisfying. On this point, Dante agrees with Highsmith, Stevenson, Mann, and James. Dante, however, takes us still deeper into the nature of evil by enabling us to understand why there are degrees of evil and why evil borders on being motiveless.

A motive is always more than a driving engine. A motive is a cognitive context or structure that enables both the agent and those who observe and judge this agent to make sense of the world.[25] A motive is a principle of interpretation. This principle may be more or less adequate, but, in every case, a motive links the person with a particular object. Since our motives grow out of universal human needs, and since these needs are many, we typically have many motives. When we cannot link a person's behavior to one of these human needs, we find it difficult to interpret that behavior. The action strikes us as bizarre and perhaps unfathomable. Dante's sinners are difficult to comprehend because they are so monomaniacal: they have only one need—a need to consummate a forbidden love, a need to consume, a need to need. The more maniacal they are—the less their actions grow out of universal, objective, and natural human needs—the more opaque their sin. Since we know what it feels like to be stung by Eros and overcome by the natural desire to be with the one whom we think we love, we readily understand Francesca's obsession. Interpreting the movement of the spendthrifts and hoarders and ascertaining how they are akin to the wrathful and sullen is more difficult.

Taking pleasure in the pursuit of something that has no value in and of itself (money), or reveling in the energy of desire itself, is even further removed from the structure of universal needs. These sins seem less motivated and more mad. We might say, therefore, that evil is the obliteration of motive.

Does it follow that the madness of sinning diminishes our responsibility for the evil we bring upon ourselves? Midgley, for example, contends that to speak of evil as madness is to excuse it. Yet she herself later refers to Iago's wickedness as "craziness."[26] How we answer the question of responsibility depends on how we understand the notion. The lives of sinners are quintessentially *their* lives. Their existence is their punishment. No sinner escapes the consequences of what he or she has done. Therefore, if we define a responsible agent as someone who has caused a particular act and should suffer the consequences of this act, then all sinners are responsible for their acts, and all are punished in a perfectly just fashion.

In another sense, though, evil does diminish responsibility. The notion of rendering a response or giving an account is implicit in the ideas of responsibility and of accountability. Those who are in hell hate their plight. Like Tom Ripley and Hendrik Höfgen, they are consumed with self-pity. Although they wish their torments to cease, they have no idea of how to alter their lives. To escape from hell they would have to be able to pursue a different object of desire. Doing that would require that they enter a world of competing motives and devote themselves to evaluating the relative merits of different objects. Obsessed evildoers who have lost the good of intellect cannot perform this evaluation. They cannot provide an account of why they do what they do, and they suffer accordingly. That is why, when victims confront their victimizers and ask why the victimizer acted as he or she did, the answer is always a variant of "I do not know." If Dante is correct about the nature of evil, this nonresponse is not disingenuous. Victimizers truly do not comprehend the meaning of their behavior. The more evil the sin, the more motiveless the victimizer's behavior and the less he or she can say about it. The sinner is like Iago, who, when Othello demands to know why Iago has ensnared his soul and body, retorts: "Demand me nothing; what you know, you know/From this time forth I never will speak word."[27] So, too, the glutton Ciacco urges Dante to remember him to those who are in "the human world" and then says, "Now, I respond and speak no more," falling back into the mire, never to wake again.[28]

So far I have been alluding to sinning or evil behavior. (I do not say "action" because sin destroys action.) But are the sinners themselves evil? Or should we speak of the sinner as one whose suffering is evil but who is not an evil person? If evil is identical to self-delusion, and if we are all deluded some of the time, is it possible to avoid doing evil unto ourselves and causing others to suffer? Dante's portrayal raises other questions: What are we to make of the fact that, although the sinners cannot give an accurate report of their sinning, Dante the poet presents himself as providing one? In what sense is his poetic account truthful? What role does his portrayal of his encounter with evil play in liberating him from it? To answer these questions, we, like Dante himself, must descend deeper into hell. If sin has its own hierarchical logic, we cannot hope to comprehend it until we have journeyed through the whole of hell and seen the entire structure of evil.

The Lower Region of Hell: Sins of Malice

Pandering and Seduction: Evil as the Loss of Individuality

Dante and Virgil cross over the marsh of rage toward a red city ablaze with fire and emitting fetid fumes. As they cross, a man covered in filth appears out of the bog to attack their boat. In the earlier circles, the two men were never assaulted. This attack signals that they are moving into the presence of a new manifestation of evil. When Dante wonders why some sinners are deeper in hell than others, Virgil cites Aristotle's *Nicomachean Ethics*:

> Don't you recall/A passage in your *Ethics*, the words that treat/Three dispositions counter to Heaven's will: incontinence, malice, insane brutality?/And how incontinence is less distasteful/To God and earns less blame/Think carefully . . . you'll see/Clearly why [those in the prior circles] are apart from the wicked here,/And why His vengeance smites them with less wrath.[29]

As we have seen, the sinners of the upper circles are guilty of incontinent concupiscence, understood as their failure to use reason to constrain their passion for sex, food, or money. Dante and Virgil have now entered the realm of the malicious. These sinners, unlike the concupiscent, do not fail to use reason. On the contrary, they reduce reason to cunning. Their cunning is extremely active, operating in ways that destroy the commonweal.

The destruction occurs through violence or fraud. Dante's journey through hell teaches him that the fraudulent are more damned than the violent. Animals can be violent. But "fraud is found/In humankind as its peculiar vice,/It angers God more: so the fraudulent/Are lower, and suffer more unhappiness."[30] Fraud takes two forms. We may defraud someone who has trusted us or someone to whom we are not especially close. Dante's hell contains both types of sinners. Those who are guilty of defrauding people with whom they have no special trusting relationship (e.g., hypocrites, flatterers, sorcerers, thieves, simoniacs, seducers, procurers, and barrators) undermine the "bonds of love that nature makes."[31] As we shall see, their behavior potentially harms other people as well as themselves. Those who sin against those who have trusted and benefited them are even worse off. They betray the special trust created by love and so reside at the center of hell.

The sins of fraud are especially intriguing. In particular, I want to consider why Dante judges fraudulent behavior to be more evil than violent deeds. Most moderns would view assault and murder as more heinous than flattery. Western legal systems certainly take this view of the matter. Yet Dante insists that fraud is the worse sin. To grasp why, we need to see how reason and desire function in each successive group of defrauders. I begin with the panderers and seducers, who occupy the first circle of Malebolge, the region of concentric pits containing the fraudulent.

The panderers prostitute others for gain or for favor, while the seducers take their pleasure with their victims and then abandon them. Both move forever in a circle, traveling *en masse*, lashed by demons with scourges. The only difference is that one group moves in a clockwise direction, the other, counter-clockwise. Both groups are condemned to traverse the same ground repeatedly. What is striking about these sinners is that they crowd together, moving as a kind of mass organism. This loss of individuality stems from the panderers' and seducers' abuse of reason. When we pander or seduce, we devote our reason to one end—getting others to trust us so that we can obtain whatever we think we need. We instrumentalize reason, reducing it to cunning. Obsessed with manipulating the truth, we never stop to consider whether we have erred in our approach to life. We are utterly lacking in insight, and insight is what individuates and distinguishes us.

To have an insight is to have truth present itself. The truth always makes itself known to a person in the way that he or she finds most meaningful. As we come to comprehend the world, we draw upon our unique experiences. We may, like Dante, feel compelled to forge a language to enable us to express these insights. Seduction and flattery destroy distinctive, meaningful language by ripping it from its moorings in the truth. The motto of panderers and seducers is "we can convert 'no' to 'yes'."[32] We become panderers and seducers whenever we proclaim, as some businesspeople do, "we will do whatever it takes to increase profits." Using euphemisms, we hide from ourselves what we are doing. Firing people becomes "right-sizing." Closing a plant is characterized as a "change in product line." We use our cunning to lie about our deceit and the untoward effects we are having upon other people.

Unchecked by any second thoughts or glimmers of insight, our drive to succeed becomes so compelling that we lose control of our lives. We respond only to this inner drive, which Dante portrays as a demon whipping panderers and seducers from behind. The image of a demon is appropriate. In selling out for the sake of the deal, we relinquish our judgment to a kind of inhuman force. We doom ourselves to be swept along with the flow when we live to minister to or to manipulate other people's desires. Like the Bolognese flatterer Venedico Caccianemico whom Dante recognizes and accosts, we rationalize our dealings by claiming that others are exactly like us.[33] Unable to defend our actions publicly, we attempt to dissolve into the crowd. It takes a Dante or a Virgil to break into the relentlessly revolving mass, to single out a particular soul for questioning, and to put a face and name to some of the many who pass under his eyes.

To seducers and panderers, nothing appears to be forbidden, not even trafficking in human flesh. Although talk of pandering sounds a bit old-fashioned, the term still has relevance. In order to win business, local Houston businessmen invite Japanese executives to ogle women at topless dance clubs. In Asia, children are prostituted and provided to clients as part of the closing of a deal. Violence against people, in all its forms, is a tool of the trade for the panderer or seducer. Here, then, we have the first clue as to why fraud might be deemed to be more evil than eruptions of violence. The hoarders and spendthrifts clash with each other, but their conflict is a side effect of their pursuit of money. The sullen and wrathful take pleasure in getting angry, but they do not use anger to achieve their aims. Upon entering Malebolge, Dante meets the chronically irascible, who are surrounded by flames and boiling waters and who explode in anger whenever their goals are frustrated. Since these sinners have mentally endorsed rage as a valid response to suffering, they are more violent and evil than the hoarders, spendthrifts, sullen, or wrathful who fall into violence. But none of these sinners is as violent as the fraudulent. The fraudulent rationalize their violence and place it at the disposal of their cunning. In doing so, they embrace violence as a matter of policy Such violence qualifies as demonic. Unlike revenge, this violence is not a response to a perceived slight or injustice. Nor is it an effect of frustrated desire. The violence of the fraudulent is strategic in nature. The panderers and seducers, like Hendrik Höfgen, have unconsciously struck a Mephistophelean bargain. For them, casual violence functions as another instrument for accomplishing a goal.

Violence becomes an intrinsic part of the lives of those who will do whatever it takes to achieve a goal. As part of this demonic bargain, we happily pander to each other's illusion that the crowd will provide us with cover. We seducers are thereby unwittingly seduced. Our narrow focus on succeeding whatever the cost blinds us to other possibilities for action. As we cease to make independent judgments and to evaluate all our options, we become less able to achieve any lasting satisfaction while simultaneously feeling ever more driven. All we think about is who is ahead of us in the race to get ahead. Like the panderers and seducers in Dante's hell, who stare at the backs of those who precede them, our gaze is fixed on those men and women who seem to be winning. We do not realize that no one wins in this demonic game of mutual seduction. Our dealing truly is a wheeling as we travel in a circle, neurotically repeating the same losing strategy we have pursued for years.

Flattery: Evil as Living the Lie

The flatterers occupy the next circle of fraud. Like the other shades in hell, the flatterers do not converse with each other. They scream and howl as they continually strike or scratch themselves. They are utterly befouled, wallowing in human excrement. Each time they touch themselves, they dirty themselves further. The air in this trench stinks because, when the flatterers gibber, they exhale foul odors.[34]

Dante's portrayal of the sin of flattery is a mixture of the commonplace and the brilliant. Our political and business leaders routinely complain that they cannot lead effectively because they are surrounded by aides, employees, and board members who are afraid to say anything displeasing. We recognize that flatterers tell us only "the crap" we want to hear and mislead us. Listening to flatterers causes our enterprises and projects to go awry. What is less obvious—and what Dante makes clear—is the way in which prostituted speech entraps the speaker. Flatterers condemn themselves to live with falsehood. Those whom we have deceived with honeyed words wish to hear more of the same each time they meet with us. Sycophants soon find themselves trapped by the false image of themselves that they have constructed. The sinners in this circle of hell frantically touch themselves in a vain effort to be assured of their real existence. Seducers and panderers tell lies; but flatterers are lies.

Evil diminishes our humanity by distancing us from reality and truth. Like seducers and panderers, flatterers move as a group, lacking any individuality. Yet flatterers are more divorced from reality than panderers. Panderers and seducers remain aware of the facts as they cunningly maneuver their way around obstacles. Flatterers, however, speak as if there were no obstacles whatsoever, shying away from mentioning bad news or unpleasant facts. What is objectively true has ceased to matter to these sinners. Truth-seekers soon learn to avoid those of us who are obsequious. Only fellow sycophants keep us company, because our lies are their natural element. We cannot trust these companions to tell us the truth, and we probably would not know the truth even if they spoke it. Once we give into the temptation to be famous—to have our name on everybody's lips—we make our perceptions dependent on the subjective opinion of liars.

Flattery, seduction, and pandering are sins of malice not because the sinner is intentionally cruel but because he or she has become, as a matter of policy, completely indifferent to the needs, feelings, or even existence of other human beings (except insofar as they advance the sinner's career). The flatterer's cleverness is devoted to creating and maintaining an apparently pleasant illusion. This sin, like pandering and seduction, threatens the entire political system. These sinners insinuate themselves into the halls of power, where they hope their lies will be richly rewarded. Sins of malice can wreak more havoc than an incontinent sin such as gluttony. A glutton will not destroy the community by overeating. Malicious sins can undermine political regimes by causing leaders to lose their focus on the common good and the people they are supposed to be serving. Instead of building a culture with arts, education, and religion designed to help citizens understand what they should be desiring, malicious sinners dedicate their lives to devising and promulgating lies capable of entrapping innocents. By destroying the natural bonds of trust among citizens and their belief in the value and worth of their community and its regime, those in Malebolge perpetuate an unjust fraud on the commonwealth. At the same time, their callous neglect of their fellow citizens renders them less human.

Divining: Evil as Distraction from the Present

The next group of sinners—the diviners, who presume to know and to foretell the future—move at a liturgical pace, weeping but mute. Although they proceed forward, their bodies are grotesquely distorted. Their heads are turned completely backwards, so they are unable to see where they are moving.[35] Their reliance on cunning has made them purposeless. What is more, they seek to draw the rest of us into their realm of useless speculation.

Diviners abound in the modern world. We are surrounded by what Gore Vidal has called the "chattering classes"—journalists, corporate strategists, and economic forecasters who predict doom and gloom and who advise us how to forestall disaster. Each of us is something of a diviner. We experience anxiety as we worry about whether we will keep our jobs under the new CEO or whether the stock market will rise at a rate sufficient to fund a comfortable retirement. Our anxiety is our punishment. When we become obsessed about foretelling future events, we cease to attend to the life we are creating for ourselves in the present. By agonizing about what's in store and refusing to let the day be sufficient unto itself, we ignore the true task at hand—the need to discover our true joy. Eager to avoid future disasters, we misunderstand the human meaning of suffering. Suffering is not necessarily bad. It can make us pay attention to what we are doing and can lead us to explore why we are doing these things that cause us such pain. However, in order to engage in this journey of self-exploration, we must delve into the nature of suffering. When we presume to know or to divine that some consequences or events are bad, and dare to prophesy which awful outcomes will come to pass, we become, in Dante's terms, "impious" and "mute" about the things that matter most.[36] We treat events themselves as evil and neglect to evaluate our representations of these events. In so doing, we defraud ourselves of meaning in the here and now.

Pandering harms us because we adopt too narrow a focus, losing ourselves in our frantic dealings and efforts to be successful. Flattering others makes it hard for us to get trustworthy information about the world and ourselves. Divining places us at a still greater remove from reality. When we devote all our thinking to figuring out what will happen to us in the future, we completely overlook what we are doing to ourselves in the present and thereby make it impossible for us to progress toward the truth about the best way to live.

LESSONS ABOUT EVIL FROM THE LOWER CIRCLES OF HELL

Additional circles contain those who have committed sins of malice—the simoniacs, thieves, and barrators, to name a few. But we have witnessed enough to know that lower hell continues and extends the pattern we saw in the circles of upper hell. In every case, evil is self-inflicted injury, a distortion of our humanity. The perversion is more extensive in the lower circles. Here the malicious not only act upon corrupt appetites, but also pervert their reason by making it serve these appetites in cunning ways. This dual perversion deprives the sinners of the contact with reality that they need in order to realize fully their individuality. The malicious sinners blend into a mass organism. The hypocrites hide behind their cloaks, trying to fade into anonymity. In the circle of the falsifiers, the sinners must lean upon each other for support. The thieves are so deprived of individual substance that they continually morph into each other.[37] In addition to costing us our individuality, malicious sinning diminishes our power of action. While Francesca and Paulo cannot initiate actions, they can at least move with the wind. The sinners of lower hell are trapped in pitch or collapsed into heaps of flesh.

   This pattern of increasing passivity is clear. What is not so obvious is that, at each level of hell, Dante succumbs to the sin and suffering he is witnessing. Having recognized a flatterer as a fellow Florentine, Dante is so bewitched by the man's appearance and words that he feels he must address him. He toadies up to the flatterer in the hope that the sinner will return the favor by acknowledging Dante's fame. When he sees the lustful Francesca, he experiences a great desire to have her by his side and to share in her romantic story of love. In the marsh of the wrathful, Dante vents his spleen, raging against his old enemy Filippo Argenti. Amid the gluttons, he feels the weight of their misery and gets bogged down in his fruitless effort to get and digest more information from one of the sinners. When he weeps over the torments of the twisted diviners, he, too, assumes a misshapen form. Dante keeps trying to turn around to gaze back on the equally distorted diviners until Virgil draws him onward by reminding him of the passing hours and the limited time allotted to each of us to discover who we are and what is truly worth knowing: the "way of wisdom for men is wholly separate from that of spells and incantations and prognostications which men have trusted in their ignorance and practiced in their guile . . . it is to be found only in the discipline of reason and conscience."[38]

   What does Dante's reenactment of these sins tell us about the nature of evil? It shows, first, how easily we slip into sin, with little awareness that we are doing so. We more readily discern the sins of other people than our own shortcomings. Yet, we share in the appetites and passions of those whom we deem evil. Our shared humanity is what enables us to perceive and assess the way in which sin diminishes a person's humanity. If we did not have these things in common, we would view these inhabitants of hell as bizarre, not as sinful. Given this commonality, we should be careful when we judge lest we be judged. That caution does not entail that we should never judge. Only if we correctly assess sin can we take steps to alter our behavior. However, we should proceed with compassion. As the words over hell remind us, all of these sinners, and hell itself, were created in eternal love.[39] As he progresses, Dante learns that true happiness consists in loving as God loves—namely, loving every part of the universe as an element of the whole. It would seem to follow that we must love even the lustful, gluttonous, flatterers, hypocrites, and all the rest insofar as their sins point the way to salvation, disclosing the workings of divine justice and revealing the actions we must avoid if we are to escape the eternal torment of sinning.

Another point can be made: although Dante behaves like the sinners, he is not irredeemable. Every time Dante is in danger of getting stuck in sin, Virgil moves him along. Often Virgil helps by disclosing the underlying reason for the spectacle Dante is witnessing. Sometimes, though, he commands Dante to follow. At some junctures, he physically carries Dante to the next circle. Always, however, the two men advance because of Dante's beloved Beatrice. It was she who, appealing to the Virgin Mary, intervened to save Dante when he found himself lost in a dark wood, and she who sent Virgil as his guide. When Dante despairs, Virgil urges him forward by holding out the promise that Dante will soon see his beloved Beatrice. Dante can progress because he retains the ability to love and be loved. *The Inferno* intimates that we are saved from evil—the loss of our humanity—through love. Dante's message is not merely that we should love others. We ourselves are in need of being loved. The human love of a particular person will rescue us if this love imitates divine love, the love that maintains the harmonious order of the entire universe. Beatrice invites Dante to see himself in relation to the structure of the whole. Dante overcomes his despair by accepting that invitation.

Loving means ordering our souls in accordance with the structure of the cosmos. Evil or sin is hateful for it disorders our being in one of two ways. We destroy our inner harmony and compromise the peace of our community either (1) by giving primacy to our passions, which should be subordinate to reason, or (2) by devising and rationalizing wiles that divorce us and our fellow citizens from the truth and from divine love. Those who love us as Beatrice loves Dante teach us to help ourselves; they encourage us to strengthen our reasoning, moderate our passions, and to appreciate the beautiful and liberating power of God, where God is understood to be what causes, sustains, and ultimately is the harmonious whole. That is why the worst form of evil is betrayal—betrayal of our loving benefactors—our friends, our country, and our God.

Betrayal: The Utmost Evil

Having passed through the different circles of fraud, Virgil and Dante arrive at the ninth and final circle of hell, the deep pit of betrayal.

Although all the frauds involve breach of trust, betrayal constitutes a quantum leap. The betrayer turns on those who have trusted and aided him or her in the past. Betrayers destroy family and country, and renounce even God. To descend into this lowest pit, Dante and Virgil need the help of Antaeus, one of the giants whose feet extend to the bottom of hell and whose torso towers above the pit. They cannot descend on their own. For sinners enter this pit only through betrayal, and Virgil and Dante have not broken trust with each other or with their benefactors.

The giants, however, have committed the sin of betrayal, believing themselves the equals of gods. Ephialtes, Briareus, Nimrod, Typhon, Tityus—all fought with, and sought to supplant, the divine. Now they are in chains, unable to move. Having mistakenly conceived of themselves as divine, they cannot develop any of their human powers. Bereft of self-awareness, they have enslaved themselves. Virgil describes the giant Nimrod as stupid, because Nimrod speaks a language no human being can interpret.[40] The language of those who have mistaken the human for the divine is a kind of gibberish. For such people, there exists no world apart from their grandiose sense of themselves. To make human sense, language must refer to the human experience. When we equate ourselves with the divine, we cease to be humanly intelligible. Like these giants, we make ourselves dumb.

Only the giant Antaeus, who never went so far as to mount an attack on the divine, retains any power of movement. Antaeus derived his power from his connection with the earth. As long as he stayed grounded on the earth, he could not be defeated. But Antaeus did not understand the limited quality of his power. Heracles was able to overthrow him by lifting him up and severing his contact with the earth. Still, that prior connection has served to moderate his claims to be divine and preserved for him a modicum of movement. By appealing to Antaeus's sense of his greatness— Virgil suggests that Antaeus's presence on the battlefield would have enabled Hannibal's troops to win the war, and he promises that Dante will rebuild this giant's fame on earth—Virgil persuades Antaeus to pick him and Dante up and to set them down in the center of hell.

The innermost circle of hell is the darkest, coldest, and most constricted of all the circles. As we would expect, these sinners' ability to initiate action is hugely circumscribed. The lustful in upper hell may be buffeted this way and that but they can passively surf the wind.

The falsifiers in the previous Malebolgean circle "fall like rain" into hell, yet they retain enough humanity to be distinct from inanimate elements.[41] Although they descend like rain, they are not identical to precipitation. The betrayers, by contrast, are immobile elements, frozen into a lake created by their tears of self-pity. Here we see evil in its most extreme form: if evil is the self-inflicted diminution of our humanity, the betrayers are the most inhuman. Dante compares these sinners to a series of animals. It would have been better for them to have been born as sheep or goats than to have lived these barely human lives.[42] All the betrayers share several features. Although their bodies may still be moving on the surface of the earth, they are spiritually dead. Their hatred of others and of the world has utterly immobilized them. We find those whose heads are above the ice insisting that they are better than everyone else. One attacks Dante for being inept; another disdains to tell Dante his name. When a fellow betrayer reveals the disdainful man to be Bocca, Bocca retaliates by shouting the names of all who are frozen alongside him. Bocca betrays them to Dante because he thinks that, if he himself is to live in infamy, so should these others. These betrayers are so full of bestial hatred that they wish to see even their relatives join them in hell.[43]

These sinners are the most deluded. They are so at one with their sin that they are completely unaware that they have sinned. Since they implicitly conceive of themselves as giants who are better than everyone else, including their victims, they minimize the wrong they have done. Like Tom Ripley and Hendrik Höfgen, they are always more sinned against than sinning. Like the falsifiers in the preceding circle, they misrepresent their deeds. But they go a step further. Not content with falsifying their past, they ask others to ratify, and become party to, their delusion. Count Ugolino tells his story so that Dante will know how the Archbishop Ruggieri, on whose head Ugolino is gnawing, horribly wronged and betrayed the count. Unable to entertain the possibility that he, too, may have committed an injustice, Ugolino wants Dante to affirm his innocence.

We betray ourselves, others, and divine love when our resentments so eat at us that we think of nothing apart from ways to inflict our pain on those we deem enemies. We view others as objects with no value other than their ability to satisfy our desire to fill the terrible void within. For Ugolino, Ruggieri is nothing but the bone he eternally and mechanically chews in a futile attempt to assuage his hunger for revenge. This bone is Ugolino's world, and he would make it ours as well.

If we are not careful, we fall into Ugolino's trap. Generations of readers have shared Dante's horror when they hear how Ruggieri locked Ugolino and his small children into a tower. Deprived of food, the children soon starved to death. On the seventh day, Ugolino's hunger overcame his grief, and he ate his children. When Dante hears this sad tale, he calls down a curse on Ruggieri's city of Pisa: the whole city should be drowned on account of Ruggieri's sin. In damning the city, Dante elevates himself into God and presumes to mete out divine justice. Dante proposes that thousands of innocents die in a flood because Ruggieri murdered four helpless children. Later Dante opines that the whole city of Genoa should be expunged because of the sin and corruption of Fra Alberigo.[44] Like Ugolino, Dante allows his anger toward another person to become an obsession. Dante forgets that Ruggieri has already received divine justice. Ruggieri is forced to live his sin of betrayal, eternally frozen alongside Count Ugolino in the inner circle of hell.

Utmost evil ensnares us in a second way. The sin so divorces us from truth that we mistake illusion for reality. Most commentators, as well as Dante the traveler, take Ugolino's tale at face value. However, given that the betrayers are still more removed from the truth than the falsifiers, we should suspect the count's story. Although the falsifiers in the previous circle minimize what they have done, they at least concede the fact of their deceit. The counterfeiter Master Adam admits to the charge of having forged currency.[45] Gianni Schicchi pretends to be someone that he is not—he counterfeits a personality—to obtain another's legacy, but Schicchi still knows who he is.[46] The falsifiers of the *Inferno* create images, but at some level they still know the difference between the image and reality. Their clever plots depend upon this knowledge and this difference. If Master Adam did not know the difference between real coins and his fake currency, he could not have made a fortune by substituting the fake coins for the real ones.

By contrast, the betrayers at the center of hell are so deluded that they can no longer distinguish their projections from reality. Unlike those who have become unhinged through disease or trauma, the betrayers' complete identification with rage at their suffering causes them to create a world that justifies their hatred. They rationalize their point of view with no consciousness of having done so. Ugolino relates how he had a dream while imprisoned. He dreams that a man

> appeared as a lord of the hunt: he came/Chasing a wolf and whelps, on that high slope/That blocks the Pisans' view of Lucca. With him/his lean hounds ran, well trained and eager: his troop/Gualandi, Sismondi, Lanfranchi—had been sent/To ride in front of him. With no escape,/After a short run, father and sons, seemed spent:/I saw their flanks, that sharp fangs seemed to tear./I woke before dawn, hearing the complaint/Of my own children, who were with me there,/Whimpering in their sleep and asking for bread.47

Ugolino assumes that the dream must apply to Ruggieri, who had formed alliances with Gualandi, Sismondi, and Lanfranchi. According to Ugolino, Ruggieri is the pursuer, Ugolino the pursued. However, since Ugolino also intrigued with these three men, he, too, has been a pursuer of fathers and sons. The identification of the father and sons with the wolf and whelps is striking. The wolf has fangs as well as the dog, and Ugolino is the one who will soon tear into his children's flesh. Ugolino does not understand that he dreams himself.

Upon awakening and seeing his children, the count reports that his "heart began to dread."48 What did it dread? Not that his children might die. That possibility has been present from the moment he and his offspring were locked into the tower. I would suggest that he has begun to suspect that he will eat their flesh. When the children ask Ugolino what ails him, Ugolino stays silent and gnaws on his hand. This feeding on his flesh lays bare what is in his heart. Then Ugolino hears his children say an extraordinary thing. He claims that they all suddenly rose and said "Father, our pain . . . will lessen if you eat us—you are the one who clothed us in this wretched flesh: we plead for you to be the one who strips it away."49 Those readers who uncritically accept Ugolino's report fall into the trap of helping Ugolino ratify his unconscious, cannibalistic wish. How likely is it that four small children would spontaneously and in complete unison offer themselves up as a living feast for their father? Ugolino is projecting his desire onto his children and then having them give him permission to do what he wants. In effect, he has his children tell him that he will be doing them a favor if he eats them!

After hearing his children's plea, Ugolino sees the image of his face in their visages. The children, like Ruggieri, have ceased to have any independent existence for the count. At the center of hell, our world is identical to our fancy. Image and reality are no longer separate and distinct. Ugolino's children wear his face because he has already committed himself to gnaw on his flesh. On the seventh day of his torment, he becomes the anti-creator: instead of resting in contemplation of the world, he destroys it, consuming those whom he most loved.

That moment marks the end of his humanity. Having reached a point when we can no longer distinguish between world and self, we cannot use our reason to discern the structure of the universe and our human place in it. We become incapable of loving the world and those who share it with us. Ugolino's destiny, like that of the rest of the sinners, is thoroughly just. Finished with his self-justifying speech, the count resumes his mechanical gnawing upon the head of his archenemy Ruggieri. Bereft of human self-consciousness, Ugolino has silenced himself and become a mad dog, a Cerberus; or worse still—an eternal chewing machine.

The Satanic Center of Hell

Finally, we arrive with Dante and Virgil at the center of hell, the expressive essence of evil in its most extreme form—Satan. Dante's Satan is like a gigantic windmill, with one crucial difference. A windmill turns with the wind; this machinery generates its own chilling and killing gusts. Dante's mechanical metaphor is a good one, for the deeper we progress into hell, the more machine-like the sinners become. To sin is to be trapped in behaviors the sinner is condemned to repeat. Betrayal is the most hopeless sin, the most evil because furthest removed from the creative and life-giving universe (God). Betrayal strips the person of his or her soul, traditionally understood as the source of human action. The sinners in this innermost circle are lower than animals, or even plants. They are but pieces of straw frozen in the glassy tears of self-pity.

All betrayers reside in the realm of Satan, the great hater and opposer. By twisting reason into cunning and by convincing themselves that they are in no way to blame for their suffering, they victimize themselves. Their sin of converting themselves into gods and taking it upon themselves to avenge the sins of others is the revolving mechanism that relentlessly produces the suffering they unconsciously embrace. Since all sin is, for Dante, self-redounding, the figure of Satan extends beyond the pit of betrayal, reaching up through the uppermost levels of hell. The betrayers are closest to Satan because they are most akin. Like Satan, they have opposed themselves to the divine, within and without. However, insofar as all sin destroys our power to love, every sin embodies satanic hatred. Satan is present in every region of hell and in every sin.

Dante's Satan has three heads. Virgil informs Dante that one head is chomping on Judas Iscariot, the other two on Brutus and Cassius. As the heads chew, they weep tears that mix with blood to create a ghastly, ruddy foam. Satan masticates in silence: the betrayers of God and country say not a word. For his part, Virgil matter-of-factly reports on the scene and urges Dante to join with him in departing. Having seen the whole, the time has come to leave hell behind. As Barolini perspicuously notes, Dante deliberately presents Satan as a "non-engaging, non-involving, [and] non-present anticlimax."[50] Dante the journeyer may be inclined to stay, but there is nothing more to see. If evil is the destruction of reality; and if the sin of betrayal diminishes our humanity to the vanishing point, then Satan as a positive presence in human life is mere illusion. The center of hell is the absence of love.

At this extremity, words fail Dante. As they must. Words gain their power by truthfully portraying reality. In the region of the betrayers of God, country, and family, there exists no reality. All is illusion. Ugolino hopes to persuade Dante that his self-pity is merited and that Dante should join in his grief. However, Ugolino's account of himself and his past is a lie. To leave the inferno, the realm of grief, we must name the count's tale for what it is—a deceit that will never know it is a lie—and move on in our search for truth.

Lessons about Evil from the Center of Hell

Evil is the self's suffering of the loss of its humanity, a loss that is self-caused. Such suffering is equivalent to the loss of the ability to move forward and to develop our human potential. Evil or sin also can be described as the loss of the ability to love anyone or anything. Evil makes it impossible for us to love even ourselves. In sinning, we destroy the self.

That said, we now can address the question I posed earlier: is the sinner evil, or is only the sin evil? If Dante is right about the nature of evil, this question requires a nuanced answer. In one sense, the sinner is evil. For if sin is evil to one degree or another, we become evil when we reduce ourselves to our sin. But, insofar as evil converts the human person into a machine, and insofar as machines cannot be evil, sinners should not be described as evil. We should be suspicious of the question. Some may pose the question in order to justify their attacks on sinners. Yet, given that sin is irredeemable, little is accomplished by blaming sinners. Blaming may itself prove pernicious. As Stevenson saw, our self-righteous propensity to condemn other people's acts can strengthen sin. We romanticize those whom we take to be purely good (Jekyll) and condemn those we perceive as purely evil (Hyde). We throw society's weight behind the purely good, repressing talents and parts of our human personality not valued in that particular society. We soon start to live vicariously through society's sinners, never acquiring insight into what we need if we are to fulfill our human potential. Dante agrees with Stevenson: salvation never comes through politics, but only through a deepening appreciation of the nature of reality and the dynamic structure of sin.

We should be wary of demonizing others, given that we all are capable of sin. To attack sinners for their sin (as Dante is wont to do on his journey through hell) is to risk becoming sinful. In self-righteously attacking others, we indulge our passion of hatred instead of sharpening our reason by focusing on the nature and structure of the different sins. Passion easily gains ascendancy and destroys our inner harmony and order, impairing our ability to develop insight and to achieve peace. Our ability to see something of ourselves in those who are in hell is, in a way, proof of our humanity. Those who are identified with their sins lack such empathy. The Ugolinos and Ruggieris of this world have gigantic egos. They think that they are super-mortals or gods who never sin and are superior to their fellow human beings. This attitude, which is part and parcel of their sin, makes it impossible for them to empathize with others. The betrayers readily condemn their fellow sinners as evil. Do we want to join them in their paralyzing hatred? If not, we should check our propensity to blame or stigmatize the sinner.

Dante's exploration of evil clarifies as well why suffering per se is not evil. Being harmed by another person is not pleasant, but it does not deform the soul in the way that sinning does. The only victims in hell are self-victimizers. Dante himself was falsely charged with selling offices and betraying public trust, and expelled from Florence. Living apart from his family, friends, and countrymen could not have been easy. As he travels through hell, his bitterness repeatedly erupts. But he is able to leave that obsessive hatred behind as he takes the hand of Virgil, a hand extended in friendship. By heeding the guidance of Virgil, studying philosophy, meditating on the nature of sin, and reflecting on the meaning of the love he felt in and for the person of Beatrice, he progressively acquires a vision of what is truly good and beautiful. Dante, the philosophical poet, finds rest.

His *Inferno* brings together many of the threads examined in the previous chapters. If sin destroys the human capability for action, we can characterize Hendrik Höfgen as a sinner. Having sold his soul to obtain public approval, Hendrik Höfgen loses all discipline and ceases to be able to portray any stage character but Mephisto. He succeeds in that role because he has become Mephisto. Or, as Dante might put it, Hendrik has entered the realm of Satan. Hendrik ends like all betrayers—weeping tears of self-pity and blaming other people for his woes. Tom Ripley has a similar fate. Desperate to escape the emptiness of his life, he settles for an illusion, murdering his friend Dickie Greenleaf and assuming Dickie's identity. The edifice of illusion Tom constructs always verges on crumbling, prompting him to take greater risks to assure himself that he truly is the "talented Mr. Ripley." Tom Ripley thinks he is a giant. He, too, ends up as all sinning giants do—in the center of hell, wailing that the world will not leave him alone.

Along with Henry James and Stevenson, Dante understands that evil has what might be termed an "escalating structure." The logic of human suffering tends toward madness. Recall that James's governess slips into paranoia as she gives her imagination free rein. Each successive encounter with the "evil" figure of Quint or Miss Jessel reflects the imbalance in her person, while laying the ground for yet another, and more dangerous, encounter with horror. As her imagination tries to master the portentous (which has no form and cannot be grasped and controlled), the governess unconsciously transforms herself from the children's tutor into their tormentor. What is striking is that James's narrator does not blame the governess for her behavior. Recall that he describes the governess as "an agreeable woman . . . worthy of any [position] whatever."[51] Dante's Francesca and Ciacco likewise are not bad or vicious people. They are, however, sinners. Both statements can be true, because evil or sinning is not a personal character flaw. Instead, evil is a self-escalating process of destruction of the human person, a process that can enmesh any of us.

Dante and James agree in locating evil in a passionate, cunning imagination unconstrained by reason. Like the sinners at the center of hell, James's governess comes to believe that she is equal to any task, including that of defeating the devil himself (Quint). The story concludes ironically with the governess becoming demonic. Before he dies in her "loving" arms, Miles shouts "you devil!"[52] The governess, like Ugolino, destroys the people she professes to love. Sin always has a kind of infernal irony about it. Having severed our ties with reality by submitting to our imagination, we are drawn inexorably downward. To speak of the "gravity of our sins" is, as Cogan observes, no mere pun. Dante's hell has bridges connecting different sins, because one act of sinning leads to another. Having alienated those who could have helped us and destroyed the faculty of reason that links us to reality, we have nothing left to check our slide into illusion. As this gap between reality and illusion widens, our existence becomes increasingly ironic. Irony is the gap between what truly is and what we perceive it to be. The supreme irony is that the sinners in hell are oblivious to the fact that they lead a perfectly ironic existence.

Again I stress that none of us is immune to this irony. We readily fall into the trap of believing everything the governess says and do not realize until the third or fourth reading that the governess most probably has killed Miles. So, too, we support Dante's self-righteous attacks on sinners as he progresses through hell. We forget that the perspective of Dante the embittered journeyer—Dante the work in progress—is, by definition, partially deluded. The Dante who crafts this poem about sin both is, and is not, the Dante who goes through hell. Dante can write his tale of enlightenment only after he has seen heaven, that is, experienced and understood divine love and the rational structure of the universe. Only then can Dante the poet show the hierarchical structure of sins and create an ironic portrayal of Dante the journeyer. Although Dante the journeyer accepts Ugolino's story as true, Dante the poet creates an encounter between the two men that can be read at many levels. How we read that exchange depends upon how well we understand sin and our ability to delude ourselves.

As I observed in the introduction, the ironic quality of evil makes poetry and literature especially well suited for portraying the truth about evil. Literature can show, as well as tell, sin. By exhibiting his encounter with sinners, Dante invites us to interpret what is happening. Dante the journeyer has one interpretation; we may have another. Each party's account of the depicted evil reflects the state of his or her soul. As it becomes apparent that Dante the angry journeyer is not a completely reliable narrator, we are forced to develop an interpretation of our own. In doing so, we shed some of our passivity and become more actively thoughtful. If all sin or evil is, as Dante thinks, passive, this transformation draws us away from evil and toward the truth.

As we start to reflect, we gain some distance from Dante's sensual drama depicting the sounds, sights, and smells of hell. This distancing is crucial for our happiness. Our imagination always uses what we have sensed to create projections or representations. If sin is our overidentification with our imaginative projections, then putting some distance between ourselves and our sensations is the only way to curtail self-inflicted suffering. Leaving hell requires that we realize how truly unsensational even the worst sins are. When we experience that epiphany, we cease to be mesmerized by the sins and sinners we encounter and can move on.

With the weakening of our attachment to our sensual imaginings, we become more adept at intuiting the intellectual structure that the sensual sin exemplifies. That is why we find Dante becoming increasingly mobile and agile as he moves closer toward heaven. The developing ability of Dante the poet to fuse the intellectual, hierarchical logic of sin with its sensible, progressive manifestations is what makes his rendering of evil powerful, persuasive, and true. As Andrew Delbanco has argued, "most people, if they are honest with themselves, will admit that they yearn for a world in which each action of the soul becomes meaningful . . . complete in meaning—in sense—and complete for the senses."[53] Dante's poem satisfies this yearning of every engaged reader. What is more, by creating this poem, Dante overcomes the black depression that set him on his journey in the first place. He finds fulfillment and achieves blessedness, which, for Dante, consists not in performing good deeds but in realizing one's human potential.[54]

A cold wind is blowing through our world. Self-inflicted suffering and frustration are real and have a structure and a logic all their own. In that sense, evil is impersonal. However, it works only through us. Evil is present whenever we sin. Since we are incarnate beings, we are always liable to become enamored with what we sense and imagine. Our reasoning can become twisted, our appetites deformed. Still, by becoming aware of the structure of sin and of its stakes—our humanity is at risk—we may be able to climb with Dante and Virgil out of hell and see the stars.

7

EVIL AS SATANIZING SELF, OTHERS, AND GOD

You always empower the demons you fight.

—Anthony de Mello

THE NEW TESTAMENT GOSPELS CONSISTENTLY IDENTIFY EVIL WITH SATAN. Jesus Christ defeats Satan and thereby liberates us from the forces of evil. How does Jesus understand the satanic or demonic? Dante suggests that we fall into the jaws of Satan whenever our identifying with our suffering causes us to be driven by our passions and seduced by our cunning. With this identification, we forfeit the possibility of freedom and become like machines. Does Jesus, like Dante, think it operates in a mechanical fashion? In what way does Jesus' message free us from evil? Are we freed from doing evil, from suffering it, or from both?

THE TEMPTATION TO CONVERT OTHERS INTO ENEMIES OR OBSTACLES

The Gospels of Matthew, Mark, and Luke, begin with an account of Satan's temptation of Jesus. This starting point defines Jesus' mission: "The reason the Son of God appeared was to destroy the devil's work."[1] Christianity traces sin back to the devil. The murderer Cain "belonged to the evil one."[2] Only those who have been born of God can avoid sin and be shielded from the power of Satan: "We know that we are children of God, and that the whole world is under the control of the evil one."[3]

The Gospels' emphasis on the temptation of Jesus suggests that evil enters our life not through a frontal assault, but through the back door of seduction. These texts impute no physical body to Satan. Instead, Satan is identical with the devious voice and logic of temptation. How does this temptation work? What are we tempted to say, do, or think that qualifies as evil? Since the canonical Gospels set such store by the temptation of Jesus, placing the account immediately after Jesus' baptism by John the Baptist and immediately before the beginning of Jesus' ministry and preaching, we may that infer this account discloses not only the meaning of temptation and sin, but also the way in which we should resist both. The attempted seduction by Satan places us "in the presence of one of those events dominating the ages which fits into the gigantic struggle between Good and Evil, between Love and Hatred."[4]

The Gospel of Matthew tells us Jesus is "led" into the wilderness of Judah, not far from the Jordan River where he has just been baptized.[5] The Gospel of Mark uses stronger and more violent language: the Greek text says that Jesus is "thrown" or "driven" into the wilderness.[6] Both texts suggest he has not voluntarily left the presence of his friends and family but has been thrust from them. By whom? Mark tells us that the *pneuma* or spirit drove Jesus into the desert. As I argue later in this chapter, *pneuma* is the word used for the devil or the spirit of opposition. Although his persecutors remain unknown, it is not farfetched to assume that Jesus winds up in the wilderness because others have treated him as if he were a demon or monster to be expelled from the community. He is akin to the scapegoat on whom the Jews annually piled their sins and then led or drove into the desert.

Just as Israel wanders for forty years in the desert, so Jesus spends forty days in prayer and penance, enduring a self-imposed fast. When Jesus becomes hungry, Satan makes his first appearance. The tempter comes to Jesus and says, "If you are the Son of God, tell these stones to become bread."[7] Satan's approach is subtle. He begins by calling attention to Jesus' hunger and slyly encourages Jesus to blame God for his starving condition. After all, fathers show love and compassion for their children. Jesus himself will later demonstrate concern for the starving masses by feeding them. According to satanic logic, God the Father should not stand by while his son Jesus weakens from hunger.

Satan, whose name means "obstacle" or "stumbling block" in Hebrew, tempts us to treat God as an impediment to our well-being and to blame or satanize the divine.[8] It may not be possible to define God. Yet we can say there is part of us that craves meaning and needs some sense of how we fit it into the vast universe that existed before we were born and that will continue after we die. I understand the divine to be the source of such meaning, a meaning in which we participate, no matter how dimly. A divine spark exists within each of us. Satan tempts Jesus to turn both this godhead and divine spark into an enemy. If we do succumb to this temptation, we lie to ourselves in two ways. To blame God is to ignore the way in which we are the cause of our condition. Yes, Jesus is hungry, but he is starving *because of his self-imposed fast*. Furthermore, what human beings most need is not mere physical nourishment but self-knowledge. If Jesus had craved bread, he could have stayed away from John the Baptist and kept a low profile living in his parents' house. He begins to fast because he understands the need to meet and to know himself if he is to cope with the communal forces that have driven him into the wilderness. Blaming God for our hunger prevents us from attending to what our souls need. To accuse the divine is to repeat the process of scapegoating that has driven us away from others in the first place. Instead of getting caught up in this blame game, we should use the silence of the desert (our aloneness) to think about our suffering.

By staying focused on our true needs, those recognized by the divine spirit within us, we can resist the tendency to satanize others. Jesus fights Satan by heeding the words of this divine spirit: "It is written: 'Man does not live by bread alone, but by every word that comes from the mouth of God.' " Satan would have us concentrate on what we put in our mouths; Jesus reminds us to attend to what comes out of the mouth— words. If we characterize the divine as an obstacle, instead of letting it be our inspiration and helper, we slip into suffering. We experience evil. Evil means destroying the self through a failure to heed our human need to develop, to love and to be loved, to rejoice, and to be more than an animal body. Jesus himself experiences this temptation to satanize. If we do not resist the temptation, self-deception and hatred will leave us stranded in a wilderness of loneliness. Jesus' ministry to others begins with this encounter with himself. Self-knowledge enables him to leave the desert and rejoin his fellow human beings in a spirit of love and compassion.

The devil responds to Jesus' refusal to turn God into an obstacle with a second temptation. Satan takes Jesus to the pinnacle of the temple in Jerusalem and says, "If you are the Son of God . . . throw yourself down. For it is written: 'He will command his angels concerning you, and they will lift you up in their hands, so that you will not trip over a stone.' "[9] This time Satan turns rabbinic, quoting Scripture just as Jesus did previously. Taking the Scripture literally, Satan suggests Jesus should be willing to throw himself from the highest point of the temple. Again, Satan appeals to a father's love for his children. If Jesus is truly the obedient Son of God, he would not, Satan insinuates, hesitate to put himself in harm's way because God will look after him.

Satan abuses Scripture and asks Jesus to do so as well. The text Satan quotes does not say we should test the divine by voluntarily inflicting harm on ourselves. On the contrary, the lesson to be learned from the first temptation is that we should avoid harming ourselves by blaming others, including God, for our dissatisfaction. What the scripture does say is that God will enable us to avoid "tripping over a stone." The allusion to the stone is suggestive. *Nomos*, the Greek word for the law that constitutes and regulates the city, originally referred to the stones demarcating the city's boundary. The Mosaic Law is written on stone tablets, and the ancient Hebrews stoned to death their adversaries and those they deemed to have transgressed Mosaic Law. These judges literally threw the book at those condemned as sinners. The passage Satan cites should be read as a warning against judging others for their supposed transgressions of the moral law. The divine lifts us up so that we will not stumble over obstacles.

In the first temptation, Satan encourages Jesus to make God into an obstacle, adversary, or tripping stone. The tempting voice tries to get Jesus to live on a diet of stones ("turn those stones into bread"), instead of on the manna of spiritual insight. Jesus brushes aside this temptation and avoids tripping over that obstacle or *satan*. The second approach seeks to persuade Jesus to treat his fellow citizens as obstacles. Drawing on the popular belief that the Messiah would appear to the Jews at the high point of the temple, he takes Jesus to the holy city of Jerusalem and places him at exactly this point.[10] He entices Jesus to see himself as the Messiah. If Jesus were to heed Satan and throw himself from the temple, he would be attempting to force God to save him. Moreover, he would be seeking to compel his fellow Jews to accept him as the Messiah of whom Hebrew scripture and law speaks. If the worshippers at the temple were to see the angels save Jesus, these people would have to believe he was their savior.

But what would happen if some still refused to accept Jesus as the Messiah? It is crucial to remember that this time spent in the desert marks the beginning of Jesus' ministry. He must decide how to proceed. He can try to manifest the loving spirit of the divine, inviting belief in God by casting out the demons that make people sick. Or he can seek to compel belief by providing listeners with all sorts of proofs. He wisely chooses the first course. It is impossible to make people believe if their hearts are hard and stony. As Jesus later claims, only those with "ears to hear, and eyes to see" will appreciate his message.[11] Those who spend their lives blaming other people for their unhappiness will have difficulty grasping what Jesus is telling them about the dangers of satanizing others. In fact, after Jesus casts out some demons, some witnesses waste no time in accusing Jesus of being a devil.[12] If Jesus were to try to force people believe his message, he would end up hating the very individuals he is trying to help and berating them for failing to accept his proofs. In effect, he would cast his fellow human beings in the role of adversaries. At that point, he would be no different from Satan, the great adversary. He might even blame God for anointing him as the Messiah and then refusing to give him the power to compel others to believe in him.

During his subsequent ministry, Jesus travels to Jerusalem and meets his accusers in the temple courts. When Herod the Great rebuilt the temple, he extended the courtyards by building a huge platform out over the southeast corner, where the land fell off sharply. The temple courts, supported by an enormous retaining wall, were on this platform and were the temple's "highest point."[13] When Jesus appears in these temple courts, some of his fellow Jews try to bait him. They see him as the enemy and attempt to trick him into making some damning statement they can use to have him condemned by the political authorities. Jesus avoids their satanic subterfuges by refusing to descend to their level. Standing at the highest point of the temple, Jesus refuses either to insult his questioners or to give them a sign or proof that he is their Messiah. Instead, he quotes the Jewish precepts in which the member of the audience profess to believe. If they have ears to hear they will recognize and take to heart the spiritual wisdom embodied in these passages. If not, so be it. Nothing is to be gained by hurling himself from the highest point of the temple. So Jesus leaves his accusers behind. Prophets are always without honor in their country and are likely to be expelled or even murdered.[14] "O Jerusalem, Jerusalem, thou that killest the prophets, and stones them which are sent unto thee."[15] This crucial insight concerning the limits of teaching gets crystallized during Jesus' second encounter with Satan, enabling him to repulse Satan by quoting the Torah: "Do not put the Lord your God to the test."[16]

The voice of temptation entices Jesus a third time. In the first case, Satan plays on Jesus' physical nature, his hunger, in an attempt to lure him into satanizing God. In the second, Satan plays upon the desires of the human heart to persuade Jesus to adopt a course that will lead him to satanize his fellow Jews. The third deception seeks to draw Jesus into the demonizing that is characteristic of political life in general. The tempting voice drops the taunting and doubting phrase "If you are the son of God" and portrays itself as a powerful ally capable of helping Jesus realize political aspirations. Whisking Jesus to the top of a very high mountain, Satan shows him the kingdoms of the world in all their splendor. "All this I will give you," Satan says, "if you will bow down and worship me."[17]

Jesus can rule the entire world, but only if he is willing to pay the price demanded of every would-be ruler—he must be willing to view everyone in the world as a potential enemy. All political aspirants think they can do a better job than those who went before. Even people who start out with noble aspirations, including the desire to order the city or state in accordance with the will of God, fall prey to the tendency to describe fellow citizens as incompetent, selfish, wicked, and so on. Since people differ as to how best to govern a state, rulers soon find themselves opposed at every turn. They are tempted to slander, imprison, or even murder anyone who dares to stand in their way. History records how often rulers invent foreign enemies to justify domestic oppression and the imposition of martial law. This favorite ruse inevitably fuels domestic opposition. Every one of those "splendid kingdoms" Satan asks Jesus to envision eventually falls prey to strife. Nations and empires succumb to internal or external bloodshed. This "thirst for conquest, human ambition in all its forms [is] . . . the very substance of universal history, from the beginning right up to the present time."[18] If Jesus were to attempt a political coup, he would become enmeshed in the same dynamic. Just as Jesus cannot use proofs to force listeners to believe what he is saying, neither he nor anyone else can compel members of the community to share a single vision of a well-ordered state. The third temptation, then, is an invitation to believe the false claim that political power can be achieved without encountering any stumbling stone and that every opponent can be made into an ally.

Such an illusion is perhaps the greatest obstacle in the path to salvation. Our drive to realize even the noblest of political aspirations leads us to do whatever it takes to realize our goal. We suffer along with our victims. Judas's political aspirations lead him to betray his friend Jesus. Judas soon finds, however, that this quest for political power takes him nowhere. Overwhelmed with horror and guilt, Judas converts himself into an obstacle and commits suicide.

Jesus' ministry begins with resistance to evil, where evil is understood not as malice or sadism but instead as our tendency to lie to ourselves and to convert potential friends into enemies. In indulging this tendency, we can be said to do evil. But again, we must not forget that the evil we do is the evil we suffer. Although we may think satanizing others will bring us lasting happiness, it does not. The blaming never ends, and we are left stewing in our rage. In the words of John Milton, "Thus they in mutual accusation spent/The fruitless hours, but neither self-condemning/And of their vain contest appear'd no end."[19] Our rage, in turn, prevents us from acquiring the self-knowledge and from performing the acts of love and generosity that bring enduring peace. Jesus continually reminds us we have yet to "enter life."[20] We are dead to true, satisfying life because we are caught up in trying to acquire power and in blaming others for our unhappiness. In satanizing others, we kill a bit of ourselves. Judas takes the satanic logic to its final conclusion.

Jesus' subsequent ministry reflects the wisdom he has acquired through combating the temptation to satanize God, himself, and the whole of humanity. The three-fold satanic temptation in the desert, at the temple, and on the mountaintop exactly parallels key incidents in Jesus' ministry. This ministry begins in the desert encounter with Satan. Later, Jesus confronts his opponents at the highest point of the temple. His ministry ends with Judas's kiss of betrayal in the garden atop Mount Olivet, overlooking Jerusalem. This parallel is not accidental. Jesus' ministry has one main message: the only way we can escape the satanic dynamic of blaming others for our unhappiness is to realize true power lies within us. Contrary to what the voice of temptation claims, no one else can give us power. As human beings, we have the ability to empower ourselves by refusing to play the political game of accusation and counterclaim that leaves us so at odds with ourselves and with others. When some followers seek to entice Jesus to declare himself a political ruler, Jesus neatly sidesteps the temptation, reminding them of the scriptural injunction to "render unto Caesar what is Caesar's, and unto God what is God's."[21] Confusing political power with spiritual strength always weakens the individual and tends to destroy the state as well. The moment we come to believe we know the secret to getting and maintaining power, we place ourselves in opposition to anyone possessing an alternative vision. Strife ensues. Satanic rule and splendid kingdoms are mutually exclusive propositions.

Recognizing this simple, yet hard to grasp, truth suffices to destroy the temptation. Jesus repulses Satan not through violence but by stating the truth: "Away from me, Satan! For it is written: 'Worship the Lord your God and serve him only.' " After Jesus insists upon the impossibility of serving two masters, Satan disappears. This power to repel temptation is ours as well: "Where believers go, these signs shall go with them: they will cast out devils."[22] Can we refrain from railing at our fellow citizens or mistaking political power for real spiritual power? If we can avoid these temptations, we can cast demons from our lives. We will no longer see the adversary at every turn.

LEGALISM

Someone may object, "Yes, it's true that human beings are wont to demonize each other. But the law can prevent or, at least, contain such evil." I do not deny that relying on the law to settle disputes is generally better than resorting to violence. Still, the temptation to portray other people as enemies is strong. We should not be overly sanguine about the ability of the law to curtail violence. That is why Jesus warns us to avoid courtrooms: "Make friends quickly with your opponent at law while you are with him on the way, so that your opponent may not hand you over to the judge, and the judge to the officer, and you be thrown into prison."[23] The Gospels pair the account of Jesus' time in the wilderness with the story of Herod Antipas and the beheading of John the Baptist. As this tale shows, the law often functions as another means by which people lock themselves in opposition to each other.

The tetrarch Herod Antipas is the ruler of Galilee and Perea (where the locals called him "king"). King Herod lusts after his brother Philip's wife Herodias and, as soon becomes apparent, after Herodias's daughter Salome as well. John the Baptist consistently opposes Herod's desire to have Herodias, warning the king "it is not lawful for you to have her."[24] Herod wishes to murder John but is afraid to do so because so many consider John a prophet. The result is a stalemate, with John languishing in the tetrarch's prison while Herod suffers John's taunts. Matters reach a crisis on Herod's birthday, when Salome dances so seductively that Herod swears to give her whatever she wants. Urged by her mother Herodias, Salome demands the head of John the Baptist on a meat platter. The king is distressed, but because he has sworn an oath, he grants her request. John the Baptist is beheaded, and Salome delivers the trophy to her mother; John's disciples retrieve the remaining portion of the body and bury it.

Although Herod's oath embodies what John the Baptist sees as an unlawful desire, it is nevertheless legal under both Mosaic and Roman law. Moses proclaims that God has commanded that if a man "takes an oath imposing an obligation on himself, he shall not break his pledge; he must carry out all that has crossed his lips."[25] Under Mosaic Law, what Herod has sworn he must do, even though his lust for Herodias and Salome violates other Mosaic strictures and will certainly cause his brother Philip to hate him. Under Roman law as well, Herod, like the Persian and Medean kings who preceded him, cannot retract an oath once given. The Jewish law recognizes this fact: "No decree or edict that the king issues can be changed."[26]

Reliance on the law forces Herod and John the Baptist into opposing positions impossible to reconcile. It hardens their hearts. The Mosaic Law on which John the Baptist relies to vilify Herod is at odds with both secular law and itself. The king both is and is not bound to do what his lust is urging upon him. Being the source of the conflict, the law cannot resolve it. The law dooms Herod and John the Baptist to satanize each other. Although only John is beheaded, all the parties to this conflict, in a metaphorical sense, lose their heads. In each case, the law functions as the executioner's sword.

The lustful Herod is so utterly bewitched by Salome that he stupidly, yet perfectly lawfully, promises to give her whatever she asks. He thereby incurs the enmity of the disciples of John the Baptist, the group whom he has feared to anger. When the enraged Herodias sees Herod shift his attention away from her to her daughter Salome, she takes revenge by using Herod's binding oath to force the king to act against what he perceives to be in his self-interest. Her plot is equally ill conceived. As long as Herod rules, he need only declare her to be his queen to make the union lawful. The king's word is law. However, if Herod's enraged subjects revolt and depose Herod, Herodias loses her one chance to become the lawful queen. Consumed with rage, she fails to discern that she will suffer along with Herod. Salome completely abdicates any responsibility to use her head, deferring entirely to her mother. Although she pleases her mother in the short term with her lawful request, she is left in the debt of a lascivious Herod. If he becomes her father, she may find her lawful demand has ensnared her in an illegal, incestuous relationship.

The parties use the law in an effort to overcome those whom they have turned into obstacles, only to discover this same law throws up other obstacles. Hatred and anger get embodied in the law, and parties use the law to extract their pound of flesh from each other. Tensions escalate to the point that all those involved in the conflict take leave of their senses. Our actions may be entirely lawful, yet our rage consumes us as we busy ourselves in serving up the heads of our supposed enemies on a legal platter.

Zero-Sum Thinking

How great is the contrast between this satanic dish and the feast Jesus provides for the crowd that has come to hear his message. Upon learning of the beheading of John the Baptist, Jesus immediately withdraws by boat to a solitary location.[27] The crowds, though, will not leave him alone. Pouring out of the towns, they follow him to the lake. When Jesus lands, he faces a mob of people. All the Gospels state there are about five thousand people; Matthew specifies five thousand men, in addition to women and children.

King Herod fears the crowds, for good reason. The king's tendency to place himself in opposition to other people invites violence. Jesus, by contrast, views the large crowd with compassion and heals the sick by driving out demons that have taken over their souls (e.g., by countering our impulse to satanize each other). While he is busy ministering, the disciples, like Herod, are keeping a worried eye on the crowd. As the sun goes down, the people begin to stir restlessly. They are hungry. The disciples fear that the crowd will turn into an angry mob. The twelve urge Jesus to send the people away to forage for food, but Jesus disregards their advice, refusing to treat the crowd as potential enemies. Instead, he tells his disciples that the people do not "need to go away. You give them something to eat."[28] The disciples protest it would cost too much to buy food and, at present, they have only five loaves of bread and two fish to offer.

The Gospel of Mark tells us Jesus directed the disciples to seat the crowd in groups of hundreds and fifties. The detail is odd. Why would Jesus array the crowd just like a Roman legion, which typically consisted of four to five thousand men deployed in groups of hundreds and fifties? A suggestion: Jesus wants to show us how to avoid turning our fellow human beings into instruments of violence and war. Although the group is arrayed like a military legion, Jesus, the disciples, and the many coalesce into a peaceful community. They break bread together and share fish. No one gets angry or becomes accusatory. The miracle here is not that Jesus feeds people bread. Although it is true we need to eat, recall that Jesus himself rejects Satan's temptation to turn stones into bread because "man does not live by bread alone." The true miracle is that a huge and restless crowd does not panic and become a mob. It stays calm because Jesus rejects the demonic response of viewing the crowd as an enemy. Treated as friends by Jesus, the people befriend each other, and no one goes hungry.

Each person receives what he or she truly needs through Jesus' spontaneous gesture of blessing and then sharing the fish and loaves. When Jesus tells his disciples to feed the crowd, their immediate inclination is to engage in a legalistic debate. Feeding so many people would require, they argue, eight months of a man's wages. They press Jesus for a rabbinic answer: "Are we really to go out and spend that much on bread and give it to them to eat?"[29] The disciples expect Jesus to engage in the all too familiar political debate. They anticipate that he will order priorities and then establish which good should trump all others. Given that people do not agree on their priorities, this type of political debate inevitably generates conflict and produces enmity. Jesus nips the debate in the bud by acting. He shares what he has with others, and everyone gets fed. In fact, there is so much bread left over that the disciples, using their lunch baskets, collect twelve basketfuls of leftovers. This numerical detail shows there was enough food all along. Instead of looking to Jesus for a solution, all the disciples had to do was to open their twelve hearts and share their food.

According to the Gospels, evil is the process of turning potential friends into enemies. Whenever we convert a fellow human being into an obstacle, that person ceases to have any independent existence. The individual can teach us nothing. He or she becomes merely an impediment to some course of action to which we are already committed. Evil consists in thinking inside the zero-sum box: if I give my food to you, I will have nothing to eat, and vice versa. Zero-sum thinking leads us to believe our options are limited and necessarily involve trade-offs. Once we embrace this satanic logic, we have no incentive to be open to what our fellow human beings might propose, or to think creatively about how to accommodate everyone's interests. Like Jesus' disciples, we get locked into looking for ways to protect our interests from the predation of our "enemies." Jesus' feeding of the crowd is wonderfully creative. Evil, by contrast, is mechanical. We know the commonplace debates and stratagems and their utterly predictable results—charges, countercharges, and blame, culminating in verbal or physical violence.

Jesus is not obligated by law to feed his followers. The juxtaposition of Herod's legal beheading of John the Baptist with Jesus' spontaneous gesture of compassion highlights the crucial difference between legalism and wisdom. Since the law is a box, legalistic thinking reinforces our tendency toward zero-sum thinking. The law can never serve as a completely effective check on our almost mechanical demonizing of other people. Once Herod utters his oath, he is legally bound to honor it, regardless of the consequences. Creative practical thinking, on the other hand, opens up new possibilities and helps us to avoid escalating battles of the will. Preserving this freedom is key, which is why Jesus warns against swearing any oath:

> Again, you have heard that it was said to the people long ago, "Do not break our oath, but keep the oaths you have made to the Lord." But I tell you, Do not swear at all: either by heaven, for it is God's throne; or by the earth, for it is his footstool; or by the Jerusalem, for it is the city of the Great King. . . . Simply let your "Yes" be "Yes," and your "No," "No"; anything beyond this comes from the evil one.[30]

True Power

We are deluded if we think the law, civil or moral, will enable us to combat and overcome evil. The law easily enmeshes us in the dynamic we must avoid if we are to be truly free. It takes "one greater than the temple" to defeat Satan.[31] The Gospels give us many examples of Jesus successfully expelling demons. Why does Jesus' way have a power over evil that institutionalized religion and morality lack? All four Gospels relate the beheading of John the Baptist or John's preparing the way for Jesus, and then describe the miracle of the feeding of the five thousand. Shortly after this miracle, Jesus walks on the water in the middle of a storm to calm his disciples.[32] The sequence of events is crucial, for the culminating story contains the key to how we can avoid evil.

After everyone is fed, Jesus sends his disciples ahead by boat to Bethsaida. He goes up the mountainside to pray and to escape the crowd that now desires to crown him king of the Jews.[33] While on the mountain, Jesus watches to see how his disciples fare on their own. The twelve are adrift in the middle of the lake. They cannot progress because the stormy winds are against them. Since Jesus cares for his friends, he is concerned to see them struggling so. But he allows them to be tested.

The disciples are forever deferring to Jesus. Like the crowd, they try to turn him into their political leader, into their private "king of the Jews." Without him, these fishermen can make no headway. We are told the "wind" is against them.[34] The Greek word for wind is *pneuma*, a word also meaning "breath" or "spirit." In this context, *pneuma* is more than the wind; it is the spirit of demonization and opposition. When Jesus casts the devil out of the man in Gerasene, he expels spirits or *pneumata*. The Aramaic tradition also applies the term *pneuma* to devils. The Lord tells Enoch that the giants who have intercourse with human women and generally wreak havoc all over the earth are "evil spirits" or *pneumata ponera*.[35] When we harden our hearts and turn others into obstacles, then, as the story of Herod and John the Baptist shows, we find ourselves buffeted hither and thither by the force of our rage and bitterness. Watching the disciples struggle with the opposing *pneuma*, Jesus is checking whether they have learned anything about how best to grapple with the satanizing spirit within. However, the men seem unable to escape the storm. Why?

When the period of the fourth watch arrives, Jesus walks out on the water. He is about to pass the disciples by but "when they saw him walking on the lake, they thought he was a ghost. They cried out, because they all saw him and were terrified. Immediately he spoke to them and said, 'Take courage! It is I. Do not be afraid.' "[36] Although the Gospels of Matthew and Mark appear to diverge as to what happens next, both texts are illuminating and, I think, complementary. According to Mark, Jesus climbs into the boat, and the wind dies down at once. The disciples are amazed "for they had not understood about the loaves; their hearts were hardened."[37] The disciples do not understand the power Jesus has over opposing forces because they did not comprehend his spontaneous feeding of the five thousand. Just as their hearts were previously turned against the hungry crowd, they now convert Jesus into an obstacle or tripping stone. They are angry with him for having frightened them out on the lake. They forget it was they who deemed him a fearful demon or ghost.[38] Jesus had been content to pass by unnoticed and to let the men continue to try to make progress on their own. The men terrify themselves through their customary satanizing of those around them, including their friend Jesus. They constitute the biggest obstacle to their spiritual development. By disclosing the disciples' demonizing tendencies—Jesus gets into the boat and the men suddenly see that this "ghost" is their friend—Jesus enables the men to escape the terrible storm and to cross over to safety.

According to Matthew, Peter courageously responds to Jesus' injunction to be brave. He replies, "Lord, if it's you . . . tell me to come to you on the water."[39] Jesus does so, and Peter leaves the boat, joining Jesus to walk on the water. By resisting the temptation to satanize the world, Peter escapes the force of the opposing wind. Peter takes a risk and treats the phantasm as a potential friend: he will join the ghostly spirit if it invites him to do so. But the moment Peter "sees the wind," he becomes afraid and starts to sink into the stormy surge. Peter's fear of his imaginary adversary is the true enemy. No "wind" impedes his progress until he creates an obstacle. Only at that point does he sink like a rock.

Peter calls out to Jesus to save him. Peter's experience of being able to walk on the water—of containing the impulse to satanize—has removed all doubt as to the identity of the ghostly figure. This figure who has shown Peter the way to be free of fear is their savior. Yet old habits die hard. Peter doubts the power of his newfound wisdom against the imagined demon wind. He slips back into looking for a leader who will save him from himself. Although Jesus reaches out his hand and walks Peter back to the safety of the boat, Jesus reprimands Peter for having so little faith. If Peter had continued to treat the spirit as a friend, he, like Jesus, could have crushed the stormy water (sometimes referred to as a "dragon") under his heel. Upon welcoming Jesus as a friend and taking his proffered hand, Peter finds he is again able to walk on water. Each of us shares Jesus' power to avoid being swamped by evil. To share this power, we need only alter our perspective. When we stop satanizing those around us, our dread and anxiety immediately disappear.

When Peter and Jesus return to the boat, the other disciples fall down and "worship him." The text is ambiguous—whom are they worshipping, Jesus or Peter? At this juncture, the two are the same in power and stature. Each man walks on water—that is, each man acts freely in accordance with his understanding and faith. Neither is propelled by the wind or spirit of opposition. The disciples, though, have failed to learn the lesson Jesus is trying to teach. Instead of looking within themselves, they idolize Jesus and then are enraged when they think he has failed them. This storm sequence shows how easily our idol turns into an obstacle or *satan*. No one can give us the power to lead our own lives. Looking to others to assume a responsibility that is ours alone, we experience disappointment. Inevitably our idols fail us. If we are not careful, we start to blame them for our lack of courage and convert them into enemies. Unless and until we expel from ourselves the tendency to see demons everywhere, we will never be safe. Weighed down by fears and disappointments, we, too, will sink like stones.

The Desire for High Status

The Gospel of John offers us a still more explicit example of what happens when the satanizing spirit enters into a human being. John's account of possession begins innocently enough. As Passover draws near, Jesus acts to show the full extent of his love. Knowing that he has come from God and is returning to Him, Jesus wraps a towel around his waist and washes the feet of all of his disciples.[40] When Peter resists having Jesus wash his feet, Jesus insists "unless I wash you, you have no part with me."[41] The Gospel prefaces this tale of foot washing with what initially appears to be an unrelated, false note. We read "the evening meal was being served, and the devil had already prompted Judas Iscariot, son of Simon, to betray Jesus."[42] What does this tale of foot washing have to do with Judas' temptation by the devil and subsequent betrayal of Jesus? Is it significant that Jesus washes the feet of Judas as well as of the other eleven disciples? Is Peter's resistance to Jesus itself demonic in some way?

If we take a closer look, we discover that this reference to satanic temptation is central to the meaning of Jesus' act of foot washing. In the scene just described, Peter places himself in opposition to Jesus. Since Jesus is the teacher, Peter assumes Jesus must be higher than the disciples. They are mere students; Jesus alone is the rabbi. As such, he should never stoop to serve his students. The scene reveals the disciples' tendency to idolize Jesus. This idolatry produces a great irony. Although they insist upon Jesus' rabbinical status, their worship of his person impedes their ability to learn. In fact, Peter's certainty that a rabbi would never wash the feet of a student leads Peter to cast himself as Jesus' superior—he will tell Jesus what a rabbi should or should not do!

Jesus responds as a true teacher, freely abasing himself in order to teach them how to love: "I have set you an example that you should do as I have done for you. I tell you the truth, no servant is greater than his master, nor is the messenger greater than the one who sent him."[43] In the quest to find and to live the truth, there are no higher and lower human beings. By washing the feet of Judas as well as of Peter, Jesus shows the extent of his love. He refuses to shun anyone, even those whom he suspects of betraying him. This service inverts the traditional Passover ritual. Instead of washing his hands, a gesture preceding the ritualized eating of the sacrificed lamb, Jesus cleanses his disciples' feet. If we satanize others, we will have blood on our hands, even if we wash them as our morality and law prescribe. Only if we refrain from suspecting and hating our neighbors and instead serve them can we enjoy a communal meal.

By refusing to allow Jesus to wash his feet, Peter not only forces Jesus into the role of an authority figure but also elevates himself. Later, Peter argues that he loves Jesus so much that he alone among all the disciples would never betray him. In this foot-washing scene, Jesus firmly rejects Peter's adulation. The quest for high status inevitably leads us to oppose our fellow human beings, while our hubristic belief that we are especially insightful makes us unteachable. In this respect, Peter's resistance is akin to Judas' subsequent betrayal. Both men would manipulate Jesus for their political ends, rather than heed his loving message to serve each other.

Yet Peter differs from Judas in one crucial respect. Peter overcomes his initial resistance and eventually allows Jesus to bathe his feet. Judas, by contrast, cannot accept Jesus' refusal to act the part of a political ruler or king. Jesus' voluntary abasement before the disciples appears to harden Judas Iscariot's heart and to fan the fire of resentment, tempting him to betray his friend. For immediately after Jesus has lovingly washed his disciples' soles, Jesus announces "he who shares my bread has lifted up his heel against me."[44]

The disciples are confused and do not understand to whom Jesus is referring. Their confusion is understandable because all of them have been sharing Jesus' bread. Jesus here intimates that every one of us is, to some degree, an enemy of the divine message of love. Like the disciples, we attach ourselves to the person of Jesus, confusing the messenger of love with the divine itself.[45] Consequently, we do not comprehend the meaning and significance of Jesus' voluntary abasement and so cannot comprehend his teaching. The twelve disciples take in Jesus' words along with the bread, but they do not, and will not, admit their ignorance. Instead, they fall back on familiar but dangerous political stratagems. Aghast at Jesus' revelation of pending betrayal, Simon Peter looks at the disciple reclining against Jesus— "the one whom Jesus loved"—and demands that this "favorite" ask Jesus to whom Jesus is referring.[46] Leaning back even further into Jesus (i.e., relying still more on his status as the especially beloved friend), this disciple follows Peter's bidding and asks Jesus who the betrayer is.

> Jesus answered, "It is the one to whom I will give this piece of bread when I have dipped it in the dish." Then, dipping the piece of bread, he gave it to Judas Iscariot, son of Simon. As soon as Judas took the bread, Satan entered into him. "What you are about to do, do quickly," Jesus told him, but no one at the meal understood why Jesus said this to him. Since Judas had charge of the money, some thought Jesus was telling him to buy what was needed for the Feast, or to give something to the poor. As soon as Judas had taken the bread, he went out. And it was night.[47]

Although the disciples think they must maneuver Jesus into telling them who the betrayer is, Jesus responds straightforwardly. He gives them the key to interpreting his actions: the betrayer is the man to whom he gives a particular piece of dipped bread. Jesus then dips and gives a piece of bread to Judas Iscariot. The disciples, though, cannot interpret the action. They expect political subtlety or surreptitiousness and do not take Jesus at his word. They are so concerned to spot any sign of favoritism that they believe Jesus has given Judas some special charge connected with the disciple's privileged role as the keeper of the collective funds![48]

They cannot see Judas Iscariot as a betrayer, because they cannot view themselves as such, despite Jesus' earlier suggestion that each of us is a spiritual traitor. All the disciples, including Judas, stare at each other, bewildered by Jesus' charge. They fail to perceive the evil of their daily calculations of who is in and out of favor. When Jesus dips the bread in the bitter herbs and holds it out to Judas, Judas cannot resist what appears to be a distinguishing gesture of honor. The Lord is offering him—Judas—a hand-dipped piece of bread! Contrary to what some interpreters seem to think, Judas does not take the bread because he is satanic. The text is clear: only at the moment that Judas takes the bread, believing it to be a token of preferment, does Satan enter into him.[49] Each of us is tempted, at one time or another, to join in the game of social one-upmanship. We behave satanically or evilly when, like Judas, we show ourselves willing to do anything, even murder our friends, in order to improve our status. Then the night of suffering truly does descend upon our souls.

The Hard and Narrow Way

The Gospels warn us against satanic evil. We participate in such evil whenever we convert another into a *satan*. Our desire for status and honor within the community often leads us to demonize our fellow human beings, the world at large, and even God. If we act to eliminate those whom we have portrayed as obstacles, we relinquish our true, inner power, a power far greater than that possessed by political authorities. Political power comes and goes. Our ability to make progress in realizing our genuine self is ours for the using. We forfeit this power of development when we idolize other individuals, deluding ourselves into thinking that they can give us freedom; when we use different machinations to try to advance our cause at the expense of our supposed enemies; or when we presume our motives are above suspicion. These maneuvers serve only to fuel our anxiety and dread, drawing us ever more deeply into the social game of one-upsmanship and into the intellectual trap of zero-sum thinking. We work to trip up our supposed enemies. They retaliate by satanizing us. Our evil acts come back to haunt us as we lose status, mourn our loss, and plot anew to reclaim our besmirched honor. One evil deed leads to another. Soon we are caught in a "vicious circle of mutual reproach."[50]

Our rage at another redounds upon us, causing us to get locked in an unending, mechanical cycle of fury. This self-caused cycle of suffering is the true evil. On this point, the Gospels agree with Dante, Mann, Highsmith, Stevenson, James, and, as we see in the next chapter, with Socrates. Although others may inflict pain upon us, there is a sense in which they cannot hurt us. Such pain is passing and does not destroy our humanity. Treating potential friends as enemies is far worse. To treat people in this way is to commit injustice. And acting unjustly does damage our humanity by undermining our ability to act creatively and spontaneously. Committing an injustice increases, rather than allays, our fear and dread. Unable to escape the consequences of our sinning, we enter a living hell: "[I]t is better . . . that a millstone were hanged about the neck [of the unjust], and that he were drowned in the depth of the sea."[51] Our hardened and violent spirit is this millstone: "And a mighty angel took up a stone like a great millstone, and cast it into the sea, saying, Thus with violence shall that great city Babylon be thrown down, and shall be found no more at all."[52]

The message of the Gospels is a simple one. The only way to avoid doing or suffering evil is to refuse to convert God, our neighbors, and ourselves into stumbling blocks. Satanic evil is both personal and impersonal. It is personal insofar as it always works through individuals. It is impersonal inasmuch as our tendency to demonize one another is enshrined in our culturally transmitted worldviews and practices. In this sense, the demonic haunts the world, forever on the lookout for an opportunity to wreak havoc. The Gospels are right to portray the satanic spirit as a force larger than you or I.

We are taught from an early age that the world is dangerous place, teeming with threats. Having learned this lesson, we warn our children not to talk to strangers, who might be evil people. We report those engaged in suspicious behavior and enroll in self-defense classes so that we will not be at the mercy of predators. Within limits, such behavior is prudent. Other things being equal, nobody wants to fall victim to violence. The danger is that, in focusing on external threats, we ignore the way in which our daily demonization of others fosters a cycle of violence. Our inherited, fearful outlook opens the door for Satan to enter our lives.

By overcoming his fears, Jesus exposes our evil: in our fear, we support and sanction the murder of innocents who have done nothing to harm us. Like Judas Iscariot, we all come from a region at the edge of the desert. Jesus' sacrifice shows a way to escape from this demonic dynamic. Like him, we must enter the wilderness of our souls and examine why we persist in treating other people as our enemies and priding ourselves on our superiority. We must take a hard look at all our attitudes, including our supposed humility. As Reinhold Niebuhr has noted, "there is no temptation so seductive as the temptation to be humble and proud at the same time."[53] Before we try to change the world, we need to remove the mote from our own eye. If "you change first then you'll get a good enough look at the world so that you'll be able change whatever you think might be changed."[54] Should change seem in order, we should proceed cautiously, always suspecting anyone—including ourselves—who lays claim to superior goodness and to a right to have the best place, the greatest honor, the most wealth, and the like. The wise person never forgets that God "maketh his sun to rise on the evil and on the good, and sendeth rain on the just and on the unjust."[55]

Only after we acknowledge the existence of our dark side can we see the world with a clear eye and take steps to live in harmony with our fellow human beings. Only after we realize that doing injustice is far worse than suffering pain at the hands of others can we claim our freedom and move into the light. Opting for this hard and narrow way does not guarantee our salvation. We do not have a magic key to lock the door of our hearts and to bar the spirit of opposition from entering. Jesus asks that we be forgiven because we know not what we do.[56] The Gospels bring our neuroses and the different sources of our dissatisfaction to the surface. The Christian message redeems, but it does not promise smooth sailing. We must do the hard work of casting light upon the dark recesses of our hearts if we are to enter life and know lasting peace.

8

EVIL AS FANATICAL IMPIETY

Men are not flattered by being shown that there has been a difference of purpose between the Almighty and them. To deny it, however, . . . is to deny there is a God governing the world.

—*Abraham Lincoln*

THE WORLD WAS STUNNED BY THE SEPTEMBER 11 BOMBINGS OF THE WORLD Trade Center and the Pentagon. What is perhaps even more shocking is that this bombing was not that unusual. In 1995, Timothy McVeigh blew up the federal building in Oklahoma City. During the past few years, American authorities have identified and foiled other terrorist plots hatched by United States citizens. A Florida militia planned to destroy a nuclear power plant, while Michigan militia members made arrangements to bomb two federal buildings. A group in Missouri plotted to kill thousands at the opening of a military base in Fort Hood, Texas. Meanwhile, militia in northern Montana amassed machine guns and pipe bombs to be used to murder a score of local officials. Anticipating that the National Guard would be summoned to restore order, the militia planned a second attack on the rescuers. They apparently hoped that other right-wing militants would join them in a revolution to overthrow the United States government and establish a new regime controlled by white Christians.[1]

Although domestic and foreign terrorists describe themselves as "true patriots" or "martyrs," most of us would call them "fanatics" because they are so obsessed with an idea or cause. The fact that every region and regime has its share of fanatics suggests that each of us has the potential to become obsessed. I do not think, therefore, that fanaticism is the special province of the mad. Or, if it is, we are all a bit crazy.

This chapter explores the nature and mechanics of fanaticism. Fanaticism is a form of obsession, but not all obsessions appear to be equally destructive. Those of us who obsessively consume food may harm ourselves, but typically do not maim others in the process. Do we become dangerous to our fellow citizens only when we begin to believe we know the correct way to live and that God is on our side? Is it at that point that we cross the line from obsession to full-blown fanaticism, from unhealthy fixation to evildoing? Is fanaticism one among many evils? Or is it more correct to say that all evil is fanatical? If fanaticism is to be avoided, how can we prevent ourselves from becoming too attached to a thing or a cause?

Case Study

Plato's dialogue the *Euthyphro* serves as a perfect case study for examining fanaticism and its relation to evil. The dialogue portrays the fanatic Euthyphro in motion while simultaneously disclosing the beliefs and fears underpinning fanaticism. Fanatics, like the characters analyzed in the preceding chapters, need not *intend* harm to others. Euthyphro views himself as a defender of the community and as a protector of the moral order. Youthful fanatics may not have lived long enough to wreak havoc. But even if fanatics intend no harm and have not injured anyone, we nonetheless shiver slightly when we encounter people who are certain that they alone know the truth about the best way to live. Socrates' conversation with Euthyphro illuminates why we experience this *frisson* of fear.

The Fanatic's Certainty

Socrates meets Euthyphro in the outer courtyard of the king's palace, the center for legal justice in ancient Athens.[2] A young man named Meletus has charged Socrates with introducing new gods and thereby corrupting the state's youth. Socrates is at the palace filing his response to Meletus's capital indictment accusing him of impiety. Euthyphro is present to lodge a charge. He is accusing his father of murder, a capital offense.

Socrates is surprised by Euthyphro's charge. He exclaims that most people would never dare to prosecute a family member because they would "not know how they could do this and be right."[3] In an effort to understand why Euthyphro is proceeding against his father, Socrates ventures that the victim must be a member of Euthyphro's family. Euthyphro responds with a sententious scolding:

> It is ridiculous, Socrates, that you think it matters whether the man who was killed was a stranger or a relative, and do not see that the only thing to consider is whether the action of the slayer was justified or not, and that if it was justified one ought to let him alone, and if not, one ought to proceed against him, even if he share one's hearth and eat at one's table. For the pollution is the same if you associate knowingly with such a man and do not purify yourself and him by proceeding against him. In this case, the man who was killed was a hired workman of mine, and when we were farming at Naxos, he was working with one of our house slaves, and butchered him. So my father bound [the workman] hand and foot, threw him into a ditch, and sent a man here to Athens to ask the religious adviser what he ought to do. In the meantime he paid no attention to the man as he lay there bound, and neglected him, thinking that he was a murderer and it did not matter if he were to die. And that is just what happened to him. For he died of hunger and cold and his bonds before the messenger came back from the adviser. Now my father and the rest of my relatives are angry with me, because for the sake of the murderer I am prosecuting my father for murder. For they say [my father] did not kill him, and if he had killed him never so much, yet since the dead man was a murderer, I ought not to trouble myself about such a fellow because it is unholy for a son to prosecute his father for murder. Which shows how little they know what the divine law is in regard to holiness and unholiness.[4]

Euthyphro's self-justifying answer reveals him to be a man who is completely certain of his position. Fanatics are convinced that an issue has only one dimension and that they fully understand it. While their positions may appear logical or well reasoned, their rationality is one-sided. We might advance numerous reasons for why Euthyphro should not prosecute his father. We could argue that children owe a special debt to their parents, who devoted their lives to raising them. Instead of prosecuting their fathers and mothers, sons and daughters should reciprocate parental concern by caring for their aging parents. Since our parents are older and more experienced, we should consult with them and take what they say seriously before running off to the courts to sue them. Or we might contend, as Euthyphro's relatives do, that justice was served in this case because the murderer himself died at the hands of those whom he injured.

Fanatics, however, dismiss other people's counterarguments and concerns as stupid or ridiculous. Refusing to entertain any objections, they insist upon the rightness and justness of their cause and approach. Euthyphro proclaims that all human actions and choices are to be directed toward one goal and judged by one standard alone: have we acted justly and kept our community pure? Note that Euthyphro presents his standard as universal. Fanatics claim to have discovered a way of life that is unquestionably best for all human beings. They assume that all people (or all those to whom they accord the status of human being) are capable of adopting this way of life. Fanatics recognize no natural barriers to the application of their universal principle. Although they may concede that their principle is not natural in origin, they always tacitly believe it accords with nature.

Socrates turns this tacit presupposition back against Euthyphro. Only those who are certain of the soundness of their moral principle would dare to dismiss natural familial bonds as morally irrelevant. After all, one thing we know to be true is that none of us would exist if we had not been born. We would not have lived if our parents had not nurtured us. If we assume that human beings have duties, rooted in the need to preserve the community, we have a responsibility to look after our parents. Socrates asks after the identity of the victim because Euthyphro's lawsuit against his father would make more human sense if the victim were one of Euthyphro's relatives. Socrates is not implying that every moral duty must derive from natural bonds of affection or that murdering strangers is less unjust than killing one's relatives. He is not even defending the idea of a moral duty. Socrates is simply amazed by Euthyphro's inhuman confidence that no compelling arguments exist for why a person should not prosecute a parent on a capital murder charge. To ensure that he has understood Euthyphro's position correctly, Socrates asks about Euthyphro's relationship to the victim: is Euthyphro truly willing to destroy his father's life on the grounds that every person who unjustifiably kills another must be removed from the state? Euthyphro's answer is an unqualified "yes." Despite the principle's lack of clarity—Euthyphro has not specified when a murder is justified or when a death is a murder, instead of manslaughter or an accident—Euthyphro is utterly convinced that his morality is sound and that his father should be executed or exiled from Athens.

Since fanatics need the support of other people in order to enforce their universal vision of the best way to live, they speak the language of universal justice. They talk as if they were concerned about the welfare of every member of the community, whose interests they claim to represent. Yet they have no real concern for strangers or genuine interest in seeing that all who contribute to the proper functioning of the whole get their share of communal goods. Euthyphro makes no effort to feed or protect the hired hand his father has bound and thrown into the ditch. Euthyphro has not taken any steps to look after the families of the dead day laborer or the murdered household slave. The fanatic lurking in our hearts is not interested in seeing true justice done, but only in enforcing our supposedly universal moral rule, code, or vision. Moral language functions as a subterfuge or proxy for our will to power. By appealing to a universal rule that admits no exceptions, we seek (consciously or unconsciously) to render any opposition illegitimate. Only we know where right lies; we alone speak for all right-minded people when we interpret and impose our rule on the community.

Winston Churchill once described a fanatic as "someone who won't change his mind and who won't change the subject."[5] We talk compulsively in order to convince ourselves that our opinions are correct and our soul is sound. Talking about our beliefs and insisting upon our moral expertise is our way of feeling alive. We feel justified in claiming to know the best way to live because our moral vision is nothing other than our will to power, cunningly tricked out as a rational policy. In more precise terms: we are driven to insist that we know what is right, good, and just because we have identified our self with our beliefs, especially our beliefs about the best way to live. Some part of each of us joins Euthyphro in saying: "I must be an expert. Because if I am not an expert, then I am nothing."[6]

If we were to admit that our moral principles might be erroneous, we would forfeit the only identity we have ever known and lose public support. The two losses are intertwined. To ratify our self-image, we need other people to join us in enforcing our principles. Were our neighbors and associates to refuse to be our allies, we could not realize our universal vision. What is even more serious, we might start to suspect that we have badly misjudged what is good. It scares us to think we might have devoted our entire lives to pursuing an illusory good or goal. That is why Euthyphro fears being ridiculed more than being wrong, why he tries to co-opt Socrates as a political ally, and why is he is so keen to attack and silence anyone who questions his position.[7]

All obsessed individuals believe what they are doing will make them happy. Like other obsessions, fanaticism derives from dread. The fanatical and the obsessed cling to established practices and habitual modes of behavior in order to maintain their identity. But fanatics differ from the obsessed in one crucial respect. Fanatics convert their private obsession into a supposedly universal moral rule and a political position. At that moment, they become intent upon imposing their moral vision and persuading or forcing other individuals to join forces with them. Fanaticism is more destructive than mere obsession. Fanatics are willing to prosecute and persecute anyone who dares to oppose them or to doubt their moral expertise. Euthyphro is so keen to prosecute his father, in part, because his father consulted a religious exegete in Athens, instead of asking his "expert" son about what should be done with the bound man in the ditch.

The evil of fanaticism is not a vice. Evil lies in the self's propensity to identify itself with something that it is not. Every obsession involves a false identification. The obese person says: "I will be happy only if I eat the entire cake." Consuming the cake leads not to happiness but to emptiness. This emptiness, in turn, forces the question of whether our self-understanding is correct. In response to this doubt, we seek to justify our identification. Obsessions thus convert easily into fanaticism. Since moral positions lay claim to a kind of universality and thereby serve to preempt dissent, we seek to bolster our position by casting it as moral truth. Morality assists us in this dubious venture. Moralities always use praise to promote some behaviors and blame to suppress others. They encourage us to find and root out the flaws in other people. Feeling that the entire weight of morality is on our side, we counterattack in an effort to suppress the doubt we are feeling. We pride ourselves on our rectitude.

But we are not home free. Others may ridicule us and refuse to support our vision of universal justice. At that point, our confidence suffers an additional blow and dread returns. Two types of response are possible. We can rethink our commitments and adopt a new approach, rooted in an awareness that our most cherished beliefs about who we are may be in error. Or we can cling to our old way of certainty, lashing out at critics. The first option does not initially appear very appealing. What it involves is not obvious: what does it mean to live a life of knowing that we do not know? How should we conduct ourselves? We are more comfortable with the second approach. After all, the assumption that we know how best to live has guided us from early childhood. So we hold ever tighter to our false identity.

Yet, once a crisis of belief has occurred, this familiar way cannot satisfy us. If we continue to be certain that we are experts, we burden ourselves with the same suspect self-image that precipitated our identity crisis. From the perspective of the wisdom tradition, adopting a new set of supposedly infallible beliefs can never resolve the crisis. What if these new beliefs are mistaken as well? This doubt engenders another round of the dread described in chapter 7, trapping us in a neurotic hell of our making. Like the sinners in Dante's *Inferno*, we identify ourselves with our sin or false self-image and relive our unhappiness forever.

The Fanatic's Divinity

Plato's genius lies in his understanding that we cling to our belief in our moral expertise with a religious fervor. The Euthyphro inside each of us is a self-styled expert on the will of the gods and on divine law. To speak of religious fanaticism is redundant. All fanaticism has a religious aspect because fanatics everywhere implicitly imagine themselves to be doing the will of the divine. To see why, let us return to the case of Euthyphro.

Euthyphro maintains that his prosecution of his father is not merely right and just. His cause is holy, and his action embodies divine law. When Socrates asks Euthyphro to define "the holy," Euthyphro replies that holiness

> is doing what I am doing now, prosecuting the wrongdoer who commits murder or steals from the temples . . . whether it be your father or your mother or anyone else . . . and, Socrates, see what a sure proof I offer you . . . that this is established and right and that we

ought not to let him who acts impiously go unpunished. . . . Men believe that Zeus is the best and most just of the gods, and they acknowledge that he put his father in bonds because he wickedly devoured his children; yes, and that that father had in his turn castrated his father for similar reasons. Yet me they are angry at for indicting my father for his injustice. So they contradict themselves: they say one thing about the gods and another about me.[8]

In other words, whatever is permitted to the supreme deity, be it Zeus or Chronos, is equally permitted to Euthyphro—because he, too, is a god! By implication, he is as omniscient and omnipotent as the divine. Therefore, like the other gods, Euthyphro is entitled to administer law and justice.

Although fanatics claim to be applying the moral law, their "law" never functions as an independent, effective check upon their behavior. Once we decide that we unquestionably know the best way to live, we need no law to guide us. The law is whatever our gods, or we, will it to be. Although Euthyphro invokes the justice of Zeus' and Chronos' actions, he provides no independent definition of justice or lawfulness. Neither does he give us the option of interrogating the sacred texts to learn what the gods mean when they praise or denounce particular actions. The Euthyphros of this world would have us do whatever the gods (i.e., these fanatics) command because their god possesses an invariably correct will. To put the point bluntly: individuals act fanatically whenever they turn themselves into gods, project their will to power into the heavens, and unilaterally decide that they are the sole, correct interpreters of the law of heaven. Since this law means exactly what the fanatics take it to mean, they are not bound by anyone else's interpretation of divine will.

If we follow Euthyphro's assertion to its logical conclusion, Euthyphro would be justified in castrating his father because Zeus emasculated Chronos. Euthyphro glosses over this implication, presumably because Athenian law did not permit individuals to castrate their fellow citizens. To claim the right to castrate would raise the crucial question the fanatic always suppresses: what is the relationship among divine action, human understanding, and human justice? Is justice identical with whatever some god is portrayed as doing (e.g., castrating a father, eating a child)? Or would a reasoned inquiry establish that even the godhead is constrained to act in accordance with the demands of objective justice, truth, and goodness? If so, no one has a reason to feel obligated to imitate divine actions as portrayed in sacred texts. We cannot know how the divine acts unless and until we know what justice is and what demands justice places upon the godhead, as well as on human beings.

I develop this point later in this chapter. Here I want to call attention to our bad faith. At the same time that we claim to know what is holy and just, we suppress the very questions we would need to address in order to establish our expertise. Instead, we zealously and self-righteously proclaim ourselves to be moral experts. This proclamation is merely a variant of our fanatical belief that we are divine. After all, who is the "expert," if not someone who is wiser than other men and women and better able to do what is right and good for the individual and the collective? And who could be more expert, powerful, and beneficial than a god? When Socrates suggests that Euthyphro should be careful lest some powerful person decide to prosecute him, Euthyphro contemptuously retorts that he would smash anyone who dared to bring him to trial. Fanatics think their actions and speeches are the thunderbolts of Zeus, capable of destroying any and all opposition. This belief gives them the confidence and strength to hold on to their suspect, dread-inducing beliefs.

Religious fervor and certainty characterize fanatics, even those who deny the existence of the divine. Avowed atheists make their disbelief into a holy cause. Their quest to prove that God does not exist serves as their god. Plato is interested in exploring what the holy is, not because all fanatics admit to being religious but because they all fervently worship one god—themselves. Whatever they believe about themselves, they project this belief with a vengeance onto their cause/god out of desperation to preserve their self-image. As a result, the fanatic's god always assumes a savage aspect, regardless of what the sacred texts of the fanatic's culture say about the divine.

Cultures attribute manifold aspects to the godhead. In the case of monotheistic cultures, these aspects get expressed as multiple dimensions of a single god (Allah [Adonai, God] is merciful, just, compassionate, righteously angry). Polytheistic religions depict the aspects as distinct gods (Shiva is god of creation and destruction; Saraswathi is goddess of learning). The god of fanatics, though, has no tolerant, loving, or compassionate aspect. Their god always desires the annihilation of those whom fanatics take to be their enemies. Euthyphro displays none of

Aphrodite's eroticism or Hermes' quick wit. He does not exhibit the kindness of Zeus, god of friendship. The fanatic embodies only the raging will of Zeus the destroyer. Just as Zeus would destroy his father god Chronos, so, too, would Euthyphro obliterate those whom he judges to be unjust. Just as angry Chronos would remake the world in his image by swallowing his children, who represent the varied aspects of the divine, so, too, would the fanatic inside us remake the divine in our narrow, dogmatic image.

Again I stress that atheistic, as well as theistic, fanatics project their will to power into the heavens. Self-professing atheists equally see themselves as avenging gods who are justified in destroying the stupid fools who think the godhead exists. Their insistence that they have never experienced the divine becomes a self-fulfilling proposition. As Abraham Lincoln observed in the passage I quote at the beginning of this chapter, when men and women turn themselves into gods, they eliminate the distinction between the two and thereby expel the divine from their lives. The fact that the atheist does not experience the divine does not prove that it does not exist. Having overthrown the godhead and installed themselves as rulers of the heavens, atheists can have no sense of the divine.

Fanaticism as the Unreasonable Repudiation of Reason

When Socrates asks Euthyphro whether he believes everything the sacred poetic texts say about the gods, Euthyphro insists that every word is true. All fanatics are literalists. Acknowledging no independent standard by which to assess what human beings write and say about the divine, they maintain "the text speaks for itself." That is another way of saying that the text means only what they, the expert interpreters, claim that it means. The text becomes, in Euthyphro's terms, a self-sufficient "proof."

Atheists on a holy mission to prove the nonexistence of a god are equally literalists. They take at face value everything said and written by like-minded men and women. Atheistic tracts function as their scripture. Theistic and atheistic religionists substitute their will to power for truth and wisdom as they fashion a god/no god in their image. The character of this fanatical projection is especially clear in Euthyphro's case. Euthyphro's gods are not infinitely wise beings who know the truth about the right way to live. His literalism transforms the gods into overly zeal-ous, angry men intent on destruction, men equipped with bodies to be bound, with throats to swallow children, and with genitals to be castrated.

Having replaced truth with willfulness and having embraced a dogmatic literalism, the fanatic has no solid basis for reasonably discrimi-nating among courses of action. When Socrates presses Euthyphro to state what holiness is, Euthyphro can only equate holiness with what he happens to be doing now, "prosecuting murder and temple theft and everything of that sort."[9] Since whatever fanatics do or say is just and right in their eyes, they see no reason to demonstrate why one course of action is better than another. Although they offer impassioned defenses of their cause, this appeal to reason is illusory. In reality, they have banished reason from their lives. They subsequently attempt to fill this gaping hole with their passion, especially with their rage at a world that stubbornly refuses to recognize the legitimacy of their cause.

When Socrates presses Euthyphro to define holiness, not merely to offer a list of holy actions, Euthyphro describes the holy as "that which is dear to or beloved by the gods."[10] This description has the merit of succinctly expressing the worldview of the fanatic. Having made ourselves into gods, our divine eyes perceive whatever thing or cause we happen to love as "holy." But as a definition of the holy, Euthyphro's response is useless for three reasons.

First, if the holy is whatever the divine happens to love, it cannot serve as a standard for discriminating infallibly among courses of action. This characterization of holiness merely restates the fanatic's tacit equation "truth equals whatever I say it is." For who decides what is dear to the gods? The fanatic! And if the holy is whatever we fallible human beings deem it to be, appealing to the holy to ascertain how we should behave is a charade. We might as well say, "This course of action is just because I prefer to act this way." Far from liberating us from illusion, this notion of holiness condemns us to persist in the error of our ways. It simultane-ously turns the gods into strange beings. If the holy is what the gods love, then the gods are holy only insofar as they love themselves. The fanatic transforms the omniscient divine into an omnipotent spoiled brat.

Second, the belief that the holy is identical with what the divine loves leads to insoluble conflicts. Different cultures have different gods. These gods do not always agree about what is just, beautiful, and good. One god may love a just thing or cause hated by another god. Therefore, if divine love suffices to make a thing holy while divine hate makes it unholy, then the same object will be simultaneously holy and unholy. The fanatic tries to save the holy by arguing that his or her god is the one and only true god. However, since fanatics in other countries or sects do the same, this appeal to the true god does not resolve conflict. Instead, it serves as a rallying cry for fanatics on each side to join forces and to attack those heathens who worship a false god.

The problem of disagreeing gods is acute in a polytheistic culture like that of Athens. When pressed, Euthyphro concedes that the Olympian gods are at war with each other because they disagree about what is just and unjust, beautiful and ugly, and good and evil. Instead of functioning as a standard for guiding choice and resolving disagreements over what is good or evil, the definition of holiness as that which is dear to the gods leaves us at odds with others and with ourselves. As Socrates notes, Euthyphro's certainty that he knows where right and justice lie places him at the mercy of disagreeing gods:

> Euthyphro, it would not be surprising if what you are now doing in punishing your father were dear to Zeus, but hateful to Chronos and Uranus, and loved by Hephaestus, but hateful to Hera, and if any of the other gods disagree about it, the same will be true of them.[11]

Monotheistic Westerners may be tempted to pity poor polytheistic Euthyphro, whose gods are forever disagreeing. However, we should not be smug. Socrates' argument applies to all members of the world community. This larger community is as polytheistic as ancient Athens. Buddhism's god is not the same as that of Christians or Jews. The problem is even worse. To the extent that we view ourselves as gods, we must be said to live among several billion contending deities. Euthyphro's plight is ours. At war with ourselves and our neighbors, we expend our energy in asserting our righteousness, instead of thinking about why we are so angry. This misallocation of time leaves us feeling anxious and teetering on the brink of violence. No wonder Socrates invokes Zeus, the god of friendship, whenever he points to a difficulty with Euthyphro's understanding of virtue and holiness.

The dialogue suggests a third reason why a fanatical understanding of holiness and justice cannot serve as a practical standard. We would need to know who or what the divine is to adjudicate among religious experts claiming to know the will of god. We need a standard for infallibly identifying a true god. Unless and until we know for certain what the divine is, we cannot know which god speaks and acts truly. If we cannot distinguish between a false and true god by appealing to a standard that makes a true god be such, then we cannot know which religious authority merits our trust. Since fanatics are utterly unaware of the existence of any standard, they have no inkling as to how to provide a satisfactory answer to Socrates' initial question: what is the holy? They can only point to a feature of the holy—the holy is beloved by the gods. They acknowledge the fact of discrimination—the gods love some things and hate other things—but cannot offer any basis for this discrimination. Divine love appears to be utterly arbitrary and irrational. It appears as unmotivated and unjustified as fanatics' love of their beliefs.

Even if all the gods in the world agreed in loving one thing or person, it still would not follow that this beloved object is holy. Any agreement might be accidental and might change at some point. Until we understand the basis for this divine love, we have no reason to characterize a particular thing, or person, or being as truly holy. Knowing that something is loved or hated by the divine is not helpful. We need to know *why* the gods love or despise this thing. Knowing why entails understanding the procedure by which the divine discrimination is made. This discriminative procedure must be one that human reason finds compelling. If the gods arbitrarily love one thing and hate another, it does not matter in which god we place our trust. Every god is equally true or false; and every human choice is arbitrary. There would be no point in looking for divine guidance in such circumstances. We do not need the god's assistance to act arbitrarily. We can do that by ourselves.

What procedure, then, enables the gods and human beings to distinguish infallibly between that which is holy and worthy of being loved and that which is unholy? Appealing to consensus will not suffice, because (1) neither the gods as depicted in sacred texts nor we agree as to what should be loved, and (2) even if we could point to some consensus, the mere fact that consensus happens to exist would not satisfy our reason. How, then, can we hope to discern what is truly holy? Or—what amounts to the same thing—how can we overcome the fanaticism lurking in our hearts?

Overcoming the Fanatic within

Although the discussion between Socrates and Euthyphro centers on the holy, the fundamental issue is one of standards. Each of us, fanatic or not, desires to know the best way to live. We differ on how we define a satisfying life. Some equate happiness with being wealthy; others with having fame, knowledge, or power. Despite the difference of opinion, we all want to live a genuinely satisfying life. In order to live such a life, we need to be able to discriminate between better and worse ways of thinking and acting.

Earlier I said that the fanatic's rationality is one-sided. In fact, truth is more damning: reason has no force in the lives of fanatics. The moral standard they endorse is not a standard at all. A standard is a nonarbitrary method sanctioned and used by reason to resolve an issue about which human beings may or do disagree. Given that a fanatical moral vision merely recapitulates the will to power, such a vision cannot help us find the best way to live. Overcoming our incipient fanaticism requires that we identify what, if anything, qualifies as a standard for acting and speaking well.

In light of our quarrels over this issue, we should begin by asking: do we have any reason to think such a standard exists? Yes, for we routinely employ a nonarbitrary way of settling disagreements. As Socrates points out, when we disagree over which of two sums is greater, we quickly settle the matter by counting. If our dispute with another turns on which is the larger or the smaller, we turn to measurement to resolve the issue. In cases where we disagree about the heavier or lighter, we go to a balance. Although all three of Socrates' examples involve numbers and mathematics, they possess a normative dimension. We believe we *should* turn to counting or to measurement to resolve our disputes instead of resorting to violence. We choose one action (counting) over another (striking each other) because we comprehend that what is at stake is not something that can be decided satisfactorily by force or will power. I may think seven plus eight is greater than eight plus eight, while you may insist on the reverse. I can beat you into submission with a speech or with a hammer, but my will to power can never make fifteen be greater than sixteen. We both understand that we should turn to counting to arrive at a good or satisfying answer to the question of which sum is larger. Why is counting the better course?

Counting is the repeated application of a standard or unit, a unit we call "one." We give a unique name to each successive application of this unchanging standard. We call the first iteration "two," the second "three" and so on. Each integer is a named application of this unit one, which the ancient Greeks insisted, was not a number like two or three. Since one is the standard by which a number is that number, one cannot itself be a number. We grasp that "one" has the being necessary for it to be a standard: one is always one, regardless of who thinks it or when or where they do this thinking. We posit the unit one as the standard and then use it repeatedly to number all integers (i.e., all applications of the standard).

The crucial point is that, each time we count, we acknowledge (1) that a standard exists, and (2) that the standard is a standard only insofar as it never alters. If the unit one were to change from iteration to iteration, then numbers would not be comparable or orderable. The fact that the standard is fixed and unchanging through all applications and is known to be such is what qualifies it to be the standard. We could say that reason is able to use this standard to resolve disputes over the relative quantity of numbers. But we would speak more accurately if we said that the repeated, unchanging, self-conscious use of reason is the standard by which we resolve any dispute over quantity. When we count, we knowingly and consistently apply the unit one, the unit of unchanging and unified being that reason intuits we must use if numbers are to be numerable. Each use of the unit is simultaneously an application of a standard and a disciplined movement of reason.

The same logic applies to measuring and balancing, the other examples Socrates cites. To compare lengths or weights, we must define a specific piece of wood or mass as the unit of length and weight, respectively. The material unit is a matter of convention. The designated length may be an inch or a centimeter, the designated weight, an ounce or a gram. However, the fact that we can use these conventional units to compare lengths and weights is not a matter of convention. To compare we must count, and counting is the repeated, unchanging application of reason— the unit "one"—that serves as a standard because of its objective features. Since the standard is self-identical and invariable, it serves to measure the length (weight, etc.) of any object in the world. Although the material objects we wish to count or measure may change in their dimensions over time, the being of a standard never alters, and its universality enables us to rely upon it in a variety of contexts.

The standard is not only a source of being but also of truth. Counting makes sixteen be greater than fifteen and causes it to be true that sixteen is greater than fifteen, regardless of the context. Socrates refers to a universal standard that is the source of being and of truth as an *eidos* (plural *eidē*). Socrates always asks his interlocutors to specify the *eidos* of the subject under discussion so that he can assess how wise they are. If Euthyphro truly knows that prosecution of his father is holy, then he ought to be able to state the *eidos* of the holy:

> What sort of thing do you say the pious and impious are, with respect to murder and other things as well? Or is not the holy, [taken in] itself, the same in every action? And the unholy, in turn, the opposite of all the holy—is it not like itself, and does not everything which is to be unholy have a certain single character (*eidos*) with respect to unholiness?[12]

Socrates is not asking for a synonym or feature of holiness or for a list of holy things. He wants the standard of holiness. Only by knowing the *eidos* or standard of the holy/unholy can we correctly distinguish between actions and speech that are holy and those that are not.

Socrates grants that many things are holy. In asking about the *eidos* of the holy, he wants to learn what is responsible for these things being unquestionably and invariably holy.[13] Euthyphro initially does not understand Socrates', question. His confusion is understandable. Since fanatics believe something is right because they say so, they have no conscious experience of the *eidē*. Euthyphro's first instinct is to provide Socrates with examples of his supposedly holy actions. The fanatic's examples of holy actions are of no use to reason because he or she provides no standard for ascertaining why these cited actions are holy while others are not. Instead of advancing our understanding of what is holy, Euthyphro's list—his "proof"—short-circuits any attempt at reasoned discussion. We are supposed to accept that something is true merely because the speaker—a religious expert, a poet, a text, or a tradition—insists on the point.

Given that we are human beings who are prone to error, this appeal to authority is not compelling. How do we know that the authority in question can be trusted? The problem of the standard for right behavior has been shifted to another locus. We need a standard or *eidos* of authority that will enable us to discriminate infallibly among the many who claim to know the truth. If this *eidos* of authority is responsible for making an authority truly an authority, then this or that particular authority cannot be the *eidos* or standard we are seeking. The fanatics' appeal to a particular authority is another ruse of their will to power.

When we indulge our desire for power, we repudiate the use of reason. This repudiation, like the other actions of the fanatic, is in bad faith. When we count or perform any sort of measurement, our reason implicitly acknowledges the existence of an objective standard that is one with itself, always the same, and universal in its applicability. We invoke this standard daily to answer all sorts of contentious questions: is the federal deficit larger or smaller than it was in the previous year? Did our butcher provide us with more or less than the quantity of meat we requested? How many weapons of mass destruction are there in Iraq? We cannot live without the standard that makes such comparisons possible. Yet, when we disagree with someone about what is just, courageous, noble, or holy, we suddenly act as if we know for certain that there exist no *eidē*—no standards of justice, beauty, courage, or holiness—applicable to human disputes.

Our certainty and bad faith cause us to misunderstand why we are disagreeing. Like Euthyphro, we imagine that disagreement reduces to a clash of wills. Socrates offers a different interpretation of the source of conflict. Our disagreement and mutual enmity, he suggests, is a consequence of our failure to use our knowledge of what a standard is (the knowledge we use whenever we count or measure) in the search for the *eidos* of the thing about which we are quarreling. We inevitably fail to find this standard of holiness or justice because we have not gone looking for it. On this score, Plato agrees with Aristotle: evil is a failure to exert ourselves. The difference between the two thinkers is that Plato sees evil as a lack of self-knowledge stemming from our propensity to assume that we fully understand who we are, while Aristotle locates evil in a blameworthy, voluntary failure to accept responsibility for the deeds we initiate.

To search for *eidē* is not quixotic. When Socrates pushes Euthyphro to give a proper definition of the holy, Euthyphro does not object that such a definition is impossible. On the contrary, he quickly abandons his list of particular holy actions and abstracts a feature that looks more like a standard—the holy is whatever is loved by, or dear to, the gods. When that definition is shown to be inadequate because it lacks the objective being of a standard, Euthyphro and the reader are able to join Socrates in trying a new line of thought. We may not know the answer to Socrates' question of whether the "the holy is part of the just" or "the just is part of the holy," but we do understand the question. Socrates postulates an abstract relation (part/whole) between two *eidē*—holiness and justice—and asks us to judge which standard is more inclusive, the holy or the just. Like Euthyphro, we are able to orient ourselves toward these two *eidē* and to start thinking about their relationship because we already have some apprehension of what a standard or *eidos* is.

To determine whether holiness is part of justice or the reverse, we must use our tacit knowledge about standards of holiness and justice. Given that we proceed with this analytical task without balking, we must think ourselves equal to the task. Our reason immediately grasps that using these two *eidē* to analyze the relationship between them is a job for reason. Therefore, if we refuse the challenge, the problem is our fanaticism, not our reason. If we already possess some knowledge of the *eidē* or standards of holiness and justice, we need only clarify our thinking to grasp them. Performing this clarification requires thinking of the standard as a standard. Doing that entails relinquishing our certainty that our beliefs are completely correct. Our opinions must be examined to see whether they conform to a standard and so qualify as reliable guides for the best way to live.

The moment we relinquish our certainty, we can start to make progress in understanding what is holy or just. Progress becomes possible for two reasons. First, we can engage with friends and colleagues in discussions aimed at learning about the just, the holy, the beautiful, and so forth. When both of us understand that the will to power can never function as the requisite standard, we can have a pleasant, sustained conversation that does not degenerate into a shouting match. Each party can benefit from the other's insights. As the Greek proverb has it, "two see farther than one." In addition, our understanding can deepen because suddenly we have room in our lives for divine inspiration. Socrates repeatedly alludes to how dependent he is on his divine voice or *daimon* to guide him in life. It appears that turning away from fanaticism is a turning toward the divine.

What is meant by the divine in this context? Socrates' question about the relation between the just and the holy provides the clue. Let us begin by assuming that justice is, roughly, the practice of rendering to each relevant party that which is his or her due. Justice appears to be the wider notion, so let us hypothesize that the holy is a part of justice, instead of the reverse. If so, holiness must consist in rendering to the divine its due. But what can we human beings render to the divine? Socrates and Euthyphro reject the notion that human beings and the gods are engaged in a business transaction, with each side giving the other what it desires in return for being provided with what it needs or lacks. Such a view destroys the divine by assimilating it to the human. The divine is complete. Since it lacks nothing, we cannot serve the divine by giving it what it needs.

Perhaps, though, Euthyphro is on the right path when he tells Socrates that human beings owe honor to the divine. Many peoples do honor the divine by praying for guidance and sacrificing to the godhead. True to form, Euthyphro interprets such acts as holy on the ground that the gods desire and are pleased with our prayers and sacrifices. This interpretation cannot be correct. It takes us back to our unsatisfactory starting point, that is, the holy is whatever the gods love, the unholy, whatever they hate. There is, however, an alternative interpretation of prayer and sacrifice. Socrates suggests that we come before the godhead in reverence. The *eidos* of reverence is, according to Socrates, the fear and dread of being accused of acting unjustly. Accused by whom? By the gods. As Socrates argued previously, how our fellow citizens view us is of little moment. Their perception may be wrong. Meletus has accused Socrates of introducing new gods into the state and of corrupting the young. Socrates denies both charges, maintaining that Meletus and others like him are the ones who are guilty of injustice and impiety. Given that human opinions frequently are in error, we feel reverence for the divine, not for our fellow citizen. Our reverence makes sense only to the extent that the divine apprehends the truth about justice and justly determines whether we are guilty of wrongdoing.

For our shame before the divine to be warranted, god must have infallible knowledge of which acts, speech, and thoughts are truly shameful. Recall that the *eidē* makes a thing or statement be true. Consequently, the divine must be that which apprehends the *eidē* of everything figuring in human action, speech, and thought. Any true god apprehends all *eidē* and acts in accordance with this apprehension. Socrates, therefore, is right to be skeptical about Euthyphro's description of warring gods. God is not some Titan or superhero residing on Mount Olympus. The fact that human beings are capable of reverence shows that the true divinity lives inside us. We feel shame and dread when we are accused of wrongdoing by the god whom we call our conscience and whom Socrates refers to as his *daimon*.

According to Socrates, the god within never gives us positive orders or directives.[14] The divine warns against some courses of action by prompting us to have second thoughts about the wisdom of performing the action we are proposing. This negative or arresting quality follows from the divine's *eidos* as that which apprehends the *eidē* of all things. Recall that the *eidos* of a thing is its source of being. A just action or law is just by virtue of the *eidos* of the justice. Every thing in the world is what it is because the *eidē* are. The *eidē* are not material beings; they are logical or necessary beings. The *eidē* are the *eidē* only when they compel thinking about being, including the being of the *eidē* themselves. For the godhead to know infallibly the truth of all things, it must apprehend continually all the *eidē*. Without this apprehension, nothing would have being or be knowable. Even the divine must submit to eidetic necessity. The *eidē* compel human thinking by orienting our inquiry toward what must be and by revealing themselves more fully as we use them to formulate increasingly better hypotheses about holiness, justice, goodness, and beauty.

Insofar as they guide our thinking about what is, the *eidē* must exist prior to our grasping them. Once we commit to searching for the *eidē* of justice and holiness, we begin to glimpse them more fully and start to have second thoughts about the justice and holiness of our actions. Since each *eidos* is related to all other *eidē*, a clearer apprehension of one *eidos* forces us to widen and deepen our understanding of all *eidē*. We find ourselves arrested and compelled to think before we proceed. That accounts for why our conscience warns against actions but never proposes them.

If this reasoning is sound, we can understand why Socrates takes such pains to establish that the holy is not the holy because it happens to be loved by the gods. The gods love the holy, he argues, because it is the holy. We can only love that which is. The holy (and any other *eidos*) is lovable because, and insofar as, the holy is an *eidos* or source of being of all that is holy, including the holy itself. This eidetic being motivates divine love. The divine has a reason to love the holy, the just, and the good because their eidetic being enables the divine to be all-knowing. If it were not for the *eidē*, the divine would have nothing to be wise about and, therefore, would not be divine. Conversely, if the divine did not continually think the *eidē*, the *eidē* would not be the thought-constraining logical entities that they are.

Unlike us, the godhead thinks all *eidē* at the same time. Limited human nature prevents us from apprehending the whole universe in all its aspects. We catch glimpses of an *eidos*, which gives us some sense of how this *eidos* is connected to the other *eidē*. At best, we can intuit the whole under a single aspect—for example, under the aspect of holiness. But the infinite divine does not provide us with a complete set of rules for how to live our lives. Fanatics think they have such rules because they conflate the finitely human with the infinitely divine. Like Hendrik Höfgen, Tom Ripley, and James's governess, fanatics shrink the universe to the size of the self. The nonfanatical among us must settle for glimmers of the just or the holy, those second thoughts that a problem, question, or situation may be more complicated than we originally thought, and that we had better stop and think before acting. Once we sacrifice our arrogant certainty that we are wise, the divine answers our prayer for guidance by inviting us to join it in the activity of thinking. But no genuine alternative to engaging in the hard work of thinking and self-examination exists.

Reluctant to relinquish his expertise, Euthyphro does not realize that he and Socrates have been circling around the holy the entire time. Reflecting upon the arguments considered up to this point, we discover that we have caught sight of the holy. The holy is the totality of being, a totality necessarily and continually thought and loved by the divine because being is eidetic. Since the godhead loves the standards or *eidē* of all things, human beings rightly revere the divine as the source of great blessings. Eidetic being—the being of a standard—is what enables us to grasp progressively what is truly in our interest and to arrive at genuinely satisfying answers to practical disputes. The holy gives us a reason to exchange our supposed expertise for a love of wisdom and to abandon our illusion of omnipotence. Real reverence means letting the divine be godly by refusing to conflate the human with the divine.

Why Fanaticism Should Be Judged Evil

All religions portray the world as a battleground for the human soul: we live a good or an evil life. The above analysis of fanaticism supports this claim. We either orient ourselves toward the *eidē*, or we persist in identifying ourselves with suspect, unstable beliefs about how best to live. Fanaticism or false piety becomes a way of life, what Christian scripture describes as the broad and easy path of damnation. When we mistake false piety for true reverence of the divine, we err with respect to the most important thing in life. We fail in the eternal task imposed upon every man and woman, the charge immortally expressed in the carving upon the temple of the oracle at Delphi: "Know thyself." Mistaking ourselves for gods, we fail to be human.

To be human is to share intermittently in divine contemplation of unchanging objective standards. To be human is to be like a god but never to be one. In practicing false piety, we victimize ourselves. Evil is, first and foremost, unwitting self-destruction. In our deluded state, we may or may not harm another living being. Self-injury, though, is inevitable, because our certainty removes us from the truth we need in order to live well. As in the case of satanic evil, our evil is less "a purposing of what is *not good*" and more what the theologian Martin Buber describes as a "*not purposing of what is good.*"[15] Our certainty that we already know the best way to live locks us into neurotic and unsatisfying patterns of behavior. It prevents us from using the insight we already possess to arrive at a more defensible understanding of the self and the world in which we must operate.

This ignorance of who we are makes us violent. Believing ourselves to be divine, we are tempted to attack our fellow citizens. Certain that our cause is unquestionably just and right, we have no patience with anyone who objects to our position. Whatever we say and believe must be true because we want it to be so. That which we desire is, in our eyes, necessarily good. Our zeal prevents us from perceiving those whom we maim or kill as we set about enforcing our universal moral vision. For the Osama bin Ladens, Timothy McVeighs, and Euthyphros of this world, the people they kill are mere "collateral damage." Although Euthyphro knows that Socrates is facing a capital charge and may soon be dead, he blithely (and with no sense of irony) promises to talk with Socrates at greater length in the days ahead. Socrates and his fate are invisible to Euthyphro who rushes away to attend to his business of prosecuting his father.

In lashing out at others, we inadvertently victimize ourselves. Euthyphro prosecutes his father on the ground that anyone guilty of an unjust murder should be put to death or exiled. As the dialogue progresses, it becomes clear to the lover of wisdom that Euthyphro himself may be guilty of plotting the unjust murder of his father. Euthyphro unconsciously demonstrates how little he has thought about any standard, much less about what justice is. Euthyphro would be more just if he devoted less energy to prosecution and more to inquiry. As it stands, Euthyphro, not Socrates, appears to be the one who has polluted the city through injustice. According to the dictates of his own fanatical vision, Euthyphro deserves to die. Our ignorance of who we are results in our being hoisted on our moral petard.

To lack self-knowledge is to expose ourselves to irony. Other people can discern what we cannot: namely, that our self-proclaimed benevolence masks naked, deadly ambition. Our falsely pious actions are not only ironic but also comical. We look ridiculous as we bring about the very danger we have promised to avert. Although fanatics portray themselves as holy protectors of family and national values, the lovers of wisdom (men and women like Socrates) are the ones who qualify as truly pious preservers of the state. Fanatics feel no reverence. They have no fear that they will stand before the divine, accused of injustice. A man like Euthyphro is not in the least concerned that he may be acting unjustly in charging his father with murder. In mounting this prosecution and repudiating the bonds of natural affection, Euthyphro does what he imputes to Socrates' accuser Meletus—he strikes a blow at the "heart of the city."[16] If, as Euthyphro insists, the divine keeps our families and state safe from danger, then the politically unwise actions of men like Euthyphro and Meletus must be judged to be violations of divine law. Socrates draws this conclusion explicitly in the *Apology*.[17] The fanatic, not the lover of wisdom and dialogue, is the one guilty of introducing new gods into the state. Euthyphro elevates himself to the pantheon when he argues that he is entitled to perform any action that scripture imputes to the gods. Socrates' sardonic remark that Meletus should be prosecuting Euthyphro for impiety, not him, rings true. The modest, humble lover of wisdom is far more conservative than those who claim to have the knowledge and power necessary to preserve the status quo.

False piety brings in its wake all the forms of suffering we have seen in connection with other manifestations of evil: dread, paranoia, rage, dissatisfaction, alienation, the loss of the power to act creatively, a propensity toward violence. If we do not orient ourselves toward the *eidē*, we come to resemble Dante's sinners who feel no reverence and experience no shame. We become as moralistic as Tom Ripley who coolly murders while presuming to judge other people's behavior. The fanatic in us shares Hendik Höfgen's narcissism as well: we start to depend on other people for our self-esteem. To realize their vision of a moral order, fanatics need followers. Without adherents, the fanatic in us is nothing. Our self-esteem is as fragile as a mirror.

Since fanatics deem themselves gods; and since they define evil as that which is hated by the divine, they think everyone whom they spurn must be wicked. By hating and fearing almost everyone, our inner Euthyphro populates the world with enemies. Through satanizing others, we justify our paranoia and our self-proclaimed status as saviors of humanity. Having cast ourselves in this salvific role, we subsequently feel entitled to do whatever it takes to rescue humanity from demons. Like James's paranoid governess, we hope thereby to garner the respect of our fellow citizens, respect that we need to assure ourselves that we are not ridiculous. In our effort to avoid ridicule, we descend into madness.

A Double Approach to Resisting Evil

I come to the last question I posed at the beginning of this chapter: how should we resist evil? There are no guarantees that we can defeat fanaticism once and for all, or that we will not ourselves be guilty at one time or another of false piety. Nonetheless, we can take some modest steps to combat the fanatic within.

Embarking on a quest for self-knowledge and truth about how best to live is the first step. People must discover for themselves a way to begin this quest. I prescribe no particular starting point. I have found it useful to pay attention to my outrage. Whenever I begin to feel incensed about anything, I ask myself whether my rage is justified. Usually it turns out that I have some opinion or commitment that needs to be examined. Outrage engenders obsession, which readily converts into fanaticism. It may be an overstatement to say that all evil is fanatical. But, insofar as evil consists in the self's false identifications, all evil tends toward the fanatical because the self feels driven to silence anyone who appears to threaten its suspect identity. I have also found it helpful to interrogate the unease I feel whenever I am in the presence of those who will not shut up and who will not change their minds. With the help of Plato, I have come to understand that this unease arises from an apprehension or intuition of the *eidos* of the holy. The holy invites us to seek after the *eidē* of things and to resist any suggestion, external or internal, that truth is merely whatever we desire it to be.

If Socrates is right about fanaticism harming us, we should take a second step. We should structure our educational system so that our children will have an experience of necessary truth. By receiving formal training in pure and applied mathematics, children learn what it means to think in a disciplined way. Using the *eidos* of number, children learn to construct addition and multiplication tables. As they age and become more adept at abstract manipulation, they can employ axioms and definitions to prove the existence of properties of numbers and figures and to show why some statements are necessarily true while others must be false.

This experience of formal necessity can be helpful in later life. For, apart from some training in mathematics, political regimes do not provide citizens with much practice in fashioning a disciplined life. Instead, they instill in us a mishmash of conflicting opinions. We mistake this inheritance of contradictory opinions for lasting knowledge and then build our identity upon its shifting sands. Not realizing that we could turn to the *eidē*, we remain mired in our confusion. Having little practice in examining our opinions with a view to finding an unimpeachable basis for them, we discover, under questioning, that our opinions are self-contradictory and our identity unstable. Socrates likens us to Proteus, the shape-shifter, who could not be pinned down. Our words are like the works of Daedalus, the sculptor who formed statues out of rock and then animated them. After investing ourselves in our beliefs—animating them—we find that everything we "propose goes round in circles on us and will not stand still."[18] Our opinions will never stand still, and we will never rest easy, until we have examined our beliefs with a view to uncovering the *eidē* of the just, the beautiful, the good, and the holy. Failing that, we will be as anxious as Euthyphro, who scurries away when Socrates presses him to try once more to state what holiness is.

If we are serious about resisting evil, we need to consider ways to make public discourse more disciplined and eidetic. Checks and balances are a step in the right direction. They force the branches of government to speak with each other and encourage individuals to make and evaluate arguments. A free press is helpful, if it behaves responsibly. Our newspapers do us no service when they print stories for shock value or when they pander to the public's sense of outrage. Journalists should ask public figures not only to state and to defend their positions but also to define their terms precisely. As it now stands, citizens and leaders accuse each other of injustice and impiety without ever being held accountable for defining these terms. We get away with sloppy speech. As a result, we fail to examine our opinions and behaviors.

Justice, like charity, begins at home. If we fear doing injustice, we should refuse to spread malicious gossip and should be wary of prosecuting other people. Euthyphro remarks in passing that he is surprised to see Socrates in court. He would never have suspected Socrates of filing a charge against anyone. However, Euthyphro does not bother to wonder why Socrates is so reticent. Given the above argument, we can comprehend the reluctance of the lover of wisdom to accuse his or her fellow citizens. Just as Jesus warns that we should remove the mite from our eye before attempting to improve the vision of others, so Socrates asks us to examine whether we truly know what justice is. Before we assume responsibility for the souls of other people, we should look to the health of our own. We can judge soundly only if we are oriented toward and actively inquiring after the *eidē*. So our energy should be devoted to seeking out those who have some insights into such matters, instead of persecuting people who may or may not be guilty of wrongdoing. As the poet Rainer Maria Rilke writes, we should be concerned about whether we are leading a life in accordance with "the law" of our self's development, not worrying unduly about whether other people are realizing their true selves.[19]

If all regimes consist of people who are mistaken about who they are, confused about what is most important in life, and prone to behave unjustly toward others, does it follow that communities should stop enforcing their laws? A lover of wisdom will give a nuanced answer to this question. On the one hand, a community needs to impose rules of behavior. A community cannot exist, much less prosper, unless some behavioral norms are observed. No community can allow its members to murder with impunity or to rob each other of the means to stay alive. Those who flout the law must be restrained so that individuals can thrive. It may be true, as Socrates argues elsewhere, that no one else can ever truly harm us. We alone determine how we stand with respect to the *eidē*. Therefore, we alone determine whether we are living a good life. However, we cannot investigate the truth of this claim if we are harassed continually and prevented from enjoying the leisure we need to think. Our children need safety and security to develop the discipline described above. Perhaps that is why, in his talk with Euthyphro, Socrates never questions the state's right to prohibit murder or to punish those who have polluted the city. The state has a right to protect its citizenry, regardless of whether the accused act in ignorance (I use "act" loosely, because, as we have seen, evil destroys the ability to act) or with intent to harm. People are not less harmful merely because they have acted without knowledge or intent. People with highly infectious and life-threatening diseases intend no harm, yet we grant the state the right to quarantine such individuals.

On the other hand, if we act unjustly and impiously out of ignorance, then the way to improve the community is to create a space in which philosophy can be practiced and in which people can be encouraged to be as thoughtful as possible. Education, rooted in the *eidē*, disciplined dialogue, and moderating religious or ethical beliefs (e.g., "love thy neighbor," "turn the other cheek") should be promoted at the same time as laws are promulgated and enforced. This double approach is crucial. No political regime can endure long if it must resort regularly to extreme punitive measures to control behavior and create a semblance of harmony. Without education and civil religion, we will continue to harm ourselves in the ways described above. That harm is real and, if we fail to devote ourselves to the truth, certain. Education is crucial because the existence of evil raises questions that the state cannot address by means of fiat, questions about the basis of the state's authority. As I noted above, whether anyone else has the power to harm us—whether the assumption underlying a regime's legal system of punishment is sound—is an open question. Confucius, Lao-tzu, as well as Socrates, have argued that we alone have the ability to hurt ourselves; no outsider can truly harm us. This claim may or may not be true. I do not pretend to resolve it here. The question, though, does merit consideration. Exploring and answering it requires that we use our reason in a disciplined way. Consequently, if we are serious about resisting evil, we should insist that our communities promote education aimed at encouraging such reason.

In addition to encouraging education, disciplined discourse, and salutary religious precepts, a regime should consider the conditions under which its laws are legitimate. Elsewhere I have argued that laws are most lawful and binding when those who are to be bound by the statutes have an opportunity to know and shape those laws, have received some benefits from the laws, and are granted a legal and viable right to exit the regime in the event they believe the laws are unjust.[20] Reason recognizes as binding only those laws that acknowledge the possibility that the laws themselves may be in error. If we demand that our community's laws be legitimate; and if we seek the *eidos* or standard of legitimacy, we will have taken a key step toward resisting evil. There remains the perennial danger recognized by Christian scripture that parties will use the law as an instrument of coercion. We cannot in conscience naively rely upon the law to save us from evil. Yet dispensing with the law is not feasible. It falls to us to demand that our laws meet the standard of legitimacy. If we do not make this demand, we are saying, in effect, that law is nothing but an embodiment of some party's will to power. When law is nothing but power, law does not exist.

All of these modes of resisting evil require that we admit that we are finite beings. Our knowledge of justice and evil is incomplete. We are not certain about the legitimacy of our laws or the basis of the prerogatives we grant to the state. Having spent most of our life assuring ourselves that we know exactly who we are and how the world works, it comes as a shock to realize that our stock of opinions is a house of cards. We can learn, but only if we orient ourselves toward the *eidē* and then use these objective standards of things. By doing that, we can gain insight and progress toward truth and justice. Still, we will never have a god's total comprehension of the universe. Unless we admit that we are merely human, we will continue to deify ourselves. And those who believe themselves to be gods soon become worse than beasts.

9

FINAL THOUGHTS

There is only one thing that I dread: not to be worthy of my sufferings.

—*Fyodor Dosteyevski*

WHEN I BEGAN THIS BOOK, I THOUGHT I WOULD BE ABLE TO SYNTHESIZE A single, all-inclusive definition of evil, specifying its genus and listing and ranking its species. Having thought about the subject for several years, I now believe that this hope was misplaced. Specifying the genus of evil is possible because the different expressions of evil share one or more attributes. If there were no shared essence, we could not distinguish evil from other topics and could not speak sensibly about it. When we spoke of "evil," we might be referring to "chocolate" or "clothes hanger." There must be, therefore, some invariable, core meaning of evil. However, it does not follow that we can specify all the manifestations of evil. As we have seen, evil expresses itself in a remarkable variety of ways. It may appear as a desire to escape boredom, to gain respect, or to save other people; as the social repression of the self, hubristic piety, or unconscious sin. It appears as if evil has as many forms of expression as there are individuals in the world.

Does that mean that the quest to apprehend the nature of evil is doomed? Or does the very multiplicity of the manifestations of evil reveal something important about the nature of evil? Here the wisdom tradition offers insight that moralities do not afford. Unlike moralities that equate evil with vice, malice, intentional sadism, or specific harms, the wisdom tradition conceives of evil as the frustration of the individual's desire for what is lastingly satisfying. From this perspective, evil or frustration necessarily has many forms because what individuals take to be good and desirable varies, depending upon their history, position, circumstances, and adequacy of understanding. James's governess desperately wants an opportunity to govern. Through governing, she hopes to prove herself worthy of her employer's trust and earn the income she needs to escape an unhappy home life. Her investment in her position as governess generates and sustains the threatening figures she requires if she is to prove to her employer that she can govern. For the governess, evil is whatever threatens her post. Dr. Jekyll/Mr. Hyde desires the freedom to indulge whims so that he can discover what he genuinely enjoys doing. However, he also craves the respect of his tight-laced peers. Since he is so conflicted, he experiences a dual evil or double frustration of desire. In Jekyll's eyes, the free, animal spirit of Hyde is evil; for Hyde, the hypocrisy of Jekyll and Jekyll's professional peers threatens his freedom. In Hyde's eyes, this hypocrisy is wickedness.

The difficulty in articulating the nature of evil is compounded because we, the interpreters of these examples, also have a desire. Our desire to know the nature of evil has led us to pay close attention to possible commonalities in the way in which evil operates. This focus on the *eidos* of evil has enabled us to discern certain trajectories or mechanisms not perceived by those who are trapped in these trajectories. As a result, evil looks different to us than it does to the parties whose perspectives and actions we have been analyzing. We perceive what the governess never does: her propensity to imagine the worst drives her into madness and costs her the very post she has fought to keep. Dr. Jekyll thinks his problem is a defect in his character, yet we can see that social forces cause him to split in two.

Those who read James, Stevenson, Dante, Highsmith, and Mann with an alternative question in mind may well perceive a different expression of evil. Unlike James's governess, I make no claim to have "fixed" or "gotten hold" of every possible appearance of evil. All is not lost, though. These appearances seem to share one feature: in every case, evil is the frustration of the individual's desire to obtain or realize what appears truly desirable to him or her, a frustration growing out of the person's attempts to preserve an inadequate conception of the self. If that is so, evil has a genus—frustrated desire. Individuals have unique desires and experience equally unique frustrations. There are as many species of evil as there are people in the world. Evil will have gained a hold on us if we come to believe that we completely comprehend its manifestations. The Greeks knew that such arrogance—*hubris*—is a kissing cousin to evil. Hubris derives from the Greek word *huper. Huper*, like *übel*, the German word for evil, means "to be beyond" or "to exceed." Evil in all its forms will be a mystery beyond us for as long as we are an enigma to ourselves. In this respect, evil resembles prime numbers. We can state what a prime number is without currently being able to determine in every case whether a given number is, in fact, prime. Primeness may not adhere to a pattern. Numbers may be, in some deep sense, individuals. So, too, we may not always be able to tell whether we are in the presence of evil, despite our best efforts to observe and analyze what individual human beings are doing and suffering.

The Genus of Evil: Evil as Frustrated Desire

With this caveat in mind, let us focus on the genus of evil—frustrated desire. The attitudes, stances, commitments, failures, and worldviews I have characterized as evil or as causes of evil impede human thriving in some profound way. Human beings thrive insofar as they satisfy their desires. Our desires have many objects. Some of us lust after wealth, others pleasure, still others pursue honor or knowledge. These four objects—thoroughly discussed by moralists—do not begin to exhaust the range of our desire. Like Dr. Jekyll/Mr. Hyde, we may desire to express and explore hitherto unacknowledged dimensions of our self. In that case, we might be said to crave integration. Or, like Tom Ripley, we may feel overwhelmed by a dreadful boredom and seek to be free of it. Relief becomes the object of our desire.

Regardless of the particular object of desire, we all want one thing: satisfaction for the self. I emphasize the self-referential quality, because every human desire is rooted in the desirer's concept of his or her self. This conceptual component distinguishes human desire from largely instinctive animal desire. While all living things desire to persist and thrive, human desire grows out of a concept of the self. I do not mean that we are always fully aware of who we are. On the contrary, we are typically not aware of the role our self-conception plays in causing us to behave or react in a specific way. What I mean is that, in seeking satisfaction, adults and children act upon a tacit or latent conception of the self.

To take but a few of the cases we have examined: Höfgen requires an audience because he implicitly believes that he is nothing if he is not reflected in the eyes of other people. James's governess devotes herself to protecting the children from Quint and Miss Jessel because doing so gives her life meaning and definition. Dr. Jekyll manufactures a transforming drug because he wants to realize underdeveloped, hidden potentials that he takes to be an essential part of who he is. Having built his entire life around his belief that he understands the will of the gods better than anyone else, Euthyphro wants to eliminate anyone who doubts his expertise. None of these individuals expressly states the self-conception driving him or her to act in specific ways. They are all at the mercy of these desires precisely because they have not examined their assumptions about who they are.

Concepts of the self derive from many sources. Our belief that the self should be preserved comes from nature. From birth, we experience thirst and hunger and act to satisfy our cravings for food and drink. Whatever appears to enable us to endure we call "good." Although we may differ as to who or what the self is, we agree that the good enables the self to thrive. We cannot repudiate this embodied idea of a persisting self; we live it in every fiber of our being. As Kant has observed, even people who commit suicide do so out of the belief that it would be better for them if they were to die instead of continuing to live. They presuppose (unwarrantedly, Kant thought) the continuation of the self at the same time as they act to end their lives.[1] The same holds true in cases of self-sacrifice.

Our inchoate concept of our selves as persisting beings is innate. But the specific content of our self-understanding comes from experience. Falling into a hole teaches us that we are subject to gravity and are capable of feeling pain. Our parents and siblings shape our self-identity through instruction and admonition. Other dimensions of identity grow out of communal expectations. Dr. Jekyll and his friends Utterson and Lanyon have been socialized into a view of what it means to be a professional. Sometimes we posit who we are in an effort to resist other people's attempts to mold us. When Ripley's aunt treats the boy as a loser and a sissy, Ripley sets out to prove his aunt wrong. Reflection and interpretation also contribute to our self-conception. We develop and alter our notion of self by thinking about it. Friends and strangers can help us in this process by asking us tough questions and demanding honest answers. Socrates unsuccessfully encourages Euthyphro to join in this reflective process.

These are but a few of the sources of our self-conception. My interest here is not in listing every source but in arguing that the self is a work in progress. We are forever identifying with different concepts of the self. This is in no way unnatural. Making such identifications is part of what it means to be a living human being. But to say that identification is natural does not make it unproblematic. Given that we are finite human beings who do not have a complete understanding of the world and our place in it, we are forever confusing the self with something that it is not. Euthyphro takes himself to be a god, though he is only a man. James's governess becomes convinced that she is the children's savior at the same time that she evolves into their tormentor. Our mistaken identifications involve us in contradictions that lead us to act in ways that leave us dissatisfied. Dante's hell-bound sinners endlessly repeat the very deeds that they find so tormenting. Perceiving themselves as victims, Jesus' disciples wind up victimizing themselves. Euthyphro's certainty that he understands the divine results in his knowing far less about the divine than Socrates, who claims no special expertise.

We ultimately desire one thing and one thing only—that the self be satisfied. Yet desire is complex because we are two selves—the empirical being we think we are at any particular moment and the transcending being who is forever seeking a more satisfying existence. So what I just said must be qualified. We are a work in progress insofar as our self-conception continually evolves. But we are also unchanging in one crucial respect: regardless of circumstances, the self always desires lasting satisfaction for itself. This ever-present desire drives our development. Even supposedly selfless altruists act in order to satisfy their desire to be the sort of people who benefit their fellow human beings.

No one desires to be satisfied only for a second. At every point of time, we desire to be satisfied for the foreseeable future. We implicitly want what will satisfy us in an abiding way. Only something that provides lasting satisfaction is truly good. And there's the rub. Although each of us strives for satisfaction, our unexamined desires contain the germ of dissatisfaction. Lacking self-knowledge, we pursue what appears good but fails to end our craving. Realizing the genuine good requires self-knowledge. Yet, knowing the self is not easy. Only by attending to what we are experiencing and reflecting on the causes of our frustration can we arrive at a more adequate view of the self and bring our empirical and transcending selves into greater harmony.

What constitutes an adequate view of the self? This question is difficult to answer. An adequate account would recognize how frequently we misjudge what will satisfy us. It would acknowledge that we are affected by many external causes; are buffeted this way and that by our strong passions and misleading imaginings; and are prone to identify with sufferings, roles, positions, loves, and a host of other things that we are not. Since how we think about ourselves is partly a function of the narratives and traditions our community makes available to us, the account would explore the relationship between self and community. A good account would also stress our ability to use reason to free ourselves from these misconceptions and to minimize the extent to which we are subject to external causes and pathological dynamics.

While much more could be said about the self, rendering a full account would take us far afield from the goal of understanding the genus of evil. The main point is sufficiently clear: as long as our self-conception is inadequate, we will find ourselves frustrated. This frustration and suffering, which is exacerbated by an erroneous notion of the self, constitutes evil. From the wisdom perspective, evil is not an external entity or malevolent force. Evil is better understood as an adjective—as *frustrated* human desire—than as a noun. To experience evil (either as the victim or victimizer) is to suffer from a lack of something that satisfies. *Poneria*, one of the Greek words for evil, expresses the nature of evil well. The word is cognate with *penia*, meaning poverty or penury. Possessing an impoverished notion of ourselves, we fail to find fulfillment.[2]

Possible Objections

Objection 1: Pain Is Evil in and of Itself

Someone may object: "You cannot be serious. If you were being tortured, you would experience evil. Evil is excruciating pain, pain to which you have contributed nothing. In such a case, your self-conception is irrelevant to what you experience. In fact, pain destroys the human self. That is why we refer to it as 'brute' pain. Under torture, you become a jangle of nerves or one long scream."

My response has several strands. First, no one writing in the wisdom tradition denies the existence of either physical or emotional pain. In fact, they insist upon it, since pain is suffering. Pain is a sensation we desire to discharge but cannot. As a species of frustrated human desire, pain qualifies as a manifestation of evil. It does not follow, though, that we contribute absolutely nothing to our pain. Buddhists have long observed that we make pain worse when we resist it, instead of letting it be what it is.[3] Suffering or *dharma* is resistance that intensifies pain. Our self-conception comes into play as we fight other people or bemoan our circumstances. Some people endure physical torture relatively well. What they abhor is the humiliation of being stripped naked or forced to live in their filth. Such cases suggest that, insofar as we identify the self with the being whom the torturer is trying to humiliate, we intensify our pain and cause the self to suffer.

The second point is that we do not have to make that identification. The fact that we say, "I am *in* pain," instead of "I *am* pain," shows that there exists a disjunction between the "I" and the pain. Much evidence suggests that the self can maintain and exploit this disjunction. For example, women make the pain of childbirth endurable by saying "this pain I feel now is nothing compared to the lasting joy I will experience by having a child." Through education, even small children can be taught to minimize their pain. We say to the crying child, "There, there. Your hurt is not so bad. Be brave and stop crying." When the child listens and ceases to attach the self to frustration, the pain subsides and the child stops crying. Since pain is self-interpreted suffering, we should be wary of talking about a person's pain as though it were an absolute quantity to which we as outside observers can assign a degree of evil. Individuals react to situations quite differently and their suffering varies accordingly.

Objection 2: All Evils Are Not Equal

A related objection runs along the following lines: "By defining evil as frustrated desire, you make it sound as if all evils are equally bad. They are not. Some evils are monstrous or horrific, while others are merely bad. We can rank evils based upon the intensity and extent of the pain caused, the permanence of the injury, or the number of people hurt. You yourself have argued that degrees of evil exist. Following Dante, you argued that the evil we suffer is greater the more our humanity is diminished."

This objection is confused. All evil is necessarily one and the same in its being. If evil in all its expressions did not share the same essence, it would make no sense to attempt to rank evil in the manner contemplated by our objector. Without a shared essence, we would have no assurance that we were comparing apples with apples. Furthermore, for talk about evil to be meaningful, we must talk about evil as experienced by someone in particular. Each of us, however, tends to experience our suffering as total. Every experience of evil is world-shaking for the one who is frustrated. In the words of the psychologist Viktor Frankl, a survivor of Auschwitz:

> A man's suffering is similar to the behavior of gas. If a certain quantity of gas is pumped into an empty chamber, it will fill the chamber completely and evenly, no matter how big the chamber. Thus suffering completely fills the human soul and conscious mind, no matter whether the suffering is great or little. Therefore the "size" of human suffering is absolutely relative.[4]

That is why onlookers find it absurd, or even obscene, when two people fight over who has suffered more. These battles over who has been most victimized never produce a winner. All evil is every bit as horrific as the sufferers feel it to be. There exists no evil apart from our experience of frustrated desire.

In this respect, evil is like blueness. When we say that some things are bluer than others, we do not mean that blueness per se is variable. Insofar as a light blue and dark blue thing are both blue, they share the same blueness. Blueness does not admit of degrees; what varies is the extent to which the thing exhibits a blueness that is invariably blue. Those who argue for the existence of degrees of evil mean to say (1) that a thing or being embodies the invariable essence of evil to a greater or lesser extent; and (2) that they can offer a convincing, nonsubjective standard by which to assess the extent of this embodiment.

I have no quarrel with the first assertion. Evil is self-compounding frustration, which increases the more we identify with a misconceived or inadequate view of the self. The more complete our identification with this erroneous identity, the more we embody evil (i.e., suffer) and the more dangerous we become to other people to whom we unwittingly try to transfer our pain. Although each of us tends to experience any frustration as world-shaking, we can use our reason to draw distinctions and to avoid identifying the self with something that it is not. When we are upset, we can say, "In the scheme of things, this frustration may not be so great. I am alive and still have my health. I should take a deep breath and try to figure out why I have allowed these events to upset me so much." By using our reason to locate the cause of our rage or fear, we can free ourselves from its grip. If you cut in front of me with your car, I may get angry. But if I tell myself, "There's been no harm done," my rage immediately evaporates. I may even take the next step and ask: Why did I allow myself to become so enraged in the first place?

Frustration is frustration, regardless of the circumstances. What varies is the extent to which we dwell on the frustration, instead of seeking its cause. The less we use our reason, the more our passions control us and the more evil (frustration) we experience. Given that we implicitly desire to be satisfied completely, we are more or less content, depending upon how successfully we achieve what our heart desires. A theorist could devise a scale representing the extent to which people's reason is corrupt and their passions in control. Dante's distinct levels of hell are just such a scale. This scale, though, is inescapably subjective. Dante argues that some conceptions of our self put us more in touch with reality. Others divorce us from it, making it more likely that we will continually experience dissatisfaction. Those residents of hell who uncritically identify with their suffering or injury do not recognize a transcending self at all. Count Ugolino is nothing but his rage. He is thus frozen, utterly unable to develop. Every sinner at every level of hell operates on some concept of the self, a concept functioning as an embodied, lived worldview for that person. Although the extent of the sinners' identification with their suffering varies, every sinner Dante encounters thinks his or her torment is the worst imaginable. And the torment *is* the worst—for the person with that self-conception.

My quarrel is with the second part of our objector's claim, with the assertion that we can set up an absolute, objective scale for ranking evils.

Those who argue for such a scale refer to "evils." Use of the plural implies that evil is a thing or a noun. That evil is a thing must be shown, not merely assumed. There is a second problem. Theorists who rank evils always begin by abstracting from the lived experience of particular people. Yet, they then proceed to talk about the degree and extent of specific individuals' suffering. In attempting to rank evils, they presuppose the existence of some neutral, disembodied spectator point of view from which a judge can assess other people's suffering and demonstrate the degree of evil they have suffered. No such point of view exists. Human beings are not neutral observers. We are engaged participants.

Suppose we try to rank evils according to the intensity of pain they cause. An excruciating war injury would count as a worse evil than the pain caused when the dentist administers a shot of Novocain. Pain, though, is notoriously subjective. Some people fall apart in the doctor's office when they see the needle, while others endure maiming with barely a whimper. Pain is inextricably bound up with subjective suffering. The sufferer gets lost in his or her frustration and can imagine nothing worse. Dante meets one sinner after another who cries out that his or her pain is worse than anyone else's. Prisoners of war, knowing full well how subjective pain's intensity is, make it endurable by telling themselves that the torture they are undergoing could have been worse.[5]

Suppose, then, that we rank pains according to their duration. The pain we experience in the dentist's chair passes quickly, while a war injury may plague us for the rest of our life. The war pain thus qualifies as a greater evil than the discomfort we experience at the dentist. But is it greater? Some people relive minor pains ("minor" in whose eyes? The mythical objective observer has again entered the picture!) for the rest of their lives, whereas others are able to let their pain go. Pain has a psychic dimension, which is why we can educate ourselves to endure pain. Dante appears to be right: we suffer in a hell of our own making for as long as a false conception of the self frustrates our desire. A similar insight has led the Dalai Lama to suggest that suffering in the West is greater than in Tibet. Although the Tibetans are more frequently hungry and cold than Americans, the Tibetans accept material deprivation as part of existence, deal with it, and enjoy the available food and warmth.[6] They have not made the mistake of tying their self-conception to the acquisition of an ever-increasing number of material goods. They can enjoy life in the present, while many Americans defer happiness into a mythical future when they believe that they finally will have obtained enough things.

I would urge another consideration: to whom would a ranking of pain and suffering be meaningful? It would never persuade those who do not share the ranker's conception of the self. How we conceive of the self depends, in turn, on the progress we have made in overcoming our erroneous notions of who we are. Individuals progress in their own way and at their own pace. We cannot prove to other people that their suffering is insignificant compared with that experienced by another party. Various individuals would understand any proof we might offer in differing ways, depending upon how they view themselves and their history. There is no independent, demonstrable standard for establishing the degree to which some experience is evil.

Undaunted, our objector plays the trump card: "Surely the Holocaust or the genocide in Cambodia is more evil than any single injury. A child may fall down a well and die a painful, lonely death. But that injury does not compare to the anguish and torment suffered by millions at the hands of a Hitler or Pol Pot." Note that our objector has now switched the basis of the ranking. Previously the objector focused on the quality of pain—its intensity and duration. This time the objector appeals to the quantity of people who have suffered. I readily concede that genocide involves more cases of frustrated desire than the case of a single injured child. But to say that some instances of frustration involve more individuals does not prove that these cases constitute a greater evil because of the larger number of victims. Hannah Arendt, for example, refuses to locate evil in the number of Nazi victims. She argues, instead, that the Holocaust was significant because it marked the first time that a state put its whole apparatus in the service of obliterating an entire people. The Holocaust was horrifying because it constituted a crime against humanity and against the order of nature.[7] Humanity by its very nature consists, Arendt contends, in diversity. To seek uniform humanity is, for her, a contradiction in terms and a wrong committed against all human beings. Although she sees the Holocaust as a new expression of evil, she refrains from suggesting that it was more evil than other types of suffering. For, if more dead or maimed lives necessarily means a greater evil, then we would have to say that the murder of two million and one people is more evil than the murder of two million. Few are willing to make this sort of claim because it sounds so obscene.

Objection 3: Some Desires Ought to Be Frustrated

Our objector mounts a third offensive: "You equate evil with frustrated desire. But some desires should be frustrated because they result in harm to others. Communities are right to punish convicted murderers, rapists, and child molesters. A desire to murder or to rape ought to be suppressed."

As I said earlier, it may be necessary for communities to define and punish vicious, criminal acts. Without some mechanism in place to check human passions and to curtail the impulse toward revenge, communities would be torn apart by civil war. The fact that violent, sadistic, and paranoid actions stem from confusions about the self does not make the violence any less socially disruptive. Nor should an understanding that someone's behavior arises from a mistaken notion of the self prevent us from taking some steps to limit the havoc we think such a person may cause. In this respect, the violently sadistic person is like someone with a deadly contagious disease. While we understand that persons infected with smallpox have suffered the misfortune of being exposed to the virus, we feel justified in quarantining them in order to protect other members of the community. Our sympathy for those who have unintentionally become dangerous to others does not, and ought not, to preclude us from taking appropriate steps to protect the community.

The critical question, though, is what our objector means when he or she maintains that curbing some desires is a good thing. The objector must mean that doing so is desirable. Desirable in whose eyes? Society's eyes. Since society consists of individuals, the objector is claiming that the members of the community want to curtail desires that they believe prevent them from satisfying their desires. That statement is true. A given society's rules appear legitimate to the extent that citizens think these rules will increase their power to act and to realize themselves. If such development does not appear to be the focus of a society's policies and laws, members become disgruntled and seek to change the regime.

Every society has a prohibition against murder. To transgress this prohibition is to act criminally, for a crime is defined as a serious violation of communal norms embodied in rules and laws. If we wish to go a step further and to claim that society is justified in criminalizing murder, we must state the basis for the prohibition. In stating this basis, we must account for why the prohibition against murder strikes us as desirable. We characterize murder as criminal because we do not want to be frustrated in our desire to live. Therefore, when we insist that a desire to murder or to rape is evil, we are not merely claiming that the desire violates some prohibition. We are claiming that curtailing this desire is a good thing because the desire leads to behaviors that interfere with the thriving of both the victims and the malefactor. Torture, for example, brutalizes not only the victim but also the torturer. Indeed, it may harm the torturer even more. The torturer is typically completely identified with the act of inflicting pain, a deed that brings no lasting satisfaction to the torturer. The victim, though, may be able to separate the self from the pain and retain a measure of satisfaction in his or her life.

So, when we analyze this third objection, we discover that that the objector implicitly agrees that evil is frustrated desire. And if evil is frustrated desire, the murderer, as well as his or her victim, must be said to have experienced evil. The frustration of the Hydes, Ripleys, and Höfgens of this world is what leads them to assault others. Given that we cannot read each other's minds, society's focus on disruptive deeds is appropriate. But it does not tell the entire story. Human behaviors are not random. To grasp why some behavior has occurred, we need to look at the individual's self-conception and how that conception has shaped desire and led to unsociable behavior. Literature provides us with one way to perform this analysis. Self-analysis is the other option. When we examine our self-conceptions, we discover that violence is symptomatic of frustration. Murderers are violent because their concept of who they are (a notion produced by the many factors touched upon above) interferes with their ability to attain lasting satisfaction.

The objection that evil cannot be identical with frustrated desire because some desires ought to be curtailed is problematic in a second respect. The objector does not specify how allegedly vicious desires are to be curtailed. Just as no one else can prove a geometrical proof for us—we must prove it for ourselves if we are to understand and be convinced by it—so, too, only we can check our desires. Others can forcibly restrain us, making it impossible for us to act upon our desires. Or they can seek to make us fear and dread the consequences of our actions so much that we try to avoid those behaviors society judges to be bad. But they do not thereby eliminate the desire in us. That is why drug and aversion therapies have not proven very successful, except when those being treated wish to be rid of a particular desire. What, then, is a person to do to overcome or eradicate a corrupt desire? The objector implies that we should use our willpower to curb particular desires. However, willpower is not effective. We cling to the only identity we know. Our desires can be altered, but only if something happens to change our self-conception. The transforming impulse may come from within or without. We may persist in a behavior until the point at which it fills us with self-revulsion. Having "hit bottom," we may be open to a new, more satisfying conception of who we are. Or we may receive a major external shock. The September 11 bombings caused many people to ask themselves whether what they were doing was meaningful and satisfying. Suddenly they were able to imagine other things to do with their lives. Earlier they may have felt vaguely dissatisfied with their work. After the bombings, these employees viscerally understood that they needed to overcome their unhappiness while they still had time to do so. This insight led them to change their lives.

Sometimes change results from an apparently random event that speaks to us in some way. Robert Stroud, the man whose true-life story is depicted in the powerful film *Bird Man of Alcatraz*, was convicted of murder. While in prison, he murdered again. Filled with anger, he violently resisted the prison warden's efforts to make him conform to prison rules. Stroud's self-conception was largely negative: he had little idea of who he was, but he was certain that he was not merely a cog in the prison machinery. One day a storm blew a young bird into the prison courtyard. In taking care of this young bird, Stroud discovered within himself an aptitude for caring for animals and for close observation. The bird's plight and its reluctance to leave the prison cell resonated with Stroud. He received permission from the new warden to raise many birds and eventually became the world's foremost authority on bird diseases. By heeding this calling—by attending to the resonance the fearful baby bird produced in him—Stroud completely lost his rage.

Internal and external causes can lead us to comprehend and then to change our self-conception and the attendant desires. Demanding that people willfully repress their desires or that they accept an identity the collective wishes to foist upon them strengthens their allegedly aberrant desires. These individuals' frustration grows until it explodes. As a society, we react to the symptoms of frustration—as we must. We need to be clear, though, that we cannot purge our passions through an act of individual or collective will. As Stroud found, the rage we feel dissolves away only if we accept responsibility for learning who we are.

If we honor and attend to the resonance we experience at different points in our lives, we can better understand who we are. Examining desires is better than repressing them. Stroud did not develop by stifling his rage. He acquired dignity as he discovered that he had no desire to murder. Neither did he desire to be angry or to vent his rage. He did want to find his way in life, to become educated, and to use his learning to improve the world. As he excavated his desires with a view to discovering who he was, he began to experience more lasting satisfaction. He published his book on bird disease and was finally able to break away from his controlling mother. His old angry self disappeared.

If we do not replace our erroneous sense of who we are with a more adequate conception, our misconception will lead us to react to external events and internal passions in unhelpful ways. These symptoms proliferate and intensify as we dig ourselves ever deeper into a personal hell of unhappiness. The Chinese ideogram for evil appropriately depicts evil as a person who is tumbling into a deep hole. Frustration breeds frustration, regardless of what we will ourselves to do or to refrain from doing. Self-understanding is needed to achieve lasting peace.

EVIL IS RELATIVE TO HUMAN DESIRE

If evil is frustrated desire, evil exists only in relation to human desire. The philosopher Paul Kashap observes that nothing could be "described as 'good' if no individual were disposed or inclined or attracted toward it."[8] Conversely, nothing could be termed "evil" if no human being were repelled by or indisposed toward it. Human beings are the only animals capable of consciously evaluating their situation and of identifying and naming the satisfaction and frustration they experience. We can talk, by analogy, about other animals experiencing evil. If, however, we were not ourselves conscious of what it means to be tormented by dissatisfaction, we could not recognize such distress elsewhere in the animal world.

Humanly experienced evil or suffering has a logical primacy, although we clearly are not the only animals that experience frustration.

In the absence of human desire, there would be no evil. Describing evil as autonomous, then, can be misleading. There is no free-floating evil force roaming the world, only failed desire. Ralph Waldo Emerson comes closer to the truth than his friend Henry David Thoreau. Emerson characterizes evil as an absence, while Thoreau takes evil to be an entity, a lurking "reptile . . . attached at one mouth of his burrow" that, when stymied, "shows himself at another."[9] Failure is not an entity; it is more of a lack or absence of satisfaction. However, Thoreau is not entirely incorrect. Talk of devils or demons is appropriate insofar as we, in our dread, behave in ways that lead to ever greater frustration. Unwittingly, we devise and spring the traps that snare us. The traps strike us as the product of a devious mind because they are such. We cunningly devise these snares and then hide from ourselves what we have done. Since we do not recognize ourselves as the moving engine, we try to place the blame on some external malignant agency—call it the "devil" or "Satan." Talk of the devil makes symbolic sense in a second way. Both the law and politics can lock us into antagonistic relations and drive us to satanize each other. As a result, we come to feel that we are being victimized by a demonic superhuman agency. This feeling is not completely misplaced. The social dynamics contributing to our inadequate self-conception and pain are beyond any single individual's control.

Neither way of thinking about the demonic implies that evil exists as a separate entity apart from human desire. Nor does such usage commit us to viewing demonic evil as something that we will or choose. We are frustrated in our desire and suffer because our conception of who we are is confused. Evil is lived ignorance. In our ignorance, we react to our frustration in ways that compound the problem and leave us, like Dante's sinners, unconsciously traversing the same ground over and over again. We fall into a trap of our making, but not of our willing.

Good and Bad versus Good and Evil

Once we grasp that evil is nothing but our experience of frustrated desire, we can see why human beings employ two distinct pairs of evaluative terms: good/bad and good/evil. "Good" and "bad" are terms of social discourse.

Every society establishes rules and develops mores with a view to helping its members live together in what the regimes takes to be a mutually advantageous manner. Whatever accords with its rules, mores, and expectations the regime calls "good"; whatever violates them, it labels "bad."

Social groups have evolved because we have found that we are better able to prosper as a collective than as isolated individuals. Since the morally good and bad have their roots in our shared natural desire to obtain what is in our interest, our application of these terms is not completely arbitrary. Nevertheless, these moral terms are limited in their reference. Conventionally determined beliefs about goodness and badness reflect and reinforce communal notions about identity and freedom and about the conditions that must be met in order for that particular society is to endure. Even transcultural mores have a relativistic dimension. For example, every society recognizes that trust is a form of social capital, that the young must receive some form of civic education if the community is to endure, and that justice is an intergenerational virtue. There are some behaviors and habits that all peoples recognize as desirable or good, because these things enhance our ability to act and to be free. Yet, widespread practices and understandings vary considerably in their application. Although every society requires that its citizens respect the dignity of their fellow human beings, what is meant by a term such as "dignity" is specified in quite different ways. Although the Chinese and Americans can agree that dignity is equivalent to personal worth, they diverge dramatically in how they interpret that worth. For the Chinese, dignity is acquired, alienable, and inheres in personal relationships. Americans, by contrast, tend to think of dignity as innate, inalienable, and resident within individuals. Concepts of dignity and integrity are always elaborated by members of a particular culture. How they get implemented depends, in turn, upon the history of a people and even upon the geography of the country where the culture has developed. What gets deemed desirable and undesirable always depends, in part, upon such factors and reflects the experience and prejudices of those who shape the community's opinions and write its laws.

Like every finite person's point of view, a particular society's conception of the self, imbedded in that group's laws and mores, is necessarily inadequate and partial. The group's mores are designed to develop traits in common and then to preserve this hard-won commonality. The norms of the good and the bad treat human beings as interchangeable members of society. But we are not interchangeable. Each of us has unique experiences and must find his or her own way through life. As the examples of Dr. Jekyll/Mr. Hyde and Höfgen illustrate, what society, even educated or high society, deems good may not be good for the individual. In fact, what society thinks desirable almost always frustrates individual desire to some extent. In that respect Paul Ricoeur is right to claim that the "state is legitimate violence."[10] Individuals understandably chafe at the state's rules and mores. We need a vocabulary for talking about human beings' efforts to transcend this frustration.

The search for this vocabulary leads the philosophically inclined into the realms of psychology and theology, the spheres in which talk of "good" and "evil" is most at home. Psychology and theology are not primarily concerned with social mores. They focus on individual development. The psychologist aims at helping the individual patient, not at curing social ills. The theologian tries to save individuals, not regimes. Psychologists and theologians employ symbols, allegories, and parables to stimulate patients and penitents to consider practices and interpretations designed to relieve their suffering. That is why therapists and theologians have long had a great affinity with literature, which is intrinsically symbolic and suggestive.

If the psychologist is successful, the patient discovers strategies for coping. Sometimes these strategies irritate the patient's family and friends. They may even run counter to societal norms. We should recall that Dante's psychological theology does not correspond to common legal notions of criminal badness. Societies imprison killers, but not hypocrites. Dante, by contrast, thinks that hypocrites and falsifiers are more damned than those who murder out of rage. These latter two types are, Dante suggests, less honest with themselves and thus further removed from reality than, say, angry lovers.

Scripture likewise asks us to distinguish the political from the personal. Rendering "unto Caesar what is Caesar's and unto God what is God's" becomes possible only if we admit that the claims of the two are not identical. The morally good and bad belong to the social arena, Caesar's realm. Good and evil, by contrast, describe how we stand with respect to the universe of which we are a part. The more our self-understanding accords with the way in which the universe operates, the more satisfied we are, and the more our lives seem good. If we persist in divorcing ourselves from this larger whole or denying its impact upon us, we suffer anguish and begin to behave in antagonistic ways. We can experience genuine, lasting happiness only if we move into harmony with the whole universe. This whole is, by definition, bigger than any particular state. No guarantee exists that the community will understand or appreciate those who have attained a wider view and a corresponding measure of harmony. If history is any guide, the community will find the original perspective of a Socrates, Jesus, Gandhi, or Confucius bizarre, if not downright threatening.

Therefore, so-called primitive peoples are right to think that the word "evil" possesses great power. Proclaiming something or someone "evil" packs a powerful emotional wallop, one that can disrupt society and upset the status quo. To speak of evil is to broach the question of what truly satisfies us as individuals and of what it means to be human. This question takes us beyond social, conventional norms. Now we are asking what we have a right to do to fulfill ourselves as individuals. Psychology and theology address this question differently. Therapists use evolving models of human functioning—models that are transcommunal and thus not tied to the experiences of any single group of citizens—to counsel people about ways to escape their neuroses. Religious teachers speak to the question by offering teachings believed to be divinely inspired. Still, both therapists and religious teachers aim at helping individuals arrive at a better and more satisfying understanding of who they are and of what they owe, and do not owe, society. These are the questions that lie at the heart of the wisdom tradition.

Lovers of wisdom would have us draw insights from these disciplines to structure society and to evaluate which regimes are most conducive to the development of individuals' souls. The wisdom tradition views evil as a more fundamental and radical notion than conventional badness or vice. Good and evil provide the basis for criticizing the status quo and its conventions. On this score, lovers of wisdom agree with the primitives. To name evil is "more than an expression of opinion: it is an act of great power and authority."[11]

Evil Is Not Vice

At this point, I want to return to the discussion of Aristotle begun in chapter 1. Recall my argument that Aristotle, like most moralists, equates evil with volitional, criminal vice. Now we can see why this equation is mistaken. In the first place, much of what society calls wicked or evil is, in reality, merely bad (i.e., a violation of mores). For years small towns in America pushed to keep stores closed on Sunday. Town leaders argued that the Sabbath should be observed and that storekeepers needed their rest. Working moms and other people who pushed for stores to be open were condemned as depraved. As large chain stores moved into rural America and as more women entered the workforce, expectations and mores altered. Most people stopped viewing Sunday shopping as a vice. Social dancing and playing cards likewise were once deemed vices and are still judged wicked by some social groups. Yet these behaviors are not evil. A person for whom dance is a vocation will find dancing to be a truly fulfilling experience. Instead of being evil, the prohibited behavior or vice is, for this person, genuinely good. We should be careful, therefore, not to mistake violations of mores for evil. If we are not clear on this point, we will wind up arguing—as some moralists do—that the state may legitimately prevent people from realizing their vocations.[12] (It is worth noting that Aristotle never mentions a single individual by name in the *Nicomachean Ethics*. His morality serves to deny that individuals have a moral claim to realize their individuality. There is no talk here of vocations or of special inner Socratic voices. According to Aristotle, people's moral virtue lies in habituating themselves to exhibit courage, temperance, wit, magnificence, and justice as understood by the political community.) Any antivocational argument is, from the wisdom perspective, suspect because citizens have a stake in participating in communal life exactly to the extent that they believe this life benefits them. If the state has a right to keep its citizens from realizing who they truly are, it is hard to see how such a state can be said to be acting in their interests.

Sometimes we use the term "vice" to refer not to a violation of a particular rule ("thou shalt not dance") but to a socially undesirable character trait, such as churlishness or stinginess. Aristotle thinks of vice in this second way, and he is partly correct. Some character traits are more conducive to a pleasant, easy social life than others. We prefer the company of the amiable to that of boors. Societies, which need harmony in order to persist, quite naturally encourage their citizens to be friendly toward each other. But, as I have argued, blaming people for character flaws is itself a dangerous practice. If we get caught up in satanizing them, we fail to understand why they have acted badly. Not every instance of truculence is properly understood as an antisocial character defect or vice. Continually persecuted, Shakespeare's character Shylock finds it difficult to summon a ready smile. Labeling his behavior "vicious" tells us nothing about why the Jewish moneylender is angry. It is far more enlightening to ask why he is so enraged. Shylock and his tormentors find that their desires are thwarted. Both their habits and their character traits are largely irrelevant to their unhappiness. What *is* relevant is the social and satanic dynamic of scapegoating examined in chapter 7, a dynamic about which moralities are notably silent.

Moralists see society and its rules as saving us from ourselves. In thrall to different passions and trapped in demonic trajectories we do not understand, we come into conflict with each other. A thinker like Aristotle will insist upon the need for law if we are to be truly free and powerful. I concede that laws may help contain violence, especially if they foster many competing forces—educational, religious, economic, and civic. The more we are subject to a variety of such forces, the more likely we are to discern incongruities and inconsistencies in what we are being told. As a result, we may start to think for ourselves, a crucial first step toward living a satisfied life. Laws, therefore, can promote individual development. However, social laws and mores frequently cause conflict, confusion, and illusion. We use the language of virtues and vices to categorize various forms of behavior. Having pigeonholed these behaviors, we then feel justified in praising and blaming people whom we judge to be behaving well or badly. This social practice of categorization, although a necessary concomitant of law and morality, often prevents us from discerning what is at stake in a particular situation and from coming up with solutions to our social problems. From the wisdom perspective, praise and blame readily become a *satan* or obstacle to achieving real satisfaction. In that respect, moralistic language verges on evil.

The relation of wisdom to morality is complex. One might say that social moralities offer an image or simulacrum of wisdom. Moralists rightly emphasize that our actions have consequences for us. By rewarding and sanctioning particular behaviors, morality drives this point home. As children, we learn that some of these consequences are more attractive than others. This perception encourages us to develop our powers of discrimination. As we mature, we find that it is better to think before we act, and we start to distinguish between acting and reacting. By using our natural desire for pleasure and aversion to pain and our drive to preserve the self, morality can make us reflect. Reflection, in turn, sparks insight.

By continually reminding us that we are part of a larger social organism on which we depend for our livelihood, opportunities, and education, morality steadily draws our eye outward toward the universe of which we are a part. When we act antisocially, we weaken this social organism and thereby compromise our ability to thrive. It could be argued, therefore, that vices (laziness, rudeness, cowardice, and so on) are forms of frustrated desire. I am not hostile to this line of argument. But I would still contend that the moralistic response to vice is just as likely to hinder as to aid our development. The central problem is that moralities do not fully appreciate individual differences and will never be able to do so.

An individual is a part of the universe. The wisdom tradition conceives of the entire universe as alive or animated. Infinitely complex, its parts are "mutually adapted in their activity and disposition to one another as required by the principle of order constituting the whole."[13] Everything is subject to this principle of order. To be lastingly and genuinely satisfied, we must apprehend this principle of order (to the extent that it is possible for our finite minds to do so). Only with this knowledge can we adequately comprehend how we are affecting and being affected by other people and things. As Socrates would put it, unless we comprehend the *eidē*, we are doomed to be locked into patterns of reactions and unable to be free agents. The effort to regulate our mind in accordance with the universe's order takes us far beyond conventional morality. Societies are but a small part of the universe, and they, too, are ultimately subject to this more encompassing principle of order. To put the point paradoxically: from the wisdom perspective, we can stand in the right relation to our fellow citizens only to the extent that we understand that morality does not provide the final word on what this right relation is.

As we reflect upon the possibilities and limits of morality, the virtues and vices take on a different aspect. Aristotle equates cowardice with the failure to take a stand on the battlefield against the city's enemies. Plato's Socrates, by contrast, argues that cowardice is the failure to devote one's life to the most necessary of all tasks—the quest for life-guiding wisdom. If we do not move beyond morality—beyond good and bad—we remain at the mercy of illusion and half-truth. As a result, we suffer. Morality cannot help us here, because morality's equation of evil with badness/vice is the source of our difficulty. Our happiness depends on getting to the point where we can distinguish the two. Hence, my insistence that evil is not vice.

A second reason for not conflating evil with vice is that doing so makes evil volitional. Morality treats the person as the blameworthy originator of the vicious act. While some moralists will concede that certain acts involve ignorance on the part of the agent, they typically deem the agent to be the blameworthy cause of his or her ignorance. As Aristotle puts it, the drunkard acts in ignorance, but it was once open to the drunkard not to be such. When we perform vicious actions out of self-caused ignorance, these deeds, moralists contend, should be judged to be quasi-intentional. Viewing vice as evil leads insensibly to the notion that all evil is a matter of malicious intention. The problem with this approach is that human beings do heinous things without a speck of malice. Hendrik betrays his friends out of a desire to gain societal respect. James's governess kills her charge Miles while acting on an apparently commendable desire to save him. Dr. Jekyll/Mr. Hyde murders an old man almost as a reflex action. Euthyphro accuses his father of injustice out of a pious desire to purify the city. These literary cases are not outliers. Most Americans would concede that our government (with the tacit support of citizens) committed a grave injustice by impoverishing and interring completely innocent Japanese Americans. While our government may have acted hysterically, no one imputes active malice to it. Even the Nazis appear not to have acted out of malice. Adolf Eichmann, a Nazi official who sent Jews to their deaths, saw himself as simply doing his job. As Neiman observes, in this respect Eichmann did not differ much from his compatriots:

> Sadists, and particularly venomous anti-Semites, were present among the murderers, but the SS sought to avoid using those who took obvious pleasure in murder, and most of it was carried out as routine. Vicious hatred was far less evident than might be expected among the lower echelons of those who took over the killing. The opportunity to avoid being sent to fight in the front enlisted far more concentration camp guards than did the opportunity to torment Jews. At the highest levels, not only malice, but also a clear view of the consequences of one's actions was often missing as well.

Eichmann is only the most famous Nazi official whose initial goals had nothing to do with mass murder and everything to do with petty desires for personal advancement.[14]

Other murderers seem to act in a fog of unknowing. Dennis Nilsen, who seduced and murdered fifteen men, refers to obscure "things" in lieu of naming his deeds:

> When I voluntarily go out to drink I do not have the intention at that time to do things. Things may happen afterwards drinking but they are not foreplanned. I'm certainly not consciously aware of what [the police] are saying. I seek company first and hope everything will be all right. . . . I do not feel like an evil person. I doubt if I could kill someone now, even under orders with lawful authority. I am about the least likely killer that I know.[15]

The self-pitying Nilsen intended or planned nothing. "Things" just happened in his world. I see no reason to doubt his passivity. We suffer frustration and become serial killers or rapists precisely because we are compelled by causes we do not comprehend.

Neiman has argued that it is only relatively recently that we have become aware that evil need not involve intention. I think that she badly misreads history. This awareness is the living heart of the ancient wisdom tradition. Socrates' claim that "no one knowingly acts unjustly" and Jesus' impassioned plea to God to "forgive them for they know not what they do" explicitly equate evil with ignorance. Both thinkers deny that either malice or forethought is a necessary component of evil. Having worked through numerous examples of evil in the previous chapters, we can appreciate Socrates' and Jesus' perspective. Individual acts of injustice such as murder or theft are not evil. The real evil is suffering—frustrated desire—that expresses itself as paranoia, narcissistic rage, or self-pity, all of which induce more suffering. The wisdom tradition admits the existence of evil and explores its suffering-producing dynamics in great detail without invoking choice, will, or intention. Moralistic writers overlook these dynamics and, consequently, fail to appreciate the magnitude of human pain. As Nel Noddings has noted, suffering enters the moralistic equation only when it can be imputed to deliberate or negligent (i.e., voluntary) human agency.[16]

Evil Is Not a Violation of the Natural Order

If evil is not intentional, the moral approach faces a difficulty: what can evil possibly be, if it is not a distortion of intention or defect of will? Arendt is one of the few moralists to face this difficulty head on. She attempts to resolve it by treating evil as a violation of the natural order of things:

> Foremost among the larger issues at stake in the Eichmann trial was the assumption current in all legal systems that intent to do wrong is necessary for the commission of a crime. On nothing, perhaps, has civilized jurisprudence prided itself more than on this taking into account of the subjective factor. Where this intent is absent, where, for whatever reasons, even reasons of moral insanity, the ability to distinguish between right and wrong is impaired, we feel no crime has been committed. We refuse, and consider as barbaric, the proposition "that a great crime offends nature, so that the very earth cries out for vengeance; that evil violates a natural harmony which only retribution can restore; that a wronged collectivity owes a duty to the moral order to punish the criminal." . . . And yet I think it undeniable that it was precisely on the ground of these long-forgotten propositions that Eichmann was brought to justice to begin with, and that they were, in fact, the supreme justification for the death penalty.[17]

But were these propositions "long-forgotten"? Or did we set them aside because we sensed that they were, in their own way, every bit as dangerous as identifying evil with intent? Arendt's casual reference to vengeance should worry us. The "earth" does not cry out for vengeance; people scream for revenge. The human collective is always more than ready to extract its pound of flesh from a supposed offender and to do so on almost any terms. A 2001 survey, though perhaps not scientifically valid, shows the problem. When asked whether Osama bin Laden, if located, should be tried in court or assassinated, 70 percent of Americans, the most constitutional people in the world, urged assassination.[18] We are apparently ready to dispense with the machinery of justice in order to get the result we think desirable.

As René Girard has shown, whenever social harmony is disturbed, members of the collective attempt to restore order by finding a person to scapegoat.[19] Arendt's "wronged collectivity" is only too happy to discharge what it takes to be its moral duty: the body politic will restore order by finding someone to punish and will not allow itself to be distracted by doubts or scruples. It could be argued that Arendt's redefinition of evil as a disturbance of the natural order is exactly the notion hit upon by our Puritan forefathers when they initiated witch-hunts. In fact, they thought the earth itself called out for vengeance. When they heard voices coming out of the earth, they dug up graves to drive stakes into the hearts of alleged vampires so that the vampires' dead victims could finally rest in peace.

If our moral duty to the earth entails putting all offenders against natural harmony to death, where exactly will the killing end? If the Nazi bureaucrat Eichmann merits the death penalty, and if millions of Germans were no more or less guilty than Eichmann of participating in the Nazi killing machine, we are driven to conclude that the Allies would have been morally justified in putting all these Germans to death. How many people can the enforcers of the moral order justifiably and judicially kill? Twenty percent of a given community? Seventy percent? Do we not risk destroying the social order we claim to want to save?

The problem with the natural harmony argument is greater than Arendt realizes. She assumes that a reformed system of international law could be used to restore harmony to the world. She overlooks the way in which the law contributes to suffering. I do not mean that laws sometimes sanction human rights violations. Political theorists and moralists, including Arendt, are well aware that conventional laws may be corrupt. I mean rather that society uses both written and unwritten laws to promote specific behaviors and, in the process, causes people who have committed no crime to suffer. Every legal system normalizes some behaviors and personas and stigmatizes the rest. Robert Louis Stevenson's genius lies in his clear perception of the way in which society creates criminals by pitting us against ourselves. Recall that Mr. Hyde becomes vicious only after the self-righteous lawyer Utterson starts persecuting him. Hyde is Utterson's shadow self, the part of his personality that Utterson's ego refuses to acknowledge because it does not correspond with society's view of who a professional is. Utterson's obsession with exposing and punishing the deviant Hyde and protecting the upright Jekyll sets into motion the series of events culminating in a murder, suicide, and death by trauma.

The fact that Utterson's generative role has gone completely unnoticed by generations of readers and critics interested only in seeing the (allegedly) monstrous Hyde get what is coming to him supports my point. Our moralistic and legalistic mindset is part and parcel of the problem. We do not perceive our complicity in the suffering we create. That is why Socrates argues that a legal system is truly legitimate only to the extent that it allows for a viable right of exit.[20] Allowing for such an exit is a sign that members of a society recognize how easily the moral desire for justice becomes a motive for oppression. Yet few, if any, regimes have provided for a viable right of exit.

Arendt herself toys with the idea that Eichmann was led astray by an unthinking devotion to Kantian moral duty.[21] However, in the passage quoted above, she turns right around and asks us to endorse a view of moral duty quite Kantian in spirit. Evil is an offense against nature (what Kant would term a violation of the "universal law of nature"). Doing the right thing means restoring the natural balance by removing the victimizer from the world. This quasi-mechanical prescription—whenever an offense occurs, remove the offending member—is not far removed from Eichmann's banal devotion to duty.

Euthyphro's justification for prosecuting his father is curiously Arendtian as well. Euthyphro contends that his father must die because, in killing the family's hired hand, his father polluted the city. This offense against the natural order must be rectified. Who, though, should rectify the offense? The natural order argument dictates that only agents who are completely pure are fit to do so. Only by acting harmoniously in accordance with the natural order can we restore harmony. By definition, criminal offenders lack this harmony. If they had conformed to the natural order, they never would have violated it. Accused defilers, therefore, can play no role in the restoration of the world. Balance must be restored by those (e.g., Euthyphro) who deem themselves to be entirely in compliance with nature.

As Socrates questions Euthyphro, the philosophic reader starts to see how self-perpetuating and self-insulating human certainty is. Anyone who dares to challenge the avenging savior's point of view gets written off as an enemy. These avengers have no qualms about characterizing opponents as offenders against the natural order. The moralistic effort to silence the earth's supposed cry for vengeance engenders another round of prosecutions, punishments, and killings.

"Vengeance is mine," saith the Lord. The wisdom tradition takes this statement seriously and interprets it in two senses. First, we ought not to presume to a certainty and purity that we do not have. We do not fully comprehend the whole and so cannot know what constitutes natural balance. Only a divine being who knows the relation of all the parts is in a position to maintain the universe. Since Socrates knows that he does not know, he never casts himself in the role of prosecutor.[22] The same can be said of Jesus. When asked to bless the stoning of a woman who had committed adultery, Jesus responds, "Let him who is without sin throw the first stone."[23] In so speaking, Jesus lays bare the entire logic of the moralistic concept of evil as a violation of the natural order. Restoration of the order must be by one who is pure. Therefore, let the stone thrower step forward and publicly proclaim, "I am without sin." To make that claim is equivalent to maintaining that one never has done, and never will do, anything to upset the natural order or balance of the universe. Although most people will not come out and say, "I am God," natural order moralities implicitly presuppose that we are divine.

Second, in casting ourselves as moral avengers, we presume that the universe needs our help to preserve its natural harmony. In one sense, the claim is true. We are part of the whole. The whole cannot be in complete harmony unless each of us is in balance. It does not follow, though, that we should cast ourselves as heroic defenders of society's moral order. Any moral order that represents itself as pure is suspect because we are finite beings prove to erring. Instead of appointing ourselves protectors of the natural order, we should examine ourselves to make certain that we are thinking and acting in ways that conform to the way the world is. That means we should seek to discover what must be true, what we can say about the universe without fear of contradiction. Learning to use what we already know to arrive at necessary truth is a task sufficiently difficult to occupy us for a lifetime. If we spend our time leveling charges at other people, we never get around to this task. Confucius urges us, therefore, to make ourselves trustworthy before we accuse other people of breaking our trust.[24] If we do that, we can perhaps achieve a modicum of inner peace. We can rest easy (1) because we are not be harming others in examining ourselves, and (2) because we are not trying to bring the world into conformity with our idealized vision of how it ought to be and then berating ourselves for our failure to secure perfect justice.

If the wisdom approach can yield such peace, it is no small achievement. The moralistic alternative of harshly punishing or killing criminals gives victims little satisfaction and frequently yields no closure. American support for the death penalty has diminished steadily over the past thirty years. Fewer people think that the death penalty deters would-be criminals; many worry about the unfair application of the law and the possibility that the innocent will be executed. What is even more interesting is that about 40 percent of Americans polled now reject the view that the death penalty is fair because it gives closure.[25] Families of victims describe how this myth of closure made them sick and unhappy. They hung on to their anger, thinking it would disappear when the killer of their loved one was finally executed. When they discovered that their rage and sadness persisted, they had to turn elsewhere for relief. These grieving survivors found that forgiving offered the only route to peace.

By forgiving, I do not mean setting aside or ignoring an offense on the ground that the harm is insignificant. Forgiveness is an acceptance that what is done is done and that letting go of anger is the only way for the living to return to health. We forgive for ourselves, not for our murdered or maimed loved ones. Understanding that murderers, thieves, rapists, and torturers act out of a profound ignorance eases the way to forgiveness. We give up blaming the victimizer, since that practice makes sense only if the blamed party is in a position to alter his or her behavior. Those who do not comprehend what they are doing cannot change it. That is why the Tibetan Buddhist justice system, which is grounded in the wisdom tradition, tailors every punishment to the offender: punishment is designed to help the particular offender achieve transformative insight into the self and the world. Perhaps that accounts for why Tibet experiences less recidivism than America.

By equating evil with vice, malice, or willed wrongdoing, moralities compound the pain of survivors. They encourage us to get to the bottom of our victimizers' motives, to force them to confess why they acted to hurt us, and to get them to commit to acting differently in the future. Yet, as Fred Alford found when he interviewed prisoners convicted of capital crimes, victimizers do not know why they acted as they did. Given that they do not know what is driving them to act in some way, our quest to plumb their motives and to get them to pledge to change their behavior proves fruitless. Morality does not point the way to peace; the way of wisdom does.

Evil Is Not Trespass against Others

Undaunted, our objector launches another volley: "Yes, I concede that evil is not malice or a violation of the natural order. However, evil always involves harm to other people. Evil is a trespass (willed or unwilled) against a fellow human being, which is why we pray that we be forgiven for our trespasses just as we have forgiven those who have trespassed against us."

Defining evil as harming others obscures more than it clarifies. We can experience evil or frustration without trespassing against someone else. If we have mistaken an illusion for our true self and are in the throes of panic, rage, and nagging anxiety, we can be said to have inflicted evil upon ourselves. Both Dante's voyage through hell and Socrates' conversation with Euthyphro reveal that evil can take the form of a pain we visit upon ourselves.

Most religions condemn suicide as evil. Although this condemnation can sound shrill and dogmatic, it contains a seed of truth. Suicide is an attempt to rid the self of feelings of dread by destroying the self. In attempting suicide, we confuse an apparent good (relief from suffering at whatever cost) with the real good (understanding the reason for our torment). Suicide drives a permanent wedge between the transcending self and the empirical, confused self that is engaged in neurotic behavior. Self-murder cannot yield the integration we crave. Having mistaken who we are, we come to believe that we will never thrive. In killing ourselves, we make this belief a certainty and thereby cause ourselves to experience evil.

Chapter 1 revealed our tendency to assimilate evil into crime. However, the real danger is not that we will commit a felony but that we will become our destiny. The ancient Greeks had an excellent feel for the true nature of evil's threat. Their word for danger—*to deinon*—means suffering or an awe-producing, uncanny, numinous, or strange terror. None of these meanings implies that we feel endangered because we have harmed another person or because we have been the victim of a trespass. They instead

emphasize human anguish. The Greek word *kakia*, which is usually translated as "evil," refers to anything that is baneful, including disease. Disease
certainly is not a form of criminal trespass; however, it is evil in the sense
that it is a form of thwarted desire or dis-ease.

Our objector forgets that a deed is not evil because it is criminal.
Deeds are deemed criminal because they are judged to be evil. Euthyphro
is not evil because he has trespassed against his father; he is proceeding
against his father because of the fanatical impiety in his heart. Even if his
prosecution fails, Euthyphro will continue to do whatever it takes to
reinforce his image of himself as divine. His antisocial rage and violent
proclivities are symptomatic of his frustrated desire (i.e., his experienced
evil), not identical with it.

Since aggression is symptomatic of frustrated desire, it is easy to
mistake violent trespass for evil. A moment's reflection suffices to show
our mistake. Animals such as chimpanzees are capable of planned and
opportunistic aggression, but they are not evil.[26] They are driven by a
frustration they cannot understand. That is why their battles and wars are
more difficult to stop than human conflicts. Human beings, by contrast,
can mediate their actions through thought. We can reflect on our self-
conception and refine our sense of what it will take to satisfy us. No such
mediation is possible in the case of living beings lacking a symbolized
image of the self.

Not defining evil as aggressive trespass makes sense for a second reason.
The fact is that we are not especially troubled by death and destruction
per se. We raise no alarm when the fish devours the shrimp. A natural
order of birth, suffering, and death does not disturb us. We may even find
the inevitable cycle of death and rebirth reassuring. We accept suffering
when it appears part of the larger order. That is why some theorists define
evil as *unnecessary* suffering. We become anxious only if we suspect that the
order of how things are and should be has been compromised, perhaps
irrevocably, thereby threatening our ability to thrive and prosper. The
ensuing feeling of dread can be unbearably tormenting. Both the Hebrew
and Greek words for evil—*ra^c* and *kakia*—stress terror. Evil was reduced
to vicious or malicious intent only later as theologians tried to codify it:

> Like *ra^c*, *kakia* means . . . pain, sickness, suffering, misfortune, and
> loss. Some Gnostic Christians, such as Valentinus, stressed the origin

of *kakia* in the "anguish and terror" of being human. . . . It was only
the orthodox Christians who insisted that *kakia* was a moral category,
a condition of the heart which leads to trespass against others.[27]

Since there are as many forms of thwarted desire and suffering as there are
people in the world, evil cannot be codified. Redefining *kakia* to mean
trespass misses the point. Suffering occurs because we are finite beings,
vulnerable and prone to error. Evil is part of the human condition; it is not
a trespass performed by some vicious individual.

Any attempt to define evil as violent trespass should be opposed for a
third reason. Trespasses are readily identified, described, and documented. Evil, by contrast, is nightmarish precisely because the nature of
our frustration is often not easy to describe. Evil eludes our grasp, leading
us to think that we are being pursued by a demon lurking in the shadows.
Conflating evil with trespass prematurely forecloses the question of what
evil is and serves to insulate us from the dread we are feeling.[28] It thereby
prevents us from understanding our suffering and intensifies our dread
and anxiety.

Does Good Come from Evil?

Having explored what evil is and is not, I want to shift gears and consider
the implications of the idea that evil is frustrated human desire. If evil is
frustrated desire, it could be argued that good comes from evil. After all,
if our mistakes provide an opportunity for us to learn who we are and to
become better able to attain peace and lasting satisfaction, does it not
follow that good (satisfaction) comes from evil (frustration)?

Here we must be very careful. Good is eternally what it is: goodness is
that which lastingly and permanently satisfies human desire. Evil, too, is
eternally what it is—frustrated desire. Since these two are forever distinct,
good never transforms itself into evil or vice versa. In Platonic language, the
eidē of good and of evil do not change. We should also be suspicious of
claims that evil necessarily leads to good or that the human race is progress-
ing toward a future in which all evil will be overcome. This romantically
optimistic view seeks to eliminate the contingency of evil. Hegel favored
such a position, arguing that philosophy's sole aim is to eliminate the contingent. Although this elimination might be possible in mathematics, we

cannot overcome the contingency of horror. Every horror has something new about it.

The Lisbon earthquake stunned people by its scale and the relentlessness of the destruction. The quake destroyed most of the city. As houses fell, the wood ignited massive fires, killing many who had been lucky to survive the earthquake. The conflagration destroyed the artwork and valuables the citizens had worked so hard to retrieve from the rubble. Then the sea turned into an enemy as massive tidal waves smashed ships and drowned those who had taken refuge from the fire along the waterfront. There seemed to be no escape from earth, fire, or water. The residents of Lisbon felt pursued by a merciless nature. Although weapons have steadily evolved over thousands of years, Hiroshima marked a new phase. The dropping of the atomic bomb demonstrated that we now have the means to destroy the entire human race. The Soviet gulags introduced a surreal dimension. Men, women, and children were imprisoned and murdered for no reason whatsoever. In the past, human beings could hope to avoid persecution by following certain rules. Under Stalin and his successors, there were no rules. The imprisoned went crazy trying to remember what they might have said or done that led to their suffering. Auschwitz boggled the mind, because never before had a political regime set out to exterminate millions of its own citizens and to do so even if it meant weakening the regime's ability to wage a war it had initiated. The Oklahoma City bombing taught us that a few people could commit themselves to a private war against the state and convert ordinary technology (fertilizer and a truck) into a weapon of mass destruction. September 11 demonstrated that a dedicated few could use another converted weapon (airplanes) to terrorize an entire nation.

I do not intend this list to specify everything that is unique about each of these events. My point is that both nature and mankind repeatedly surprise us. There is no reason to think that this contingency is going to disappear in the future. The contingency of suffering is inevitable, because an infinitely large number of causes interact in ways that we cannot fully grasp. It would be a mistake, therefore, to try to reconcile ourselves to suffering and pain by claiming, as Hegel does, that we must accept individual misery as a byproduct of history's march toward a necessary culmination. As long as the world confounds us with unimaginable horrors and terrors, talk of steady, necessary progress borders on madness.

As Neiman puts it, "every Hegelian avenue is blocked [after Auschwitz] by the production of corpses."[29] In Arendt's words: "Who would dare to reconcile himself with the reality of extermination camps, or play the [Hegelian] game of synthesis-antithesis-synthesis until his dialectics have discovered 'meaning' in slave labor?"[30]

Nietzsche tries to save the day by positing that evil is the suffering we bring upon ourselves by a failure of nerve or willpower.[31] He thinks we are unhappy because what is occurring has diverged from our ideal of what ought to be happening to our loved ones and us. We resent the present because it does not conform to our vision of what it should be. The solution to overcoming such resentment is to stop living in the future and to will the present as it is. Only by fully and unconditionally embracing our current state can we be happy. Through willpower, we can, Nietzsche believes, close the gap between ideal and real, and eliminate our suffering. By willing whatever is to be good, we can imbue the contingent with a kind of necessity. Our life must be good because we will it to be so.

On this Nietzschean view, we should be willing to return to the past and enthusiastically relive whatever has occurred. Through nerve, we supposedly can live in the best of all possible worlds. This technique, though, is just another parlor trick for eliminating contingency. No one who has survived torture or rape would gladly sign up for another round of abuse. The sinners in Dante's hell disprove Nietzsche's theory of the "eternal return." They relive their past and, in some cases, do so with passion and gusto. Yet none is happy. If they were, they would not be in hell.

Speaking of evil as necessarily redemptive leads us down the dangerous path of denying contingency. Such talk makes me uneasy for another reason. To make this claim, we must categorize the effects of suffering. Categorization, in turn, can lead to the notion that suffering redeems by bringing about a greater good. Yet, as we have seen in the preceding chapters, individuals frequently get caught up in their suffering. In these cases, suffering does not improve people's lives. When they identify with suffering, it becomes their lives. Suffering can be purely destructive. Auschwitz and Mauthausen did not build character. Camp survivors frequently assert that the best individuals were the ones who did not make it: "whatever depth or wisdom or humanity was intact after Auschwitz remained not through but in spite of it."[32] For some in the death camps, seeking meaning in suffering seemed a positive disadvantage. To survive it was better not to think.[33]

Thinkers committed to the notion that suffering is necessarily redemptive try to save the argument by appealing to the notion of collective redemption: the few who die make life better for the rest of us. Such talk is cheap. Although martyrs may improve life for future generations, that possibility is a small consolation prize for those "immolated on the alter of history."[34] The concept of collective redemption instrumentalizes the individual. It is but a small step from "good comes from the death of a few" to "better that a few die so that the many may live." As Caiphas (trapped in Dante's eighth circle of hell) discovers, the latter platitude is easy to utter but harder to endorse when we are the ones who get sacrificed for the good of the many.[35]

For all these reasons, we should be cautious about any attempt to show that evil necessarily leads to good. It is possible, however, to err on the other side and to underestimate the role suffering plays in human development. Although suffering is not necessarily redemptive, it can provide an opportunity for insight. Some who were stricken with AIDS have claimed that the disease woke them up to life. They had been going through life on autopilot until AIDS brought them face to face with their mortality. The pain did not make them wise, but it did function as an invitation for them to examine their lives with a view to discovering what would make life worth living. Nelson Mandela's years in prison enabled him to develop into a leader who could act to heal a nation divided by years of apartheid. Lucy Dawidowicz documents the efforts of the Polish underground to preserve civilization during the German occupation. The deprivations endured by these underground members were huge, but the war made them realize the importance of culture. They instilled in ghetto children a tremendous discipline of mind, enabling the children to acquire the "habits of a civilized existence."[36]

Nor is it true that everyone who survived the camps did so by refusing to think. Bruno Bettelheim found evidence that political prisoners in the camp who could theorize about what was happening to them were less devastated than those who were not able to do so.[37] Many prisoners of war returning from Vietnam have described their imprisonment as a "growth experience."[38] Even in the camps, some people found vocations. The Polish writer Mordechai Strigler taught children, whispering poems and snatches of history "to keep their minds from dying."[39] While interred, Viktor Frankl evolved his theory that suffering expands to fill the available space, a concept that became the basis for his psychiatric theory of logotherapy. Still others who survived the camps saw an opportunity in the cruelty and injustice. They could not change the past, but they were free to respond to, and interpret, the past. One survivor who had been a child in the camps describes his life as a proof that that misery need "not consume us with hatred to the point of destroying our own and other people's lives." [40]

The human rights activist Natan Sharansky discovered that the very techniques the KGB used to try to break him strengthened him:

> The KGB made a big mistake when they put me in the punishment cell. Their objective, of course, was to intensify the psychological pressure, and at first their plan succeeded. But gradually, in this harsh setting, with no distractions and no human companionship, I was able to focus all my energies into new strategies of resistance. As I paced around the tiny punishment cell during the final forty-eight hours of my confinement, my thoughts were of how to recover some self-control, which I felt I had lost in recent sessions. I saw two possible responses. The first was to barricade myself in my own world and to terminate all communication with the KGB. I admired the simplicity of this approach, but how long could I maintain such a position? Moreover, I was reluctant to follow an inflexible strategy that left no room to improvise. The second alternative was more elegant, but also more perilous: I would seek some kind of proof that they were lying to me. If I was successful, I could throw away my doubts and regain control of the interrogations. At the same time, I couldn't allow myself to start bargaining with them—as in "Give me a face-to-face confrontation with X and I'll tell you something"—for such arrangements were invariably a prelude to concessions. Could I possibly discover whether they were lying to me without making any deals? [41]

People experience suffering in different ways. To try to qualify the human experience of suffering as inevitably redemptive or nonredemptive is to ignore or repress human individuality. So many factors determine individuals' responses to suffering that we cannot discover some rule that specifies how people will react. Contingency is present not only in events but also in people's responses to their suffering. If we claim to know what insights other people will or will not glean from their frustration, we repeat the same mistake made by Hegel and Nietzsche. We appropriate the experience of others in our effort to prove that this experience is necessary.

Is there any sense, then, in which it might be true and safe to say that good can come from evil, although it need not do so? We can make such a claim if we remember that evil is frustrated desire. Overcoming evil in order to lead a more satisfied life requires that we assess how adequate our concept of our self and our world is. We cannot gain such self-knowledge without making mistakes. Only by identifying with inadequate concepts of the self do we gain the material upon which our understanding can work. Without these forays into self-knowledge is, incomplete and erroneous though they may be, self-development is not possible. Coming to perceive a mistake as a mistake is how we know that we have learned something in the interim.

The suffering we experience when our desire is frustrated can motivate us to examine our presuppositions, refine our notions about who we are, and alter any unrealistic aspirations. Evil understood as a lack of satisfaction can lead us to a deeper appreciation of the causes of human behavior, including our own. This progress, though, does not occur in isolation. In Buber's famous phrase, we do not achieve salvation "by the subtraction of the world."[42] We continually affect and are affected by the world. The world provides many opportunities for us to teach ourselves something about who we are and about the nature of the universe. We may believe that we are completely in control of our world. Then one day, while we are walking to the grocery store, a car jumps the curb and hits us, paralyzing us for life. We can either complain that the world is unjust because it failed to recognize our right to be in total control, or we can rethink what kind of control a person can have in a world in which accidents occur. Those who reduce themselves to victims become angry or depressed. Those who rethink this identification have an opportunity to develop through suffering.

To put the point more succinctly: as long as human beings are capable of interpreting their suffering, they can develop. Past habits or vices do not determine a human being's fate. The psychotherapist Frankl, who survived the concentration camps at Dachau and Auschwitz, provides a striking example of this point:

> [Dr. J] was the only man I ever encountered in my whole life whom I would dare to call a Mephistophelean being, a satanic figure. At that time he was generally called "the mass murderer of Steinhof" (the large mental hospital in Vienna). When the Nazis started their euthanasia program, he held all the strings in his hands and was so fanatic in the job assigned to him that he tried not to let one single psychotic individual escape the gas chamber. After the war, when I came back to Vienna, I asked what happened to Dr. J. "He had been imprisoned by the Russians in one of the isolation cells of Steinhof," they told me. "The next day, however, the door of his cell stood open and Dr. J. was never seen again." . . . Recently . . . I was consulted by a former Austrian diplomat who had been imprisoned behind the Iron Curtain for many years, first in Siberia and then in the famous Lubianka prison in Moscow. While I was examining him neurologically, he suddenly asked me whether I happened to know Dr. J. After my affirmative reply he continued: "I made his acquaintance in Lubianka. There he died, at about the age of forty, from cancer of the urinary bladder. Before he died, however, he showed himself to be the best comrade you can imagine! He gave consolation to everybody. He lived up to the highest conceivable moral standard. He was the best friend I ever met during my long years in prison!" This is the story of Dr. J., "the mass murderer of Steinhof." How can we dare to predict the behavior of man?[43]

As this case illustrates, we do not know all the causes that lead a person to behave one way instead of another. We should be dubious, therefore, about the assertion that someone is irredeemably wicked. Individuals have an incentive to change. Since suffering is painful, we try to escape from it. Escape is possible only if we interpret suffering by unearthing its cause. By becoming more aware of the contribution we have unwittingly made to our suffering, we empower ourselves to stop at least some of the pain. We escape these traps of our own making not by dwelling on our unhappiness or by making some Herculean effort of will to embrace it, but by excavating our false assumptions and identifications.

As we correct our misidentifications, our concept of human freedom alters. Real freedom does not consist in being undetermined or in being able to use one's willpower. We are truly free only to the extent we use our reason to become progressively more aware of the causes of our behavior and of the stakes for which we are playing. Freedom is the knowledge of these causes. Insofar as erroneous self-conceptions cause us to be unhappy, freedom is equivalent to self-knowledge. To the extent other factors (e.g., lack of education, persecution, overly rigid role expectations) are adding to our suffering, human freedom consists in identifying and understanding these contributing factors. As our comprehension improves, so does our ability to work with these causes. With this increase in power, our ability to satisfy our desires is correspondingly enhanced, and evil is reduced.

Free individuals are concerned with themselves, but not to the exclusion of other people. As we free ourselves from rage and fear, we see other people more clearly. Recognizing that each person must find his or her way to self-understanding, we are less inclined to meddle in their lives or to condemn their activities. This tolerance liberates us, because we cease to waste precious energy opposing others' attempts at self-realization. This energy can go toward helping each other. The more free each of us becomes, the better we grasp the causes of other people's suffering. If they should ask for aid, we can draw upon this knowledge to help them remove these impediments to lasting satisfaction.

Transcending suffering is identical with reflecting on what is causing our unhappiness. This cause is always some feature of the universe, some aspect of the way in which the world and the self are operating in tandem. Transcending entails accepting factual features of the universe. Again I would stress that individual development does not occur in isolation. The ideas of those who have identified the true causes of their suffering begin to converge.[44] In knowing and developing ourselves, we inevitably come to know something of the concerns of other people. As our increase in freedom causes our ideas to converge with those of others who are similarly liberating themselves, we discover that we can collaborate to create civic institutions devoted to enriching human understanding. Instead of standing on the sidelines blaming other people, we can become a force for positive change.

True freedom is equivalent to experiencing greater satisfaction in life. By helping us to understand the universe and our place in it, the disciplines of religion, psychology, and philosophy, help us to escape or, at least, minimize our suffering. If, however, we get stuck in a misconception of who we are, then we, like Dante's sinners, become little more than a succession of passions or sufferings.

Should We Resist Evil?

Earlier, I suggested that the best way to resist evil is to seek to discover who we really are. Having considered the genus of evil, we are in a position to say a little more about this tricky issue. The question of whether, and how, we should resist evil takes on a completely different complexion as we come to a deeper understanding of the nature of evil and human freedom. Substituting "frustration of our desire" for "evil," the question becomes: should we resist the frustration of our desire? So phrased, the question borders on the nonsensical. Given that every human being craves lasting satisfaction, our lives are devoted to avoiding frustration. No normative issue exists. We always naturally strive for satisfaction.

The normative issue arises with respect to what it means to resist evil. If our frustration is bound up with false ideas about the world and self, our energy should be expended not in fighting our frustration but in grasping its cause. The wisdom tradition focuses on the subjective or variable component of each person's experience of suffering and says, "You are affecting your satisfaction by how you interpret the causes of that experience. Be careful, therefore, to examine and test that judgment. Test it repeatedly. Consider whether it is as self-evident and necessary as you are making it out to be. Think whether you can interpret the suffering in other ways. As you do all of these things, you will gradually realize that you are not a passive victim. You, too, are functioning as a cause of your experience. The more deeply you understand your experience, the more self-causing you will be. You will see where you have power and where you do not. Then you will be able to use your power more effectively than if you keep on responding unthinkingly to everything that happens to you."

James's governess, Ripley, Hendrik, and Dante's sinners do not adopt this approach. As a result, they are condemned to an anguish-filled existence. Socrates, by contrast, does embrace this way of thinking. Doing so enables him to go cheerfully to his death.[45] Since he knows that he cannot know what death is, he realizes that to fear death is hubris. We presume to know that death is the greatest threat. But, for all we know, death may be nothingness or a state akin to a deep and pleasant sleep. Instead of doing whatever it takes to escape the death penalty, Socrates concentrates on understanding why he is being unfairly prosecuted and on determining what he must do if he is to avoid committing injustice. He devotes his energy to figuring out what sort of power he does possess and discovering where he has a measure of control over how satisfying his life will be. Confucius adopts a variant of the same strategy. When told that someone was ill disposed toward him, Confucius retorted: "Heaven is the author of the virtue that is in me. What can Huan T'ui do to me?"[46] Socrates and Confucius did not have to fight "evil" people, because they saw that their persecutors posed no real threat to them. What other people did or said would not alter Socrates' or Confucius's grasp of the truth or disturb the inner peace that accompanied their insight into the world.

Let me be clear. The way of wisdom is not the same as Stoicism. Or, since Stoicism takes many forms, I should say that wisdom repudiates the Stoical view that we ultimately control nothing but our own willpower. This version of Stoicism would have us focus on mastering our selves and our response to external events. It argues that it is within our power to *will* ourselves to view things in a less upsetting way. If we are unhappy, it is only because we have failed to exercise our will. The wisdom tradition, makes no reference to the will or to willpower. It equates freedom to correct understanding. In comprehending that we cannot know what death is, Socrates simultaneously apprehends that he cannot live a satisfying life as long as he takes his bearings from a fear of death. His life will never be peaceful unless he allows himself to be guided by reason. When we let reason be our guide, we find that it is not necessary to control our passions or emotions through an act of will. Thinkers in the wisdom tradition view emotions, such as fear and rage, as confused reasoning. Passions do not have to mastered. These sufferings disappear of their own accord as our understanding of our place in the universe improves. Our first obligation, then, is to examine ourselves and to overcome the frustration within. While moralities direct us outward, encouraging us to locate and blame others who have violated rights, duties or laws, the way of wisdom turns our attention inward. The novelist David Duncan says this about the inward turn:

> As a lifelong student of the world's wisdom literature, it is my duty to inform students that "ridding the world of evil" is a goal quite different

from any recommended by Jesus, Buddha, or Mohammed, though not so different from [that] recommended by Joseph Stalin, McCarthy, or Mao Tse Tung. In wisdom literature the principal evil to be attacked by the person of faith is the evil in oneself, and a secondary evil to be opposed is the power of anyone who victimizes the weak.[47]

Only by examining ourselves can we see the world clearly. Before we intervene in the world, we ought to know with what we are dealing. In the words of Anthony de Mello, "You change first. Then you'll get a good enough look at the world so that you'll be able to change whatever you think ought to be changed."[48]

To return to an example considered earlier: our erroneous supposition that murderers are sadistic prevents us from seeing murders as they happen under our very nose. The governess in *The Turn of the Screw* is, according to the narrator, "a most charming person" and "the most agreeable woman I've ever known in her position; she'd have been worthy of any whatever."[49] As we read the story, we see no evidence that the governess is vindictive. Learning of events through her eyes, we are sympathetic toward her. She appears to have the best of intentions—to save two innocent children from being corrupted. Only if we are sufficiently self-aware to realize that each of us sees the world through the lens of our desire will it occur to us that the figures the governess encounters may be representations produced by her own desire. As soon as this thought occurs to us, we start to entertain the possibility that the governess unwittingly murders the child Miles as she tries to save him from a figure she sees at the window. If we do not pay attention to the self-frustrating quality of the governess's desires, we take the governess to be the savior she paints herself to be. Enthralled by the same passions, convictions and good intentions that trap the governess, we uncritically accept her representations. Although we do not think of ourselves as evil people, we cheer her on as she murders a child. If the governess is evil, what does that make us?

Self-examination is crucial if we are not to reproduce the behavior of those whom we condemn. It is well known that many police share the same psychological profile as the criminals they arrest. Gabriel Utterson and Enfield, the two men who hunt down Dr. Jekyll/Mr. Hyde, exhibit the double nature of the man they have demonized. At every stage of Dante's journey through hell, the poet repeats the sin of those whom he has previously chastised. On the lookout for malefactors, we satanize other people without being aware that we are doing so. I have not found a single commentator who has remarked upon the extensive similarities between Dr. Jekyll and his lawyer friend Utterson. None has observed that the "barely human" Hyde turns nasty only when Utterson and Utterson's cousin Enfield start to hound him. Critics similarly view Dante as pure and virtuous. They excuse his vicious verbal and physical attacks on sinners, contending that Dante has completely "weaned himself from evil practices" and that sinners in hell are so evil that Dante is justified in assaulting them.[50] James's tale works by leaving its values blank. The reader imagines the worst, and thereby unconsciously joins the governess in her mad speculations. Although James explicitly states in his introduction to *The Turn of the Screw* that he has laid a trap, almost forty years elapsed before the critic Edmund Wilson suggested that the figures the governess encounters are her projections. Wilson was vilified by readers and critics who were certain that the governess was a reliable, pious, and virtuous narrator and that the menacing figures of Quint and Miss Jessel were real ghosts. The vitriol elicited by Wilson's hypothesis confirms James's central insight: our certainty that our interpretation is the only correct one turns us into an enemy akin to the one we wish to obliterate. It is in this context that we should view Jesus' recommendation that we turn the other cheek. He is not urging passivity but showing us a way out of this demonic dynamic.

We are on the path to wisdom when we can start to see how our unexamined opinions, including many of our most cherished moral beliefs, lead us to act like those whom we attack. While moralities stress justice and enforcement of the law, the wisdom tradition praises compassion, love, and mercy. Given that we, too, are sinners, we ought not to judge others too harshly. Does that mean that we must be silent in the face of injustice? Quite the reverse. Those who are clearest about their limitations are best positioned to speak truth to power. If we know that we do not know what death is, we can perhaps resist authorities without the fear of dying. Socrates followed the argument wherever it led, even when it meant opposing the civil authorities. Hildegaard von Bingen, who was exceptionally clear about human finitude, was one of the few courageous enough to confront the emperor Frederick Barbarossa. When the emperor banished music from the church, she dressed him down, warning him that he should not presume to know and judge what the divine finds pleasing.

Mello speaks of a Master who lived life to the full but who was also known to take great risks. This Master condemned the tyranny of government, thereby courting arrest and death. He also led a group of his disciples to serve a plague-stricken village.

> "The wise have no fear of death," he would say.
> "Why would a man risk his life so easily?" he was once asked.
> "Why would a person care so little about a candle being extinguished when day has dawned?" he replied.[51]

Mello's Master implies that we can be human candles, illuminating the darkness. Through devoting our energy to becoming enlightened, we fulfill our mission on earth and have no reason to fear death. At a deeper level, the Master reminds us that the universe has its own rhythms and ways of dispelling darkness. The universe produced us, not the reverse. The dawn comes whether or not we contribute our measure of light. Wise individuals do not rail against dying, because they know that they are part of a universe that will continue to unfold after they are dead. They understand that their first duty is to grasp the limited role played by human beings in the totality of creation. Their second duty is to act in accordance with this understanding—to be a burning candle, not to attempt to assume the powers of the sun.

In fulfilling these two duties, we find that our courage grows as we accept our limitations. We may even uncover power in what the world perceives as weakness. No one understood this point better than Mahatma Gandhi. He intuited that the human spirit would revolt at the sight of the strong (armed British soldiers) repeatedly brutalizing the weak (unarmed Indian civilians). Drawing upon reservoirs of compassion that we might not even have been aware existed, we would be able, he realized, to make use of suffering to end it.

P. D. Ouspensky liked to say, "We live in perilous times. One works at one's own risk." Every era has its dangers. The natural world continually surprises us, and we create terrors as we unwittingly empower the very demons we fight. Even if we manage to engage in the work of self-examination, we are not home free. The resulting changes in our outlook can be seismic. What's more, these world-shaking changes do not occur merely once or twice. Our empirical self—that mass of beliefs and accompanying emotions—gets reshaped repeatedly as our understanding of the causes of our suffering improves. We are always at risk in our work. The risk, though, is worth taking. Once we cease to have new thoughts and emotions, we become dead to life. What we should most fear is not being abused by other people but failing to be worthy of our sufferings.

NOTES

INTRODUCTION

1. Immanuel Kant, *Groundwork of the Metaphysic of Morals*, trans. H.J. Paton (New York: Harper & Row, 1956), pp. 69–83; Onora O'Neill, *Towards Justice and Virtue* (Cambridge: Cambridge University Press, 1996), pp. 60–65.
2. Aristotle, *Nicomachean Ethics*, trans. W.D. Ross, ed. Richard McKeon, *The Basic Works of Aristotle* (New York: Random House, 1941), bks. 1–7.
3. Ibid.
4. Anthony de Mello, *One Minute Wisdom* (New York: Doubleday, 1985), p. 1.
5. Plato, *The Republic of Plato*, trans. Allan Bloom (New York: Basic Books Inc., 1968), bk. 1.
6. Rob Campany, "Cosmogony and Self–Cultivation: The Demonic and Ethical in Two Chinese Novels," *Journal of Religious Ethics*, http://www.fsu.edu/religion/~religion/jre/arc/14–1/index.html.
7. See chapter 7, pp. 187–206.
8. Gandhi quoted at www.ieer.org/latest/oct2quot.html.
9. Mary Midgley, *Wickedness* (London: Ark Paperbacks, 1984), p. 1.
10. W.H. Auden, "Herman Melville," http://jclarkmedia.com.
11 *The Book of Job, NIV Study Bible*, ed. Kenneth Barker (Grand Rapids, MI: Zondervan, 1985).
12. Kenneth Cauthen, *The Many Faces of Evil* (Lima, OH: CSS Publishing Company, 1997), p. 46.
13. John Knowles, *A Separate Peace* (New York: Macmillan, 1959), p. 186.

1

1. C. Fred Alford, *What Evil Means to Us* (Albany, NY: Cornell University Press, 1997), pp. 3, 67, 70.
2. Ibid., p. 67; Elaine Pagels, *The Gnostic Gospels* (New York: Random House, 1979), passim.
3. Alford, *What Evil Means to Us*, pp. 67–68; Sandra Bloom, "Trauma and the Nature of Evil," *Community Works*, November 1996, p. 3; Donald Taylor, "Theological Thoughts about Evil," ed. David Parkin, *The Anthropology of Evil* (New York: Basil Blackwell), pp. 26–41.
4. Paul Ricoeur, *The Symbolism of Evil*, trans. Emerson Buchanan (Boston: Beacon Press, 1969), pp. 20–41.

5. Gerald Messadié, *A History of the Devil* (New York: Kodansha America, Inc., 1996), passim.
6. Bloom, "Trauma and the Nature of Evil," p. 4.
7. Susan Neiman, *Evil in Modern Thought* (Princeton, NJ: Princeton University Press, 2002), p. 3.
8. Ibid.
9. Aristotle, *Nicomachean Ethics*, trans. W.D. Ross, ed. Richard McKeon, *The Basic Works of Aristotle* (New York: Random House, 1941), 1098a1–1101b5.
10. Alford, *What Evil Means to Us*, p. 67.
11. Aristotle, *Politics*, trans. Benjamin Jowett, ed. Richard McKeon, *The Basic Works of Aristotle* (New York: Random House, 1941), 1253a1–1253a2.
12. Aristotle, *Politics*, passim.
13. Aristotle, *Nicomachean Ethics*, 1109b30–1109b35.
14. Ibid.
15. Ibid., 1109b35–1110a4.
16. Ibid., 1110a5–1110a10.
17. Ibid., 1110a9–1110a19.
18. Ibid., 1110a20–1110a25.
19. Ibid., 1100a29–1100a31.
20. Ibid., 1116a15–1116b3.
21. James Boswell, *Life of Samuel Johnson* (New York: Alfred A. Knopf, 1993), entry for June 3, 1784.
22. Aristotle, *Nicomachean Ethics*, 1113a10–1113a13.
23. Ibid., 1112b31–1112b35.
24. Ibid., 1150b35.
25. Ibid., 1110b15–1110b17.
26. Ibid., 1110b24–1110b35.
27. Ibid., 1110b24–1111a20.
28. Ibid., 1110b27–1110b31.
29. Vince Lombardi, http://www.brainyquote.com/quotes/authors/vincelomba 132105.html.
30. Aristotle, *Nicomachean Ethics*, 1101a1–1101b6.
31. Ibid., 1151a15–1151a30.
32. Ibid., 1151b1515–1151b1522.
33. Ibid., 1151a10–1151a30.
34. Ibid., 1150a1–1150a77.
35. Ibid., 1150b35–1150b36.
36. Ibid., 1114a10–1114a25.
37. Friedrich Nietzsche, *Samtliche Werke: Kritische Studienausgabe*, ed. Giorgio Colli and Mazzino Montinari (Berlin: De Gruyter, 1980), p. 69.
38. Garrath Williams, "Blame and Responsibility," *Ethical Theory and Moral Practice*, vol. 6, p. 429.
39. Christopher Kutz, *Complicity: Ethics and Law for a Collective Age* (Cambridge: Cambridge University Press, 2000), p. 254.
40. Conversation with John Cornell about the New Testament.
41. Henry David Thoreau, "A Week on the Concord and Merrimack Rivers," *The Writings of Henry David Thoreau*, vol. 1 (New York: Houghton Mifflin, 1906), p. 236.

42. Oliver Goldsmith, *The Good Natur'd Man*, Act 1 (Reprint Services Corp. 1921).
43. Aristotle, *Nicomachean Ethics*, 1111a20.
44. Victor Hugo, "Thoughts," *Postscriptum de Ma Vie*, trans. Lorenzo O' Rourke (New York: Funk and Wagnalls, 1907); William Shakespeare, *The Merchant of Venice*, *The Complete Works of Shakespeare* (New York: Scott, Foresman, and Company, 151), Act 3, sc. 2, 1. 81–82.
45. Amitai Etzioni, *The New Golden Rule: Community and Morality in a Democratic Society* (New York: Basic Books, 1996), pp. 222–229.
46. Aristotle, *Nicomachean Ethics*, 113b20–113b35; 1144a30–1144a35.
47. Hannah Arendt, *On Revolution* (New York: Viking Press, 1963), p. 99.
48. Williams, "Blame and Responsibility," p. 432.
49. Flora Tristan quoted in *Victorian Women*, ed. Erna Olafson Hellerstein, Leslie Parker Hume, and Karen M. Offen (Stanford: Stanford University Press, 1981), p. 90.
50. Richard Steele, *The Spectator*, no. 266 (1732), http://www. tabula.rutgers. edu8080:/cocoon/.
51. Oscar Wilde, "The Soul of Man Under Socialism," *Fortnightly Review* (February 1891).

2

1. Simone Weil, "Morality and Literature," *Cahiers du Sud* (January 1944), p. 160.
2. Aristotle, *Nicomachean Ethics*, ed. Richard McKeon, *The Basic Works of Aristotle* (New York: Random House, 1941), 1128b10–1128b35.
3. Ibid., 1128b10–1128b36.
4. Leon Kass, *Toward a More Natural Science* (New York: Free Press, 1985).
5. Klaus Mann, *Mephisto* (New York: Penguin Books, 1977), pp. 11–16.
6. Ibid., pp. 64–65.
7. Ibid., p. 68.
8. Ibid., p. 17.
9. Ibid.
10. Klaus Mann quoted in Publisher's Note to *Mephisto*, p. v.
11. Mann, *Mephisto*, pp. 52–53.
12. Ibid., p. 53.
13. Ibid., p. 50.
14. Ibid., p. 52.
15. Ibid.
16. Ibid., p. 147.
17. Ibid., p. 16.
18. Ibid., p. 50.
19. Mason Cooley, *City Aphorisms*, First Selection (New York: n.p., 1984).
20. Mann, *Mephisto*, pp. 9, 17.
21. C. Fred Alford, *What Evil Means to Us* (Albany, NY: Cornell University Press, 1997), pp. 39, 54.
22. Mary Midgley, *Wickedness* (London: Ark Paperbacks, 1984), p. 13.
23. Mann, *Mephisto*, p. 75.

24. Ibid., p. 72.
25. Ibid., p. 165.
26. Ibid., pp. 184–192.
27. Ibid.
28. Ibid., p. 148.
29. Ibid., p. 168.
30. Ibid., pp. 113–114.
31. Ibid., p. 245.
32. Ibid., p. 189.
33. Ibid., p. 195.
34. Ibid., p. 243.
35. Ibid., p. 197.
36. Ibid., p. 135.
37. Ibid., p. 90.
38. Ibid., p. 168.
39. Ibid., p. 87.
40. Ibid., p. 112.
41. Ibid., p. 110.
42. Ibid., p. 123.
43. Ibid., p. 220.
44. Ibid., p. 221.
45. Ibid., p. 94.
46. Ibid., p. 97.
47. Ibid., pp. 250–251.
48. Ibid., p. 254.
49. Ibid.
50. Ibid., p. 255.
51. Ibid., p. 256.
52. Ibid., p. 263.
53. Ibid., p. 178.
54. Ibid., p. vii.
55. Henry David Thoreau quoted in Andrew Delbanco, *The Death of Satan: How Americans Have Lost the Sense of Evil* (New York: Farrar, Strauss & Giroux, 1998), pp. 101, 105.
56. Ibid., p. 101.

3

1. Patricia Highsmith, *The Talented Mr. Ripley* (New York: Vintage Books, 1992), passim.
2. Margaret Sönser Breen, "Reading for Constructions of the Unspeakable in Kafka's *Metamorphosis*," *Understanding Evil* (Amsterdam: Rodopi Press, 2003), pp. 43–56.
3. John Gray, "An Encounter with Evil: Patricia Highsmith, a Book Review of *Beautiful Shadow: A Life of Patricia Highsmith*," *New Statesman* (June 30, 2003), http://www.findarticles.com/cf0/m0FQP/4644132/105366852/p1/article.jhtml.

4. Highsmith, *The Talented Mr. Ripley*, p. 8.
5. Ibid., p. 9.
6. Ibid., p. 23.
7. Ibid., p. 186.
8. Edmond De Goncourt and Jules De Goncourt, *Pages from the Goncourt Journal*, ed. Robert Baldick (Oxford: Oxford University Press, 1988), entry for July 30, 1861.
9. Findings of Professor Jack Levin of Northeastern University reported in *USA Today* (July 1, 1996), pp. 1A–2A.
10. Highsmith, *The Talented Mr. Ripley*, p. 14.
11. Patricia Highsmith, *Ripley's Game* (New York: Vintage Books, 1993), pp. 8–28.
12. Highsmith, *The Talented Mr. Ripley*, pp. 4, 85, 100.
13. Ibid., p. 35.
14. Ibid., p. 53.
15. Ibid., p. 127.
16. Ibid., p. 249.
17. Ibid., p. 192.
18. Ibid., p. 250.
19. Ibid., p. 237.
20. Ibid., p. 12.
21. Ibid., pp. 31–34.
22. Ibid., p. 13.
23. Ibid., p. 19.
24. Ibid., pp. 70, 168, 179.
25. Ibid., p. 175.
26. Ibid., p. 257.
27. Ibid., p. 157.
28. Gertrude Stein, *Everybody's Autobiography* (New York: Exact Change, 2004), p. 289.
29. Highsmith, *The Talented Mr. Ripley*, p. 33.
30. Ibid., p. 37.
31. Ibid., p. 92.
32. Hannah Arendt quoted in Maurizio Passerin D'Entreves, *The Political Philosophy of Hannah Arendt* (London: Routledge, 1993), p. 30.
33. Highsmith, *The Talented Mr. Ripley*, p. 79.
34. Ibid., p. 221.
35. Ibid., pp. 261, 272.
36. Mason Cooley, *City Aphorisms*, First Selection (New York: n.p., 1984).
37. Highsmith, *The Talented Mr. Ripley*, p. 160.
38. Ibid., p. 180.
39. Ibid., p. 92.
40. Ibid., p. 200.
41. Ibid., p. 263.
42. Ibid., p. 3.
43. Daryl Koehn, *The Ground of Professional Ethics* (London: Routledge, 1994), pp. 20–28.
44. Highsmith, *The Talented Mr. Ripley*, pp. 58–59.

45. Highsmith, *The Talented Mr. Ripley*, p. 8.
46. Ibid., p. 40.
47. Ibid., pp. 206–207.
48. Ibid., pp. 20–21.
49. Ibid., p. 100.
50. Highsmith, *Ripley's Game*, p. 5.
51. Highsmith, *The Talented Mr. Ripley*, p. 92.
52. Ibid., p. 183.
53. Ibid., p. 282.
54. Ibid., p. 285.
55. John Berryman, "Life, Friends, Is Boring," *The Dream Songs* (New York: Noonday Press, 1982), Song #14.
56. Andrew Delbanco, *The Death of Satan: How Americans Have Lost the Sense of Evil* (New York: Farrar, Strauss & Giroux, 1998), p. 27.
57. Highsmith, *The Talented Mr. Ripley*, p. 129.
58. Ibid., p. 254.
59. Ibid., p. 290.
60. Ibid.
61. Primo Levi, *The Drowned and the Saved*, trans. Raymond Rosenthal (New York: Summit Books, 1988), pp. 48–49.
62. Wendy Lesser, *Pictures at an Execution: An Inquiry into the Subject of Murder* (Cambridge, MA: Harvard University Press, 1993), p. 67.

4

1. Robert Louis Stevenson, *Dr. Jekyll and Mr. Hyde*, ed. Leonard Wolf, *The Essential Dr. Jekyll and Mr. Hyde* (New York: Penguin Group, 1995).
2. Ibid., p. 115.
3. Ibid., p. 118.
4. Ibid., p. 122.
5. Ibid., p. 118.
6. Ibid., p. 41.
7. Ibid.
8. Ibid., p. 50.
9. Ibid.
10. Ibid., p. 51.
11. Ibid.
12. Ibid., p. 109.
13. Ibid.
14. Ibid.
15. Ibid.
16. Ibid., p. 121.
17. Ibid., p. 115.
18. Mary Midgley, *Wickedness* (London: Ark Paperbacks, 1984), p. 119.
19. Stevenson, *Dr. Jekyll and Mr. Hyde*, pp. 55, 115.
20. Ibid., pp. 123, 119.
21. Ibid., p. 67.
22. Robert Louis Stevenson, "Letter to Myers," *The Essential Dr. Jekyll and Mr. Hyde*, ed. Leonard Wolf (New York: Penguin Group, 1995), p. 272.

23. Stevenson, *Dr. Jekyll and Mr. Hyde*, p. 99.
24. Mary Midgley, *Wickedness*, p. 122.
25. Stevenson, *Dr. Jekyll and Mr. Hyde*, p. 35.
26. Ibid., p. 36.
27. Ibid.
28. Ibid., p. 128.
29. Ibid., p. 36.
30. Ibid., pp. 37–38.
31. Ibid., p. 35.
32. Ibid., p. 38.
33. Ibid., p. 33.
34. Ibid., p. 31.
35. Ibid., p. 32.
36. Ibid.
37. Ibid., p. 33.
38. Ibid.
39. Ibid., p. 32.
40. Ibid., p. 118.
41. Ibid., p. 33.
42. Samuel Butler, *The Way of All Flesh*, http://www.classicreader.com/read.php, ch. 26.
43. Stevenson, *Dr. Jekyll and Mr. Hyde*, pp. 38–39.
44. Ibid., p. 128.
45. Ibid., p. 127.
46. Ibid.
47. Ibid., p. 63.
48. Ibid., p. 62.
49. Ibid.
50. Ibid.
51. Ibid., p. 63.
52. Ibid.
53. Ibid.
54. Ibid., p. 32.
55. Ibid., p. 66
56. J.A. Sanford, *Evil: The Shadow Side of Reality* (New York: The Crossroad Publishing Company, 1998), p. 65.
57. Stevenson, *Dr. Jekyll and Mr. Hyde*, p. 129.
58. Ibid.
59. Ibid.
60. Ibid., p. 132.
61. Ibid., pp. 115–136.
62. Ibid., p. 33.
63. Ibid., p. 48.
64. Ibid., p. 52.
65. Ibid., p. 53.
66. Ibid.
67. Ibid., p. 46.
68. Ibid., p. 47.
69. Ibid., p. 44.

70. Ibid., p. 47.
71. Ibid., p. 34.
72. Ibid., p. 119.
73. Ibid., p. 121.
74. Ibid., p. 67.
75. Ibid., pp. 124–125.
76. Ibid., pp. 97–99.

5

1. Henry James, *The Aspern Papers and The Turn of the Screw*, ed. Anthony Curtis (London: Penguin Books, 1984), p. 39.
2. Ibid., passim.
3. Ibid., p. 40.
4. Ibid., p. 42.
5. Ibid., p. 164.
6. Ibid., p. 165.
7. Ibid.
8. Ibid.
9. Ibid., p. 167.
10. Ibid., p. 169.
11. Ibid., p. 170.
12. Ibid.
13. Ibid., p. 171.
14. Ibid., pp. 173–174.
15. Jeffrey Burton Russell, *The Prince of Darkness* (Ithaca, NY: Cornell University Press, 1988), pp. 114–115.
16. James, *The Turn of the Screw*, p. 178.
17. Ibid.
18. Ibid., p. 176.
19. Ibid., p. 179.
20. Ibid., p. 180.
21. Ibid., p. 181.
22. Ibid., p. 182.
23. Ibid., p. 170.
24. Ibid., p. 184.
25. Ibid., p. 185.
26. Ibid., p. 39.
27. Ibid., p. 194.
28. Ibid., pp. 195–196.
29. Ibid., p. 199.
30. Ibid., p. 184.
31. Ibid., p. 182
32. Ibid., p. 216.
33. Ibid., pp. 200–201.
34. Ibid., pp. 204–205.
35. Ibid., p. 22.
36. Ibid., p. 220.

37. Ibid., pp. 220–221.
38. Ibid., p. 232.
39. Ibid., p. 234.
40. Ibid., pp. 234, 238.
41. Ibid., p. 240.
42. Ibid.
43. Ibid., pp. 244–245.
44. Ibid., p. 248.
45. Ibid., p. 198.
46. Ibid., pp. 253–256.
47. Ibid., p. 253.
48. Ibid., pp. 255–256.
49. Ibid., p. 256.
50. Ibid., p. 258.
51. Katherine Anne Porter, Allen Tate, and Mark Van Doren, "James: 'The Turn of the Screw,' A Radio Symposium," ed. Gerald Willen, *A Casebook on Henry James' The Turn of the Screw* (New York: Thomas F. Crowell Company, 1969), p. 165.
52. James, *The Turn of the Screw*, p. 147.
53. Ibid., p. 260.
54. Ibid.
55. Ibid.
56. Ibid., p. 42.

6

1. Dante Alighieri, *The Inferno of Dante*, trans. Robert Pinsky (New York: The Noonday Press, 1994). I cite the canto and then line numbers in these endnotes.
2. Michael Welner, "Defining Evil: A Depravity Scale for Today's Courts," *The Forensic Echo*, 2:6 (1998), pp. 4–12.
3. Dante, *The Inferno*, 3:9.
4. Ibid., 11:22–23.
5. Marc Cogan, *The Design in the Wax* (Notre Dame, IN: University of Notre Dame Press, 1999), p. 23.
6. See the order of the virtues in Aristotle, *Nicomachean Ethics*, bks. 3–5.
7. Dante, *The Inferno*, 5:2–3.
8. Cogan, *The Design in the Wax*, p. 9.
9. Dante, *The Inferno*, 1:46–109.
10. Ibid., 5:38–39.
11. Ibid., 5:30.
12. Ibid., 5:112–124.
13. Ibid., 5:90.
14. Ibid., 6:33.
15. Ibid., 6:25.
16. Aristotle, *Nicomachean Ethics*, bk. 7.
17. Dante, *The Inferno*, 6:53.
18. Ibid., 6:71–75.

19. Ibid., 6:105–109.
20. Dante, *The Inferno*, 7:20–30.
21. Robert Pinsky, Notes to *The Inferno of Dante* (New York: The Noonday Press, 1994), p. 316.
22. Cogan, *The Design in the Wax*, p. 51.
23. Dante, *The Inferno*, 7:110.
24. Cogan, *The Design in the Wax*, p. 77.
25. Mary Midgley, *Wickedness* (London: Ark Paperbacks, 1984), pp. 142–144.
26. Ibid., pp. 71, 147.
27. William Shakespeare, *Othello*, *The Complete Works of Shakespeare* (New York: Scott, Foresman, and Company, 1951), Act V, sc. 2, 1. 300.
28. Dante, *The Inferno*, 6:80–85.
29. Ibid., 16:78–87.
30. Ibid., 11:24–27.
31. Ibid., 11:56.
32. Ibid., 18:59–61.
33. Ibid., 18:57.
34. Ibid., 18:95, 109.
35. Ibid., 20:8–10.
36. Ibid., 20:30.
37. Ibid., 29:70–75.
38. John D. Sinclair, *The Divine Comedy of Dante Alighieri* (London: Oxford University Press, 1971), p. 258.
39. Dante, *The Inferno*, 3:1–10.
40. Ibid., 31:72–77.
41. Ibid., 30:94–96.
42. Ibid., 32:14–16.
43. Ibid., 32:150–153.
44. Ibid., 33:148–149.
45. Ibid., 30:10–120.
46. Ibid., 30:39–44.
47. Ibid., 33:25–35.
48. Ibid., 33:37.
49. Ibid., 33:56–59.
50. Teodolinda Barolini, "Narrative and Style in Lower Hell," *The Undivine Comedy: Detheologizing Dante* (Princeton, NJ: Princeton University Press, 1992), ch. 4, http://www.dante.ilt.columbia.edu/books/undivine-com/ udc4.html.
51. Henry James, *The Aspern Papers and The Turn of the Screw* (London: Penguin Books, 1984), p. 147.
52. Ibid., p. 261.
53. Andrew Delbanco, *The Death of Satan: How Americans Have Lost the Sense of Evil* (New York: Farrar, Strauss & Giroux, 1998), p. 16.
54. Cogan, *The Design in the Wax*, p. 169.

7

1. *1 John*, *3:8*, *NIV Study Bible*, ed. Kenneth Barker (Grand Rapids, MI: Zondervan, 1985).
2. Ibid., 3:12.

3. Ibid., 5:19.
4. Nicolas Corte, *Who Is the Devil?* (New York: Hawthorne Books, 1958), p. 37.
5. *Matthew*, 4:1.
6. *Mark*, 1:9–15.
7. *Matthew*, 4:3.
8. Neil Forsyth, *The Old Enemy* (Princeton, NJ: Princeton University Press, 1987), pp. 287–292.
9. *Matthew*, 4:6.
10. Bruno de Jésus–Marie, *Satan* (New York: Sheed & Ward, 1952), p. 232.
11. *Luke*, 10:24; *Matthew*, 13:13–17; *Mark*, 4:9.
12. *Mark*, 3:22–30.
13. See *NIV* footnotes to *Matthew*, 4:5; *Luke*, 4:2.
14. *Matthew*, 13:57; *John*, 4:44.
15. *Matthew*, 23:37.
16. Ibid., 4:7.
17. Ibid., 8:4–9.
18. Corte, *Who Is the Devil*, p. 41.
19. John Milton, *Paradise Lost*, bk. 8, p. 132, http://www. sliteraturepage.com/read/paradise-lost-132.html.
20. *Matthew*, 19:17.
21. Ibid., 22:21.
22. *Mark*, 16:17–18.
23. *Matthew*, 5:25.
24. Ibid., 14:4.
25. *Numbers*, 30:2.
26. *Daniel*, 6:14–15.
27. *Mark*, 6:31; *Matthew*, 14:13; *Luke*, 9:10.
28. *Matthew*, 14:16.
29. *Mark*, 6:37.
30. *Matthew*, 5:33–37.
31. Ibid., 12:6.
32. Ibid., 14:22–32.
33. *Mark*, 6:46; *John*, 6:14–15.
34. *Mark*, 6:48.
35. Neil Forsyth, *The Old Enemy*, p. 171.
36. *John*, 6:20; *Mark*, 6:50.
37. *Mark*, 6:51.
38. Ibid., 6:49–50.
39. *Matthew*, 14:28.
40. *John*, 13:2–4.
41. Ibid., 13:8.
42. Ibid., 13:2.
43. Ibid., 13:15–16.
44. Ibid., 13:18.
45. Ibid., 13:16.
46. Ibid., 13:22–24.
47. Ibid., 13:29–30.
48. Ibid.

49. Ibid., 13:27.
50. Andrew Delbanco, *The Death of Satan: How Americans Have Lost the Sense of Evil* (New York: Farrar, Strauss & Giroux, 1998), p. 155.
51. *Matthew*, 18:6.
52. *Revelations*, 18:21.
53. Reinhold Niebuhr, *Law and Justice* (Louisville, KY: Westminster John Knox Press, 1992), p. 120.
54. Anthony De Mello, *Awareness* (Garden City, NY: Image Books, 1990), p. 151.
55. *Matthew*, 5:45.
56. *Luke*, 23:34.

8

1. Nicholas D. Kristof, "All–American Osamas," *New York Times* (June 7, 2002), http://www.nytimes.com/2002/06/07/opinion/07KRIS.html.
2. Plato, *Euthyphro*, trans. Harold North Fowler (Cambridge, MA: Loeb Classical Library, 1971), 2a1–2a3.
3. Ibid., 4a1–4a2.
4. Ibid., 4b1–4e2.
5. Tom Kuntz, "Who Let the Bulldog Out?" *New York Times* (September 23, 2001), sec. 4, p. 3.
6. Plato, *Euthyphro*, 5a1–5a2.
7. Ibid., 2c1–5c1.
8. Ibid., 5a1–6a4.
9. Ibid., 5d8–5e5.
10. Ibid., 6e5–7a2.
11. Ibid., 8b1–8b3.
12. Ibid., 5c1–5d2.
13. Plato, *The Dialogues of Plato: Euthyphro, Apology, Crito, Meno, Gorgias, Menexenus*, ed. R.E. Allen (New Haven, CT: Yale University Press, 1985), p. 29.
14. Ibid., p. 18.
15. Martin Buber, *Good and Evil* (New York: Prentice Hall, 1980), p. 87.
16. Plato, *Euthyphro*, 3a3–3a4.
17. Plato, *The Apology*, 35d.
18. Plato, *Euthyphro*, 11b9–11b10.
19. Rainer Maria Rilke, *Letters on Cézanne* (New York: Fromm International Publishing Corporation, 1985), p. 5.
20. Daryl Koehn, *Rethinking Feminist Ethics* (New York: Routledge, 1998), ch. 4.

9

1. Immanuel Kant, *Groundwork of the Metaphysic of Morals*, trans. H.J. Paton (New York: Harper & Row, 1956), p. 89.
2. *Ecclesiastes*, 12:1.
3. Lama Surya, "The Second Noble Truth: The Cause of Suffering," http://www.dzogchen.org.
4. Viktor Frankl, *Man's Search for Meaning* (New York: Washington Square Press, 1984), p. 64.

5. Interview with prisoners of war, *National Public Radio*, Evening Edition, April 9, 2003.

6. Dalai Lama, *The Art of Happiness: A Handbook for Living* (New York: Riverhead Books, 1998), p. 147. See also Dalai Lama, *Ethics for the New Millennium: His Holiness the Dalai Lama* (New York: Riverhead Books, 2001).

7. Hannah Arendt, *Eichmann in Jerusalem: A Report on the Banality of Evil* (New York: Viking Press, 1963), p. 277.

8. S. Paul Kashap, *Spinoza and Moral Freedom* (Albany, NY: State University of New York Press, 1987), p. 113.

9. Andrew Delbanco, *The Death of Satan* (New York: Farrar, Strauss & Giroux, 1995), p. 233.

10. Paul Ricoeur quoted in Bernard Dauenhauer, *Stanford Encyclopedia of Philosophy*, http://www.plato.Stanford.edu/entries/Ricoeur/ #3.6.

11. David Parkin quoted in Subniv Babuta and Jean-Claude Bragard, *Evil* (London: Weidenfeld and Nicolson, 1988), p. 24.

12. Jean-Christophe Aeschlimann and Jean Halperin, *Ethique et Responsabilité, Paul Ricoeur* (Neufchâtel: A la Baconniére, 1994), p. 16.

13. Errol Harris, *Substance of Spinoza* (Amherst, NY: Humanity Books, 1995), p. 86.

14. Susan Neiman, *Evil in Modern Thought* (Princeton, NJ: Princeton University Press, 2002), pp. 270–271.

15. Delbanco, *The Death of Satan*, p. 37.

16. Nel Noddings, *Women and Evil* (Berkeley: University of California Press, 1989), p. 5.

17. Arendt, *Eichmann in Jerusalem*, p. 277.

18. Netscape poll taken on November 20, 2001 and reported on Netscape website.

19. René Girard, *The Scapegoat*, trans. Yvonne Freccero (Baltimore, MD: Johns Hopkins University Press, 1989), passim.

20. Natan Sharansky and Stefani Hoffman, *Fear No Evil: The Classic Memoir of One Man's Triumph Over a Police State* (New York: Public Affairs, 1998), p. 121.

21. Plato, *Crito*, trans. Harold North Fowler (Cambridge, MA: Harvard University Press, 1971), 51a–51e1; Daryl Koehn, *Rethinking Feminist Ethics* (New York: Routledge, 1998), pp. 100–150.

22. Arendt, *Eichmann in Jerusalem*, pp. 136–137.

23. Plato, *Euthyphro*, 1b1–1b10.

24. *John*, 8:7–8, *NIV Study Bible*, ed. Kenneth Barker (Grand Rapids, MI: Zondervan, 1985).

25. Confucius, *Analects*, trans. D.C. Lau (Hong Kong: The Chinese University Press, 2000), bk. 1, analect 4.

26. Babuta and Bragard, *Evil*, p. 103.

27. C. Fred Alford, *What Evil Means to Us* (Albany, NY: Cornell University Press, 1997), p. 67.

28. Ibid.

29. Neiman, *Evil in Modern Thought*, p. 262.

30. Hannah Arendt, *Essays in Understanding 1930–1934*, ed. Jerome Kohn (New York: Harcourt Brace & Co., 1994), p. 444.

31. Neiman, *Evil in Modern Thought*, pp. 213–227.

32. Ibid., p. 266.

33. Primo Levi, *The Drowned and the Saved* (New York: Summit Books, 1988), p. 142.
34. Georg Wilhelm Friedrich Hegel, *Introduction to the Lectures on the Philosophy of World History*, trans. H.B. Nisbet (Cambridge: Cambridge University Press, 1975), p. 43.
35. Dante Alighieri, *The Inferno of Dante*, trans. Robert Pinsky (New York: The Noonday Press, 1994), 23:110–118.
36. Lucy Dawidowicz, *The War Against the Jews* (Hammondsport: Penguin, 1983), p. 317.
37. Bruno Bettelheim, *Surviving & Other Essays* (New York: Vintage Books, 1980), passim.
38. W.H. Sledge, J.A. Boydstun, and A.J. Rabe, "Self-Concept Changes Related to War Captivity," *Archives of General Psychiatry*, vol. 37 (1980), pp. 430–443.
39. Mordechai Strigler is described in an obituary written by Lawrence Joffe, "Memories of Yiddish," *The Guardian* (May 27, 1998).
40. Survivor Ben Helfgott quoted in Bill Williamson, "Learning in Extremis," www.erill.uni-bremen./de/lios/sections/s7_williamson.html.
41. Sharansky, *Fear No Evil*, p. 121.
42. Martin Buber, *Between Man and Man* (London: Fontana Books, 1969), p. 88.
43. Frankl, *Man's Search for Meaning*, pp. 154–155.
44. Genevieve Lloyd, *Collective Imaginings* (London: Routledge, 1999), pp. 93–95.
45. Plato's, *Apology*, trans. Harold North Fowler (Cambridge, MA: Harvard University Press, 1971), 40c1–42a4.
46. Confucius, *The Analects*, bk. 7, analect 23.
47. David James Duncan, "When Compassion Becomes Dissent," *Orion Online* (January/February 2003).
48. Anthony de Mello, *Awareness* (New York: Doubleday, 1990), p. 151.
49. Henry James, *The Aspern Papers and The Turn of the Screw*, ed. Anthony Curtis (London: Penguin Books, 1984), pp. 146–147.
50. C.H. Grandgent in Dante, *La Divina Commedia*, ed. C.H. Grandgent (Cambridge, MA: Harvard University Press, 1972), p. xxxii; Patrick Cummins, *Dante Theologian: The Divine Comedy* (St. Louis, MO: B. Herder Book Co., 1948), p. 422.
51. Anthony de Mello, *One Minute Wisdom* (New York: Doubleday, 1988), p. 159.

WORKS CONSULTED

Aeschlimann, Jean-Christophe and Jean Halperin. *Ethique et Responsabilité, Paul Ricoeur*. Neufchâtel: A la Baconniére, 1994.

Aho, James. *This Thing of Darkness: A Sociology of the Enemy*. Seattle: University of Washington Press, 1994.

Alford, C. Fred. *What Evil Means to Us*. Albany, NY: Cornell University Press, 1997.

Aristotle. *Nicomachean Ethics*. Translated by W.D. Ross. Edited by Richard McKeon. *The Basic Works of Aristotle*. New York: Random House, 1941.

———. *Politics*. Translated by Benjamin Jowett. Edited by Richard McKeon. *The Basic Works of Aristotle*. New York: Random House, 1941.

Arendt, Hannah. *Eichmann in Jerusalem: A Report on the Banality of Evil*. New York: Viking Press, 1963.

———. *Essays in Understanding 1930–1934*. Edited by Jerome Kohn. New York: Harcourt Brace & Co., 1994.

———. *On Revolution*. New York: Viking Press, 1963.

Auden, W.H. "Herman Melville," http://jclarkmedia.com.

Babuta, Subniv and Jean-Claude Bragard. *Evil*. London: Weidenfeld and Nicolson, 1988.

Barolini, Teodolinda. "Narrative and Style in Lower Hell," *The Undivine Comedy: Detheologizing Dante*. Princeton, NJ: Princeton University Press, 1992, pp. 74–98.

Berryman, John. "Life, Friends, is Boring," *The Dream Songs*. New York: Noonday Press, 1982.

Bettelheim, Bruno. *The Informed Heart: A Study of the Psychological Consequences of Living Under Extreme Fear and Terror*. New York: Free Press, 1960.

———. *Surviving & Other Essays*. New York: Vintage Books, 1980.

Bloom, H. "Introduction," *English Romantic Poets*. Edited by H. Bloom, New York: Chelsea House Publishers, 1986, pp. 1–20.

———. *The Lucifer Principle: A Scientific Expedition into the Forces of History*. New York: The Atlantic Monthly Press, 1995.

Bloom, Sandra. "Trauma and the Nature of Evil," *Community Works* (November 1996), pp. 1–34.

Boswell, James. *Life of Samuel Johnson*. New York: Alfred A. Knopf, 1993.

Breen, Margaret Sönser. "Reading for Constructions of the Unspeakable in Kafka's *Metamorphosis*," *Understanding Evil*. Amsterdam: Rodopi Press, 2003, pp. 43–56.

Buber, Martin. *Between Man and Man*. London: Fontana Books, 1969.
———. *Good and Evil*. Upper Saddle, NJ: Prentice Hall, 1952.
Butler, Samuel. *The Way of the Flesh*, http://www.classicreader.com/read.php, chapter 26.
Campany, Rob. "Cosmogony and Self-Cultivation: The Demonic and Ethical in Two Chinese Novels," *Journal of Religious Ethics*, http://www.fus.edu/religion/~religion/jre/arc/14–1/index.html.
Cauthen, Kenneth. *The Many Faces of Evil*. Lima, OH: CSS Publishing Company, 1997.
Cogan, Marc. *The Design in the Wax*. Notre Dame, IN: University of Notre Dame Press, 1999.
Confucius. *Analects*. Translated by D.C. Lau. Hong Kong: The Chinese University Press, 2000.
Cooley, Mason. *City Aphorisms*. First Selection. New York: n.p., 1984.
Corte, Nicolas. *Who Is the Devil?* New York: Hawthorne Books, 1958.
Cummins, Patrick. *Dante Theologian: The Divine Comedy*. St. Louis, MO: B. Herder Book Co., 1948.
Dante. *Inferno*. Translated by Robert Pinsky. New York: The Noonday Press, 1994.
Dawidowicz, Lucy. *The War Against the Jews*. Hammondsport: Penguin, 1983.
d'Entreves, Maurizio Passerin. *The Political Philosophy of Hannah Arendt*. London: Routledge, 1993.
Delbanco, Andrew. *The Death of Satan: How Americans Have Lost the Sense of Evil*. New York: Farrar, Strauss & Giroux, 1998.
Duncan, David James. "When Compassion Becomes Dissent," *Orion Online* (January/February 2003).
Duster, T. "Conditions for Guilt-free Massacre," *Sanctions for Evil: Sources of Social Destructiveness*. Edited by Nevitt Sanford and Craig Comstock. San Francisco: Jossey-Bass, Inc., 1972, pp. 25–36.
Etzioni, Amitai. *The New Golden Rule: Community and Morality in a Democratic Society*. New York: Basic Books, 1996.
Forsyth, Neil. *The Old Enemy*. Princeton, NJ: Princeton University Press, 1987.
———. "The Origin of 'Evil': Classical or Judeo-Christian? Perspectives on Evil and Human Wickedness," *Wickedness*, 1:1 (January 2002), pp. 17–52.
Frankl, Viktor. *Man's Search for Meaning*. New York: Washington Square Press, 1987.
Gilligan, J. *Violence: Our Deadly Epidemic and Its Causes*. New York: G. P. Putnam's Sons, 1996.
Goncourt, Edmond de and Jules de Goncourt. *Pages from the Goncourt Journal*. Edited by Robert Baldick. Oxford: Oxford University Press, 1988.
Girard, René. *The Scapegoat*. Translated by Yvonne Freccero. Baltimore, MD: Johns Hopkins University Press, 1989.
Goldberg, C. *Speaking with the Devil: Dialogue with Evil*. New York: Viking, 1996.
Goldsmith, Oliver. *The Good Natur'd Man*. New York: Reprint Services Corp., 1921.
Gray, John. "An Encounter with Evil: Patricia Highsmith," review of *Beautiful Shadow: A Life of Patricia Highsmith*," *New Statesman* (June 30, 2003), http://www.findarticles.com/cf0/m0FQP/4644132/105366852/p1/article.jhtml.

Harris, Errol. *The Substance of Spinoza*. Amherst, NY: Humanity Books, 1995.

Hegel. *Introduction to the Lectures on the Philosophy of World History*. Translated by H.B. Nisbet. Cambridge: Cambridge University Press, 1975.

Herman, J.L. *Trauma and Recovery*. New York: Basic Books, 1992.

Highsmith, Patricia. *Ripley's Game*. New York: Vintage Books, 1993.

———. *The Talented Mr. Ripley*. New York: Vintage Books, 1992.

Hugo, Victor. "Thoughts," *Postscriptum de Ma Vie*. Translated by Lorenzo O'Rourke. New York: Funk and Wagnalls, 1907.

James, Henry. *The Aspern Papers and The Turn of the Screw*. Edited by Anthony Curtis. London: Penguin Books, 1984.

Jésus-Marie, Bruno de. *Satan*. New York: Sheed & Ward, 1952.

Joffe, Lawrence. "Memories of Yiddish," *The Guardian* (May 27, 1998), p. 6.

Kant, Immanuel. *Groundwork of the Metaphysic of Morals*. Translated by H.J. Paton. New York: Harper & Row, 1956.

Kashap, Paul S. *Spinoza and Moral Freedom*. Albany, NY: State University of New York Press, 1987.

Kass, Leon. *Toward a Natural Science*. New York: Free Press, 1985.

Kavolis, V. "Civilizational Models of Evil," *Evil: Self and Culture*. Edited by M.C. Coleman and M. Eigen. New York: Human Sciences Press, 1984, pp. 17–35.

Knowles, John. *A Separate Peace*. New York: Macmillan, 1959.

Koehn, Daryl. *The Ground of Professional Ethics*. London: Routledge, 1994.

———. *Rethinking Feminist Ethics*. New York: Routledge, 1998.

Kristof, Nicholas. "All American Osamas," *New York Times* (June 7, 2002), http://www.nytimes.com/2002/06/07/opinion/07DRIS.html.

Kuntz, Tom. "Who Let the Bulldog Out?" *New York Times* (September 23, 2001), section 4, p. 3.

Kutz, Christopher. *Complicity: Ethics and Law for a Collective Age*. Cambridge: Cambridge University Press, 2000

Lama, Dalai. *The Art of Happiness: A Handbook for Living*. New York: Riverhead Books, 1998.

———. *Ethics for the New Millennium: His Holiness the Dalai Lama*. New York: Riverhead Books, 2001.

Lesser, Wendy. *Pictures at an Execution: An Inquiry into the Subject of Murder*. Cambridge, MA: Harvard University Press, 1993.

Levi, Primo. *The Drowned and the Saved*. Translated by Raymond Rosenthal. New York: Summit Books, 1988.

Lifton, Robert. *The Nazi Doctors*, New York: Basic Books, 1986.

———. "Understanding the Traumatized Self: Imagery, Symboliztion, and Transformation," *Human Adaptation to Extreme Stress: From the Holocaust to Vietnam*. Edited by J.P. Wilson, A. Harel, and B. Kahana. New York: Plenum Publishing, 1988, pp. 7–31.

Lloyd, Genevieve. *Collective Imaginings*. London: Routledge, 1999.

Mann, Klaus. *Mephisto*. New York: Penguin Books, 1977.

Mello, Anthony de. *Awareness*. New York: Doubleday, 1990.

———. *One Minute Wisdom*. New York: Doubleday, 1985.

Messadié, Gerald. *A History of the Devil*. New York: Kodansha America, Inc., 1996.

Midgley, Mary. *Wickedness*. London: Ark Paperbacks, 1984.

Milton, John. *Paradise Lost*. At http://www.literaturepage.com/read/paradise-lost-132.html.

Mora, G. "Reification of Evil: Witchcraft, Heresy, and the Scapegoat," *Evil: Self and Culture*. Edited by M.C. Coleman and M. Eigen. New York: Human Sciences Press, 1984, pp. 36–60.

Neiman, Susan. *Evil in Modern Thought*. Princeton, NJ: Princeton University Press, 2002.

Niebuhr, Reinhold. *Law and Justice*. Louisville, KY: Westminster John Knox Press, 1992.

Nietzsche, Friedrich. *Samtliche Werke: Kritische Studienausgabe*. Edited by Giorgio Colli and Mazzino Montinari. Berlin: DeGruyter, 1980.

NIV Study Bible. Edited by Kenneth Barker. Grand Rapids, MI: Zondervan, 1985.

Noddings, Nell. *Women and Evil*. Berkeley: University of California Press, 1989.

O'Neill, Onora. *Towards Justice and Virtue*. Cambridge: Cambridge University Press, 1996.

Pagels, Elaine. *The Gnostic Gospels*. New York: Random House, 1979.

Pattison, E.M. "Psychoanalysis and the Concept of Evil," *Evil: Self and Culture*. Edited by Marie Coleman Nelson and Michael Eigen. New York: Human Sciences Press, 1984, pp. 61–88.

Peck, M.S. *People of the Lie*. New York: Simon & Schuster, 1983.

Pinksy, Robert. Notes to *The Inferno of Dante*. New York: The Noonday Press, 1994.

Plato. *Apology*. Translated by Harold North Fowler. Cambridge, MA: Harvard University Press, 1971.

———. *Crito*. Translated by Harold North Fowler. Cambridge, MA: Harvard University Press, 1971.

———. *The Dialogues of Plato: Euthyphro, Apology, Crito, Meno, Gorgias, Menexenus*. Edited by R.E. Allen. New Haven, CT: Yale University Press, 1985.

———. *Euthyphro*. Translated by Harold North Fowler. Cambridge, MA: Loeb Classical Library, 1971.

———. *The Republic of Plato*. Translated by Allan Bloom. New York: Basic Books Inc., 1968.

Pocock, D. "Unruly Evil," *The Anthropology of Evil*. Edited by D. Parkin. New York: Basil Blackwell, 1985, pp. 42–56.

Porter, Katherine Anne, Allen Tate, and Mark Van Doren. "James: 'The Turn of the Screw,' A Radio Symposium." Edited by Gerald Willen. *A Casebook on Henry James' The Turn of the Screw*. New York: Thomas F. Crowell Company, 1969, pp. 160–170.

Ricoeur, Paul. *The Symbolism of Evil*. Translated by Emerson Buchanan. Boston, MA: Beacon Press, 1969.

Rilke, Rainer Maria. *Letters on Cézanne*. New York: Fromm International Publishing Corporation, 1985.

Russell, Jeffrey Burton. *The Prince of Darkness*. Ithaca, NY: Cornell University Press, 1988.

———. "The Evil One," *Facing Evil: Light at the Core of Darkness*. Edited by P. Woodruff and H.A. Wilmer. LaSalle, IL: Open Court, 1988, pp. 47–60.

Sanford, J.A. *Evil: The Shadow Side of Reality*. New York: The Crossroad Publishing Company, 1998.

Shakespeare, William. *Othello, The Complete Works of Shakespeare*. New York: Scott, Foresman, and Company, 1951.

Sharansky, Natan and Stefani Hoffman. *Fear No Evil: The Classic Memoir of One Man's Triumph Over a Police State*. New York: Public Affairs, 1998.

Sinclair, John. *The Divine Comedy of Dante Alighieri*. London: Oxford University Press, 1971.

Sledge, W.H., J.A. Boydstun and A.J. Rabe. "Self-Concept Changes Related to War Captivity," *Archives of General Psychiatry*, vol. 37 (1980), pp. 430–443.

Southwold, M. "Buddhism and Evil," *The Anthropology of Evil*. Edited by D. Parkin. New York: Basil Blackwell, 1985, pp. 1128–1141.

Steele, Richard. *The Spectator*, no. 266 (1732), http://www.tabula.rutgers.edu8080:/cocoon.

Stein, Gertrude. *Everybody's Autobiography*. New York: Exact Change, 2004.

Stevenson, Robert Louis. *Dr. Jekyll and Mr. Hyde*. Edited by Leonard Wolf, *The Essential Dr. Jekyll and Mr. Hyde*. New York: Penguin Group, 1995.

———. "Letter to Myers." *The Essential Dr. Jekyll and Mr. Hyde*. Edited by Leonard Wolf. New York: Penguin Group, 1995.

———. "The Rajah's Diamond," *The Complete Short Stories of Robert Louis Stevenson*. Edited by Charles Neider. New York: Da Capo Press, 1998, pp. 110–196.

Taylor, Donald. "Theological Thoughts About Evil," *The Anthropology of Evil*. Edited by David Parkin. New York: Basil Blackwell, 1985, pp. 26–41.

Thoreau, Henry David. "A Week on the Concord and Merrimack Rivers," *The Writings of Henry David Thoreau*, vol. 1. New York: Houghton Mifflin, 1906.

Turner, A.K. *The History of Hell*. Orlando, FL: Harcourt Brace, 1993.

Watson, Lyall. *Dark Nature: A Natural History of Evil*. New York: HarperCollins, 1995.

Weick, K.E. "Small Sins and Large Evils," *Facing Evil: Light at the Core of Darkness*. Edited by Paul Woodruff and Harry A. Wilmer. LaSalle, Il.: Open Court, 1988, pp. 83–92.

Weil, Simone. "Morality and Literature," *Cahiers du Sud* (January 1944), pp. 160–163.

Welner, Michael. "Defining Evil: A Depravity Scale for Today's Courts," *The Forensic Echo*, 2:6 (1998), pp. 4–12.

Wilde, Oscar. "The Soul of Man Under Socialism," *Fortnightly Review* (February 1891).

Williams, Garrath. "Blame and Responsibility," *Ethical Theory and Moral Practice*, vol. 6 (December 2003), pp. 427–445.

Williamson, Bill. "Learning in Extremis," www.erill.uni-bremen./de/lios/sections/s7__williamson.html.

ABOUT THE AUTHOR

Professor Daryl Koehn holds the Cullen Chair of Business Ethics at the University of St. Thomas in Houston, Texas. She has written many articles on ethics and five books on the subject—*Trust in Business: Barriers and Bridges;* / *The Ground of Professional Ethics;* / *Corporate Governance: Ethics Across the Board;* / *Rethinking Feminist Ethics: Care, Trust, Empathy;* / and *Local Insights, Global Ethics for Business.* Her book *Rethinking Feminist Ethics* was the subject of an hour-long interview on National Public Radio. Her writings have been translated into Chinese, Spanish, Japanese, and Bahasi. In addition to teaching at UST, Professor Koehn has been a Visiting Professor at the University of Chicago and a Visiting Research Fellow at Hong Kong Baptist University. She has been appointed a Special Research Fellow at Shanghai Academy of Social Sciences. She has been profiled in *Life* and *Time* magazine and is regularly quoted in the *New York Times, Business Week, LA Times, Harvard Business Review,* and *Houston Business Journal,* on National Public Radio, and in other media outlets.

She serves on the editorial boards of several major ethics journals. Her popular writings have appeared in the *Harvard Business Review, Houston Business Journal,* and *Dallas Business Journal.* She is at work on a new book on finding joy.

INDEX

action, 2–3, 11–12, 19–22, 24–26, 28,
  31–33, 44–45, 50–51, 59–61, 98,
  197–198, 213, 217, 225–229,
  256–257, 261–263
  involuntary action, 3, 18–19, 22
  power to act, 19, 45, 229, 246
  voluntary action, 3, 18–19, 22, 28; vs.
    unwitting enslavement, 3–5
Alford, C. Fred, 281–283
alienation, 81–82
  alienated boredom, 64–67
ambiguity, 36, 125, 129, 136, 141,
  158, 201
  attempt to master, 144–149
angels, good and bad, 45–48
approval, 36–37, 40–43, 46–47, 54–56,
  61, 70, 104–105, 108, 117, 128, 183
Arendt, Hannah, 30–31, 73, 83, 245,
  259–261, 268
Aristotle, 2, 5, 11–12, 17–31, 33–36, 42,
  45, 67, 90, 152, 155–156, 159, 167,
  223, 253–257
asymmetrical judgment, 32
Auden, W.H., 10, 281

Balzac, Honoré de, 27
Barbara (*Mephisto*), 38–39, 44, 46–48,
  55–57
Barolini, Teolinda, 181, 290
Berryman, John, 81, 286
betrayal, 39, 48, 57–58, 60, 156,
  175–176, 178, 180–181, 193,
  202–203
  as the utmost evil, 175–180
Bettelheim, Bruno, 269, 294
Bloom, Sandra, 15

boredom, 63–67, 69–75, 77–79, 81, 83,
  85, 235, 237
  alienated boredom, 64–67
  connection to violence, 75–81
Buber, Martin, 228, 271
Buddha, 3
Butler, Samuel, 101, 287

Campany, Rob, 281
Carew, Danvers (*Strange Tale of
  Dr. Jekyll and Mr. Hyde*), 90, 95,
  104, 106–108, 113
Cauthen, Kenneth, 12, 32
certainty, 124–125, 127–128, 130, 134,
  136–138, 142, 148, 202, 208, 213,
  215, 218, 223–224, 227–228, 239,
  261–262, 264, 277
  self-righteous certainty, 128–131
  violative certainty, 124–128
  see also fanaticism
Christianity, 7, 15, 32, 156, 187,
  206–207, 218, 228, 234,
  265–266
Churchill, Winston, 211
civilization, 9, 83, 95, 106, 259, 269
coercion, 7, 22, 127, 234
Cogan, Marc, 156, 184, 289–290
community, 3, 7–9, 17–18, 21–22, 25,
  27–29, 33–34, 44–45, 54, 94,
  105–106, 172, 175, 188, 192, 197,
  204, 208, 210–211, 218, 232–234,
  240, 246, 251, 253, 260
  true community, 8–11
conflict, 4, 25, 170, 195–197, 217–218,
  223, 231, 236, 255, 265
Confucius, 3, 7, 9, 233, 253, 262, 275

convert, 13, 36, 73, 81, 99, 103, 143–144,
    159, 163, 169, 180, 182, 187, 193,
    198, 200–201, 204–205, 212, 230, 267
counting, 220–221
courage, 6, 21, 26, 31–32, 36, 53, 80,
    94–95, 115, 126, 128, 133, 135–136,
    155–156, 175, 188, 190, 200–201,
    212, 223, 231, 233, 239, 241,
    254–255, 263, 277–278
  genuine courage, 21
  political courage, 21
cruelty, 31, 90, 98, 270
Crysostom, St. John, 15
cunning, 35, 40, 42, 52, 73, 97, 117, 131,
    137, 139, 154, 168–173, 180, 184,
    187, 211, 250

Dalai Lama, 293
Dante, 3, 12–13, 62, 151–162, 164–171,
    173–178, 180–187, 205, 213, 230,
    236, 239, 242–244, 250, 252, 264,
    268–269, 274, 277
dark side, 50, 87, 96, 133, 206
Dawidowicz, Lucy, 269, 294
degradation, 47, 71, 92
Delbanco, Andrew, 185
democracy, 8–9, 64
demonization of others, 8, 11, 13, 27, 33,
    98, 106, 113–114, 182, 192, 194,
    198–200, 204–206, 277
  and our complicity in evil, 34, 83,
    102–103, 116, 261
depression, 73, 135, 185
desire, 34, 49, 55, 58, 73, 94, 97–99,
    106–113, 117, 143–144, 147,
    157–170, 192, 199, 215, 220, 225,
    236–239, 243, 246–249, 255, 258,
    273, 276
  frustrated desire, 5, 137, 236–237,
    240–250, 264–266, 271, 274
  obsessive, 67–71
  repression of, 5, 52, 82, 87, 88–101,
    103–109, 111–115, 182, 235,
    248–249, 270
development, 7, 33, 45, 76, 94, 103, 119,
    128, 200, 232, 239, 253, 255–256,
    269, 271, 273
deviance, 27–28, 31, 33–36, 65, 88, 260

devil, 23, 40, 42, 49–52, 54, 56, 60–62,
    81, 104, 109, 127, 144, 147–148,
    184, 187–188, 190–191, 194, 199,
    202, 250
  evil one, 50–51, 187–188, 198
  see also Satan
dignity, 31, 36, 38–39, 41, 50, 60, 115,
    249, 251
dissatisfaction, 40, 49, 57, 64, 66, 88,
    163, 190, 206, 240, 243, 248–249
Divine Comedy (Dante), 151, 156, 158
  hierarchy of hell, 152–156, 181, 243
  Inferno, 13, 62, 151, 155, 164, 175,
    178, 183, 213
  lessons about evil, 164–167, 173–175,
    181–186
  three regions of hell, 152–153
divine voice, 224
divinity, 9–11, 13, 16–17, 43–47, 88,
    151–158, 160, 164, 172–178, 181,
    184, 189–191, 203, 209, 213–219,
    224–230, 239, 253, 262, 265, 278
  true divinity, 225
Dostoyevsky, Fyodor, 235
dread, 4–5, 31–33, 36, 60, 75, 77, 80, 83,
    88, 93, 100, 111, 118, 122, 126,
    130–136, 141, 149, 151, 179, 201,
    205, 212–215, 225, 229, 235, 237,
    248, 250, 264–266

education, 18, 32, 115, 172, 231, 233,
    241, 251, 255–256, 273
Eichmann, Adolf, 257–258
eidos, 222–229, 231–234, 236
Emerson, Ralph Waldo, 250
enemies, 8, 12, 21, 124, 142, 144, 177,
    187–194, 196–198, 201, 204–206,
    215, 230, 256
Enfield (The Strange Tale of Dr. Jekyll and
    Mr. Hyde), 89–91, 95–96, 98–106,
    109–112, 276–277
Etzioni, Amitai, 29
Euthyphro, 208–218, 220, 222–225,
    227–233, 238–239, 257, 261,
    264–265
evil
  as attempt to master ambiguity,
    144–149

comical narcissism of, 54–56
concepts of, 4, 15–16, 42, 64, 262
as creation of enemies, 142–144
danger of equating with vice, 25–34
as denial, 140–142
as deviance, 33
doing evil, 45, 72, 167, 187
face of, 130, 134, 136
fictional evil, 35
as frustrated desire, 237–249
and human desire, 249–250
as human presence, 131–135
imagined, 132, 135
as mad courage, 135–137
as manipulative control of vulnerable
    people, 137–140
nature of, 1, 10, 12–13, 83, 139, 149,
    152, 165–166, 182, 235–236, 240,
    264, 274
overcoming, 5–8, 136, 139
ranking, 235, 242–245
real evil, 35, 258
resisting evil, 13, 141, 230–234,
    274–279
romanticism of, 52–54
satanic evil, 204–205, 228
as threat to identity, 119–124
as vice, 1–2, 15–33, 236, 253–258, 263
as violation of natural order, 259–264
as violative certainty, 124–128

family, 24, 31, 43, 55, 65, 73, 89, 92, 96,
    99, 101, 108, 164, 176, 181, 183,
    188, 209, 229, 252, 261
mothers, 60–61, 210
fanatic, 207–225, 227–231, 233,
    265, 272
certainty of, 208–213
and divinity, 213–216
fanaticism as unreasonable
    repudiation of reason, 216–219
literalism of, 216–217
overcoming the fanatic within,
    220–227
as religious expert, 219, 222
religious fervor, 213, 215
why fanaticism should be judged evil,
    227–230

fear, 4, 20, 31, 37, 42, 44, 60, 72, 79, 82,
    91, 94, 103, 110–111, 113–114, 120,
    133–134, 145, 197, 200, 205, 225,
    229, 232, 248, 262, 274–275,
    278–279
Flora, (*The Turn of the Screw*), 118, 120,
    128–132, 135–139, 142–145
Frankl, Viktor, 242, 271–272, 292
fraud, 63, 66–67, 71, 74, 79, 82,
    168–170, 172–173, 175–176
freedom, 3, 8–10, 12, 32, 81, 122, 146,
    153, 155, 187, 198, 204, 206, 236,
    251, 272–275
friends, 10, 18–19, 23–24, 43, 48–49, 51,
    55, 63, 79, 90, 95, 99, 101, 108, 155,
    175, 183, 188, 193–194, 197–199,
    204–205, 216, 218, 224, 238–239,
    252, 257

Gandhi, Mahatma, 9, 253, 278
genocide, 245
Girard, René, 259, 293
god, 9–13, 37, 43, 46–47, 54–55, 90–91,
    109, 142, 154–158, 161, 167–168,
    174–178, 180–181, 187–195,
    197–199, 201–208, 214–219,
    225–226, 228, 252, 258
cultural views of, 16, 215–216, 218
false god, 60, 218
the god within, 13, 226
Goethe, Johann Wolfgang von, 3, 35
good and evil, concept of, 2, 188, 218,
    266–274
vs. concept of good and bad,
    250–253
Gospels, identification of evil, 7,
    187–188, 194, 196, 198–200,
    204–206
Gray, John, 284
Greenleaf, Dickie (*The Talented
    Mr. Ripley*), 63–71, 73–75, 78–81,
    83–84, 183
Grose, Mrs., (*The Turn of the Screw*),
    118–119, 126–129, 131–132, 136,
    140, 142–145
guilt, 12, 52, 77, 83, 92, 108–109, 111,
    145, 153, 167–168, 193, 225,
    228–230, 232, 260

habits, 2, 7–8, 21–25, 33–34, 69, 72–73,
90, 98, 103, 153–156, 200, 251, 255,
269, 271
happiness, 24–25, 45, 50, 92, 137, 161,
174, 212, 220, 245, 257
Harris, Errol, 293
Hegel, Georg Wilhelm Friedrich,
266–268, 294
hell, 13, 25, 57, 147, 151–158, 160,
162–168, 171, 173–174, 176, 178,
181–186, 213, 243–244, 249, 264,
268, 277
  geography of hell, 155–156
  see also Divine Comedy
hierarchy, 152, 155–156
Highsmith, Patricia, 12, 63–65, 72, 78,
84–85, 87, 117, 149, 155, 165,
205, 236
Hitler, Adolf, 12, 51, 53, 245
Höfgen, Hendrik (Mephisto), 36–61, 64,
67, 69, 74, 79, 117, 122, 154, 166,
170, 177, 183, 227, 230, 238, 247,
252, 257, 274
  portrayal of Hamlet, 43, 58–60
holiness, 209, 213, 217–218,
222–227, 231
  the holy, 190, 213, 215, 217–219,
222–227, 231
Holocaust, 9, 12, 245
human rights, 36, 260, 270
humanity, 3, 21, 24, 27, 36, 40, 45, 49–51,
56, 60–61, 115, 125, 151–155,
157–163, 165, 167, 169, 171,
173–175, 177, 179–183, 185–186,
193, 205, 230, 242, 245, 268
  human action, 15–17, 25, 59, 180,
210, 225
  human desire, 3, 161, 237–238, 241,
249–250, 266
  human freedom, 8, 155, 272–273
  human suffering, 2, 11, 16–17
Hyde, Edward (The Strange Tale of
Dr. Jekyll and Mr. Hyde), 87–116,
182, 236–237, 247, 252, 257,
260–261, 276–277
  as hated self, 90–96
hypocrisy, 30–33, 51–52, 61, 87–88,
103–105, 107, 117, 236

identity, false, 2, 213
idolization, 45, 55, 106–107, 201–202, 204
ignorance, 1, 5, 7, 12–13, 19, 22–24, 29,
36, 87, 110–111, 121, 174, 203,
228–229, 233, 250, 257–258, 263
  self-caused ignorance, 22
  unavoidable ignorance, 22
imagination, 20, 35, 95, 98, 109–110,
115, 117–118, 120–122, 124, 131,
134–135, 137, 139, 141, 153,
183–185
imitation, 44, 59, 109, 156, 278
impulse, 33–34, 36, 40, 77–78, 94,
96–97, 101, 104, 106–108, 196,
200, 246, 248
individuality, 173, 254, 270
  loss of, 167–170
indulgence, 1, 22, 26, 30, 34, 49, 52–53,
88–90, 94, 96–98, 100–101, 107,
158, 182, 193, 223, 236
  indiscriminate indulgence and its
effects, 96–103
infallibility, 93, 213, 217, 219, 222, 226
inner child, 97–99
insight, 1, 5, 7–9, 41, 83, 87, 109, 152,
156, 164, 169, 182, 190, 192, 202,
224, 228, 232, 234–235, 244, 248,
253, 256, 263, 269, 271, 275, 277
integration, 93, 95–96, 100–102,
107–109, 111–112, 115, 237, 264
irony, 80, 184, 202, 228–229

James, Henry, 3, 12, 117–119, 122, 125,
132, 134, 137, 139, 144–145,
148–149, 152, 154–155, 165,
183–184, 205, 227, 230, 236,
238–239, 257, 274, 277
Jekyll (The Strange Tale of Dr. Jekyll and
Mr. Hyde), 87–115, 151–152, 182,
236–238, 252, 257, 260, 276–277
Jessel, Miss (The Turn of the Screw), 119,
131–132, 136, 139–143, 147, 149,
183, 238, 277
Jesus, 3, 7–8, 12–13, 28, 30, 156,
187–194, 196–204, 206, 232, 239,
253, 258, 262, 276–277
  as teacher, 202–203
  temptation of, 188–194

Job, 10–11
John the Baptist, 189, 194–196, 198–199
Johnson, Samuel, 21
Judas Iscariot, 156, 181, 193,
    202–204, 206
justice, 6, 16, 30, 44–45, 53, 73, 106,
    152–155, 170, 175–178, 205–215,
    218, 223–226, 229, 232–234, 251,
    254, 257–263, 270, 275, 277
  universal justice, 211–212

Kant, Immanuel, 1, 238, 261
Kass, Leon, 37
killing, 6, 24, 28–29, 63, 65, 69, 78–79,
    83, 85, 96, 98–99, 114–115, 180,
    184, 192–193, 207, 209–211, 228,
    252, 257–258, 260–264, 267
Knowles, John, 13, 281
Koehn, Daryl, 285, 292
Kristof, Nicholas D., 292
Kutz, Christopher, 28

language, 7, 23, 28, 76, 79–80, 118, 169,
    176, 188, 211, 255, 266
Lanyon, Dr. (The Strange Tale of
    Dr. Jekyll and Mr. Hyde), 90–91,
    95–96, 100, 104–105, 108, 112, 238
laws, 18, 25–33, 38–40, 76, 89–92,
    102–106, 109–110, 210, 212,
    232–234, 246–247, 250–251,
    254–255, 258–263, 275
  legalism, 194–196, 198
  moral law, 10, 32, 214
laziness, 17, 21, 24, 26, 155, 256
Lesser, Wendy, 84, 286
Levi, Primo, 83, 294
Lloyd, Genevieve, 293
Lotte (Mephisto), 37–38, 40, 43, 50, 53,
    55, 58
love, 43–44, 51–53, 55, 69–71, 151–152,
    156–158, 160–162, 165, 168,
    174–175, 177, 181, 188–190, 193,
    203, 217–219, 226–227, 233

madness, 8, 59, 116–117, 129, 132,
    136–137, 166, 183, 230, 236, 267
malice, 2, 4–5, 10, 13, 15–16, 26, 35–37,
    75, 137, 152–154, 165, 167–168,

    171–173, 193, 232, 236, 257–258,
    263–265
Mandela, Nelson, 269
Mann, Klaus, 12, 34, 36–38, 40, 42, 45,
    53–54, 56–57, 61, 87, 117, 149, 154,
    165, 205, 236
martyrdom, 207, 269
masochism, 2, 39, 41–42, 50, 52–54, 56,
    60, 64, 87
McVeigh, Timothy, 12, 207, 228
measurement, 220, 223
mechanical, 2, 21, 35, 72–73, 77, 83,
    154, 177, 180, 187, 198, 205, 261
Meletus, 208, 225, 229
Mello, Anthony de, 187, 278, 281, 294
Mephisto (Mann), 34, 36–38, 40, 45,
    49–52, 57, 59, 61–62, 170,
    183, 272
Midgley, Mary, 9, 45, 94, 96, 166
Miles (The Turn of the Screw), 63, 80,
    118–119, 128, 131–132, 137–142,
    144–148, 184, 257, 276
Milton, John, 193
money, 41, 56, 66–70, 76, 78, 80–81, 99,
    102, 104, 162–163, 166–167, 170,
    203, 255
  obsessive desire for, 67–71
mood swings, 53, 75–76
moralistic tradition, 1–5, 8, 10–12,
    17–18, 24–33, 37, 45, 56, 64, 79, 90,
    152, 230, 237, 253–263
morality, 2–3, 7, 10–11, 25, 27, 33, 37,
    48, 79–80, 83, 88, 90, 117, 122, 199,
    202, 211–212, 254–257, 264
  moral duty, 210, 260–261
  moral language, 79, 211
  moral principles, 210–211
  moral virtue, 155, 254
  moral vision, 211–212, 220, 228
motives for evil, 35–36, 58, 99, 102–103,
    139, 148, 165–166, 205, 261,
    263–264
moving principle, 19–22, 27, 32–33

narcissism, 4, 13, 33, 54, 56–57, 61, 63,
    65, 67, 69–75, 77–79, 81–83, 85,
    151, 230, 258
  comical, 54–56

Neiman, Susan, 16–17, 257–258, 268, 293
Nietzsche, Frederick, 27, 30, 268, 271
norms, 25, 27, 31, 39–41, 49, 59, 64, 79, 81, 99, 103–104, 160, 210, 216–224, 227–229, 232, 234, 242, 245, 247, 251–253
    communal norms, 27, 31, 247

obsession, 39, 45, 54, 132, 152, 165, 178, 208, 212, 230, 260
Othello, 166
Ouspensky, P.D., 278–279

pacts, 49–52, 253
    see also trade-offs
pain, 4–5, 17, 20, 29, 36, 111, 137, 151, 177, 205–206, 240–242, 244, 247, 250, 256, 263–264, 267, 269
    intensity of, 244
paranoia, 13, 33, 81–82, 84, 94, 183, 229–230, 258
passions, 4, 8, 18, 23, 53–54, 153, 158, 164, 174–175, 187, 240, 243, 246, 249, 255, 274–276
passivity, 22, 34, 65, 81, 174, 176, 185, 258, 274, 277
persecution, 97, 107, 109, 112, 188, 212, 232, 255, 260, 267, 273, 275
personality, 51, 67, 72–73, 87–88, 91, 94, 96, 101, 104, 108, 178, 182, 260
piety, false, 228–230
Plato, 1, 3, 208, 213, 215, 223, 231, 256, 266
power, 7, 11, 17–19, 36–38, 45–47, 131–132, 137–139, 156, 172–176, 181, 185–188, 191–194, 199–201, 211, 214–216, 220, 223–224, 229, 233–234, 253–255, 268, 272–278
    true power, 193, 199–201
praise and blame, social system of, 2–4, 12, 18–25, 27–29, 31–34, 42, 50, 79–80, 93–94, 180, 182–183, 188–189, 191
prayer, 188, 225, 227
punishment, 4–5, 10, 12, 16–17, 29, 32, 34, 84, 94, 122, 153, 164–165, 172, 233, 262–263, 270

Quint (The Turn of the Screw), 119, 128, 131–139, 142, 144–149, 183–184, 238, 277

rationalization, 8, 48, 50, 52, 58–60, 72–73, 97, 117, 139, 157, 169–170, 175, 178
reality, 2, 8, 45–46, 66, 69, 75, 87, 94, 102, 107, 110, 115, 131, 153, 165, 171, 173, 178, 180–182, 184, 217, 243, 252, 254, 268
reason, 1–2, 6, 9–11, 22–23, 50–52, 97–98, 118–119, 130–131, 153–154, 156–158, 160–164, 167–168, 173–175, 180–187, 214–227, 233–234, 257–259, 264–269
    genuine reason, 73
    repudiation of, 216–219
religion, 54, 92, 172, 199, 215–216, 227, 233, 264, 273
    disagreeing gods, 218
    religious concept of evil, 16
respect, 6, 8–9, 19–22, 26, 34–43, 45–47, 50–55, 59, 68–71, 74, 76, 84, 88–89, 92, 125, 130, 139, 152–153, 161, 165, 202–203, 212, 221–222, 235–239, 242, 246–247, 251–252
    ambiguous quest for, 36–39
    and masochistic anxiety/obsession with purity, 39–45
reverence, 225, 227–230
    true reverence, 228
Ricoeur, Paul, 15, 252, 293
Rilke, Rainer Maria, 232, 292
Ripley, Tom (The Talented Mr. Ripley), 63–65, 69, 72–73, 75, 79–80, 82–83, 151, 154, 166, 177, 183, 230, 237
    stealing of Dickie's identity, 63, 75, 78, 84
romanticizing evil, 52–56, 61, 69, 105, 158–159, 164, 174, 182, 266
Rousseau, 16–17
    analysis of Lisbon earthquake (1755), 16–17, 267

sadism, 2, 4, 26, 33, 41, 59, 87, 90, 98, 193, 236, 246, 257, 276

salvation, 76, 145, 151, 153, 161, 174, 182, 193, 206, 271
Satan, 91, 127, 180–181, 183, 187–194, 197, 199, 203–206, 250
satanization of self and others, 6, 13, 187, 189, 191–193, 195–197, 199–203, 205, 230, 250, 254, 277
  satanizing God, 193
  see also demonization of others
satisfaction, 3, 57, 64–65, 76, 81, 97, 106, 159, 163–164, 170, 190, 206, 237–240, 243, 247, 249–250, 255, 263, 266, 273–274
self
  alienated self, 81–82
  authentic self, 6, 10
  controlling self, 94
  destruction of the self, 72, 116
  hidden self, 93, 97, 102–103, 107–108, 111, 115–116
  irritated and melodramatic self, 72–75
  narcissistic self, 70
  objective self, 13, 65, 81, 84
  shadow self, 93, 260; see also shadow
  socially hated self, 103 106
  unintegrable self, 111–116
self, aspects of
  self-deception, 22, 189
  self-destruction, 6, 9, 228
  self-discipline, 48, 53, 153, 159
  self-elevation, 71
  self-esteem, 42, 46, 48, 61, 68, 230
  self-examination, 227
  self-image, false, 77, 213
  self-indulgence, 107
  self-knowledge, 2, 5–6, 10, 13, 67, 189, 193, 223, 229–230, 240, 271, 27
  self-pity, 50, 53, 55, 57, 60–61, 72–73, 75, 166, 177, 180–181, 183, 258
  self-understanding, 151, 238, 252, 273
September 11, 2001, 9, 12, 207, 248, 267
shadow, 42, 49, 91–93, 96–97, 100, 107–108, 122, 266
  persecuted shadow, 107–111
Shakespeare, William, 255, 290

shame, 4, 24, 34, 36–37, 47, 49–52, 56–58, 72–73, 76–78, 88, 92–94, 98–99, 108, 145, 225, 230
  false sense of, 56–57, 72
Sharansky, Natan (Anatoly), 270, 293
Shylock, 255
silence, 121, 123, 128, 134–135, 143, 145, 159, 180–181, 189, 212, 230, 261
sin, 13, 30, 106, 153–156, 159, 161, 163–168, 171–176, 178, 180–188, 213, 262, 277
  concept of, 156
  divining, 172–173
  flattery, 168, 169, 170–172
  gluttony, 159–162
  hoarding and spending wantonly, 162–167
  infernal sin, 155
  lust, 157–159
  pandering and seduction, 167–170
  sinful desire, 153
  see also betrayal
slavery, 31–32
society, and pressure on individuals, 4, 12, 21, 25, 27–28, 33–34, 87–88, 92, 94, 97, 100, 103–106, 111, 115, 117, 159, 182, 246–249, 251–255, 260–262
Socrates, 4, 7–9, 12 13, 30 31, 205, 208–210, 212–213, 215–229, 231–233, 239, 253, 256, 258, 261 262, 264, 274–275, 277
soul, 40, 52, 90–91, 106, 109, 161–162, 166, 183, 185, 242
Spinoza, Baruch, 3
Stevenson, Robert Louis, 12, 87–88, 90, 94–95, 97–98, 100, 106, 112, 115, 117, 165, 182–183, 205, 236, 260
Strange Tale of Dr. Jekyll and Mr. Hyde, The (Stevenson), 87–103, 111
  plot summary, 88–90
Strigler, Mordechai, 269, 294
subjectivity, 43, 72, 81, 130–131
  alienated subjectivity, 72

suffering, 1–2, 4–7, 9–17, 20, 24–25, 29, 34–36, 81–83, 92, 95, 125, 139, 151–156, 164–167, 170–174, 178–189, 204–206, 229, 235, 237, 240–245, 250, 252, 258, 260–261, 264–275, 278–279
  suffering evil, 5, 72, 205

talent, 6, 36, 40, 43, 54, 57–61, 70, 72, 76–77, 79, 92, 95–98, 111, 115, 182–183
Talented Mr. Ripley, The (Highsmith), 63, 66–67, 84
temptation, 25, 114, 137, 171, 187–190, 192–194, 197, 200, 202, 206
Tenab, Princess (*Mephisto*), 40–48, 52, 54–55, 60–61
terrorism, 207
Thoreau, Henry David, 28, 62, 250
torture, 20, 45, 240–241, 244, 247, 263, 268
trade-offs, 49–50, 62, 198
truth, 4, 7, 11, 13, 47, 50, 53, 60–61, 77, 79–83, 93–95, 102, 114, 137, 148, 167–169, 171, 173, 175, 178, 181, 185, 194, 202, 208, 212, 215–217, 220–222, 225–226, 228, 230–231, 233–234, 250, 256, 262, 264, 275, 277
Turn of the Screw, The (James), 118, 276–277
  "evil" apparitions, 119–120, 125, 129–130, 133, 136, 138, 145, 147
  first sighting, 119–124
  second sighting, 124–128
  third sighting, 128–131
  fourth sighting, 131–135
  fifth sighting, 135–137
  sixth sighting, 137–140
  seventh sighting, 140–142
  eighth sighting, 142–144
  ninth sighting, 144–149

Ugolino (*Divine Comedy*), 177–182, 184, 243
Ulrichs, Otto (*Mephisto*), 48, 50, 57–58, 60
Utterson (*The Strange Tale of Dr. Jekyll and Mr. Hyde*), 89–91, 95–96, 100–106, 108–112, 114–115, 238, 260–261, 276–277

vice, 1–5, 11–12, 17–18, 21, 23, 25–34, 36, 39, 42, 44, 54, 64, 83, 98, 118, 146–147, 152–155, 159, 162, 168, 197–198, 202, 212, 232, 236, 245, 253–257, 263, 266, 271
  Aristotelian vice, 17–25
  vs. self-ignorance, 1–2
violence, 1–2, 4–5, 8, 10, 13, 31, 33–34, 64, 74–79, 81, 83, 111–112, 137, 143, 168–170, 196–198, 205–206, 218, 228–229, 246–248, 252, 255, 265–266
  resorting to violence, 111, 194, 220
  see also killing
virtue, 7–8, 15, 18, 21, 26–29, 31–32, 34, 36, 44–45, 49, 66, 79–80, 93, 107, 154–156, 159, 218, 226, 251, 254–256, 275
  heroic virtue, 136

wealth, 67–70, 72, 78, 172, 206, 220, 237
  see also money
Weil, Simone, 35
will to power, 211, 214, 216, 220, 223–224, 234
Williams, Garrath, 27
Williamson, Bill, 294
wisdom tradition, 1–6, 8, 10–12, 18, 26, 30, 32, 36, 64, 151, 213, 235, 253, 256, 258, 262, 274–275, 277
worship, 43–46, 54–55, 60, 191–192, 194, 201–202, 215, 218

zero-sum thinking, 196–199, 205